Joseph Masheck, MLitt (DUBL), PhD, has tau
Professor of Art History, at Hofstra University
editor-in-chief of *Artforum*, he has been a Guggenheim renow., ~~~~~~~~~~
of Edinburgh College of Art (University of Edinburgh) and visiting fellow at St
Edmund's College, Cambridge University. Previous books include *Building-Art:
Modern Architecture Under Cultural Construction* (1993), *Marcel Duchamp in Perspective*,
2nd edn (2002), *The Carpet Paradigm: Integral Flatness from Decorative to Fine Art*
(2010) and *Texts on (Texts on) Art* (2011).

'Joseph Masheck wears his erudition with wonderful wit. His ambition to
reclaim Loos for art comes across with vigor and passion. To paraphrase Adolf
Loos, a monument isn't an everyday occurrence but something that makes you
stop and take notice. Masheck's new book is a monumental contribution to the
Loos literature – ambitiously conceived, thoroughly provocative, and deeply
insightful.'

**Joan Ockman, Distinguished Senior Fellow,
School of Design, University of Pennsylvania**

'Masheck's fresh interpretation of the work of Adolf Loos places the emphasis on
the specific nature of his architecture rather than on the cultural scope of his critical
writing. In so doing he demonstrates not only how Loos's work was influenced by
very varied traditions ranging from Biedermeier to Art Nouveau, but also how his
abstract approach to form anticipated in a specific way the discourse of American
minimalist art.'

**Kenneth Frampton, Ware Professor of Architecture,
Columbia University**

'This is a provocative take on Adolf Loos at a time when criticism has exhausted its
theoretical resources, and the near past seems almost out of reach. Each chapter
of the book disbands the established interpretive canons if only to proclaim a
diachronic affinity between Loos, Constructivism and Minimalism of the 1960s.
Joseph Masheck is cogent and persuasive.'

**Gevork Hartoonian, Professor of Architecture,
University of Canberra**

'Proto-minimalist or Architectural Dadaist? The enemy of ornament or the last
"classicist"? Who better than Joseph Masheck in this penetrating book to guide
us round the paradoxes of this dandified enemy of ornamental invention, whose
most prominent masterpiece is a bronze-and-marble colonnaded gentlemen's
outfitter!'

**Joseph Rykwert, Cret Professor of Architecture Emeritus,
University of Pennsylvania**

Frontispiece: Adolf Loos, Müller Villa,
Prague, 1928–29. Rear of the house seen
from below. Photograph by the author.

ADOLF LOOS
The Art of Architecture

Joseph Masheck

I.B. TAURIS
LONDON · NEW YORK

Published in 2013 by I.B.Tauris & Co Ltd
6 Salem Road, London W2 4BU
175 Fifth Avenue, New York NY 10010
www.ibtauris.com

Distributed in the United States and Canada Exclusively by Palgrave Macmillan
175 Fifth Avenue, New York NY 10010

International Library of Architecture: 1

ISBN: (PB)   978 1 78076 423 8
         (HB)   978 1 78076 422 1

A full CIP record for this book is available from the British Library
A full CIP record is available from the Library of Congress

Library of Congress Catalog Card Number: available

Typeset in Perpetua by freerangeproduction.com
Printed and bound in Great Britain by T.J. International, Padstow, Cornwall

In memoriam

OTTOKAR UHL

(1931 Wolfsberg in Kärnten–2011 Vienna)

CONTENTS

ILLUSTRATIONS

Every effort has been made to gain permission for the use of the images in this book. Any omissions will be rectified in future editions.

PREFACE

The buildings and writings of Adolf Loos (1870–1933) are now often enough taken, or mistaken, in the cultural sphere, as exemplary of an early modern iconoclasm which, if not downright nihilistic, was out to deny art as such, as if with some Dadaist form of anti-architecture. In spite of a longstanding interest in Duchamp, I always suspected that Loos was something more than simply the Duchamp of architecture; but how so? Considering aspects of his contribution, the present book offers makings of an answer. Not that Loos wasn't iconoclastic; but his was the witty and knowing iconoclasm of the believer, on behalf of the great art of architecture. Against the commonplace of Loos as mere ironist, part of the history of architecture possibly only as a critical curmudgeon clearing the way to modernism rather than as building and advancing it, the following thematic essays take off from the assumption that as a practitioner Loos belongs as much to the history of art as any other great modern artist.

Kenneth Frampton offers a uniquely qualified double negative, speaking of the "dissolution of classical aesthetics" by "both the positive and the negative avant-garde," sometimes to perversely sublime effect, of "Duchamp's anti-painting painting or Adolf Loos's anti-architecture architecture." He points up how Loos "makes a distinction between architecture and art" in his 'Architecture' essay of 1910, "oscillat[ing] between describing the house as conservative and the art work, art, as subversive," only to end "with this beautiful and ironic passage, 'and so the man loves his house and hates art.'"[1] Indeed there is irony there, and it is not at odds with art. 'Architecture' also salutes the great romantic-classicist of a hundred years before, Karl Friedrich Schinkel; and if the Loos of 1910 seems not to vie with Schinkel in sublimity, his genuine artfulness has been sufficiently forgotten, notwithstanding his latter-day cultural celebrity, for him to deserve in his own right, now a century later still, some of the honor of his own memorable salute to Schinkel: "May the light of this towering figure shine upon our forthcoming generation of architects!" It doesn't matter that Loos never got to build the projected public buildings which to his mind might have justified that; his informal modern formalism was the lesson which was needed, and may well be again.

In New York, Loos had to wash dishes for pocket money, and part of the time he slept in a YMCA: what a waste it would have been to struggle through that just to make jokey, one-liner art. No; Loos's sarcasm never got the better of his wit, nor his wit of his intelligence. He did as much as any other architect after Otto Wagner, the grand old Viennese master of the prior generation, to bring forth modernism at the opening of the twentieth century. A relative youngster who took to calling himself Le Corbusier was one whose art this supposed non-artist influenced. Loos showed how the end of the established academic tradition, far from implying the end of what was entitled to be considered the art, might allow the new modern architecture to inherit what truth of the old tradition deserved to survive.

Philosophically, his skeptical outlook and blunt eschewal of obfuscation sometimes affiliate Loos with the tougher-than-thou logical positivism of the Vienna Circle, which sought to clean up modern life by taking out the presumed rubbish of metaphysics. Extreme architectural functionalism, which Loos made possible but to which he himself was not constrained, was similarly framed as a truth of which only those strong enough to live value-free were worthy. However, the more one considers even his most radical architecture, the less like a standard functionalist Loos seems. If anything, he parallels less the logical positivist Rudolf Carnap than the Ludwig Wittgenstein who actually drew back from the Vienna Circle which he had helped to make possible. Even where Loos notoriously states that at least the private house should not be a matter of art, it would be as dangerous as with Nietzsche, not to mention Loos's friend Karl Kraus, to lose track of the ironist's deft control of meaning. Loos's standing caricature was inevitably encouraged by his delight in playing the outrageous avant-gardist: the posture which this really very much 'true' architect's most famous text, 'Ornament and Crime,' perpetrated to the distraction of all else.

What confuses modernists without consoling conservatives is how his obvious radicalism allowed of perpetuating some essence of the sacrosanct classical tradition 'without portfolio,' as it were, literally in his own little school, quite independently of the academic system. This must be why the less insightful moderns and the more insecure conservatives shy away from major cases where Loos was close to the gravitational center of canonical fine-art architecture but decidedly on his own, inevitably idiosyncratic-seeming terms. Thus his early remodeling of the Villa Karma, near Montreux in Switzerland, in 1904–06, is a modernist equivalent – how dare it be! – to one of the masterworks of the aristocratic Renaissance palatial type, Giuliano da Sangallo's Medici villa at Poggio a Caiano, of the early 1480s. Anyone who juxtaposes the two works can develop a list of surprising similarities. Here and now the details are not significant: what is significant is that if a house – yes, the supposedly excluded Loosian category – looks so much like a great work of architectural art, perhaps the burden of proof that it is non-art does not lie with the artist, ironist or not. The more one considers the art-historical embeddedness of his work, the less satisfied one can be with the working stereotype of Adolf Loos as anti-artist pure and simple.

To some extent the problem concerns the development of understandably anti-aesthetic 'functionalist' thinking, in more extreme form than whatever stemmed from Le Corbusier (himself ever respectful of French classical tradition), especially in Czechoslovakia and elsewhere in Central Europe in the 1920s and 1930s. But though the Czech-born Viennese Loos was eventually taken as a prophet of functionalism, he was never prepared to reduce architecture to mere functionalist-utilitarian determinism himself. His ingenious notion of the *Raumplan* ('spatial plan'), though architecturally clever, obviously had its impracticalities, including the complication and expense of an engineer collaborator, just so as to have the floors of rooms occur on discontinuous levels, not to mention the additional complexity of any subsequent alteration in response to changing needs: hardly the economy and efficiency generally advertised by functionalism. Comparing buildings by Loos with buildings by dyed-in-the-wool Czech functionalists also tends to show up the art in Loos which otherwise grateful functionalists supposedly so bravely eschewed. And still people who should know better take Loos's de-ornamentalized simplicity as simple point of origin of a general-purpose 'Bauhaus functionalism.' As may become clear by the end of the present reconsideration of Loos as an artist-architect, to extrapolate further from Loos as proto-functionalist to Loos as grandfather of 'minimalism,' meaning now, however, not the best sculpture of the 1960s and 1970s but merely a fashionably frigid decorative mannerism in repressively up-tight 'luxury' architecture and design *c.* 2000, can only betray ignorance of Loos – as if all 'degrees zero' were the same.

The present reading of the master's work should go some way to redressing a sense of Loos as not having an artistic 'personality' – ironically that was precisely how his early disciple and earliest advocate, the contemporary Loosian art historian Franz Glück, sought to introduce him to the cultural world. Ultimately, however, a few comments of the cultural critic Theodor Adorno (noted in chapter 7), possibly deriving from vexed expressions of Walter Benjamin's fairly remedial interest in Loos in the last years of the architect's life, have issued in a vague sense of Loos's being diminished as accessory to a conclusive juridical 'failure' of the modernist architecture he did much to bring about; that he must surely have gone down with the ship of modernism, except insofar as postmodernism managed to secure him a theoretical afterlife on the basis of his writings alone, above all 'Ornament and Crime' – and that's *not* 'Ornament *as* Crime' (chapter 4).

The turn against architectural modernism inevitably implicated Loos, however mistakenly. But far from incidental in this matter is a standing caricature of modernist architecture as definitively committed, whether idealistically or materialistically, to glass, whether as potentially transcendent, in line with the light-mysticism of German expressionist architects – notably in *Glasarchitektur*, by Bruno Taut's associate Paul Scheerbart (1914) – or else as, so to speak, a materially transparent material capable of rendering naked the tectonics of structure (something which has always troubled conservatives, making odd company for Adorno to keep). If Adorno preferred to oppose the latter, he doesn't seem as prepared to frame it as wittily as André Breton's Corbusian caricature of glass architecture connoting coldness and lack of privacy in his surrealist novella *Nadja* (1928): "Me, I'll continue to dwell in my glass house … where I rest all night on a glass bed with glass sheets …"[2] Eventually Adorno and his many followers will seem dismayed, spiritually affronted, by expanses of glass in (later) modern architecture as inhospitable toward human presence: presumably rejecting by virtue of slickness and reflexivity anything like 'dwelling.'

Some analysis is in order, of the critical situation in which this architect and his reputation have been implicated in this in preparation for moving on with a fresh look at Loos and his work. By 1933 Walter Benjamin might even seem to have set out some such terms, as in the section 'To Live Without Leaving Traces,' in his text 'Short Shadows II' (1933; 701–02).[3] If anything, however, Benjamin had been attracted to just such slickness as promising a fresh modern start, free of 'aura,' though a certain *topos* which he employs seems confusingly ambivalent. How Adorno, in as it were the slipstream of Benjamin, would seem not to mind effectively pinning what today is too easily taken for anti-modernist moral distaste on Adolf Loos, it would fall to Massimo Cacciari to straighten out. Let us briefly look at the critical situation more closely.

Art-historically, the problem is that, though in a developmental sense Adolf Loos's architecture did make Le Corbusier's architecture possible, and the different but still glassier architecture of Ludwig Mies van der Rohe and others, Loos simply never built or even projected any building with an unconventionally large area of glass. Hence he should not be blamed for this major feature of an increasingly hostile anti-modernist caricature of all modernist architecture as so much 'functionalism' (a category in the development of a special strain of which, the Czech, Loos had in fact played an inspiring part). Indeed, the domestic architecture of Loos, which comprises the major part of his production, is sufficiently closed unto itself to be marked, all parties agree, by a strong sense of privacy. Now if we ask where the dubious anti-modernist Loosian caricature came from, the likely answer is Walter Benjamin, whose interest in architecture seems to have blossomed in 1927, as he reports in a letter of that August to Hugo von Hofmannsthal,[4] which is to say, during Loos's fluorescence of fame a few years before his death.

Loos and Karl Kraus, the great anti-journalistic journalist (1874–1936), were like two peas in a pod, as Benjamin knew when he wrote about them, possibly by the time of a fragmentary text called 'Karl Kraus,' of 1928, but definitely by that of the substantial article 'Karl Kraus,' of late 1931, which is actually dedicated to Glück, the Loos enthusiast. In the article Benjamin appreciates Loos's basic notion of "separat[ing] the work of art from the article of use" as akin to Kraus's campaign to separate "information and the work of art" in journalistic circumstances; hence "[t]he hack journalist is, in his heart, at one with the ornamentalist" (op. cit., in n. 3; 434), meaning, for his readiness to fill pages with such fluff that it hardly matters whether it's indulgent art-for-art's sake or the most artless functionalism. (Loos may have tended to be weakly accused of the latter by Adorno and others just because he couldn't possibly be guilty of the former.) Benjamin wants to support the uncompromising criticality of Kraus towards "a society that is in the process of building houses with glass walls, and terraces extending far into the living rooms that are no longer living rooms" (438). However, no house whatsoever by Loos even approximates to this characterization, and Benjamin may even have had in mind Ludwig Mies van der Rohe's new and splendid, and broadly Loosian-boxy, Tugendhat Villa, of 1930, at Brno, Loos's home town, in the Czech Lands of the Austrian empire, with its living room wall of mammoth glass plates that in good weather could be lowered into the basement at the press of a button. A couple of years later, in 1933, 'Experience and Poverty,' in 'Short Shadows, II,' includes another critical barb against Scheerbart's "culture of glass" where Benjamin speaks quite far-fetchedly of "adjustable, movable glass-covered (*sic*) dwellings of the kind since built by Loos and Le Corbusier" (733). To read Benjamin with scrupulous scriptural attention, in search of insight into Adolf Loos's architectural art, would seem to be quite mistaken.

The Kraus essay mentions as borrowed from Goethe a memorable figure of the philistine, would-be art connoisseur running his hand over the surface of an engraving or a relief in order to feel it by gross physical sensation instead of by the sublimated detachment of sight, as the Benjamin who eschews the aura of bourgeois art and is inclined to favor the very slickness of caricaturally modernist glass architecture, would agree (even if detachment might for Adorno become a question of alienation). From an unpublished fragment dating to 1931 or 1932 it is evident that the Goethean *topos* was borrowed from the first serious book on Loos, just recently published: "While reading Goethe's rebuke to philistines and many other art lovers who like to touch copper engravings and reliefs, the idea came to him [Loos] that anything that can be touched cannot be a work of art, and anything that is a work of art should be placed out of reach" (554).[5] The source quoted and cited is the 'Outline of the Personality' of Loos by Franz Glück, prefaced to the young Loosian architect Heinrich Kulka's *Adolf Loos: Das Werk des Architekten* (Vienna: Schroll, 1931). Whether or not Loos himself ever employed the figure,[6] it relates to his despised 'graphic-art' approach to architectural design and perhaps even of scarification as a form of tattoo.

On the part of Theodor Adorno, any sense of antipathy toward Loos as straw-man of a dehumanizing architectural functionalism does seem likely influenced by Benjamin's portrayals. By the time of the posthumous *Aesthetic Theory* one might almost be reading reactions to modernist church architecture by Catholics who regret the reforms of Vatican II. If this has not been reckoned, perhaps it is only because the low-intensity engagement of both major critics with actual modern architecture acted as a passive cause, lowering critical resistance to iconoclastic anti-modernism under postmodernism. It was a wholesale postmodernism, essentially literary in thrust, that caused much 'cultural' excitement by locating architecture for the first time in the forefront of a comprehensive shift in master style, with probably the most brutal anti-modernism abroad since the ruckus that Adolf Loos caused with his 'Ornament and Crime' lecture-essay of 1909.

There is eventually a recovery from dismissiveness in the challenging but sympathetic writings of Massimo Cacciari, after Adorno's death. In the text known as 'Loos and His Angel' (1981), while certain unspecified exterior "compositional details" of the Steiner, Horner and Strasser houses, of 1910–19, seem somehow unpleasantly mechanical, even if "strictly connected to the interior rooms," the 1922 Rufer House's fenestrational "eurythmy" pleases with a "finished, classical presence" that counters modern cultural deracination (171).[7] (One hopes this claim does not owe too much to the classical figural reliefs embedded in the façade, because the fenestration of the earlier Horner House, for one, is already beautifully eurythmic.) Adorno the musicologist would have noticed the point which Cacciari makes, by means of specifically modernist music, of the happy parataxis of the Rufer fenestration: even modern "dissonance must be composed: even the extreme dissonances must be the object of composition" (172); and how he proceeds to speak of "the polyphonic dissonances of Loosian composition" (192). The facing of the Rufer House is neither a concealment nor a reflection of "the truth of the interior" (173), but is taken as an essentially linguistic disposition; and further on, where the Loosian house is typically boxy (*but opaque*), Loos's calculated perfection of the exterior is likened to Kraus as *linguistically* transparent. Moreover, there is outright denial of the openness found so alarming when mistakenly ascribed to excessive glazing: "This exterior does not express, does not produce, does not have transparences – and for this very reason it may (perhaps) enclose an interior, an authentic place of the collected. It leaves open, so to speak, the possibility of an interior" (182) – a reading which entails the essentially modernist conception of *volume* over and against mass. How mistaken even great critics have been to sloganize against Loos for a caricaturally inhuman modernist architecture of steel and glass: Cacciari is quite right to insist that "Loos cannot in any way be seen as part of Scheerbartian Glaskultur" (187).

All told, it seems risky to take as definitive Adorno's late comments on architectural modernism in *Aesthetic Theory* (1970), which are too abbreviated by over-familiarity, and possibly crabbed by disappointment, to hold up in changing circumstances – as if they stood ready to serve the undialectical abolition of modernist 'utopian' idealism by a postmodernism with nothing better – surely not capitalist materialism – to offer.[8] Better to read back through Adorno's challengingly subtle essay 'Functionalism Today' (1965), which acknowledges as point of departure a Loosian distinction of the purposeful and the artistic – which Benjamin had seen as affiliating him with Karl Kraus.[9] Surprisingly enough, in view of the position eventually imputed to Adorno, this most famous Adorno architectural text actually makes no mention of glass or steel at all, only a single theoretically useless mention of stone and concrete.

Looking back further, to Adorno's *Minima Moralia* (1951), we can see what the later anti-modernist caricatures were based on, that is, the actually more Corbusian than Loosian notion of a 'machine for living' as a supposed dehumanization of architecture by reduction to mechanical utility. By rights that should even be ruled unfair to Le Corbusier, whose call for artistic awareness has so often been conveniently, or cynically, ignored (assuming that calls for formal value are calls for a human benefit, *pace* extreme 'productivist' functionalism). "The functional modern habitations designed from a *tabula rasa*," Adorno writes here, "are living-cases manufactured by experts for philistines, or factory sites that have strayed into the consumption sphere, devoid of all relation to the occupant ..." (38; note the theme of 'bad' detachment).[10] Even forms originating by mechanical determination could be fetishized as superficial style: "From a distance the difference between the Vienna Workshops and the Bauhaus is no longer so considerable. Purely functional curves, having broken free of their purpose, are now becoming just as ornamental as the basic structures of Cubism" (39). Adorno must have faced something like the affective loss of the reactionaries. He even employs an affirmative variation on the Goethe *topos* of the caressing sweep of an appreciative hand, saying of American roads, "they are without the mild, soothing, un-angular character of things that have felt the touch of hands or their immediate implements. It is as if no-one had ever passed their hand over the landscape's hair" (48). Instances of a modern corporate architecture of glass as bourgeois-liberal charade of 'transparency' are found as well, as "the old injustice is not changed by a lavish display of light ... but is in fact concealed by the gleaming transparency of rationalized big business ..." (58). Thus it is by tracing back almost to Benjamin's demise that Adorno connects, however unreliably, with him on Kraus and, as if by induction, Loos.[11]

Without pretending that this complex affair concerning the reputation of the artist-architect Adolf Loos has been exhaustively plumbed, this account is enough to illuminate the problem of Loos as a major case of cultural critique all too estranged from art history.

Rather than contend with the received wisdom, let us refresh the question by as it were standing back and allowing Loos's work and, to some extent, even his thought, to show itself as participating in fine art as such, on the principle that if it walks like art and talks like art it may be art, not to mention surprisingly beautiful as such. I put it this way because as a college sophomore taking my first course in architectural history, with Everard M. Upjohn (grandson of Connecticut State Capitol Upjohn and great-grandson of Trinity Church Wall Street Upjohn), I could understand how Loos's work had an important place in the unfolding of architectural modernity, but I wondered if it would ever actually appeal aesthetically to me: maybe, like much Northern art, it must prove interesting *instead of* beautiful. I had seen the most accessible Viennese works as a student and liked and respected them. But I don't think I buckled down to study Loos until my thoughts were turned to Loos indirectly in confronting the eighteenth-century Berkeley House, near Newport, Rhode Island, just about a decade ago, and being inspired by it to ponder the relation of vernacular building to sophisticated architecture (and of modernism to generalized classicism), which put me squarely and firmly in mind of my never forgotten but theretofore admired only from a distance Adolf Loos.

My art-historical interest in Adolf Loos, along with my interest in Wittgenstein, and in the kindred pursuits by both of a bare-bones, uncompromised truth, had been stimulated, just as I finished an academic dissertation under Wittkower (and, when he died, Dorothea Nyberg) on eighteenth- and nineteenth-century architecture, by Allan Janik and Stephen Toulmin's then new *Wittgenstein's Vienna* (1973). There Karl Kraus, with his own terse rhetorical concision, also figures. Indeed, that is where many of us first encountered his most famous pronouncement: "Adolf Loos and I — he literally and I grammatically — have done nothing more than show that there is a distinction between an urn and a chamber pot and that it is this distinction above all that provides culture with elbow room. The others, those who fail to make this distinction, are divided into those who use the urn as a chamber pot and those who use the chamber pot as an urn."[12] Curious about what might be better than nihilistic in Loos and Wittgenstein, I wasn't yet sure that there was anything more in Kraus; but having grown to appreciate him made me wonder how the critical situation came about, as I became more familiar with Loos's work, stimulated in particular by Benedetto Gravagnuolo's *Adolf Loos: Theory and Works* (1982) and Yehuda Safran and Wilfried Wang's important Arts Council exhibition catalogue *The Architecture of Adolf Loos* (1985). These works initiated in me a sufficiently aesthetic awareness of Loos's architecture, almost without realizing it, to see that, whatever else they are, culturally speaking, his buildings definitely do not present themselves as self-evidently anti-artistic, let alone ugly, quite regardless of how charmingly naughty one might like to consider them if they did.

This book proceeds in nine thematic chapters, variously general and particular, theoretic and concrete. The first raises the problematic question of Loos as an artist-architect. While Loos might be both an artist and an anti-artist (or architect and anti-architect), any possibility that he might be exclusively an anti-artist is undermined by certain evident similarities of formal thinking with characteristically modernist works of art, including Cézanne's and other modernists' in painting. For this chapter a sense of the 'Biedermeier' is appropriate art-historical background for the bringing forth of Loos's live but unhampered awareness of tradition in architecture and design: a fine precedent of stalwart simplicity to which he was to some extent indebted without being at all beholden; and one can understand his apprehensions about its invocation, since what he was up to was anything but a stylistic revival of any sort. So let Biedermeier simplicity lend Loos's simplicity a dimension of historicity, but as nothing like a restraint or limit: on behalf of a liberating modernist formalism rather than in demure revival of a certain mode of respectable Congress-of-Vienna bourgeois-classic simplicity. That on the larger scale even such a distinction must entail art history and thereby art, means that, especially in view of commonalities with early modernist painting, our known ironist can no longer be taken so literally in asserting, for his own rhetorical purposes, that in his view almost no buildings rightly count as architectural art. Even his single most notorious executed work, the 'Looshaus' on the Michaelerplatz, in Vienna, has features in common with unqualified 'art' architecture, of both classic and modern ilk. And if it proves possible to find in the work of a disciple of Loos a direct stylistic evocation of the master, something considerably more than non-art is at stake.

The second chapter deals indirectly with the Loosian question of vernacular architecture, which, though not official fine-arts architecture, is nevertheless a problem of art at grassroots level. Whether something is architectural art or not implicates the question of classical orthodoxy as guaranteed architecture, always and everywhere, as against local homegrown vernaculars (especially with hand-me-down ornament to make them presentable). This question, which had abiding pertinence to Loos's work, is raised indirectly by centering the discussion on a pre-Loosian building, in British colonial America at that — one which would have interested the Anglophile Loos for its crafted character alone, and which may even seem broadly Loosian as one looks into its strongly vernacular aspect.

As a young architect-to-be, Loos actually lived in America for most of three years. The third chapter considers not only his origins and the complex, ambiguous ethnic identity of a young German-speaking Austrian, born in

Moravia, in the Czech Lands, and living by his wits in New York while taking in all he could about architecture; it also speculates on his relationship with the city in the mid-1890s. At the center of the discussion is his first significant building design after returning to Vienna, a projected Jubilee church for the emperor, Franz-Joseph as conceivably influenced by an important 'Beaux-Arts' classical building just rising as Loos left New York for home.

Chapter 4 takes up the ultimately Loosian question of ornament and its elimination from the new architecture. Loos the artist-architect comes into better focus as we begin to understand his theoretical opposition to ornament as not so simple after all. Yes, the people who thought that the way you make a building into architecture is by superadding ornamentation were wrong; but almost the only thing widely known about Loos is seriously flawed: that by referencing tattoo he supposedly equated ornament with primitivity and crime in the lecture-essay of 'Ornament and Crime.' Here fresh attention is given to that challenging text. Loos's second most famous text, 'Architecture,' figures in chapter 5, along with two executed architectural designs by Loos that turn out to employ ornament, contradicting any simplistic sense of its supposedly all-or-nothing theoretical elimination.

The sixth chapter concerns a project that by itself seems frankly ludic, but which might almost symbolize the encounter between the cosmopolitan but Old World classicism that was never far below the horizon of Loos's consciousness and the excitement of a new and extreme American building type, the skyscraper. We may speculate, in connection with Loos's American experience, on his understanding of Louis Henri Sullivan's role in the invention and promulgation of the skyscraper, especially through the essay 'The Tall Office Building Artistically Considered'; yet what could be more ornamental and less functionalist for the headquarters of a large urban American newspaper than to take the form of a single colossal classical column (punning, too, on the typographical meaning of that term).

The possibility of a willful 'architecturelessness' is raised in chapter 7 as a way of coming to terms with Loos's problematic theoretical denial that houses, at least, are or should be works of art, and that most buildings designed by people identified as architects (at least in his historical moment) amount to architecture at all. If in 1910 Picasso had written that because most paintings are not works of art and hence he was not going to consider himself a painter, would that have been taken at face value for the next fifty years as an effective denial that his work could be, or was ever really meant to be, art? Regrettably, this is just how the writings and buildings of Loos are still, *a hundred years later*, widely presented. Attention then turns from such grander claims to Loos's surprisingly 'green' practice in the remodeling of existing houses in the period of the Great War, and in social housing during several postwar years. Here is a humbler Loos than is usually pondered, but perhaps no less an artist and certainly no less an architect.

Chapter 8 entertains a different Anglo-Austrian question, very much a matter of Loos's work as not so styleless after all: the house that the philosopher Wittgenstein, himself a specter of sorts in Loos's itinerary, built for his sister in Vienna. This building inevitably invites the not so simple question of what it has to do with Loos, as begun by Loos's favorite pupil yet purportedly the work of Wittgenstein himself. Problematic aspects of the project concern not only whether any work of art can stand *sui generis*, outside of art history but also how mere fastidious perfectionism can bring about art.

Finally, under the rubric 'Loos and Minimalism,' the ninth and last chapter reviews some of the historical background to the problematic of so-called 'minimalism' during the last decade. True Minimalism, which was a movement in sculpture in the 1960s and 1970s, had significant historical roots in the constructivism of the period between the world wars, whose architectural counterpart was orthodox functionalism. (Despite what one hears now, it had nothing whatsoever to do with the transcendental aesthetic of 'Less Is More' propounded in architecture by Ludwig Mies van der Rohe.) Loos may in the end have a more integral affinity with original 'sixties Minimalism' – when his own work became newly appreciated – than with the 'minimal' as a critical free radical, more recently.

Other essays by the author bearing on Loos: 'Karel Teige: Functionalist and Then Some,' *Art in America* 89/12 (December 2001), 100–05, 128; 'The Vital Skin: Riegl, the Maori and Loos,' in Richard Woodfield, ed., *Framing Formalism: Riegl and the History of Art*, Critical Voices in Art, Theory, and Culture (Amsterdam: G + B Arts International, 2001), 151–82; 'The "One-Walled House": A New Facet to Loos's Dodgy Classicism?' *Word and Image* 23 (2007), 270–74; 'Stalking Loos in Bohemia in 2005,' *Kosmas: Czechoslovak and Central European Journal* 22 (2008), 100–06; 'The Anti-Architect,' *Art Monthly* (London), no. 348 (July–August 2011), 11–14.

A note on punctuation: all quotations here take double quotation marks except for quotations within quotations, which take single quotation marks, along with titles of less than book-length texts, and terms highlighted in 'scare quotes.'

ACKNOWLEDGMENTS

Certain colleagues have helped greatly to bring the present project to realization. First in time, I thank Dr Paul O'Grady, of Trinity College, Dublin, who had already shared a visit with me to the Wittgenstein House, for showing me Bishop Berkeley's house in the summer of 1998. The experience stimulated my incipient thinking as I began to relate Loos to that curious old building in preparing a lecture for the next spring at Edinburgh College of Art and in the beautiful little Mackintosh lecture hall of the Glasgow School of Art. And that led, in turn, to an extended ECA appointment as Centenary Fellow, which effectively supported the bulk of the research and writing of this book – not least by affording me an ongoing art and architecture lecture audience, including committed and conspicuously interested students, for my developing ideas.

Further collegial hospitality at Cambridge allowed me also to present there what have here grown into several chapters as lectures in the Faculty of Architecture and History of Art. For this I thank Dr Deborah Howard, Professor of Architectural History, and members of the Martin Centre for Architectural and Urban Studies, especially Dr Marcial Echenique and Dr Manolo Guerci, the latter then a research fellow and now on the staff of the University of Kent School of Architecture. In America, I thank Professor Jean-Michel Rabaté and Dr Aaron Levy for provoking a, for me, crucial lecture, since grown into chapter one, at the Kelly Writers' House of the University of Pennsylvania.

For a variety of invaluable facilitations in Vienna and the Loosian 'Crown Lands' I want especially to thank Ms Jitka Hynková; O Univ Prof Mag art Franz Lesák, of the Institute for Architectural Design of the Technical University of Vienna; Ph Dr Andreas Nierhaus, Curator of Architecture at the Wien

Museum; and Prof Ph Dr Pavel Zatloukal, director of the Muzeum Uměni, Olomouc.

Here at home I want to acknowledge a general indebtedness to Kenneth Frampton, Ware Professor of Architecture at Columbia University, for the inspiring intellectual generosity of the celebrated expert prepared to encourage an art-historical generalist. I am also especially grateful to Joan Ockman, Distinguished Senior Fellow in the School of Design at the University of Pennsylvania, for a generously responsive reading of the manuscript; and to my Hofstronian colleague in Comparative Literature, Pellegrino D'Acierno, the translator of Tafuri, I owe vital elucidations of Cacciari and much more.

My thanks extend, too, to my research assistant Alexandra Halidisz, especially for her diplomatic handling of the complexities of permissions. Also to Liza Thompson, at I.B.Tauris, for her editorial acumen, and to Paul Tompsett for his care and patience in production.

Impossible to account is the unfailing support of my wife Marjorie Welish, and her sympathetic Loosophilia-by-induction, which developed as we poked about together in search of the master's work.

Three of the present chapters have previously appeared in somewhat different form in the following journals and book, the editors of which I thank for permission to re-publish: chapter 3 as 'Imperial America in Adolf Loos's Jubilee Church Project,' *Kosmas: Czechoslovak and Central European Journal* 16 (2002), 1–20; chapter 6 as '"His Native Doric" and Other Columns: Adolf Loos and the Chicago Tribune,' *Things* (London), no. 15 (Winter 2001–02), 20–37; and chapter 8 as 'Form(alisme), function(alisme) et la maison de Wittgenstein en histoire de l'art,' trans. David Lachance, in Céline Poisson, ed., *Penser, dessiner, construire: Wittgensten et l'architecture* (Paris and Tel Aviv: Èditions de l'éclat, 2007), 45–62.

Finally: the Ariadne Press, of Riverside, Calif., has been most accommodating with respect to the many quotations from Michael Mitchell's translations of Loos's essays in *Ornament and Crime: Selected Essays* (ed. Adolf Opel), of 1998, and *On Architecture* (ed. Adolf and Daniel Opel), of 2002, volumes which have rendered much more accessible the range of the architect's writings for English-speaking readers.

ABBREVIATIONS

AAL   *The Architecture of Adolf Loos: An Arts Council Exhibition*, ed. Yehuda Safran and Wilfried Wang (1985), 2nd edn. London: Arts Council of Great Britain, 1987. Especially Loos's 'Architecture' as translated by Wang, pp. 104–09.

OA   Adolf Loos, *On Architecture*, ed. Adolf and Daniel Opel, trans. Michael Mitchell (Riverside, Calif.: Ariadne, 2002).

OC   Adolf Loos, *Ornament and Crime*, ed. Adolf Opel, trans. Michael Mitchell (Riverside, Calif.: Ariadne, 1998).

T   Adolf Loos, *Trotzdem; 1900-1930*, ed. Adolf Opel (Vienna: Prachner, 1988). Especially 'Architektur,' pp. 90–104.

1

LOOS AND FINE ART

A new overview, reappraising and reinterpreting Adolf Loos (1870–1933) can begin and perhaps end with questions of art and artlessness. For the work of this early modern architect, in theory and practice, is often enough taken as only an extreme case of nihilistic early modern iconoclasm, out to deny art as such and prove all the braver for it. Ironically, Loos is often made to sound like a Marcel Duchamp of anti-architecture even though, ironically enough, he is somehow also cast as a patron saint of ultra-rational architectural functionalism. Different in theory but likewise negative is also a persistent view of the Viennese Loos as happily heartless architectural counterpart to the Vienna Circle of 'logical positivists' in philosophy, with its summary nullifications of whatever might be accused of not being empirical as hopelessly metaphysical – that circle from which Ludwig Wittgenstein, having in some measure made it possible, walked away. Scandalously enough, Loos did make something in the order of a claim that architecture, or, rather, the private house, should not be a matter of art; though as with Nietzsche, it would be dangerous to lose track of the ironist's twists. Rather than contend with the terms of the nihilistic view we might seek to open up the question by teasing out Loos's artfulness, taking Loos more artistically seriously in a variety of aspects.

Misconstrual of Loos has only worsened now that being all too well known an artist has come to imply being a media 'star,' identifiable by performing a role in an art world that is a realm of entertainment rather than by producing notable works of art. Here Loos himself does not help his case by having been a bon vivant who liked creating a stir while managing not to ruffle the basic persona of a scrupulously groomed Anglophile (and Ameriphile) variety of the turn-of-the-century artist dandy. And as far as the art of architecture, specifically, was concerned, some ambiguity was inevitable. It had long seemed a commonplace that what made a mere non-art building into a work of architectural art was the superaddition of ornament borrowed from one or another canonical historical style (Greek, Roman, Byzantine, Gothic, Renaissance, Baroque, Neoclassical), when Loos came along and claimed that such a conception was an affront to urbanity. The sophisticated modern city-dweller should know better: applied ornamentation, like tattooing, should be evidence of low civility. Surely it was wrongheaded to think that ornament was what made an otherwise unqualified building architectural art: if anything, in modern times ornament was vain and vulgar.

In line with William Morris in theory, if not with the Viennese 'Secession' as offshoot of the Morrisonian Arts and Crafts movement, for designer-artists to be handing over to craftsmen 'artistic' designs for servile execution, no matter how up-to-date, signaled the ruination of craft traditions which had otherwise held artistic authenticity. A valid architecture should be like unselfconscious, unpretentious, local vernacular building, the praises of which are sung in his text 'Architecture' (1910). No wonder confusion set in about it being a fine thing for a building to amount to art, and about what, if anything, was to be the role of an architect who agreed with what Loos was saying.

His signature building as architecture-as-such

Vital to the question of Loos as artist-architect is the case of his signature building, known as the 'Looshaus,' on the Michaelerplatz in central Vienna, designed in 1909 and built in 1910–11. It is true that in the time of this building he was already calling into question in 'Architecture' whether architecture as such, as some say, or at very least whether a house, ought to be conceived as a work of architecture and hence as a work of art. For the time being, we can accept Loos's 'masterpiece,' with the Goldman & Salatsch men's tailoring emporium on the lower two floors and private apartments above, as at least eligible to be counted as architecture. After all, a collective apartment house may have at least the dignity of an individual house (one might even say, 'of many mansions').

Because this heroic upstart of a modern building has stood like a bulwark against the notion that pseudo-historical ornamentation is what qualifies a building to count as architecture and hence art, and its author as an artist-architect, it seems to have been all too embroiled in ritual controversy and insufficiently regarded as enmeshed in art history as a work of art. Evidence is ample of the work's artistic affiliations, ignored in the standard approach to the building, with its classy urban tailor shop below and supposedly brutishly fenestrated apartment walls above. Loos himself seems to have enjoyed the metropolitan scandal, at least as what he would have called an English 'good sport.' Now that the building is a century old we may be able to assess it more fairly as the textbook masterpiece it became – first of the modern as true, good, and beautiful, during the mid-twentieth century, later for essentially literary postmodern cultural generalization.

Suppose it is true, first of all, that the emperor, whose imperial front door it faced, disliked looking at the Looshaus's supposedly ever so radically plain upper stories, which Loos himself once reputedly likened to vernacular plainness. Well, then it is also true that the plainness of those upper stories was hardly different from the plainness of the fenestration – which is to say, the disposition of the windows in a façade – along prominent stretches of courtyard within the precincts of his own palace, notably the east end of the court between the Imperial Chancellery wing and the Leopoldine wing. As a matter of fact, just such plain fenestration, with grids of windows having few or no frames, can be seen as a nice old *Goethezeit*, Neoclassic-to-Biedermeier thing, as traditional as neatly pressed linens (as the eighteenth-century scientist and writer Georg Lichtenberg is sometimes invoked for in his sheer aphoristic critical terseness as anticipating Karl Kraus or Wittgenstein).

Instead of thinking of the Looshaus as rudely and artlessly interjecting the horrid modern world into charming Vienna, let us try thinking instead of the Looshaus, as it rose, politely keeping its counsel about a certain gross stylistic anachronism across the way. For though the 'Michaelertrakt,' as that wing of the palace is called, with the great entrance portal to the Hofburg, was designed by Josef Emanuel (son of Johann Bernhard) Fischer von Erlach in the early eighteenth century, nobody had actually gotten around to building it until 1889–93, when it must have looked more revivalist than authentic. To exaggerate for emphasis: the moment the Looshaus went up facing it across the square, as a perfectly decent modern counterpart to the plainer stretches of the palace, the Michaelertrakt should have blushed for looking like a young person dressed in vintage clothes. The trouble was, everybody except the moderns was in on the historical charade of, in this case, 'Late Baroque Classicism.' Only because charades of the kind were precisely what was meant at the time by architectural art did Adolf Loos make a point of negating all such talk.

1. David Gilly, Vieweg Press, Brunswick, Germany, 1800–07.

Fortunately, modern art, including architecture and even this particular building, was coming into its own historical conviction. So when we hear Loos, in the same moment as the Looshaus, seemingly denying architecture the status of art, we ought to keep the polemical circumstances in mind.

Purportedly it was the shamelessly unadorned simplicity, as if *undressed*, of the unrelieved, gridded fenestration of the whole upper façade that had everybody in a stir. A well-known journalistic cartoon could liken it to a flipped-up storm-drain grate in the street in front of it only because, to most people, it looked ignobly lacking in the bourgeois grandeur that made for serious architecture, architecture worthy of the name. But despising historicism – the parasitic dependence on historical stylistics – is not the same as denying art history. Besides the overlooked affinity with other parts of the supposedly offended Hofburg, the building has quite decent art-historical ancestors in its own right. There is an urbane similarity between the façade of the Looshaus, with its plain upstairs, with recessed Roman Doric porch between two converging streets, and the walls with evenly spaced square windows bending back left and right from a rounded corner with recessed

2. Adolf Loos, Looshaus (or Michaelerhaus),
Vienna, 1909–11.

Roman Doric porch, in Baldassare Peruzzi's (Mannerist) Palazzo Massimo
alle Colonne, in Rome, begun in 1532. That is a valid if relatively arcane
art-historical point, if not all there is to the case, especially in view of the
nearness in time as well as Central European space of the earnestly simple
Biedermeier.[1]

Again, the burghers of 1910 really must have wanted to have their
tantrum of rejection because the Looshaus could easily have been welcomed
on proto- or quasi-Biedermeier terms as happily akin, for instance, to
a certain classicizing commercial building with chaste Doric porch, built
likewise on the corner of a tapering site a century earlier in Brunswick
(Braunschweig), Germany, by David Gilly, teacher of the famous ultra-
classicist Karl Friedrich Schinkel: the publishing establishment Vieweg
Verlag, of 1800–07 (the firm, which left Brunswick only in 1974, published
a book on Loos's Müller House in Prague, by Christian Kuhn, in 1989).

Gilly was a major architect belonging to that restrained, so-called 'Zopf' tendency in Middle European culture *c.* 1800, named after women's tight hair braids of 'upright' connotation: the cultural set-up, in a sense, for the Biedermeier. Gilly's building, too, was dual-purpose, if not so private/public disjunct as tailoring and housing: as an industrial and office building housing both printing and publishing functions. Formally, the volumetric articulation of the three-bay central portal of Gilly's long flank with flush doorway and flanking windows below, all without disturbing the smooth façade plane, has a Loosian ring. A large, typically Gillian but also pre-Louis-Sullivanian, sweeping semicircular arc, here somewhat hidden behind the portico on the building's shorter side, would also one day cut smartly through the otherwise quite regimented fenestration of a late Loos hotel project of 1931. With such art-historical connections available, making a scene for publicity might even save the cause of art.[2]

Beyond Biedermeier overtones, the wider stylistic relations of the Looshaus (artistic style being intrinsically a matter of art) are richer than its usual characterizations allow – the question of art as style, and style as ornament, being itself not as simple as a mere presence (below) or absence (above) of classical columns. There is not only a significant British feature, sometimes acknowledged, but a relevant American parallel of overall form, all the more significant after Loos's direct experience of early modern Chicago architecture, including a major possibility of Sullivan from outside Chicago. On the first point: the inset bay windows of the second floor (American style; 'first floor,' European), are accepted as reminiscent of the British Victorian 'oriels' referred to by Loos himself ("English bow windows"; *OA* 96). In aspects of disposition, the Looshaus has been seen to compare with two recent American office buildings with which Loos might have acquainted himself in Chicago, namely, S. S. Beman's Studebaker Building (now Fine Arts Building), of 1884, and The Rookery, 1885–66, by Burnham and Root (Czech and Mistelbauer 108). Apropos of the latter, Frampton sees "two-storey inlaid columnar peristyle" of the Looshaus entrance façade as "a simplified version … of the very similar treatment devised by Burnham and Root for the street-level façade of their Rookery Building" (Frampton, 'In Spite' 216). Loos would have understood that he was, if anything, returning to Burnham and Root's thinking before they took on the dubious job of imposing Imperial Roman classicism throughout the World's Columbian Exposition – which Loos had come to America to see – except, ever so notably, for Louis Sullivan's Transportation Building (by then already demolished).

Particularly Sullivanian, however, seems the crisp, unmodulated conjunction of cylindrical-columnar and boxy-beam forms in the lower, commercial part of the Looshaus, with, between the shorter bay windows of the entrance wall, each square pier between bays answering a column immediately beneath. This disposition follows an uncannily similar interplay of round and squared elements at the ground and first floor of Sullivan's Guaranty Building, in Buffalo, New York, of 1894–95. Loos was interested in Sullivan; and when Rudolf Schindler, one of his two most famous disciples who emigrated to America (the other being Richard Neutra) tried unsuccessfully to help Sullivan publish his *Kindergarten Chats* in Austria or Germany, between 1918 and 1922, Loos, in 1920, thought that possibly the Quakers of Vienna might be able to help (see McCoy). Sullivan parallels which have already been noticed include his Union Trust Company Building, at St Louis, 1892–93, and a Loos project of 1925 for an office building on the Boulevard des Italiens, in Paris, whose eleven storeys of unframed windows between a plain tall ground floor and a columned top are unabashedly reminiscent of the Looshaus (illus., Sekler 262, 263).

The Looshaus does seem to fascinate those who would rather engage with avant-garde *scandal* than with architectural art, and can deal with the *idea* of Loos's antiornamentalism but might be confused in the thick of things by Sullivan's American critical revisionist sense of ornament as hardly an all or nothing affair. In actual fact, the building never stood completely blank, even before the city fathers obliged Loos to add windowboxes on the front (which he did, in simple form but of bronze). Curiously, radical though it is, the Looshaus is one of those shake-up modernist masterpieces which prove surprisingly respectable, once invited into the serious art-historical canon, by an artist who may have spoken against the oppression of architectural historicism but who made art history one of the subjects of study in his private architectural school.

Loos's famous building is by no means artless and no stranger to the history of architectural art; and even in its plainness it is certainly not styleless. If it were, it would not have been possible for me, not long ago, to have been walking down Schleifmühlgasse, in the IV District, a street I had known since first staying there as a student forty years before, and suddenly to sense a building as uncannily Loosian, even suggestive of the Looshaus, on noticing its 'negative' oriels inset between columns on the top floor. This is the Paulaner-Haus, an apartment building at number 3, dating from 1910–11; and it turned out that its designer was Ernst Epstein (1881–1938), an engineer who built it while working with Loos supervising the construction of Looshaus. Hence

3. Louis H. Sullivan, Guaranty Building, Buffalo, New York, 1894–95. Detail of corner.

my conviction had depended entirely on a formal artistic device that simply reverses its formal equivalent on the Looshaus, and I can only have been picking up on the physiognomic character, the style, of the inverted Loosian form *qua* form. Because this was a matter of style, an essentially artistic affair, this second building, by a Loos disciple, must confirm its source, that is, the Looshaus, even beyond confirming itself, as a work of art.

It would be at least as wrongheaded to take the building as ugly, just for being largely unornamented, as to think it impudently transgressive of local convention, which it simply isn't, notwithstanding the fun that the very much 'artist' architect surely had with his scandalous struggle for the radical-progressive stance which this work as well as related contemporaneous

4. Loos, Looshaus. Detail of corner.

publicity effectively secured him. But Loos was more than a showman; he was a literate as well as intelligent artist who would definitely have liked knowing that a distinguished British Victorian critic stood behind him in the question of affirmative plainness. For English vernacular architecture had inspired the poet-critic Coventry Patmore to isolate a quality, applicable to the Looshaus, whose implications were Loosian before the fact. In an essay on 'Ideal and Material Greatness in Architecture' (1886), no doubt with Ruskin's notion of the 'Lamp of Sacrifice' (in *The Seven Lamps of Architecture*, 1849) at the back of his mind, Patmore propounds as architectural virtue a "modest ostentation" of "substantiality," which "constitutes the secret effect of many an old house that strikes us as 'architectural' though it may be almost wholly without architectural ornament." Why bother to build anything to last longer than oneself? "The answer is: Because that very 'waste' is the truest and most striking ornament," indeed, "an 'ornament' of the most noble and touching kind, which will be obvious at all seasons to yourself and every beholder, though the consciousness of its cause may be dormant; whereas the meanness of your own plan will be only the more apparent with every penny you spend in making it meretricious" (Patmore 212–13). Loos could have written that; and it applies as much to the elaborate, unseen (and surely expensive) steel trusswork which makes the great horizontal beam of the Looshaus façade possible as well as to the "magnanimously," Patmore would say, richly figured cipollino marble cladding.

One might be forgiven a certain impatience, after entertaining all this evidence, with the notion that the Looshaus is not a work of architectural art, and its author not really an architect, or, perish the thought, artist. The basis for considering a practice art, and its practitioner an artist, is its embeddedness in the great art-historical web of more- and less-related productions. For Loos's work to count as architecture pragmatically concerns, bluster aside, its participation in the ongoing history of buildings projected, built, and theorized as works in the art of architecture – one of the three 'fine arts' or 'arts of design' ('design' meaning *disegno*, which is projective conceptualization and not just drawing, as the Loos who warned against approaching architecture as merely a task in graphic design would have been pleased to emphasize). Whether Loos's productions were or were not architecture or architectural art was never simply something he was in a position to establish by mere fiat; and what really matters for the art question is the evidence of his active participation in an abiding art, still after him and even thanks to him under way, with a formidable history of more or less closely affiliated productions. Someone who knows no better may gawk at Loos's signature building as a strange, original brainstorm out of the blue; but what makes it architecture – even though Loos had reason for not appealing to that term – are its kinships with significant other buildings as (already) works of art.

The formal factor

With modernist buildings no longer subject to a classical system, the formal aspect of the building concerns, beyond its general volumetric exterior character, *fenestration* – again, the pattern of windows on its principal and other façades. Modern fenestration takes on great formal interest in its own right, but also in respect to composition in non-objective or abstract painting (which is why the abolition of the classical ornamental syntax is often compared with the abolition of tonality in music as well as of representation in painting and sculpture). Hence for Loos's fenestration to show significant relations to modern painting is one of the more ostensible ways in which his architecture shows itself as part and parcel of the 'fine arts' (i.e., painting, sculpture, architecture); and Loos shows himself especially good at handling not only asymmetrical fenestration as such, in detachment from any lingering of classically presumed symmetry, but astute combinations of symmetry with asymmetry in the same building.

The fenestration of Loos's houses, especially early on, as so many differently sized rectangular windows composed orthogonally within a rectangular wall – something other than, and more designed than a grid – is a primary formal feature that must be a matter of art, for it even finds significant counterparts in modern painting. It is no surprise for questions of symmetry and asymmetry to arise with divergences from regularity presumed to be dictated by 'functional' necessity, with variable elements non-aesthetically constrained to follow the interior disposition of a building. But that in practice that was not all there was to the matter is evident in a strong general distinction, in Loos's houses, between symmetrical fronts and asymmetrical flanks on the same buildings, which precisely as a compositional option confirms Loos's practice as that of an artist within the fine art of architecture. Even similarities between irregular but nicely ordered compositions of orthogonal elements of a single façade and comparably free orthogonal compositions in early modern painting, are questions of similarity between two fine arts.

That in the essay 'Architecture' Loos censures the approach to the task of architectural design as a "graphic art" of façade design (OA 76–78), merely in extension of the old academic way of dolling up a building façade to make it architectural, does not preclude appeal to sophisticated painting compositions, after the fact, as evidence that architecture and painting show points of constitutional similarity as visual arts. The likes of Cézanne were not mere graphic designers, and neither is Loos when his fenestration resembles such a composition by breaking with any presumption of a grid by setting windows of varied sizes in a grouping sharing an asymmetrical unity of interrelation, like a balancing of vectors. That entails something more independently aesthetic (and structuralistic) in respect to modernist painting than a merely 'graphic' sense of the façade.

Consider, from the mid-nineteenth century, Ruskin's extensive admiring description of the tolerance of irregularity (while maintaining orthogonality) on the Lagoon façade of the Palazzo Ducale in Venice, which has the last two windows at the right lower than the rest (with extra little square windows off-centered above, not even mentioned), so as to accommodate, inside, a council chamber with high, decorated ceiling. Ruskin understands the accommodation to function: "A modern architect, terrified at the idea of violating external symmetry, would have sacrificed [the internal disposition] ... But the old Venetian ... unhesitatingly raised the large windows to their proper position with reference to the interior of the chamber [comparably with what is called the 'Raumplan,' of varied floor levels in Loos], and suffered the external appearance to take care of itself." Not that the practical reason alone would be sufficient to justify a glaring awkwardness on the most conspicuous wall of the great maritime city for anyone approaching by sea. No, the last word must be aesthetic: "... I believe the whole pile rather gains than loses in effect by the variations thus obtained in the spaces of wall above and below the windows," says Ruskin in *The Stones of Venice* (1851–53; II. viii; Ruskin, *Stones* 2: 286). At the end of the century, Loos's Viennese contemporary Aloïs Riegl shows an even more affirmative sense of paratactical irregularity (which is not to say disorder) in late antique, i.e., still Roman but no longer classical, fenestration that seems practically Loosian. According to Riegl, in bringing the basilica into its own, the Early Christians were seeking "the most functional ... form," including a "straight beamed ceiling" suggestive of the flat roof advocated by Loos; but thereby, too a "thousand-year domination of form over surface ... was ... shattered," and "Now windows could pierce the walls in any way at all" (Riegl 250).

Despite anxieties of conservatives who (still) fear it as anarchic and want the reassurance of regulation as guarantee of order, the freeing up of fenestration made the actively formal 'relational' composition of modernist art possible. Now the hypotactical orderliness of absolute regularity is the stock in trade of classical architectural form, while moderns have long appreciated irregular, non-systematic or paratactical composition not only as found in Gothic but also in good vernacular building, as will be considered in the next chapter; but here 'good' vernacular architecture applies to distinctly artful anonymous compositions, not to just any structure ignorant of hypotactical rules. Likewise, Adolf Loos's liberated fenestration – which, by the way, if significant in private houses is a reason for considering them architectural art regardless of their designer's polemical remarks – is anything but a question of fenestration no longer mattering artistically. Even the 'liberated' floor levels of his *Raumplan* make, not for an easy concession that it doesn't matter where windows occur, but rather for an all the greater artistic challenge: with structural constraints less rigid than ever, and basic recourse to hypotactical order surrendered, artistically it matters more than ever where the windows go, and whether they relate to one another significantly while no longer constrained to a gridded orderliness of ranks and files. At the same time, a basic persistence of orthogonality allows for the sense of a fresh and deliberated order that is anything but anarchy, as in early abstract paintings by Piet Mondrian.

To generalize: all visible making of a point of fenestration as a matter of façade composition, whether symmetrical (hypotactical) or markedly free (paratactical), is a concrete matter of form implying artfulness. In regard to 'late modern' painting and sculpture, there has been a major critical reaction against form as made manifest in relational composition, and for some good reasons formalism itself has a bad name. Formalism taken to excess may mean fiddling while Rome burns; but what a gain there was, a century ago, when it first underwrote a definitively modern sense of the art object as having the responsible self-sufficiency of a logical proposition, independently of whether it 'applied' to anything beyond. For forms to stand in significant relations to one another was for form to stand alone as making manifest the art in art (as many a gifted vernacular artist would recognize), much like the priority contemporaneously assumed by logic as truly the philosophy in philosophy. In the heyday of Loos's architecture the great logician Bertrand Russell emphasized relations as "pure forms," symbolizable as 'x R y,' meaning the *relation* of x to y. So he could explain in 1919 how a proposition itself is relationally constituted, that in it which "remains unchanged when every constituent of the proposition is replaced by another" being its "form" (Russell 198–99).

Even early on the formal aspect is to the fore in Loos's work, notwithstanding his importance for later, purportedly anti-formal 'functionalist' tendencies. On a simple level, there is the way in which, if it formally resembles a known style of established architectural art, it must have form and is likely art. Consider the Museum Café, in central Vienna, of 1899, with its clarified version of the typical Viennese café layout, and its surfaces both plain and gently curved as planes, as finding some art-historical precedent in that accessibly *gemütlich*, sometimes oddly formally extreme mode of classical simplicity, the popular mid-nineteenth-century Biedermeier style of art, architecture and decoration. Despite alterations, the Museum Café still retains much of this character, with a rectitude that does not preclude charm. The shallow curvature of the ceiling and the dormer-like way the deep-set windows carve gently into it always remind me of a similar shallow curve over a window, as well as the simple whitewashed plainness, of a Biedermeier

5. Gustav Klimt, *Water Castle* (or *Schloss Kammer on the Altersee I*), 1908–09.

interior as conveyed, for a typical example, in an 1853 watercolor by Rudolf von Alt, *Peasant Room in Seebenstein* (Düsseldorf, Kunstmuseum).

With domestic architecture at stake in the broader question of Loos's work as architectural art, certain relevant aspects of his earlier houses can be considered, notably – even if not really a matter of architecture, if the contemporaneous claim of his 'Architecture' text be taken without irony – the Steiner House, 1910, in the inner suburb of Vienna called Hietzing (XIII District), built while the Looshaus was under construction in the city center. But witness such a contemporaneous modernist painting as Gustav Klimt's *Water Castle* (or *Schloss Kammer on the Altersee I*), of 1908–09 (Prague, National

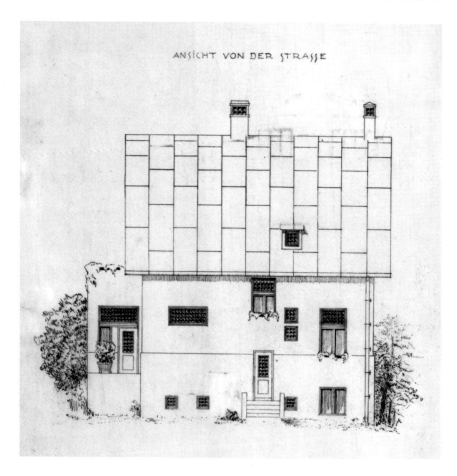

ANSICHT VON DER STRASSE

6. Loos, Horner House, Vienna, 1912. Detail of architect's submission drawing.

Gallery), whose black rectangles as well as white and yellow planes themselves constitute an asymmetric, while basically rectilinear, relational composition. On its own artistic terms Klimt's painting holds up a sophisticated, reservedly lyrical response to Austrian vernacular architecture that hardly makes one think twice about the freewheeling rectilinear fenestration of otherwise undeniable urbanity in such a Loos work in Hietzing as the Horner House, of 1912. Klimt's painting welcomes the formal art-worthiness of the simple country building into the formal context of the modern painting. In a way, its testimony marks a certain frontier or threshold of 'artliness,' for simply equating traditional Austrian domestic architecture with Loos's would be going too far, and losing the sense of the latter as a fine-art affair, here in respect only indirectly with vernacular form, while directly in respect to the compositional formalism of the modernist painter.

Indeed, the artfulness of Adolf Loos's architecture becomes evident in regard to contemporaneous paintings presenting comparable architectural forms in a sympathetic spirit. Examples by Cézanne, Klimt, and Bonnard, as well as a recurrent air of Mondrian, prove particularly telling. We understand Cézanne as concerned with what he considered the tectonic build-up of his pictorial images, compositions; and we can respect his extremely fine-tuned adjustments of a building façade that obviously proved too simplistically regular for his purposes. Bonnard, for his part, brought to more extensive graphic work the seriousness and nuance of his painting. Yet both, we find, offer such uncanny parallels to the supposedly artless Loos that we can only think, If it walks like art and talks like art, it must be art.

Loos's wonderful Steiner House, in Vienna, poses the question of fenestrational formalism as 'classically' symmetrical and/or asymmetrically relational, for there both systems, or system and non-system, coexist and interface (as it were, Social Democratically). In itself, this work is first of all peculiar in looking like a one-storey cottage with attic from the street and like a grand three-storey mini-palazzo on the rear or garden side. This anomaly was owed to zoning regulations obliging the street front to appear as small as one storey plus basement and attic, though here there was the benefit of the downward slope of the land behind. But the Steiner House proves indeed illuminating for the play of symmetry, which generally marks the public façade of the free-standing Loosian house, and the free, asymmetric fenestration which often marks its flanks.

The street front might look simply symmetrical, as the big garden front really is; but, curiously it holds interest in virtue of a subtle asymmetry. At first one might think of windows set simply a-B-a, low-high-low beside and above a central portal, like a classically styled gatehouse, with the central upstairs window projecting as a dormer from the back-rolling, quarter-round copper roof. Then one notices that the left-hand window is slightly taller than square, while the right-hand one is of about the same area but wider and does not extend as low down, while slightly horizontal in its vertical dormer element, even as the setback entrance portal breaks the façade up into its 'a,' 'B,' and 'c' single-windowed elements (two further, seeming basement windows are sunken almost flush with the pavement, withdrawn from compositional interaction). Even though these are placed as symmetrically and equidistantly as possible, the distinct rectangles chime so 'relationally' together that one

7. Loos, Steiner House, Vienna, 1910. Street façade.

8. Loos, Steiner House. Right flank and garden façade.

is always surprised to see that they all differ even as suspended together in such an artfully contrived 'intra-relational' disposition. The whole boxy, three-storey-plus-basement garden façade is so absolutely symmetrical, despite using a variety of window shapes and sizes, as to be the street front the house had 'wanted' to have.

On approach from either side, walking along the street, the typically white-rendered suburban dwelling, partly hidden in foliage, bears a general resemblance to the kind of Austrian country architecture in which the painter Klimt had been taking modernist interest. For the flanks of the Steiner have freely asymmetric fenestration, much too irregular to account for in its vertical and horizontal alignments and non-alignments. As in some musical composition by Loos's friend Arnold Schoenberg, we find ourselves too aesthetically committed to the lively, seemingly irregular order even to want to track it, so that settling on an intuited sense of simultaneous relations carries the day. There is no denying that irregularities of fenestration in the flanks of this and other Loos houses are occasioned by practical, 'functional' commitments of the spaces within; still, the lively interplay of differently sized and seemingly intuitively placed rectangles, held together in orthogonal relations, seems sought after and cultivated on Loos's part.

Consider as precedent, in the spirit of Loos, a watercolor by Cézanne which was still new when the Steiner House was built. In the handling of its architectural motif, this work of the early 1890s, long called *Mill at the Pont des Trois Sautets*, until its re-titling as *The Limekiln* by John Rewald, offers a subtly complex lesson in deviation from fenestrational regularity. This stark watercolor of an industrial building in the country shows how aesthetically engaging of our formal intuition of relations just the right irregularity can be. That the building is really a limekiln has Loosian interest both as pertaining to whitewash (which is folklorically saluted in 'Architecture') and because, for industrial purposes, at least some of the interior space was likely more than one regular storey high – like the way, within a couple of years, Loos was to loosen up interior space with his *Raumplan*, freely varying the floor and ceiling heights of individual rooms of houses as answering to distinct functional requirements, and with windows potentially capable of following suit.

The painter Erle Loran published a photograph of the original building, which no longer stands, in 1930, comparing with it Cézanne's rendition. Cézanne, a modernist on record as despising industrial and commercial encroachment on the countryside, has approached the unprepossessing industrial structure head-on, like so many modern painters, including Mondrian, who

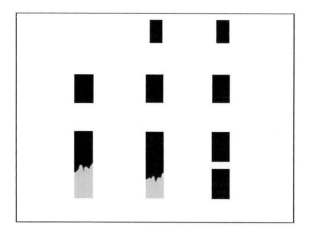

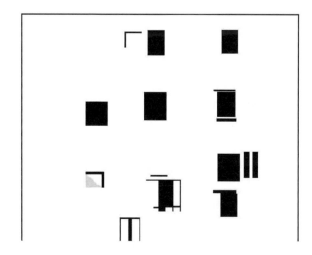

9. Diagrams showing (above) the fenestration of the building whose façade appears in Paul Cézanne's *The Limekiln* (or *Mill at the Pont des Trois Sautets*), pencil and watercolor, 1890–94; and (below) the fenestration of that building as appearing in Cézanne's rendition. Gray areas indicate form as inferred behind foliage.

have welcomed into their planar compositions the geometrically inscribed frontality of building façades. Basically, the fenestration of the limekiln's big unrelieved forward wall was given as a bilateral grid, with the position of the first top window at the left blank, like a musical line starting with a rest. But as one sees here in comparing diagrams of the original factory fenestration and Cézanne's intuited reworking of it, with adjustments so slight that each in itself might have been inconsequential, if not simply erroneous, Cézanne's rendition of the rectilinear pattern of rectangular windows breaks free in subtly calibrated deviations from the given axes, to lively asymmetric effect. Even the Cézannophile Loran did not at first notice Cézanne's transformation, writing, "the photograph is so identical with the picture that one has the illusion of being able to trace the lines of the one over the other," merely conceding that the artist had "made a few subtle changes in the placement of the windows for the sake of variety" (Loran 531), though on returning to the problem in his influential *Cézanne's Composition* (1943), his comments were more appreciative. (Adolf Loos would have been interested in how Cézanne, who had inherited his father's estate with its patriarchal manor as boxy in a bourgeois classical mode as this utilitarian limekiln, took such an active revisionist interest in the visual redaction of the given industrial structure on his own artistic terms.)

A more general analogy of asymmetric formal unity obtains between the adept fenestration of Loos façades and the asymmetric orthogonality of various rectangular forms in relational suspension in works by Piet Mondrian and others in the De Stijl movement, including some of the architect's most beautiful fenestrational dispositions, from the street façade of the Horner House, in Hietzing, Vienna, to the sporty elegance of the Rufer House, also in Hietzing, ten years later, where Loos manages to extend the same compositional acuity from face to equal face around the corners of the square house. All in all, that the compositions of the early modernist painters prove so formally compatible with Adolf Loos's early houses says something, however indirect, about the houses as works of, shall we say, artfully architectural art. Two late houses by Loos will extend this purview with rather different problems of symmetrical façades as against their freely composed flanks; but first an unexpected and overlooked parallel from early modern painting for what is always and everywhere Loos's most famous building.

Having turned to painting as a way to come to terms with the artfulness of Loos's buildings, and moved on to consider resemblances to other buildings that affiliate with it as a work within the art of architecture, it turns out to be

10. Pierre Bonnard, *Les Boulevards*, 1900. Color lithograph.

possible to supplement this approach by acknowledging a work of visual art from mere moments before the Looshaus, which bears an at least confirmatory relation to its design. For Loos's famous design startlingly resembles a work by a modern painter of such refinement that no one would ever see him in light of the supposed impertinence of the Looshaus, namely, Pierre Bonnard, who produced this color lithograph titled *Les Boulevards* in 1900, several years before Loos's signature building. Bonnard's image, thin and bracing as afternoon tea, shows a large-looming commercial building quite similar to the Looshaus, and similarly sited. Whether Bonnard invented his principal motif or endowed with elegant simplicity the façade of some actual building similarly sited on a *place* between two converging streets, is hard to tell; but his image conveys not only an aesthetic urbanity worthy of Baudelaire, Georg Simmel, or Walter Benjamin, but an uncanny adumbration, moments before the fact, of the Looshaus. And if such an architectural motif proves acceptable to the ultra-aesthetic painter Bonnard, for whom printmaking in particular "gave opportunities to refine, distill and recompose" the elements of his urban environment (Ives 127–28), it should at least be difficult to consider it at odds with art. Whatever its own source or sources, Bonnard's image adumbrated the look of the Looshaus and could even have influenced Loos: although extra copies were apparently sold in Paris, the print was actually commissioned and published in Germany as part of a portfolio put out by the Insel Press at Leipzig in 1900.[3]

In the end, there is an elegant substantiality to Loos's design which cannot be explained away by the polite deference of certain details – columns or cornice line – toward the church to the right of the Looshaus on the square. In assessing it, we are again reminded of the Biedermeier as a bona fide art-historical style; but not to dispose of the question, and certainly not to contain and repress Loos's radical modernism by trimming it to fit just another revivalist style; no, only to support even further the case that the Looshaus is a work of art with respectable genealogical claims in the history of art. Art history has been appealed to here as justification for the full-fledged fine art standing of a textbook masterpiece of the sometimes supposed anti-architect.

The answer would seem to be that Loos's formalism became subtler but never left him, to judge by an interesting feature of the house that is his greatest late building, the Müller Villa, built in collaboration with the engineer Karel Lhota in the Prague suburb of Střešovice in 1928–30. There a symmetrical, plastically articulated downhill front looks out over the city while the very flat side-street wall equivocates, in outline and fenestration, between symmetry and asymmetry – reasonably enough for a flank that also presents itself to a street. The entrance façade, on the uphill side, confronts the street less plastically and *almost* symmetrically.

But what ought by rights to be a shocking irregularity in the Müller's fenestration turns out to be almost subtle enough to overlook: a 'missing' window in the upper right-hand corner. How curiously akin this proves to be to the 'missing' upper left-hand window of the old limekiln as painted by Cézanne. The preparatory drawings for this almost but not quite symmetrical façade show that, unconstrained by the interior *Raumplan*, and even apart from interference in the planning of the fenestration by the municipal authorities, the 'Cézannesque' irregularity was definitely a free compositional decision by Loos (van Duzer 47–51). Subtly enough, it is irregular and slightly asymmetrical but non-relational – more like a musical rest allowing of syncopation: yet another telling instance, then, of dealing with compositional symmetry and asymmetry on the part of Loos as artist-architect.

Although their formal similarities to works of early modernist painting support the claim of artfulness for Loos, all the examples so far cited are quite early. What if Loos's formalism of *c.* 1910 was only a way of getting started? Doesn't the sheer boxiness of Loos's mature house designs, which is sufficiently marked to raise the question of later twentieth-century Minimal Art, preclude formalism in the initially relational compositional sense, and thereby undermine the argument that formalism is in some sense as qualifying for art as logic is for philosophy? For now: that will prove an artful anti-formalism.

Between classicism and functionalism

The opposition between classicism and functionalism is no separate affair from that between formalism and functionalism: classicism, ever concerned with formal and compositional models of perfection, is *guaranteed* formalism, and as such its most conservative mode. Conservatives see Loos's practically unornamented work as boxy and functionalist; but it cannot be the boxiness that nettles them, despite a modernist tendency to adopt that as a sign of pro-functional and anti-formal commitment. What could be boxier, after all, than Karl Friedrich Schinkel's little 1824–25 pavilion at Schloss Charlottenburg, on the edge of Berlin, which all parties admire? Loos himself salutes the great Hellenist in 'Architecture': "The last great master arose at the beginning of the nineteenth century: Schinkel. We have forgotten him. But the light of this great figure will fall on future generations of architects" (*OA* 85). As interesting as it is that Loos was prepared to plead his case in 1910, the figure of Schinkel as a precursor of modernism becomes a *cliché* when it upstages the modern potential in even Renaissance tradition: Vasari's praise for Michelozzo's Medici-Riccardi Palace, in Florence, of 1445–60, for a plainness not inciting to envy, and 'modern,' functional disposition of its interior, would also have appealed to Adolf Loos. Whatever the formal vicissitudes of his work, and whatever else he said for polemical purposes, in his lasting critical respect for classicism, Greek, Roman or Renaissance, Loos showed that he voted for form, aware that that was a vote for art. Classicism, prepared to defend even standardized form, was ultimately at odds with functionalism, which, at most extreme, denied the cult of form as an empty fetish and was proud to refuse the very condition and status of bourgeois 'art.' The latter sounds like Loos more of the time, and Loos was prepared to laugh in public at classicism of academic ilk; but the former somehow saves him from artlessness in the actual architectural results.

Sometimes the regularity and the premium on symmetry in classicism, especially domesticated Renaissance classicism, proved capable of conversion into a more or less exclusively geometric modernist simplicity. But while an emphasis on simple geometric forms in symmetrical relations has often done crypto-classical duty, a less-conservative, more freely asymmetric strain has great things to its credit from the hands of a modernist like Mondrian, in his so-called 'classic' abstract paintings of the 1920s; and much the same can be said of Ludwig Mies van der Rohe, whom in some sense Loos made possible in architecture. This more adaptable strain may find its emblematic answer to the Schinkel problem, so anchored in the symmetry and uniformity of the Parthenon, in that overshadowed neighbor of the Parthenon on the Acropolis hill, the Erechtheum, built only a decade or so later, toward the end of the fifth century BC. The suggestion is not far-fetched: Loos's notes of his 1913–14 walking tour of Viennese architecture indicate special attention to the upper part (supposedly) of a building at Herrengasse 17 (possibly the Austro-Hungarian Bank), as having, at the time of its construction in the nineteenth century, been influenced by then contemporary archaeological excavations of the Erechtheum (*OA* 22); and he even projected a house inspired by the Erechtheum: his Villa Konstandt project, for Olomouc, in Moravia, of 1919. So he cared about such a classical *artistic* anomaly, even if the general view of his work tends toward the opposite, functionalist, which is supposedly to say, the artless, extreme.

People who dislike modernity often blame Loos for all that they associate with 'the Bauhaus' as ultra-rationalist, especially what they think of as heartless rationalist functionalism – that great art school with its material-centered and task-oriented approach to architecture and design – as killing off what they could familiarly recognize as architectural beauty in the classical artistic tradition. Others, more at home with modernity, have preferred to take the 'rationalism' of such design, including its emphasis on basic geometric form, as a case of relative classicism, 'our' classicism again, as a matter of timeless beauty adapted conveniently to our time but, far from anti-artistically, as much as standing for or symbolizing art. Some later modern enthusiasts, subjectively enthusiastic about Bauhaus design for its elemental simplicity as aesthetically appealing, would be confused to learn that the Bauhaus itself came to stand on the anti-art side of Soviet 'productivism,' the form of constructivism most anxious to become anything but classical and something other than art.

The crypto-classical view might seem to have little evidence going for it in the built work of Loos (though not in his grander civic fantasies, where the point seems to be playing the next Otto Wagner to some next Habsburg). Some of his criticism of historicist style-mongering can be read in line with eighteenth-century revisionist criticisms of overdressed Baroque rhetoric as abetting an 'abstract-classical' rationalist case; and there is something to think about there, especially in linguistic terms, though Loos would have thought twice about the anti-Catholic element in the wider anti-Baroque aesthetic campaign. On this complex matter we can simply take a page from a summary remark on the neoclassical style in the fine arts in a great 1967 book on abstract art: although "harmful to artistic creation, a dead-end for art ... it did nevertheless contribute to familiarizing men's minds with the idea of form, at that time still vague ... As an ideal it perished, but the dream of a perfect [type of] form, and the formalism which it engendered, survived" (Vallier 10–11).

In a few cases of built works there is a definite classical air, thanks to a compact massing of plain elements, well before any question of classical ornamentation, even the most reserved. Yet, significantly, it is not quite a surprise to find Loos's early Villa Karma, near Montreux, on Lake Geneva, begun as a remodeling project in 1904 and abandoned when largely complete in 1906, happily comparing with a classical masterwork of the Renaissance: Giuliano da Sangallo's Medici villa at Poggio a Caiano, of the early 1480s. Nobody who looked it up would deny that Sangallo's Renaissance villa is a beautiful work of architectural art, and that it wears its classicism lightly, perhaps *despite* (Loos's trademark '*trotzdem*') certain compositional peculiarities. Probably few would deny that, juxtaposed with it, Loos's early villa looks not only unexpectedly beautiful but elusively akin.

This, so to speak, art-historically active view of Loos's work is unusual – after all, any evidence of sophisticated art-historical embeddedness must threaten the established case for Loos as anti-artist – but it is not unique. Another modernist architectural historian has already underscored how much, at least from the garden side, the Steiner House, of 1910, can been seen to engage Baldassare Peruzzi's Villa Farnesina, Rome, of 1508–10, as well as a project for a town house (not freestanding, but undeniably similar) by Karl Friedrich Schinkel (Hartoonian 49–51). Of course, our point is not to embalm the modern but, on the contrary, to inherit history, including now earlier modernist art history, on behalf of living art. No; given the early modernist struggle to overthrow academically established classicism in architecture, alongside representation (however classically idealized or naturalistic) in painting, it might be hopelessly reactionary to claim that whatever artistic truth obtained in Loos's work was only by virtue of whatever it had failed to overthrow. It is Loos's comprehensive project, however, in history and theory as well as practice, that makes him important: he was a modernist, and quasi-classicism or crypto-classicism, even his own, cannot account for his artistic significance.

What about modernist 'functionalism' as opposite extreme to formalism? Under extreme functionalist conditions form, in design, is a distraction and potential compromise or even contamination of the unimpeded execution of purposive building tasks. Clearly, as soon as one defines one of these terms in polar opposition to the other, problems arise, such as the strong but possibly unvoiced or even unconscious aesthetic tastes of engineers, or even ebbs and flows of fashion for 'high-tech' styling in object design. But one can see what Loos – who after all even influenced Le Corbusier in the matter – meant. The point is a new, free realm where architects, emulating engineers, might go the whole way and be free of art, at least in the bourgeois sense, satisfying human needs unhampered by established grammars and stale histories. As early as 1898, following Gottfried Semper in praising the Greeks for producing beauty in object design by putting function first, Loos had referenced that new invention, the bicycle, in effect modern from scratch, as a model of design with promise for the dawning new century: "Are there still people who work in the same way as the Greeks? Oh, yes. As a nation the English; as a profession, the engineers. The English and the engineers are our Greeks … These Greek vases are beautiful, as beautiful as a machine, as beautiful as a *bicycle*" (*OC* 69; emphasis in source). If a formalist appeal to modernist quasi-classicism must inevitably exclude the most Loosian and most art-historically important evidence, the prevalent attempt to make Loos the Columbus of styleless and artless functionalism proves oblivious to historicity, and could only support Loos's work, whether as art or as non-art, by ignoring statements where he speaks, however rhetorically, of classicism as the height of architecture and of his really only picking up where the classical tradition had misguidedly broken off (but really did break off). Loos's express interest in the craftsman's point of view when independent of supposedly artistic interference, often engages the category of the vernacular: in itself that might only guarantee artliness on the level of the folkloric, not of fine art; but as an architectural figure it proves to mean more.

The problem of 'Bauhaus' over-generalization needs to be set aside. Unfortunately, after a generation of anti-formalism, even well-read people today cannot tell the difference, or else seek to avoid the complications of acknowledging the differences, between Loos's art as harboring even downright subtle formal intuitions, and, on the other hand, two generations before late twentieth-century Minimal Art, the materialist sangfroid of the Bauhaus and of other functionalist and constructivist architecture and art. To speak of the Bauhaus is to invoke that great art school of the Weimar Republic, especially in the new home that Walter Gropius built for it in 1925–26, which, secondarily, has become so symbolic of modernism in the strength of not its youthful, but more its ephebic and militant phase, a phase of optimistically materialist, world-building constructivism.

While Le Corbusier's more famous functionalism was always unashamedly informed by aesthetic sense, an understandably anti-aesthetic, utilitarian functionalist practice of more marked social motivation developed, notably in Czechoslovakia, in the 1920s. Loos's importance for the formation of Czech functionalism was recounted in the heart and heat of it by Karel Teige in *Modern Architecture in Czechoslovakia*, written in 1927 and published in 1930. The Moravian-born Viennese Loos was an inspiration to the Czech functionalists; but while his work in theory and practice influenced them considerably, it is significant that he was actually not himself prepared to reduce architecture to functionalist-utilitarian determination, with an exception that proves the rule – his bare-bones housing-crisis design for the cheapest possible row housing: the project for a House with One Wall, patented like an invented device in 1921, which, however, was so much a matter of mere building in a default carpenters' mode as not stylistically to resemble even bare-bones functionalism (which depended on masonry and rendering).

Despite the anti-art thrust of functionalism, Czech functionalists, supposedly committed only to devices engendered rationally as directly answering to need, were evidently prepared to borrow forms from Loos as so many artistic motifs. A large rectangular opening at the upper corner of the right flank of Loos's Villa Müller, in Prague, of 1928–30, dramatically like a picture-window cut through a freely extended roof terrace wall (contemporaneously with a comparably conceived 'picture-frame' window in a wall of the roof terrace of Le Corbusier's Villa Savoye, at Poissy), and a form like Loos's similar but tamer roof porch of a house in Prague-Smíchov (possibly by František Zelenka, 1936); or the finely articulated post-and-lintel roof trellis of his Winternitz Villa, in Prague-Smíchov, of 1931–32, *versus* the then already built but run-on roof terrace framing of Bohuslav Fuchs' public baths at Brno, of 1927. And still people take Loos's de-ornamentalized simplicity as the point of origin of 'Bauhaus functionalism,' so called. For social as well as polemical reasons Czech functionalists often said that what they were doing was not art, and were as anti-formalist in the 1920s as orthodox Minimalist sculptors would be in the 1960s; yet they honored Loos as their principal inspiration in the generation before – an essentially art-historical genealogical relationship.

Loos's fascinating principle of the *Raumplan*, or spatial plan – articulating the building in section to allow divergent floor and ceiling heights for the various rooms with their discrete functions – is so often taken as exemplary of his supposed functionalism. But this really only shows how much more thinking must be done on these matters. As I have said before, there is the, one might have thought, practical fact of material economy that the *Raumplan* made for extra-special constructional complexity, requiring the services of an engineer. For an architect to require an engineer's collaboration, a significant extra demand in expertise as well as materials, means that in his own right he cannot be operating as an unqualified functionalist solver of practical building problems simply following functionalism's favored economy of means, but must instead take the role of designer or artist-architect. Significantly, what must be the most developed *Raumplan*, that of the Müller Villa, which necessitated the services of Lhota, a professor of engineering, was a *tour-de-force* commissioned by a building contractor. Rather than jump on this aspect of Loos's practice as impractically false functionalism, a failure of pure, anti-aesthetic efficiency, why not consider it negative corroboration of the fact that he was really more of an artist-architect after all than he was inclined, in heavily ironic theory, to admit.

It supports the art-standing of Loos's work that a conspicuous device that looks peculiarly functional or task-determined, finds an art-historical adumbration, presumably after the fact. For as independent as they are of the procession of historical styles as like so many modes of dressing up structure, the works nevertheless entail art history as a history of forms. By itself, such a building as Loos's Scheu House, in Vienna, of 1912–14, with its boldly stepped terraces set back on one side, might seem altogether ad hoc, in its intent to give individual terraces to both the family part of the house and to an upstairs rental apartment. Then we see just that feature which had seemed if anything oblivious to art, echoed, not as an exaggerated mannerism but after all as a form, fifteen years later, in a 1928 Czech functionalist house by Oldřich Starý at Brno, Moravia, Loos's home town. The stepped profile of terrace roofs so boldly foregrounded in Loos's house is retrospectively made a point of by the plainspoken terrace of its later, typical Czech functionalist counterpart. Thus the latter registers as a feature thanks to its Loosian formal precedent: so it was a form after all; in fact, it proves, as if on second thought, a more pointed one than the later allusion to it. In between the Scheu House and the Czech functionalist example stepped-back terracing recurs in several projects by Loos.

Now the point is not formal idiosyncracy, however justified by functionality, as proof of originality, but, on the contrary, the embeddedness in art history of something that might seem artlessly ad hoc. And it is just because Loos's stepped Scheu design looks so eccentric that it must be too merely ad hoc or idiosyncratic for history to pertain that it becomes all the more significant for Loos's 'non-functionalist' artfulness to discover that just such a form was already there, somewhere in the great memory bank of architectural history. In this case, the at first seemingly unique Scheu House finds a remarkable 'retroactive' adumbration, for its stepped terracing as stacked would-be gardens, in a Baroque project: Livius Creyl's hypothetical image of one of the seven wonders of the ancient world, the Hanging Gardens of Babylon, as engraved in 1670 by Coenraet Decker for Athanasius Kircher's book on the Tower of Babel: *Turris Babel* (Amsterdam, 1679). What Loos was 'functionally' erecting was indeed a modern form of 'hanging gardens'; and here the general sense of formal precedent is enough to implicate art in its historical dimension without implying a specifically causal source.

Finding so fortunate a retroactive prototype, with the dignity of a legendarily ancient idea, curiously leaves Haus Scheu looking less than ever like an exception to architecture as art. Today its large and simple, successively stepped form may even suggest now the typically boxy and impassive, an-aesthetic 'object'

11. Livius Creyl, *Hanging Gardens of Babylon*, engraving by Cornelius Decker, 1670. From Athanasius Kircher, *Turris Babel* (Amsterdam, 1679).

sculptures, only incrementally inflected, of latter-day Minimal Art. Eventually that 1960s movement will be seen (chapter 9) historically to entail denials not only of formalism but even of artistic concern, in constructivism, including Czech functionalist architecture, yet undeniably making its point within fine-art sculpture – a movement thoroughly germane to the contemporary context in which many of us late moderns discovered and took to Adolf Loos. Suffice it to say for now that this Minimalism proper was rigorously non-relational and anti-formal yet neither non-art nor anti-art, no matter what was said, even by its proponents at the time, for the simple reason that it made no sense except as art.

Loos means something different by saying, notoriously, at the close of 'Architecture,' that only the tomb and the monument may be truly architecture, presumably implying that nothing else can be. These exceptions too are pragmatically useless, as art is often accused of being by all too practical folk;

12. Loos, Scheu House, Vienna, 1912–13.

but arguably they share a *spiritual utility* that conceivably extends to art. In any case, it is more important at the start to establish that whatever formal interest and value is to be found in the work of Loos can only serve to confirm that his work is, after all, art. Notwithstanding reasons, interpretations or misinterpretations of his spare, no-nonsense, anti-ornamental art as purely and simply an anti-architecture or an art-to-end-art in a nihilistic sense, it does prove possible to find more to the formal, ostensibly artistic aspect of his work than is usually looked for. This is evident in the massing of his buildings and the dispositions of their walls, and markedly in fenestration as definitely not insignificant or irrelevant, especially once it is just about all there is to play with after the abolition of ornament – and as often enough engaging, in its disposition, relational composition as familiar from early, and contemporaneous modernist painting, as well as conventional window grids.

It is curious how many people mean by 'art,' painting – though all the more curious, some of us think, how when they say 'the arts' they will forget about painting entirely. On the level of polemic, what we need to keep in mind is that this Loos who actually loved the classical tradition and most respected it in moving beyond it – like all 'moderns,' ever since the *Querelles des Anciennes et des Modernes* — was most of all opposing the notion that buildings were architecture, and architecture was art, only insofar as the buildings in question, embellished with grammatically correct classical ornament, approximated the orthodox architectural models of Greece, Rome or the Renaissance. It must be in the true spirit of Loos that we moderns find ourselves bridling at the idea that a building can approximate to architecture, and architecture to art, only insofar as it resembles the Parthenon in its sublime hypotactical symmetry.

Somehow, the challenging modern conviction of Loos invites alternative thinking about that relatively neglected smaller, multi-cultic neighboring temple. One might curiously hesitate to call it classical, though we are told it is entitled — so daringly and beautifully asymmetrically balanced ('fearful symmetry' as anxiety about free balance): yes, the Erechtheum. In its perfect irregularity it reminds me of Loos, but also, more relationally than Loos, of the exquisite balance in a 'classic' Mondrian. Place its ground plan side by side with more than one Mondrian *Composition* of about 1922, and discover kindred artistic spirits. It might be objected that ground-plans are not architecture — except that the Erechtheum is not only winningly asymmetric in all its elevations, but in section as well, thanks to the different vertical displacements of the floor levels of its several chambers, which thus make for a peculiarly apt analogy with Loos's *Raumplan* at that. Certain points here might be open to expert qualification; nevertheless, the comprehensive point is proved: that Adolf Loos was an artist-architect whose works participate in the history of art. How reassuring, then, after first giving this essay as a lecture, to discover a late modernist text titled 'A Guide to the Anticlassical Code' (1973) in which the architectural historian Bruno Zevi, criticizing the rhetorical tendency of hypotactical or symmetrical buildings to be "symbols of totalitarian power or products of sloth or cynicism," offers as a counterexample that was never so easy for academic classicists to co-opt: "the Erechtheum, a quite irregular and asymmetrical building, so 'modern' that in a way it is a forerunner of Adolf Loos's multilevel Raumplan" (Zevi 18).

2

LOOSIAN VERNACULAR

The vernacular, which has already arisen here as an artistic matter, is a vexed subject for a category meant to concern the everyday, commonsensical, tried-and-true 'right' way basic things are locally made: a house or a stone wall, a chair or a pie. Its implications are of an essentially conventional, unlegislated rightness in contradistinction to standards of 'classical' correctness in analogy with Latin, and by extension, models in general (e.g., 'castle cooking,' *versus* ordinary folks' cooking in the Czech Lands). Vernaculars are local and exclusive, but in a curiously universal way (my grandmother's dumplings have just the same significance as my friend's grandmother's pasta sauce). The thing seems to be that they be 'taken aboard' early enough to be second-nature, unselfconscious, undetermined by an imposed grammar. We can perhaps gain some purchase on this notion, vital to Loos's modernist architectural thought though still today excessively confusing and elusive, by examining a telling eighteenth-century case in the reflected light, as it were, of Adolf Loos.

Whatever exactly the term is taken to mean, the vernacular ought by rights to stand opposed to the classical as referring back philologically to formal models, especially of antiquity, or especially in a canonical grammar of artistic form, in analogy with Greek or Latin grammar as limiting models of linguistic possibility. Yet the taken-for-granted vernacular resists being leveled to folk art: if anything, it is too transparent to notice as a mode or style, where folk art and folkloric culture are conspicuous in their self-confident independence. It is more definitive that the vernacular be like a parochial 'classic' type (relative sense), than that it owe anything to second-hand classicism (absolute sense);

yet also, in Adolf Loos's usage, that it also be unspoiled by a citified, academic notion of 'applied art.' The cosmopolitan Loos most liked the aspect of vernacular building-art which concerns the 'right' way of building, as neither toe-the-line orthodox, like so many classical buildings in the history books, nor vainly arty, 'creative,' idiosyncratic. An extreme but relevant example: from Anglo-Saxon culture Loos can even be said to have derived a notion that creativity in design might be tantamount to *rude* – as an imposition upon others.

The surprising complexity of the concept of the vernacular as germane to a people and not imperially imposed is articulately explored in Brian Friel's play *Translations* (1980), set in 1833, in which Latin lessons being given in the Irish language are interrupted by British troops changing local signage from Irish to English. Aspects of the vernacular problem include not only possible provincial decline from metropolitan classicism, as with the breaking-down of late antique Latin, but the happenstance canonization of one particular dialect in the formation of a modern language. When the eighteenth-century Anglo-Irish philosopher George Berkeley set out as a clergyman of the Church of Ireland for America to found a British colonial college for the natives, in Bermuda, the everyday administrative language of the Austrian empire was still Latin. Berkeley's supposedly national church's *Book of Common Prayer*, based on the pre-Reformation Latin Missal, had only recently been published in Irish for the first time (1712): what then would it mean to describe it as vernacular? There was something about the Berkeley of the British Empire that the Loos of the Austrian Empire would have understood – this Loos who was so Viennese, even with his Czech passport and 60th-birthday Czech pension.

It was actually an American vernacular house that George Berkeley may at least partly have designed, or re-designed, and in which he lived for a while, which first stirred the present attempts to look and think afresh about Adolf Loos. Accounting now for how that might have been will lead further into what it might mean to find this house, or any other, or anything else, Loosian. This sense will be stimulated later on in considering a later philosopher's house in something comparable to the style of Loos that was largely though not wholly designed by the philosopher himself, namely, Ludwig Wittgenstein (chapter 8). What may be gained indirectly through the Berkeley case is a sense of how the urbanity that stamps the writings, the buildings, and the persona of Loos only makes the more fascinating his engagement with its supposed opposite: the vernacular as somehow – nevertheless (Loos's '*trotzdem*') – the real thing after all.

The problematic vernacular

Critically speaking, Loos's recurrent opposition between the integrity of the vernacular craftsman and the vanity of the self-imposing designer or architect inherits a distinction first drawn by Friedrich von Schiller in his essay 'Naïve and Sentimental Poetry' (1795–96) and subsequently modified and developed by Nietzsche, but in a way worked through by Loos in practice as well as theory. By a case method of sorts, the present chapter takes as a point of reference for the question of the vernacular, ever at least implicitly important in Loos's work, an early eighteenth-century building in some sense 'by' the great Anglo-Irish philosopher George Berkeley, a house which has seemed most hospitably to engage and illuminate such, at first, Loosian inscrutables as why a house might not necessarily be considered a work of art.

'Sentimental' does not seem quite the right predicate for Adolf Loos in English; but something that deserves to be clarified at the start is how, for Friedrich Schiller, a realist 'naïve' stands, on what here counts as the vernacular side, in opposition to an aesthetic idealist 'sentimental.' Schiller's 'naïve' mode refers to art in contented accord with nature; his opposing term 'sentimental' means something like knowingly pursuing an idealization of reality by will and art. This accounts, for the moment, for the Loosian importance of a Schillerean 'naïve' vernacular in craft production and architecture alike, because, in a nutshell, Loos was an extremely sophisticated and willfully artistic ('sentimental') artist who despised most of what was being done in his time on that self-consciously artistic side of things, and identified, in compensation, as it were, with the simpler things done, almost by genetic inheritance (as 'naïve') by those craftsmen. At least, despite industrial culture, they had managed to retain a respect for something made well in some right, time-honored, non-eccentric, unaffected way.

Philosophically, Wittgenstein, who knew and respected Loos, helps us to understand what is at stake in the matter with a worthwhile parallel in his philosophical concept of the *Lebensform* ('form of life'), meaning, of the way, in human society, things simply are supposed to be done: "not agreement in opinions but in form of life," "agreement not only in definitions but also ... in judgments" (*Philosophical Investigations*, §§ 241–42; Wittgenstein 88e).

Philologically speaking, the vernacular is a generalization of the linguistic usage whereby the *vernaculus* is the plain-folk native, even in a sense of the 'home'-grown (from *verna*, for a slave born in his master's house). By rights the architectural analogue should be *anything but* (Greek to Roman) *classical* – despite conservatives' vested cultural interest in 'trickle-down' views of bourgeois classicism. Importantly for Loosian theory (chapter 4), however, neither is the vernacular a primitive condition, like barbarity before a classical overlay. Extended to art, the vernacular implies something passed on, yes, but, in the sense of book-learning, definitely *unschooled* and maintained instead by an unwritten tradition of workshop practice. The problem of the vernacular has been unnecessarily compounded by casual use of the term as a commendation for local, homegrown buildings bedecked with touches of classical cultivation – just what the true vernacular as anything-but-Latin ought to be free of. No wonder well meaning people are confused by this subject, which, however, Adolf Loos was not confused about!

We can come to a Loosian understanding of the vernacular in practice by considering an actual project, a real house (a category that supposedly Loos wants to rule out as art), at least partly old at the start and then expanded in remodeling, subsequently left to fall derelict, and finally restored. In its definitive state the house may actually have been authorially 'by' George Berkeley, one of the greatest of eighteenth-century philosophers, or else by nobody in particular; or rather – vitally for the question of the vernacular – in some sense substantially by the 'everybody' of some people collectively. Several aspects of the building in question together justify its Loosian interest by appealing to prime concerns of the architect Loos, including the priority of craftsman over artist; imperial culture; eighteenth-century British design, including its politics; and even America as an enviably but problematically open cultural field, along with the difficult overarching question of the vernacular as such.

In its general collective anonymity, vernacular architecture is made by craftsmen driven by a committed sense of rightness to task, not by artists indulging personality in the interest of idiosyncratic creation. Loos always set the integrity of the craftsman against the vanity of the self-positioned artist meddling in architecture and design. Very early on – so memorably, from the time of his distasteful reaction to the supposedly heartwarming parade of exotic nationalities at the Austro-Hungarian emperor's jubilee celebrations of 1898 in Vienna – Loos derided the wish to concoct an Austrian vernacular style in an increasingly cosmopolitan culture that ought to be going for sophistication rather than kitsch: "It would be a sin against our civilized standards to require us to give up our table manners and have the whole family eat out of one bowl like the peasants, just because our eating habits and table manners come from England." Note, however, how among practical townspeople a commonality of craft understanding obtains even across borders, *though not between the pretentious, pedantic architects*: "There is no difference between the mind of a Viennese cabinetmaker and one from London, but there is a world of difference between a London cabinetmaker and a Viennese architect" (*OC* 67).

How many times Loos's statement has been quoted in connection with his vernacularism that "[a]n architect is a bricklayer who has learned Latin," usually out of context, as if everything architectural were essentially so much borrowed classical capital, and the good simple bricklayer would hardly even understand what he meant – this Loos who was always proud of having earned bricklayer's papers in America. Consider, under the title 'Ornament and Education' (1924), where he actually writes of the bricklayer who learned Latin: "The starting point for drawing instruction should be classical ornamentation," which in Europe underpins "a common ... culture" (*OC* 187). Let us not be detained by the mention of ornament for the time being; better to bear in mind that he had already produced statements as outrageous as this, of 1898, when the bicycle was new: "Model your machines on the genuine Austrian wooden bicycle, designed by the Styrian woodcutter Peter Pinecone (was that the fellow's name?). It surely fits in better with our Alpine countryside than the ugly English ones" (*OA* 67). Or this complaint of 1912 against, in effect, imported wooden bicycles:

> *Heimat* – home, where we belong – is a fine-sounding word and the demand that we foster our own, vernacular way of building quite justified. No foreign body should dare to force its way into a townscape, no Indian pagoda flaunt itself out in the countryside. But how do the artists who call themselves *Heimatkünstler* interpret this approach to art? First and foremost by banishing all technical progress from building for all time ... It is fortunate for these architects that Stone-Age man did not insist on that, since it would mean that there would be no vernacular architecture and they would not be able to make a living from it. (*OA* 110)

Such *Heimatkünstler* (perhaps today renderable as 'homeboy artists') might be considered misguided Schillerean 'sentimentalists' affecting a condition of naïveté. Loos, after all, spoke from experience, but complex experience, having studied Latin in school before learning bricklaying in America.

He also wrote, in the 1913 mission statement for his little private architectural school, on what can be called the great subjunctive imperative of the classical tradition: the duty creatively to rise to the occasion in changing circumstances and dare to do what the Vitruvius of antiquity *would have done* here and now (which is ever more demanding than just reiterating precedents): "Since mankind has come to recognize the greatness of classical antiquity, the great architects have all had the same approach. 'The way I build,' they thought, 'is the way the Romans would have gone about it in my situation.' This is the approach I want to instill in my students" (*OA* 120). In the guidelines which he drew up alongside such comrades in the revolutionary situation of 1919 as Arnold Schoenberg (and with Wittgenstein put off by his political activism), Loos specifies: "Following the new regulations, the state may only train those to qualify as master builders and architects who have completed an apprenticeship as bricklayer, carpenter or stonemason" (*OA* 134). In other words, no 'sentimental' architecture for anyone inexperienced first in 'naïve' building; indeed, in that the famous bricklayer remark was written after all these statements means that even it comes to its own classicism through vernacular experience.

Approaching our modernist Loos in this indirect way allows us to advance on one or two of the perennial Loos-related problems: the vernacular as of all the more sophisticated interest once the superficial decorativeness of 'Secession' ornamentalism was disposed of; and just that on behalf of an authentic architectural modernity despite seeming Loosian denials of architectural art at all.

A British-colonial house in Loosian view

'Whitehall' referred to the government buildings in London which effectively comprised the 'capitol' of the new British Empire when George Berkeley wittily chose it as the name of the ample but unpretentious American-colonial or British-imperial frame farmhouse that he in some sense 'built' for himself and his family near Newport, Rhode Island. There is much to be considered about the provincial-born 'Austrian-imperial' Loos and other moderns, in respect to Berkeley's literally colonial house, its general vernacular aspect, and even about asymmetry as an anticlassical hallmark of modernism – this house in which Berkeley speculated and wrote, precociously enough, on what moderns consider unadorned 'functional' beauty. The forthright plainness of just such commendably vernacular buildings would hold modern appeal in the early years of the twentieth century when architecture, having broken free of historical styles, exercised a rationalism sometimes reminiscent of the eighteenth century.

It was in 1729, in hopes of gaining support and eventually going on to set up a missionary college in Bermuda open to native Americans, that Berkeley, eventual Anglican bishop of Cloyne, in Ireland, had come and in some measure built outside the colonial capital Newport (now it is in Middletown). As a philosopher's house Whitehall is more seriously architectural than a little *faux-primitif* backyard hut called the 'School of Philosophy' which, a century later, Emerson would build behind his otherwise normal Georgian house in Concord, Massachusetts, while considerably less ostensibly architectural than the also quite plain modernist building, now another 'celebrity' house, which the later modern philosopher Wittgenstein would build in a Loosian mode for his sister, in Vienna. In Whitehall, however, Berkeley largely composed the set of dialogues *Alciphron; or, The Minute Philosopher* (1732), which of all his writings has the most to offer in the way of architectural theory.

What it means to say that Berkeley 'built' any of his house is problematic. The account of his purchase of the property, with a farmhouse already standing on it, is vexed, owing to passages in two letters that can be read contradictorily as referring to Berkeley's subsequent building in respect to either the original house or else a new one, from the ground up (Luce 123–24).[1] Curiously, Berkeley had already speculated on the ontology of re-building in *Three Dialogues Between Hylas and Philonous* (1713): "suppose a house, whose walls or outward shell remaining unaltered, the chambers are all pulled down, and new ones built in their place; and that you should call this the *same*, and I should say it was not the *same* house: – would we not for all this perfectly agree in our thoughts of the house, considered in it self?" (Dial. III; Berkeley, *Works* 2: 248). In this case, the evidence suggests that Berkeley's 'building' project consisted of altering and expanding the existing farmhouse. No less an architectural historian than Vincent Scully testified that the present large old kitchen "may be" its surviving core (Downing and Scully 440). To this, at least, Berkeley would have added new front rooms, with upstairs bedrooms and a proper new façade. On inspection one does find a discrepancy of more than two inches in ceiling heights between a downstairs bedroom, behind the old kitchen, and the present front sitting rooms, while upstairs a shift in the floor confirms that the entire front element, consisting below of two parlors, foyer, and chimney, does constitute a discrete structural unit, supporting the idea of its being an addition.

Just such disjunctions owed to alteration make for a marked up-and-down irregularity within that no one would suppose pertained to Loos, except, come to think of it, that suggests an unexpected type of vernacular parallel for his sophisticated *Raumplan* of internal shifts in section as well as plan. A comparable literary appreciation of such is Ronald Knox's vernacularly attuned comment, in a 1926 essay on country walks, on a typical English country inn's "atmosphere of crooked passages, alternating levels, projecting beams,

13. George Berkeley (?) and local builders.
Whitehall, Middletown, Rhode Island,
c. 1729–30. Façade.

14. Berkeley (?) and local builders.
Whitehall. Left flank with additions.

which tells you that the house is old without self-conscious antiquarianism"
(Knox 280).

From the side, Berkeley's American house offers a semi-'saltbox' profile
in that 'pragmatic' New England way of accommodating additions by
smoothing them over under a longer and longer roof with lower and lower
eave. What appears so uncommon in the case of Whitehall as a saltbox
is the addition also of a new front, though the severe dereliction of the
house in the nineteenth century, when it was owned by Yale University,
followed by now already old restoration, makes it difficult to know just
what the building was like in Berkeley's day. Interestingly, however, as a
vernacular type the saltbox was no homegrown product of Yankee ingenuity
but an imported British vernacular form transplanted from southeastern
England in the early seventeenth century – as the then "newest of all English
houses, streamlined and modern" (Glassie 122, 126). In any case, the happy
adaptability of unembarrassed asymmetry on the sides of the house, even
the left (which was itself further added onto later) happens to comport with
the conspicuously more relaxed formality of fenestration on the flanks –
significantly, *versus* symmetrical façades – of the Steiner House and even of
Adolf Loos's houses in general.

One must wonder, if the pedimented and pilastered classical front
doorway embodies the disposition of *c*. 1730, if it reflects William Kent's *c*.
1727 *Designs of Inigo Jones* (Chaney 324). Newport 'Neopalladianism' centers
upon the Redwood Library and Atheneum, designed, or basically copied
from some standard Palladian source, by Peter Harrison, a sea captain, in
the later 1740s. Berkeley was sufficiently knowledgeable about architecture
for him to have been in on two prominent pre-Neopalladian projects before
leaving Ireland: as librarian of Trinity College Dublin, he must have taken
an interest in the design by Colonel Thomas Burgh of the Old Library
(1713–32), with its great run-on ranks of windows; and in 1722 he was
actually consulted in the building of Castletown, in Kildare, a major classical
country house said to have been designed in 1719 by Alessandro Galilei
(Craig 125). It would be mistaken, however, to imagine Berkeley arriving in
the woods of Rhode Island from an already Palladianized Dublin, for at the
time full-fledged Neopalladianism was still a novelty in that imperial sub-
capital, though the first volume (1715) of Colin Campbell's speculatively
financed *Vitruvius Britannicus* was already establishing the conception of the
principal block of a substantial country house as basically a plain shoe-box
with a grid of windows punctuated by a central doorway with pedimental
feature, as at Berkeley's Whitehall.

Neopalladianism was a programmatic revival, *c.* 1720, in early Hanoverian England of the High Renaissance classical architectural style of Andrea Palladio, especially for guaranteed tasteful domestic display on the part of new wealth. Berkeley was at odds with the Whig Neopalladians, as a churchly Tory with small sympathy for the classy classicism of, in a word, these first 'yuppies.' Anthony Ashley Cooper, third earl of Shaftesbury, chief ideologue of the movement, is attacked in Berkeley's *Alciphron*; and according to Wittkower (in 'Classical Theory and Eighteenth-century Sensibility,' 1966), Berkeley's radical empiricism was a fatal threat to Shaftesbury's conservatively classical aesthetics (and see Wittkower 199–200). Loos obviously had some affinity with self-made bourgeois clients, and his Anglophilia must have included some appreciation of Neopalladianism; it is even possible that the architect as "bricklayer who has learned Latin" trope, which he liked to identify with, alludes to Palladio as known to have started as an apprentice bricklayer in early sixteenth-century Vicenza. But Loos was no revivalist, not interested in domestic ostentation, and yet also incapable of mere propriety.

Aficionados of Neopalladianism must still be happy to find in the woods of New England a pedimented doorway with pilasters, which they can take as a sign of the influence of the nationalistic British style. Yet if the front door and its framing surround *are* accurately preserved or restored, they suggest workmanly resort to certain Neopalladian craftsmen's 'ponies'; for the doorway as we see it measures seven feet high by five and a quarter wide, in a nice proportion of three to four, or Palladian harmonic 'fourth,' while the doubling of the doors (with one at least now an inoperative dummy) hints at a combination of formal astuteness with craftsmanly aplomb.

However, the more one scrutinizes Whitehall, the less Neopalladian it seems, especially when moving through its ad hoc accretion of rooms. The real problem is that Neopalladianism, especially as simplified for practical purposes, derived from the literally Latinate tradition of Vitruvius and his Renaissance heirs, became so identified with not only eighteenth-century British imperial and American colonial, but also American 'Revolutionary' identities (the last thanks especially to Thomas Jefferson), as to be conflated with a homegrown vernacular (as such, *anything but* Latin), seems to have fascinated Loos. Even his collaborating with an engineer, later on, might seem like an extension of the practical empirical wisdom of the collective vernacular experience.

By the time of Whitehall it was common in British culture for carpenters to partake of Neopalladian forms by the demystified means of handbooks in which they could simply look up arithmetic dimensions standing in certified ratios, without having to understand proportional ratios as such, one of the most influential of these pocket crib books being William Halfpenny's *Practical Architecture* (2nd edn, 1724; Wittkower 108, 170). The writers not only flattened out matters of proportional theory into handy arithmetic tables of approved ratios but also "for the first time seriously challenged" the hierarchical Renaissance humanist tradition according to which "the houses of the lower classes, at the bottom of the [social] pyramid, are purely utilitarian, they cater for need, are done 'without art' and therefore not the concern of architects" (108). Thus, in Neopalladian circles in 1747, one David Garrett would publish "the first book in which classical discipline, order and rule was extended to the farm-house," followed by Robert Morris' *Rural Architecture; Consisting of Regular Designs ... in Which the Purity and Simplicity of the Art of Designing are Variously Exemplified* (1750; Wittkower 109).[2] Although these other books postdate Whitehall, whose unaffected squirishness is little different from similarly substantial yet unostentatious houses within the town of Newport, the likes of Halfpenny were already advancing a percolation down into the vernacular of formerly classier classical elements, and something more than just selected ornamental 'nouns': templates, as it were, for how not to go wrong, while set examples of ornament were also available for direct quotation in handbooks illustrated with engravings.

Just how vernacular, then, may Whitehall be? Remarkably, the basic Whitehall ground plan, with a large central chimney planted in the center and a room to either side is something which early Newport had actually not shared with the rest of Rhode Island, but which was, however, characteristic of Massachusetts and Connecticut, e.g., the Elder Williams House, likewise frame, built at Deerfield, in Massachusetts, in 1707 (Downing and Scully 32).[3] In Whitehall this special New England disposition is found not only in the presumed original core but in Berkeley's likely addition, with its own new chimney, up front. This also, by the way, has a negative consequence for presumptions of Neopalladianism in that it plants the sheer bulk of two hefty back-to-back fireplaces at the center of everything, notwithstanding that Palladio, by the almost gospel authority of his *Four Books of Architecture* (1570) – a copy of the then new Neopalladian translation of which, by Giacomo Leoni (1716–20), Berkeley is known to have had at Whitehall – always has a void, and never a solid, at the center of his every ground plan. All the more reason to suppose that Berkeley had a local builder simply do whatever he customarily did – like Loos's policy of no artistic interference in the name of art, in craft production – in enlarging a house that had probably been started by another New England but not local Rhode Island builder. Loos might have remarked, How clear such unwritten traditions prove to be!

It turns out that the new front, as executed, shows a mastery of local convention not likely within the command of an amateur newly arrived from overseas. For a major feature of Whitehall, evidently overlooked heretofore, if not glossed over as a defect in a fairly unpretentious provincial work, proves a telling and hardly inadvertent instance of vernacular formal thinking. It might have been supposed that, whether in wood or brick or stone, a symmetrical two-storey façade with two windows to either side of the door and five windows above, was just too basic, too typical of so much eighteenth-century building in Britain and the British pale in America, to matter. *Except*, that is, for the fact, apparently not noticed, that this façade is far from being symmetrical after all. The left-hand side of the house is considerably longer than the right, with the doorway somewhat off-center, in accord with an imbalance on the interior of a larger 'hall' to the left of the entrance with a smaller parlor or study to the right. Even Scully, normally keenly observant, speaks too summarily of Whitehall's "symmetrical façade." Yet the spacing of the fenestration is found to be calibrated to allow more an effect of symmetry, and a lively one, rather than, or more than, mathematical asymmetry.

Taking the present front windows and measuring them center-to-center to minimize discrepancies in replacement, I have found a remarkable series of spacings. The distance from the left corner of the façade to the center of the first window is greater by nearly a foot than that from the center of the last window to the right corner. The two left-hand windows are more than three inches further apart than the two right-hand ones, even as the inner pairing of the windows either side of the doorway is practically the same. Hence the discrepancies narrow toward equality at the center, even though what would now be called the living room, to the left, is thus given a good extra six feet in length vis-à-vis the opposite room to the right, yet without having the façade look obviously asymmetrical. The inequality might have looked wayward or careless: if anything, a lively order, rather than blunt regularity, prevails.

Quickly reviewing the likely building history of Berkeley's house: most plausibly, in front of the older core of a double fireplace stack, shared between a large kitchen on one side and what is now a bedroom on the other, there stands, thanks to Berkeley, a whole new two-storey front with, on the ground floor, one large room, or 'hall' to the left, and a somewhat smaller sitting-room or study to the right, either side of a second shared fireplace stack, with vestibule (and presumably once encased stairs) between them, up front.

Curiously, in the one architectural book besides Palladio that Berkeley is known to have possessed at Whitehall, Richard Neve specifically says in his *City and Countrey Purchaser and Builder's Directory; or, The Complete Builder's Guide*

(1703), addressed to craftspersons, that in judging a house one should consider "whether the principal Entrance be in the middle of the Front, like our Mouths; whether the Windows, as our Eyes, be set in equal Number, and distance on both sides [of] the Entrance" (qu., St George 284)[4] – an uncanny Berkeley-contemporary adumbration of the chronic postmodernist insistence on taking the façade of Loos's Moller House, in Vienna, as a punning, funny face. Not only Neve's chatty treatment of architectural pragmatics but his moralizing with a light touch on the practice of building as little more than humble carpentry, would have appealed to Loos as well as to the would-be missionary Berkeley. What about the discrepancy between the pronouncement just quoted, to have the front door "in the middle," and the facts of the remodeled Whitehall façade? The irregularity in question was too subtle to be conspicuous, even if it might please the practiced local craftsman or the odd aesthetically aware metaphysician.

How all the more interesting, then, to notice other houses of the same generation in the vicinity showing *precisely the same irregularity*, for there are several instances within the town of Newport of frame houses of the same type and vintage as Whitehall with similarly subtly but visibly irregular asymmetric fenestration, all stretching out on the left-hand side of the façades. To judge by the plan of the Jeremy Clarke House (built before 1670; demolished, 1898), the disposition had already appeared in Newport before the turn from the seventeenth to the eighteenth century. Examples occurring soon before and after Whitehall include the Wanton-Lyman-Hazard House, built by a Stephen Mumford c. 1695–1700, and probably the Thomas Richardson House (1715; demolished, 1940); and the Pitts Head Tavern, too, in Newport, probably built before 1726 and expanded in 1744 can also be mentioned.[5] By itself, each of these might seem like an insignificant deviation from symmetry, but not once the supposed deviation is itself seen as regular. Together, they indicate that the architecturally sophisticated Berkeley patronized a distinct local artisan aesthetic, proto-functionalist in its pragmatic practicality yet also pragmatic in the sense of *linguistically conventional* in regard to its formal demands: how a house ought to look as locally, 'vernacularly,' right. At Whitehall, then, as Loos would have been interested to see, it was probably an unknown local Newport builder who had the upper hand, with some collaboration from Berkeley, in the front that we see that as added to a formerly more modest farmhouse possibly by a different unknown builder from a neighboring state – like some old house in Austria that Loos, as Moravian born, could have told by looking had actually been started by a Moravian.

In front of Whitehall one might well think of what is now admired by conservatives as 'vernacular classicism,' a term that at best should apply only to the hand-me-down classical and not to anything rigged up ad hoc by clever illiterates in the provinces. However, it was in the actual historical moment of this house that in *The New Science* (1725) Giambattista Vico articulated the notion of "*vernaculae*" from this term anciently applied "to the vulgar tongues introduced by the vulgar of the peoples, that is, by the plebs of the heroic cities" (§ 1060; Vico 402). And in light of Vico, one might better describe such local work that is too fine to be considered rustic as traditional in an insider, 'townie' sense – workmanship, that is, of just the sort to be praised by Loos in 1910, the year of the Steiner House, as by far aesthetically superior to anything contaminated by the arty Arts and Crafts. Significantly, in 'Architecture' Loos is pleased to take the vernacular builder as unselfconsciously doing something in a don't-think-twice, locally generic way, much as Vico takes the vernacular affirmatively as communally produced.

A modern vernacular?

Loos can be brought into closer conjunction with Berkeley's Whitehall by way of Ruskin, in the nineteenth century, and Hoffmann in early modern Vienna. Well before Muthesius, John Ruskin, one of the prophets of architectural modernity with his Gothic of structural and ornamental integrity, had despised what he saw as the repressive regularity of the generically classical, symmetrical eighteenth-century house façade. Ruskin so despised hypotactical, i.e., rigorously orderly, classical orthodoxy that he would have had small patience even with the slightly lopsided façade of a house as respectable as Berkeley's Whitehall. In something of a neo-Edwardian moment today, with new money often enough looking yet again to a warmed-over, guaranteed Palladian taste, what is too easily forgotten is Ruskin's despising of all such architecture as empty propriety and vain pomp, as part of an alternative medievalism that was both critical of capitalism and proto-modernist – making even Hermann Muthesius's (1861–1927) more Loosian thinking possible.

Bearing in mind how under-appreciated has been the subtle irregularity of the Whitehall and related façades as vernacularly executed, the problem is the overriding strength of the disposition as all too readily schematized (with vernacular irregularities efficiently overlooked) as the whole, which hardly

warrants being called a composition, is reduced to a simplistic, doltish grid of
windows and central door –

$$w = w = w = w = w$$
$$w = w = D = w = w$$

– and how this critically resembles Ruskin's generic schematization of an
eighteenth-century classical house façade in an illustration (published under
the rubric 'Classical Architecture,' as Appendix III) to an 1857 lecture on
'Influence of Imagination in Architecture' (with brackets here and now
indicating lean-to additions of one bay on either end):

$$w = w = w$$
$$[w] \, w = D = w \, [w]$$

Obviously having a good time with this, Ruskin says, "Don't laugh; you must not
laugh, that's very improper of you, this is classical architecture. I have taken it out
of the essay on that subject in the *Encyclopaedia Britannica*" (Ruskin, 'Influence'
128; illus., 207). Anybody who wonders how Yale, as custodians of Whitehall
in the nineteenth century, could have allowed the house to fall into virtual ruin,
needs only to consider the situation in light of Ruskin's, in itself, well-founded
critical opposition to the classical vanity fair. Ruskin (following on A. W. N.
Pugin) had advanced a Gothicizing, ethico-aesthetic way to modernity that was
visually incompatible with Berkeley's more rationalist (yet in its way at least
as theological) sense of 'functional' form as showing forth a divinely ordained
purposiveness.

Besides eighteenth- and nineteenth-century approaches to the house as
architecturally proto-modern, a twentieth-century one, looking from Loos
onward, does seem possible. Yes, the Steiner House is typologically different
from Berkeley's Whitehall; but its Loosian fenestration, especially on the
flanks and the street front – ever symmetrical only on second glance – proves
much more akin to what is interesting about Whitehall than does a late house
by Loos's contemporary Viennese rival, the, to Loos, ever so decoratively
tasteful Josef Hoffmann: Knips House, of 1924–25. Loos had already built in
Vienna his radically asymmetrical Scheu House (1912–13) and Rufer House
(1922), the latter with its radical *Raumplan* and daringly free fenestration,
when Hoffmann, the Mackintosh of Vienna, built this suave but conservative
villa whose main element is a boxy block of two storeys, plus attic dormers
and a hip roof with chimneys. By a mildly daring lurch in the façade, which,

having an even number of openings, can have no central doorway, Hoffmann
replaces one window in his otherwise unruffled double row of evenly spaced
windows with a door:

$$w = w = w = w = w = w$$
$$w = w = w = D = w = w$$

Knips House is understandably taken as an exercise on Hoffmann's part in
blending in modernist plainness with the generalized-classical Biedermeier
houses of the immediate semi-suburban neighborhood.[6] Loos would say what
many weakly 'contextualizing' architects of the 1990s should have heard:
that any fool can 'blend in'; the point is compatible distinction, not a more
and more diluted blanding-out over time. By the moment of the Knips
House a more radical grounding of architecture in sophisticated, hardly
homogeneous, urban culture had already been undertaken by Loos for a
good twenty years.

   In a spirit of Loosian subtlety, attention can also be called to certain twentieth-
century American counterparts to another feature of Berkeley's house that one
might also take as a quirk if not an imperfection: the chunky, asymmetrical,
'L'-shaped chimney. It must be more than aesthetic nay-saying that keeps us
coming back to Adolf Loos's famous Steiner House, whose street façade, doing
its best to look diminutive to appease the city fathers, is vitally subtle in its
asymmetry, as well as its bolder shifting from the already subtly asymmetric
façade to the freely asymmetric flanks and on, 'meta-asymmetrically,' to the
serenely symmetrical garden façade – not unlike the more modest vernacular
situation at Berkeley's Whitehall, where the ad-hoc saltbox profile simply
excuses itself from the front and lets windows fall where they must. But for
someone so devoted to the fireside inglenook, Loos was coy about making too
homey a point of chimneys on his domestic exteriors. The Steiner flank sports
two diminutive ones, slightly asymmetrically placed at either end, while on the
street façade the end one of these takes on bulk and is repeated three more
times in a row along the crest of the barreled sheet metal roof, as Loos plays
a shell game with his row of four white stumps, any one or another of which
might be an operative chimney.

   The big Whitehall chimney looming above the peak of the shallow hip
roof is even more obviously off-axis with respect to the entrance than the
façade is asymmetrical. In head-on view its left-hand edge falls close enough
to the central axis of the entrance to lessen its inert bulk, while the mass
of the chimney is articulated as two fused blocks, set back at the left to an

'L'-shape in section. Just here, perhaps more than in any other detail, one would like to know the precise role of Berkeley in the remodeling of the house, including the chimney, which is known to be modified. For however pragmatically necessitated a design feature may be, there is latitude in effecting it; and this particular chimney disposition actually proves uncannily related to two American houses that must be, respectively, the most art-historically distinguished modernist and postmodernist houses in the United States.

Apropos of the classically modern: a similarly compounded 'L'-shaped chimney is a prominent feature – for known formal reason at that – of no less modernist a monument than Frank Lloyd Wright's Robie House, in Chicago, which at the time of its building in 1909 was something of an affront to its ersatz Georgian neighbors, theretofore happily housed in only less elegant 'colonial' classical equivalents to what Hoffmann was still doing twenty years afterward. Joseph Connors has pointed to the rationalization of this feature as a closet, as shows in a blueprint,[7] meaning that the bulking out of the asymmetrical chimney was really a formal, artistic decision for which rationalization was found after the aesthetic fact, since nobody would build such a cyclopean tower just to gain an extra bedroom closet. As for postmodernism, there is something American, even amusingly Georgian-assimilationist, in the once scandalously 'Pop'-modern house, since co-opted by postmodernists, which Venturi, Rauch and Scott Brown built for Robert Venturi's mother at Chestnut Hill, Pennsylvania, in 1962 – that famous plain frame house, tinged with a light classicism, whose articulated, off-centered chimney places it among unaccounted descendants of Berkeley's Whitehall, as well as of the more modestly plain-walled houses of Loos.

After the postmodernist likes of Venturi, it is sometimes worth reconsidering the notion of purposive functionalism that half a century ago seemed a good basis from which to propound architectural modernism. Whitehall itself may not look self-evidently modern, except in the vaguely patronizing way in which no-nonsense, efficient-looking American country things like Shaker furniture and old carpenters' tools have often been adopted by the urbane as 'honorary' modern; and young Loos himself seems to have been interested enough in such to visit a Shaker community while in America. Yet there is something persistently modern-pertinent about it that will not be exhausted by reference to adumbrations of functionalism in *Alciphron*, as where the Berkeleian character Euphranor remarks how one can "infer the excellency of animal bodies from observing the frame and fitness of their several parts" (Dial. I; Berkeley, *Alciphron* 53); he even thinks of the classical ornamental orders as condensations, of sorts, of sometime utilitarian forms (III; 69).

'Post-American' Loosian vernacularism

After seeing to the work on his temporary residence in Rhode Island, and living in it for more than two years, George Berkeley had to face the fact that he would not be supported in his Bermuda missionary effort and so would have to return home to Ireland in 1731, where in 1734 he took up the Church of Ireland bishopric of Cloyne, in County Cork. *Alciphron* (1735), with its anticipations of functionalist theory, had largely been composed in the Newport house; but soon after going home Berkeley wrote a political text, of special interest in the matter of vernacular design, in which one can pick up on spectral impressions of a vernacular Whitehall recently left behind. This is *The Querist; Containing Several Queries Proposed to the Consideration of the Public* (1735–37; *Works* 6: 87–192), in which Berkeley sets forth a polemical series of ironic, even sarcastic, observations and rants, especially on bad conditions in Ireland, as those must have struck him all the more vividly after his time in America.[8] The 'queries' (numbered as 'Q's), cast as questions but being in effect challenging statements, have echoes of Berkeley's three-year experience of Whitehall as a building, along with clues to a complex Anglo-Irish, within British imperial, identity, not unlike that of Loos, the Viennese of culturally 'German,' yet also technically Moravian, birth (as will be considered in chapter 3).

Adolf Loos would have liked Berkeley, the actual 'Querist's,' advocacy of sumptuary laws, at least as a critical polemic, provided they were focused on ostentation without discouraging simple quality in clothing: "Whether it may not concern the wisdom of the legislature to interpose in the making of fashions; and not leave an affair of so great influence to the management of women and fops, tailors and vintners?" (Q. 13; 6: 106). Tantalizing with respect to Whitehall's authorship is the query "Whether if a man builds a house he doth not in the first place provide a plan which governs his work?" (Q. 50; 6: 109), implying at least that he himself would not have built or remodeled his house without some concrete design, some form of drawing, though not necessarily rendered by himself.

Questions of local building convention arise, and evidence suggesting that, owing in part to limitations of available material, if not the technical limitations of local builders (both implying some at least supervisory role for himself), Berkeley possibly didn't really *like* his American house: "Whether tiles and plaster may not supply the place of Norway fir for flooring and wainscot?" (Q. 117; 6: 114; Norway fir being common pine); or "Whether plaster be not warmer, as well as more secure, than deal? And whether a modern fashionable house, lined with fir, daubed over with oil and paint, be not like a fire-ship, ready to be lighted up by all accidents?" (Q. 118, 6: 115). Brick and stone, even marble [on Loos's behalf we may specify green cipollino!] might have been nicer (Q. 120, 123; ibid.). There are also several remarks in a Loosian spirit on Berkeley's "English" (not even Anglo-Irish) identity as evidently only reinforced by the colonial experience, which would have pleased the Loos whose imperial Vienna, whatever else he might say, was the beloved capital of his world. Berkeley's Whitehall was not important enough to be known in Europe, but it is a good example of vernacular house-building as a category of distinctly Loosian modern interest.

It is impossible to follow Loos's work from its beginnings onward without meeting up at some point with Muthesius, the Anglophile architectural theorist of the Deutsche Werkbund, whose grand illustrated tomes *Das englische Haus* (The English House), which appeared in 1904–05, would obviously have interested Loos in the way medievalist picturesqueness gave way, in them, to 'free' composition, along with the artisanal emphasis underpinning Loos's own vernacularism. Muthesius is on some level a link between the *sachlich* or matter-of-fact, vernacular aspect of Whitehall and the *sachlich* or matter-of-fact aspect, often considered functionalist, even by early functionalists themselves, of Loos's Steiner and other houses. Before his famous picture book he had already sounded Loosian in print: "[I]n Germany today it is seriously contested whether architecture is an art at all, whether the artist is an architect or not" (Muthesius 49); and was it ever clearer how vernacularist in thrust that very question was? Although there are differences (Frampton, notably, warns against referring too much of the Loosian to Muthesius), Loos would have been curious about his view of the Zopf-to-Biedermeier taste, and obviously interested in his sense of *sachlich,* matter-of-fact simplicity (53). The book in question is *Style-Architecture* (1902); and after bemoaning the "rapid decline of craftsmanship," Muthesius adds a very Loosian comment in the second edition (1903): "Only the substratum of building production, the art of the master mason, remained healthy for a time. With it the old tradition endured, almost uninfluenced by the foolishness of high architecture, until the second half of the nineteenth century; it was overrun only when the architectural schools of a style-making academicism intervened ..." (58–59). So it was that in the earlier nineteenth century "art and the handicrafts quite naturally lost their footing, and a [N. B.] barbarism, such as our culture had not seen before, penetrated the substratum of the trades with little notice" (59). New middle-class people lacked proper bourgeois taste: "Generally, they were attracted, like the barbarian, to the gaudy and the vulgar" (60). Yet where architects proved unable to break out of classical conventions, these people "cultivated a unique and admirable bourgeois style of furniture, embodied by Chippendale [actually a Loos favorite], Hepplewhite and Sheraton"; what is more, "With this, the ground was laid for genuinely middle-class household furnishings whose early development can also be observed somewhat later on the Continent in the so-called Biedermeier time ..." (61).

With this and much else, including express distaste for the *art nouveau* or *Jugendstil*, Muthesius, who had opened an important modern German window on English domestic architecture, can seem to offer a cue card or two for Loos. But if even supposedly orthodox Loosian ideas were promulgated by this German architect and cultural attaché at the German embassy in London (1896–1903), who seems to belong to the nineteenth century but was only nine years older than Loos, many might as well trace back to Loos's own early critical reviews of crafts and industrial arts. Although these were collected in 1921 in *Ins Leere gesprochen* (i.e., 'Whistling in the Wind'), they were first published between 1897 and 1900, so that Muthesius himself might even have been aware of the perspicacious young architect and design critic from Vienna. "Architecture should follow nineteenth-century men's dress in its trend of simplification," Muthesius could write (79), precociously, one could say, except that a young writer named Adolf Loos had already been saying much the same. Even the Loosian distinction between public architecture and domestic non-architecture is there: "with the quotidian tasks, especially with the dwelling ... we surely should disallow the demand to realize a higher artwork in a closed form. Such goals are as much out of place here ... as the journalist's intention to write a newspaper article in an epic form" (81).

A Loosian vernacular?

While Berkeley's house is obviously not a modern building, and, in fact, quite the kind of reassuringly tidy, stolid box of an old frame house that people sometimes hold up to shame a seemingly steely modernism, in the sheer restraint of its marked plainness, rhetorical only at the welcoming door, it is just the sort of pre-modern, quite often anonymous, building which still a generation to two ago, in virtue of unadulterated simplicity, used to serve to corroborate a quasi-functionalist sense of fitness-to-task. Since the general waning of modernism the functionalist case has been moot, yet perhaps in a revisionist way Whitehall begins to make a new sort of claim for itself, as works of art often do.

Within the scope of Loos's production, one finds two different categories of house that broadly compare to Whitehall as vernacular. On one hand, there are his suburban Viennese renovations: the Duschnitz (1915–16), Mandl (1916), and Strasser (1918–19) Houses, which have nothing visual to do with Berkeley's British-colonial farmhouse; on the other, two rural houses.

What may be considered vernacular about the latter is the way they look like well-built versions of what might be expected after looking up generic builders in the telephone directory instead of engaging a fine-arts architect. (Loos often 'talked generic,' but never produced conventional or generic works.) Except for its luxurious scale, the Kuhner Country House, of 1929–30, at Kreuzberg, near Payerbach, might suggest, by its local, mountain-chalet handling, that formidably 'primitivist' exception to modernist rule, the 1921 log-cabin-style Sommerfeld House at Berlin, on which Bauhaus folks worked under its designer: amazingly enough, Walter Gropius. Yet closer to a vernacular spirit is that more modestly ample country house, also in Lower Austria, the oddly overlookable, even though boldly vertically striped, board-and-batten, freely asymmetrical Spanner Country House, at Grumpoldskirchen, of 1924, which nobody ever talks about. Not for any particular reason, but on principle, it seems, the Spanner is ordinary: the three-bedroom house with dining room and salon either side of an English-type 'hall,' is roughly the size of Whitehall and seems vernacular-ordinary – unfortunately all the more so today, lacking its original shutters and with added hip instead of flat roof, plus dormers.

Functionalism as adumbrated by Loos, and vernacularism as advanced by him, have much in common as eminently pragmatic modern interests; but the functionalist denial of art in architecture is not identical with the vernacularist denial, which is more a denial of the 'artist' architect. Functionalism was incapable of accounting for the art in Loos's work because it didn't want art to count, though it had its way of appreciating engineered beauty and couldn't applaud Loos enough for de-ornamentalization as a necessary if not sufficient reason for something's deserving to rate as distinctly modern architecture, not as non-architecture, (comparably to abstract or non-objective painting as *not non-painting*). As Loos maintains in 'Architecture' (1910), the way to true modernity was not that of Arts and Crafts revisionists, after all – and not for anti-vernacularist reason but because the crafts had been corrupted by artiness. The trouble with the Vienna Secession was that *ornament reformed* was still *ornament as usual*. So the architect, on Schiller's specially defined 'sentimental' side, must have the humility not only to do without affected ornament but to defer in appropriate contexts to 'naïve' craftsmen, if any can still be found, who know from the experience of generations how to effect the form called for not only by pragmatic practicality but also by immemorial pragmatic custom, which is cultural, without pseudo-artistic ado. Somewhat idealistically (another sign of Schiller's 'sentimental'), Loos imagines such a just-plain builder confronting his task, which is not so trivially executive after all: yet what he actually proposes could be described as real architecture elicited natively, without a bourgeois architect-designer:

> [W]hile the mason is laying brick upon brick, stone upon stone, the carpenter arrives and sets up his tools. His ax rings out merrily. He is making the roof. What kind of roof? A beautiful or an ugly one? He has no idea. It's just a roof.
>
> And then the joiner measures up the doors and windows, and all the other craftsmen come and measure up and go back to their workshops and work. Finally the farmer mixes up a large tub of whitewash and makes the house nice and white. He cleans the brush and puts it away. He'll need it again next Easter.
>
> His intention was to erect a house for himself and his family, or for his animals, and that is what he has done. Just as his neighbor or his great-grandfather did. Just as every animal does when it is guided by instinct. Is the house beautiful?
>
> Yes, just as beautiful as a rose or a thistle, as a horse or a cow. (*OA* 73–74)

No building procedure could be any more vernacular – not that the resultant forms have no history, but that they are innately historical, without affectation or fuss. Loos was writing in the spirit of Nietzsche when he warned ailing art-architects to give up expecting to save themselves by parasitic resort to the crafts, ordering craftsmen to follow their arty orders – as that great modern prophet says of such a would-be artist in *The Birth of Tragedy*: "Because he is unable to behold a vision, he forces the machinist and the decorative artist into his service" (§ 19; Nietzsche, *Birth* 117). No; the point has a different fulcrum: in the face of self-conscious historicisms that can never make for truly contemporary style, the builder or carpenter who knows how to discharge his task with humble care in satisfaction of necessity and custom may be by default the only decent artist around, as Berkeley, for one, probably understood at empirical first hand; which certainly need not mean the end of art, properly understood.

The distinguished Berkeley scholar A. A. Luce's apologetic accolade of 1949 that Berkeley's house "suits its purpose" is now not only truistic but curiously dated, as evocative of a high point of widespread functionalist conviction in the postwar period. Just so could Luce salute Whitehall as perhaps somehow just a little more than unprepossessing work: "simply a plain, commodious, two-storey farmhouse, with a comfortable, solid, and pleasing air" (Luce 124). Architecturally speaking, however, in view of Loos there proves to be more to the matter than that.

In the interwar period of modernist propagation the vernacular might have been useful to functionalist theory, but with a possible onus of the romantically sentimental. A 1939 survey of Rhode Island buildings by none other than Henry-Russell Hitchcock – already the author, with Philip Johnson, of the definitive Museum of Modern Art exhibition and book *The International Style* (1932) – makes no mention of Whitehall and shows some irritation with the vernacular approach, commenting on then new suburban evocations of colonial farmhouses. Hitchcock remarks that it is a mistake to take as style, reiterable as such, what belongs to a strongly vernacular typology: "The timber-framed yeoman's house of England and America in the seventeenth century was not, like the academic houses of the eighteenth century, the product of conscious stylistic intention … It is in no sense to be considered as a work of capitalized Architecture; and to imitate its visual appearance is as irrelevant as to imitate an Indian wigwam in ferro-concrete" (Hitchcock 13).[9] After all, as Adolf Loos would have emphasized, it is as if, before the modernist fact, Berkeley had said to a reputable Newport carpenter-builder: I shall not impose what I think to be fine art upon you; go and rise to the level of art just by doing plainly, unembellished, what you know best how to do best. The Loosian point, as it already seems it could have been for Berkeley in America, was to approach the art of building not as some precious bloom, at odds with the ordinary, but as the flower of the ordinary.

The emigrée modernist Sibyl Moholy-Nagy would have been ideally prepared to pick up on just the homemade vernacular eloquence of Whitehall on the terms of her *Native Genius in Anonymous Architecture* (1957) – a title later expanded by the qualification '… in North America.' This emigrée Central European modernist who held vernacular architecture to the high standard of Goethe's comment on folk art as being "like a word of God, spoken this instant" (Moholy-Nagy 44) was negatively impressed by the self-conscious display of gentility in Neopalladian 'Georgian' mansions of the United States, North and South alike: "the poor man's dream of [Colin] Campbell and [William] Kent," she wrote. Yet she was more critical still of the rather nativist New

England saltbox house, faulting the very type for lacking "specific response to local environmental conditions and uniqueness of architectural solution" and calling to task an implicit ideological attitude: "The Puritans who created this house type in the Western Hemisphere offer the peculiar historical paradox of being protesting conformers ... The early New England house was a symbol of utter conformity with the non-conforming congregation. Just as women dress to impress men, so the Saltbox was built to impress the community with the undeviating righteousness of its inhabitant" (110–11). Otherwise, however, Mrs Moholy-Nagy admired home-grown American forms quite unpatronizingly.

It used to be clearer than it is today that while radical early modernism stood against an academic tradition which indulged stereotypically classical ornamental rhetoric, it was committed to empirical knowledge of form and material as exercised traditionally in the crafts and, for that matter, in the decidedly craft-based art program of the very Bauhaus. Thus did the anonymous and supposedly out-of-left-field, non-European architecture shown in Bernard Rudofsky's *Architecture Without Architects* (1964), subtitled 'A Short Introduction to Non-Pedigreed Architecture,' carry modernist formal appeal in the West, possibly shadowed by a sense of tribal or peasant vernaculars as already everywhere in their twilight. Contemplating Whitehall provokes the thought that discourse on what is considered vernacular architecture *at all* was perhaps already vexed by the time of Pop art and the contemporaneous architectural revisionism of Robert Venturi. In respect to colonial history it might have been better to specify the term vernacular for what really was truly culturally native, using something like 'vulgate' for the canonically hand-me-down classical.

All this is a long way from eighteenth-century New England; but in Rhode Island, Berkeley in some sense adumbrated Adolf Loos in trusting an anonymous Newport carpenter-builder possibly to rise to some level of art by doing well with usual humility what he knew how to do. Regrettably, such wisdom has withered away in a new philistinism that is something like the Neopalladians without the borrowed wisdom of their Palladio. Already a decade ago, it was shocking to see rising all around Berkeley's house a flotilla of resentfully anti-modern, *pompier* 'McMansions' (so called in allusion to the global McDonald's American hamburger chain) – spanking new model-railroad cottages inflated to size 'XXXL,' all with now obligatory, factory-produced, 'pseudo-Palladian' windows (Wittkower's term). Berkeley wanted no architectural artist but just a good builder who knew how to build in a basically right way, as Loos recommended a century ago now; but in the

15. Steven Holl, Y House, Catskill
Mountains, New York State, 1999.

ignorant decadence of the present the pretentiousness of the McMansions is probably being taken for 'our' vernacular. In these circumstances, even Henry-Russell Hitchcock would probably have to concede to Whitehall the status of art, and practically proto-modern art at that.

As Loos would maintain, the proper response to such alienated ersatz folksiness as now too often sails under vernacularist colors is new art that lives up to the best of the old in the spirit of the Schillerean sentimental rather than of a faux-naïveté. A great counter-example to the many thousands of pretentious commonplaces is Steven Holl's 'Y' House, of 1997–99, in Upstate New York. Like the Steiner House of Loos, its uphill rear entrance façade understates what develops on the flanks and at the downhill rear, facing onto nature. Slim steel components are used lightly, in the manner of thin wood, but painted, as Loos would approve, an anything-but-wood red, while in the loose rectilinear fenestration of the flanks, as well as the mountain-tuned face, something of Loos (and even something not strange to Berkeley) can be understood. In an interview, Holl agreed that there is a rather vernacular aspect to the way the house splits from its front entrance into two attached cottages, side by side, as if bringing their own neighborliness with them as remotely sited in the mountains (Masheck, 'Holl' 28); and when I explained that I was writing on Berkeley's Whitehall out of concern for the vernacular in respect to Loos, he seconded the notion that discourse on the vernacular has been distorted by anti-modernist conservatives who reserve the word as a term of approbation for mere "middle-class, hand-me-down classicism" (29).

Stepping back from the problem, we might find ourselves thinking that anonymity is perhaps germane to the vernacular, not merely a circumstance of Whitehall. Vernacular art offers meaning as embedded in *langue*, to be down-loaded from a common fund of meaning, and implying a priority of community. That is how, in the Prague Linguistic Circle, of which Loos was doubtless aware, folklore could be distinguished from literature as more a matter of *parole*, the personally enunciated word. As Roman Jakobson and a colleague stated in 1929, in this situation "even the creator has no reason to view his work as his own, or the works of other contemporary creators as extraneous" (Bogatyrëv and Jakobson 39). In Vico's day Whitehall had shown in architectural practice what is implicitly at stake in vernacular production, and how the more profound reason why we cannot satisfy ourselves as to the authorship of Whitehall is not the lack of documentation but the more comprehensive truth of the way vernacular is authorship seated in the culture at large, in the Viconian sense of the Greek people as such as author of the canonical 'Homer.'

As vernaculars dried up under general cultural alienation, there was ever less scope for vernacular architecture. Loos was on an early modern cusp of sorts; but it would surely be mistaken to suppose that, together with many other modernists, he was 'part of the problem,' foisting some heartless industrial approach to architecture onto formerly craft-oriented builders. No; Loos's abiding tropism toward the essentially vernacular building-craft tradition was always for him an inspiring longing for integrity on fully modern terms.

Postscript

If it sometimes seems uncertain just what the operational limits of Loos's concept of the vernacular were, the British-colonial Rhode Island example with a Connecticut aspect may still perhaps convey a critical sense of a sort of 'bifocal' vernacularism aware, non-contradictorily, of both specifically local and culturally general (if not universal) formal dispositions. In 1906–07, while young Wittgenstein was studying engineering in Berlin, Josef Hoffmann built for the Wittgensteins at Hohenberg, in Lower Austria, a somewhat vernacular-styled country house. Although the plain façade might look to a glance symmetrical, with five supposedly evenly spaced unframed upstairs windows, the downstairs fenestration is strongly asymmetrical, with one wide window to the left, and two the same as the upstairs ones to the right; but what is perhaps more, the doorway, which Adolf Loos would have been the first to criticize as Secessionist-ornamental, is conspicuously off-centered toward the right.

Yet a certain anonymous, likely eighteenth-century Swiss farmer's house, also two storied and also five windows wide, with off-centered portal and chimneys, shows itself perhaps all the more meaningfully akin, in the gentle asymmetry of its fenestration stretching laterally on one side (in this case to the right of the door), to the farmhouse on which Berkeley must have worked while he lived and wrote in America. If anything, Nietzsche would have liked its turning out to be general 'Euro-vernacular' as well as distantly akin to what certain carpenters in New England thought was just the right way, in their known world, to build a right-looking house.

There at Sils-Maria, in the Alpine landscape of the Engadin Valley, Nietzsche summered for much of the 1880s in the bare guestroom of a plain boxy farmhouse with similarly off-centered front door. In a letter of June 1883 he writes of "the narrow parlor of a farmhouse" and wishes he could afford to build himself a little two-roomed cabin (qu. Krell and Bates 157). Yet in a great text issuing from his spare, pine-paneled room (compare Berkeley's humble "deal"), *The Genealogy of Morals* (1887), Nietzsche, who would likely have read about the adaptation of utilitarian form to purpose in *Alciphron*, makes points about asceticism which must have appealed in their Karl-Krausian iconoclasm to Loos. Today they may especially inspire discontent with the falseness and affectation of so much would-be 'minimalism' that is nothing but a tailored, repressive, corporate-world 'tastefulness' imposing itself in the illiterate culture at large, including architecture as respected as John Pawson's: so proudly frigid and "hieratic," as Nietzsche would say – the Nietzsche who in his room in this house wrote, "I do not like these ambitious artists who like to pose as ascetics and priests ..." (III. 26; Nietzsche, *Genealogy* 158) – no offense, of course to the clerical Berkeley, as proto-Loosian architectural vernacularist.

3

LOOS AND IMPERIAL NEW YORK

The obvious reason that a hopeful young Austrian architect without resources should stake everything on the chance to visit big, blustery America in the mid-1890s was to escape for a time the cultural inertia of traditional Europe and to experience at first hand the excitement and promise of modernity in the leading culture of the New World. All the more remarkable, then, that the first major project which Adolf Loos designed on his return to Vienna from an extended American sojourn should have been an Austrian imperial building just possibly inspired by a then new American project that was itself a work of 'fine,' indeed, establishment, architectural art in the ultra-European Beaux-Arts tradition, more akin to the grand Roman imperial classicism dominating the World's Columbian Exposition, which Loos had also come to see, than like anything of Louis Henri Sullivan's quite exceptional modernity there in Chicago. That seems like a curiously conservative thing to do, out of artistic character for the radically modern Loos we know and admire; but the whole situation warrants attention for its implications about Loos's developing cosmopolitan identity in his formation as an artist.

This chapter advances the sense of the budding architect assessing his historical situation by visiting America in order to orient himself and ready himself for active participation in the new modern reality, as when, a few years later, the young Picasso would break with the local ethnic modernity of Barcelona in favor of cosmopolitan Paris, though Loos was only exploring on his sojourn in the booming US, and staying for awhile in New York. His other main destination – the World's Columbian Exposition – was important in that the Chicago spectacle presented the new mass democracy under a newly assertive plutocracy with imperial ambitions, however excitingly open the society would have seemed on street level. But Loos must have been enervated by his extended stay in anarchic New York – a New York, he would have noticed, impatient to simplify as general 'German' the newly arrived Bohemians, Moravians, Slovaks and even Austrian Austrians – which makes it all the more surprising that the major new project there, which possibly influenced him, was as conservative and literally imperial Roman as everything in the World's Columbian Exposition except Sullivan's Transportation Building. Perhaps, however ironically, a curious thing about New York to the penurious but cosmopolitan Loos was its seeming something like a promising 'next' Vienna.

Carolina (Lina) Obertimpfler Loos, the architect's actress first wife, obtained a curious result in playing word-association with Adolf: "I say '*Volksgarten*,' and he gives me back 'lilac.' I say 'Paris' and he gives back 'pastry.' I say 'London' and he gives 'fried fish' and 'fog.' I say 'New York' and he gives me back 'homesickness (*Heimweh*)' …" (E. A. Loos 30). Here the notion of a *memory* of homesickness, as evidently expressed in later life in regard to New York by Adolf Loos, conceivably cuts two ways. One can simply remember, at home, being somewhere else and having been homesick *there*. Yet one might quite otherwise find oneself feeling a sentimental pang for a faraway time and place where one was youthful and bravely alone, and hence had then and there felt homesick – as if now as much as homesick for a past homesickness.

Maybe there was some of both sorts of homesickness for New York in the seemingly unsentimental Loos. If so, that would concern what America, and primarily New York in the mid-1890s, meant in Loos's experience, perhaps particularly as implicated in a major early project of the architect on his return to Vienna from America. The work in question was an 1899 competition project for a church to commemorate the jubilee of the Emperor Franz Joseph. It was projected for the Mexikoplatz, a square on the Danube Canal whose name alludes to Franz Joseph's liberal but frustrated brother, the Maximilian whose execution as emperor of Mexico in 1867 was immediately and so unsentimentally memorialized by Manet at the time. The church was to have been dedicated to Saint Elizabeth, name saint of the empress, affectionately known as 'Sisi,' who herself had only recently been assassinated in the prior, actual jubilee year of 1898. As it happened, Viktor Luntz's large but rather thin and 'big-box' neo-Romanesque jubilee church dedicated to the emperor's own 'Franz,' Francis of Assisi (finished 1913), rose on the site instead.

In view of such 'imperial-and-royal' connections at home, one might suppose that Loos had simply put his New World experience aside for the sake of entering the competition, not expecting the high classicism of Loos's imperial Austrian proposal to be conditioned by contemporary, up-to-date America, let alone a monumental Austrian imperial project as possibly influenced by anything like the ultra-academic-classical architecture of the World's Columbian Exposition of 1893, in Chicago. Such a literally imperial monumental building by an eventual modernist from Brno, Moravia, in the Czech Lands of the Austro Hungarian Empire, does not obviously intimate influence from overseas, especially from the brash new American empire of Calvinism and commerce just then developing, in part by wildly popular military aggressions against the remains of the ex-Habsburgian Spanish empire in the New World.

Yet on consideration it does seem plausible that, in leaving one imperial capital behind, Loos may well have been stimulated, against the background of his experience in Chicago, by New York as cultural capital of an up-and-coming imperial power. In substantiation of this suggestion concerning the genesis of the Vienna jubilee-church project, several factors can be considered: Adolf Loos's reactions to the Chicago world's fair; some cultural implications of his extended stay in New York, including the likely interest to him of a new building complex then under way in the city; but also the wider cultural implications of Loos's imperial commemoration project: how, at the start of a great modernist career, Loos seems with his jubilee church to have negotiated a complex problematic of ethnicity, nationality and cosmopolitanism in culturally identifying in a cosmopolitan, transatlantic way with his own imperial capital, stimulated by another, for better or worse, then rolling out to the center of the historical stage.

Loos and the World's Columbian Exposition

Adolf Loos arrived in New York in the summer of 1893 at the age of twenty-three. Before settling in, for between two and three years, he visited Philadelphia, staying with family on a farm in Pennsylvania and then traveling with anticipation to Chicago. Chicago, birthplace of the skyscraper, was already architecturally important; but then there was also the World's Columbian Exposition to see, the tremendous 'Columbian' world's fair, celebrating the 400th anniversary of the European discovery of America – though everything possible was done to expunge anything so Continental in identity as an Italian sailing for the Spanish empire, and instead, to establish a public 'American' identity of principally

British derivation. Loos, visiting from Franz Joseph's Austria, was an Anglophile in his own way, though he would have seemed 'German' foreign.

Besides being formidable and problematic as architectural spectacle, the fair may have had a role in the germination of Loos as an art critic as well as an architect. From a previous world's fair in Philadelphia, the Centennial Exposition of 1876, Franz Reuleaux, an engineer from the Zurich E.T.H., had published in Germany provocative and influential field reports in 1877 about how "*billig und schlecht* (cheap and poor)" were the German products on view (Dal Co 201–07; Frampton, *Modern Architecture* 110); and on his return to Vienna, Loos would produce the great flurry of critical reviews in 1897–98, especially of finely crafted luxury wares as against mass-produced 'applied art,' responding to exhibits at the great exposition celebrating the emperor's jubilee, that made a name for him in the Viennese avant-garde. That the reputation of the seventeen-years-younger Le Corbusier begins with a report on German art-ware productions (*Étude sur le mouvement d'art décoratif en Allemagne*, 1912) is only one of the ways in which Corbusier followed in Adolf Loos's footsteps.

The academic-classical architecture of the new World's Columbian Exposition as a whole was under the general artistic responsibility of Daniel Burnham and John W. Root – ironically enough, given those partners' distinguished contributions in the proto-modern line of H. H. Richardson and then Louis H. Sullivan in which, apart from the Beaux-Arts Disneyland of the world's fair, Chicago already excelled. To this day it seems curious that Loos, the modernist-to-be, did not rankle at all the pseudo-classicism, or, at that, pseudo-*Baroque*-classicism, and emerge a partisan of Sullivan and his lone modernist Transportation Building. Even the 'Hōō-den,' or Phoenix Villa, by Masamichi Kuru, based on a medieval Japanese prototype and decorated in later Japanese styles, with its gabled central feature connected by wings to secondarily emphasized end pavilions (cf. Lancaster), was practically Anglo-Palladian in layout. Well, it was a fair, after all, and as such an actual spectacle and not necessarily a 'Potemkin village,' in that pejorative term for sham architecture inherited by Loos from the doyen of earlier Viennese architectural modernity, Otto Wagner, the great teacher of pioneer modernists, who after all had a brass-band side himself. The sheer excitement of this footloose fellow from the Austrian empire was perhaps that of a young sophisticate open to the likes of John Philip Sousa even though he would literally wind up a friend of Arnold Schoenberg, though Sullivan had good reason for his lapidary prophecy that the Chicago exposition would set American architecture back fifty years, owing to conservative East Coast architects imposing their Beaux-Arts classicism practically throughout.

Actually, there was still some liberal flexibility in the American situation as late as the onset of the First World War, given a basic bourgeois respect for the homegrown, Richardson-to-Sullivan modernity as, maybe, not too much wilder than a freewheeling *Rundbogenstil* (nineteenth-century Germanic 'round-arch' style), through Sullivan and down to Frank Lloyd Wright, and as even the fans of Theodore Roosevelt could have said, 'progressive' in the bargain. Soon something of an ancients-and-moderns polarization would set in, especially with the publication in 1914 of two books: Morris Hicky Morgan's translation of the *Ten Books of Architecture* of Vitruvius, the only architectural text to come down from antiquity, as underwriting a plutocratic American counterpart to Edwardian classicism, practically coincidentally with Geoffrey Scott's *The Architecture of Humanism: A Study in the History of Taste* (of which Loos owned a first edition, surely savoring its ultra-Englishness). These would only facilitate an American plutocratic, 'classy' classicism, already under way, which was a beefier, more tycoonish application of Vitruvius than the elegant Edwardian equivalent epitomized in Scott. The mystique of just such hazardous categories young Loos was by then cracking, like a code; and it would probably be mistaken to presume that at Chicago he categorically rejected everything stylistically classical, including the exhibition as a whole. If anything, he always had a tropism toward classicism, though it doesn't usually matter, in view of his modernist achievement, that his most ostensibly classical projects went unbuilt.

Loos is seen beginning to articulate his viewpoint back at home, a few years later, in the Vienna *Neue Freie Presse*, writing criticism in the new context of the Vienna Jubilee Exposition of 1898. One report in particular, even as it shows the unresolved complexity of Loos's 'thinking aloud,' takes special pains with finely crafted luxury wares of leather and precious metals. The article is challenging in its, as it were, pluperfect viewpoint (not unlike the secondary sense of 'homesick'), with the writer reflecting on just how, *on second thought*, he should have been thinking (*but hadn't been*), in front of the exhibits in Chicago. Loos is in effect reconsidering, at home in Vienna in the time of his imperial jubilee-church project, what he had promisingly but perhaps mistakenly been thinking at the start of his American sojourn. Consider his train of thought as he responds to what he sees in Vienna in 1898 by reconsidering his Chicago experience five years earlier, with recollections in the third person – not unlike *The Education of Henry Adams* (1907), with its famous 'Dynamo and the Virgin' chapter recollecting the Paris world's fair of 1900 but also with the same World's Columbian Exposition in mind.

To paraphrase, in italics, with quotations intact: Travel gains one a fresh view of things at home, and though he had brought with him a presumption of the superiority of both German and Austrian to American productions, especially of Arts and Crafts ilk, that now seems too crude. The German wares shown in Chicago were "[n]othing but vulgar fakery" (*OC* 32), though of specifically Austrian work in two categories he was right to be proud, namely, fancy leatherwork and silversmithing; everything else had deserved his superior disapprobation. What is so good about Austrian luxury goods made of leather and precious metals, as should have been more apparent before? Before he had resented the simple leather luggage as mere "fashion" accessories – "Fashion! What a terrible word!" (32) – but they really were tasteful, unlike the historicizing ornamentation of whatever issued from the Viennese School of Applied Arts. Fortunately, the Viennese don't really buy much of that, for they somehow suspect it "vulgar" to embellish "articles of dress and ordinary use" (33). Now, however … "[t]he bracing American and English air has blown away all my prejudices against the products of my own time" – despite the "[u]nscrupulous people" who "have tried to turn us against our own time, telling us to look backward" (33). At least we Viennese weren't taken in by bad leatherwork or silversmithing – crafts which had benefited by the British design reforms of the mid-century. Thus, too, we have good furniture, for what's good in the Arts-and-Crafts influence never had anything to do with "acanthus ornament" (34) – a specific form whose internal logic and wide dissemination the great Bohemian-Viennese art historian Aloïs Riegl had only recently scrutinized in his *Problems of Style* (1893; see below, chapter 4). No; rather what's good in art-ware production concerns "correct form, sound material, and precise workmanship" (34). If metalworkers were not quite so unspoiled as leather-workers, nevertheless enough Austrian silver and gold offers "sufficient examples of originality, of an art which though simple, does have its origin in the firm's own studio" rather than being imposed from without by some designer (34) – a remarkably early, and surprisingly William-Morrisonian, statement of the Loosian aesthetic of design unadulterated by imposition of supposed 'art.' No doubt the leather-workers have a better record because they have never been subcontracted: letting the typical architect tell them what to do would surely turn even them into stylistic pedants of historical style too (which then must show its absurdity in a situation like the Chicago exposition).

Even in precis there is rhetorical difficulty in the build-up of qualifying statements, beyond the fact, which no one wants to assert, that Loos was actually not a very gifted writer; for the text is challenging because modernism too readily contented itself with simplistic advocacy of utility and economy, as if the mechanically simplest solution to any design problem guaranteed its necessary and sufficient, if not unsurpassable, beauty. While it is easy to accept Loos's willingness to challenge bourgeois taste, it is not easy to see why the famous radical prepared to make a clean sweep of convention should prove, as if on the other hand, so ready to bless 'style,' let alone condone it in the sense of the 'stylist,' which cannot simply be a matter of convenience – and just when all such wickedness might have been abolished. But Loos was not a puritan. Notwithstanding his rhetorical bluster, he is not going to convince anybody that his beloved English eighteenth-century Chippendale chair was some ultimately simple object-type naturally disencumbered of all superfluities through some evolutionary school of hard knocks.

Now consider how different in attitude is a contemporary response to the Bohemian presence at the Exposition in Chicago – new home to many Czechs – in a Bohemian-American journal, interesting both in its framing of the question of ethnic identity as well as for its concern with Czech art-glass production. The editor, one Josef Jiří Král, an exact contemporary of Loos, comments on how unfair it is to find "the historical kingdom of Bohemia ... a non-entity" in Chicago, in view of the fair's various "small British possessions, half-civilized savages, and extinct nations, represented by their works" (Král 12). Solidarity was not one of Král's strong points, though in fairness, it seems that any immigrant in his position who had a broader, more socialist, picture of political reality was liable to being tainted as a dangerous anarchist; and the mission of this first Bohemian-American English-language paper was really remedially nationalistic in that it was to overcome anti-Czech bias in the German-language press, which alone was conveying things Czech to America (see Chroust). The capitalist structure of assimilation saw to it that compliant types might 'do all right,' if not trouble-makers with their inscrutably complicated foreign gripes.

Those complaints boil down to three historical facts: (a) the 1866 victory of Bismarck's Prussia, which categorically detached from the 'German-German' empire, now more Protestant than ever, a German-speaking, mostly Catholic, multi-ethnic Austrian empire which had formerly been the 'Holy Roman Empire of the German Nation'; (b) the formation a year later of the dual monarchy of Austria-Hungary, and (c) the failure of Franz Joseph ever similarly to concede to the kingdom of Bohemia a constitutional identity like Hungary's, leaving the Czech Lands considerably more conflicted in respect to their imperial capital. In the circumstances, a certain

Bohemian-nationalist *ressentiment* is understandable, though, ironically, nothing seems as 'un-American' about the new paper as its soliciting paternal protection by bad-mouthing its old papa to its new one.

Král's view is: We Bohemians are especially pained, since Europe's first world's fair was that of Prague in 1791, but a century later in Chicago we only see Bohemia "robbed of political independence by Austria" as "part of that disjointed country known as the Austro-Hungarian monarchy" (Král 12–13). Very well, but there must be nationalist hypocrisy as well as pettiness in garnishing a bitter rejection of the Austrian emperor with pleas of provincial ethnic coziness even as all concerned busily file citizenship papers in a much bigger, increasingly powerful and newly imperial, as well as much more foreign, state. Why, except for the shared expediency of mutually hating Austria, should a Moravian even be interested in Bohemia? When our Bohemian-American reviewer mentions Moravia, Silesia and northern Hungary, even he only means Bohemians living there. Thus those who struck the pose of nobly refusing to play the Austrian game scrambled to posture as Americans, even presenting themselves as a rarer and more sophisticated bloom than the more common German, with whom, however, they were and often enough still are lumped together by other Americans.

But if the mother tongue of our Moravian by birth was German, Loos, for one, who also counts as a Catholic in a more considerably Protestant province, would have known very well that not only the German language but Austrian 'high' culture was something Bohemians and Moravians, not to mention Slovaks, were entitled beneficially to share. Hadn't that, even, been the position of the Jesuits, in at least as 'liberal' a pushing of the German language as that of Joseph II, in the eighteenth century? The lack of solidarity here, even with those from other Czech Lands, is all the more unhappy in view of the virulent American 'Know-Nothingism' of the later nineteenth century; and perhaps Loos, our Viennese-by-choice born Moravian, modernist despiser of all nationalistic folksiness thrown up in non-comprehension of industrial culture, learned something about this in America too, as if the abolition of indulgent ethnicity and of ornamental indulgence were one thing.

The more decent complaint of the same immigrant writer is that with Bohemian *wares* exhibited as unqualifiedly Austrian, "whatever merit there may be in Bohemian work is readily credited by the visitor to an imaginary 'Austrian' nationality except in case[s] where the industrial superiority of Bohemia has outbalanced her political dependence." Perhaps still more to the point: "The Austrian section of the Manufactures [and Liberal Arts]

Building makes an impression ... as though Austria were composed of two parts: Bohemia and Vienna." Art-glass production receives special attention, and fairly naïve admiration, there being an obvious gap – to this day even in the ongoing production of the great Moser factory, in Karlovy Vary (Karlsbad) – between the dubiously aesthetic kitsch potential in that category and the more markedly unornamented cosmopolitan wares, such as the fine leather which Loos could happily admire as Austrian in Chicago. One can imagine Loos amused by the combination of aesthetic naïveté and technical awe on the part of the all-enthusiastic Bohemian nationalist critic: "The cutting is exquisite. The incisions are so deeply made that the effect from the front surface is that of a beautifully modeled subject" (loc. cit.). As interesting as the discussions of art-wares would have been, Loos would also have been engaged by the problem of Germano-Austro-Czech-American ethnic identity in Chicago, already then and still the major Czech-American city.

The New York context

Czechs and Austrians as well as Germans as such were part of the New York social landscape in the 1890s; and questions of ethnic identity would have arisen as Loos dug in and negotiated daily life in the city. Architecturally speaking, such typical New York urban furnishings as the bar as a neighborhood facility would have defined themselves in experience. But Loos would also have noticed New York versions of contemporary architectural forms also known elsewhere. For instance, a connection has been drawn between a feature of Loos's first-built work back in Vienna, the Ebenstein tailor's salon interior, in the Kohlmarkt, of 1897, and the exterior window framing with quarter-round upper corners, on the building at 726 Chestnut Street, Philadelphia, which housed his uncle's business (see Sekler). But rectangular windows with quarter-rounded top corners may have been interestingly new in New York as well, since at least one instance dated slightly too late for him to have seen in person (1899–1901) survives: Horace Mann Hall, of Teachers College, Columbia, by Howells Stokes and Edgar H. Josselyn.

A much more significant urbanistic influence, not as yet invoked, is possible in the case of the Kärntner, or 'American,' Bar (or familiarly, 'Loos Bar'), of 1908, in the center of Vienna – a cultural influence, or at least

16. Loos, Kärtner (or American) Bar, Vienna, 1908.

affinity, that helps to account for what should, already a century ago, have seemed to make the little jewel of a bar seem somehow patently American – something more than its dissimilarity from a typical Viennese café or *Weinstube*. First: in 1898 Loos himself had been unexpectedly pleased by an American Bar, by one "Oberländer," thought to be Gerhard Oberländer, actually famous as a caricaturist, at the Jubilee exhibition in Vienna (*OC* 29–30, with 31 n. 6). What most distinguished an American bar from a British pub (or 'public house') was its physical non-segregation of social classes, and even unaccompanied women, at one bar in a common space. Apropos of which: if not by the time of his arrival in New York, where the term 'saloon' actually carried over from the classier bar area by the British system, then soon after, Loos might have been aware of Stephen Crane's scandal of literary realism *Maggie: A Girl of the Streets; A Story of New York* (1893; German ed., 1897). The bar or saloon in *Maggie* is "a glass-fronted building" that "shed a yellow glare upon the pavements ... The inside of the place was papered in olive and bronze tints of imitation leather. A shining bar of counterfeit massiveness extended down the side of the room. Behind it a great mahogany-appearing sideboard reached to the ceiling. Upon its shelves rested pyramids of shimmering glasses that were never disturbed. Mirrors set in the face of the sideboard multiplied them ... The elementary senses of it all seemed to be opulence and geometrical accuracy" (Crane 42–43). Of course, if Loos had Crane, who died in Germany in 1900, in mind, what he did in 1908, in a happy flush of moving beyond his by no means regretted New York salad days, was to produce something of the same with real leather and mahogany. In that sense the Loos Bar, including its glowing, thin-as-mica marble clerestory window of squares, is a loving, luxurious transfiguration of the 'dives' of Loos's New York.[1]

Crane's naturalism issued in a kind of architectural description whose blank, harshly *sachlich*, or 'objective,' character, mainly intended to convey an uningratiating *mise-en-scène*, also holds a different sort of Loosian interest as evoking radical simplification of architectural form. In 'An Experiment in Luxury,' a story that might have caught Loos's eye when it appeared in the *New York Press* on 29 April 1894, a young man visits a rich New York friend in his family's brownstone: "The house was broad and brown and stolid like the face of a peasant. It had an inanity of expression, an absolute lack of artistic strength that was in itself powerful because it symbolized something. It stood, a homely pile of stone, rugged, grimly self-reliant, asserting its quality as a fine thing when in reality the beholder usually wondered why so much had been spent to obtain a complete negation" (Crane 168). The Loos who qualified as a bricklayer in America would also have picked up not only on the note of 'Anglo-Saxon' bourgeois comfort as the fellow is surprised that the "effect" of his friend's casually messy room is actually "good, because the disorder was not necessary" (169–70), but also on the patriarch of the family, in a state of "abstraction, of want of care," playing with a kitten, as seeming to the young man to be "in a far land where mechanics and bricklayers go, a mystic land of little, universal emotions" (172).

Before turning to his jubilee-church and its possible missing American cousin, there should be some review of Loos's New York situation, which would have interested Crane sociologically, even to his discussion of good and bad flophouses, but especially as concerns the question of national identity – something that he as a sophisticate might take lightly at home but that would have presented itself bluntly in that great city of ever extreme ethnic multiplicity under the firm cultural control, however, of an 'Anglo' establishment just then developing a grand new commercial empire. The situation can only have highlighted that in which Czechs, which is to say, Bohemians and Moravians – but also so-called Germans of Austrian identification, including Loos, though, again, he was born in Moravia – not to mention Slovaks – were conflicted about what store to set by the high culture of Vienna, their entitled 'Rome,' *versus* more or less authentic ethnic pride in whatever national culture was also their prerogative.

Loos's amused distaste for the exotic panoply of specimen ethnics parading in costume for the emperor's jubilee is well known – though with his sense of irony he was no doubt more aware than the many who have re-told that story that it also had another dimension: that all those people from the ends of the Habsburg earth in their grandparents' Sunday-best ethnic outfits were Austrian *too*. Certainly he felt that way about food: in 1921 he expressed regret that "'Austrian cuisine' ... was made possible by the fact that a combination of states known as the Austro-Hungarian monarchy lasted for centuries"; not only vital cooking ingredients had come from the emperor's "non-German territories" but dishes as Viennese as "Bohemian *Knödel*, Moravian *Buchteln* [filled buns], (N.B.) Italian *Schnitzel (frittura)*." Now however, since 1918, "We must create our own national cuisine," using "indigenous food" – as if, ironically, for the first time (*OA* 159). In a sense there really never had been a simple Austria until, now, everything Austrian except 'Austria proper' was territorially alienated. So it is fair to assume that on his return Loos was not competing to memorialize a sovereign he had serious Moravian or Czech reason to *resent*, but rather, simply exercising the entitled advantage of his situation as a worthy artist from the imperial provinces. Insofar as that meant something rather better than being locked into the category of provincial art, empire had its rewards.

In the New York that received him in the 1890s, at best as Viennese, there were enough Czech- and German-speaking people for this bright foreigner not to have seemed to come from outer space, even if the crude 'German' *cliché* would have been rolled out daily − caricatural pay-back to the sophisticated humor of Loos about the eastern province of Bukovina as land of country bumpkins, beyond even Slovakia.[2] From a boyhood in Vienna around the time of the empire's end, Ernst Gombrich would never forget the visits of a Slovak embroidery trader, initiated, significantly enough, by a relative of sufficiently modernist inclination to have had founder of Czech functionalism, Jan Kotěra, build a villa (chapter 8). If Loos might have been interested in what Gombrich rightly saw as the William Morris aspect of such an enthusiasm, and even the publication of examples in *The Studio*, in London, he would have had small patience with the culturally conservative aspect wherein "these pieces were doubly precious since they could never be produced again," not only owing to the inferiority of aniline dyes but because "the style of life which supported these homecrafts was disappearing" (Gombrich vii). Loos would not have been so sensitive about such things had they not compromised, by an incorrigible ethnicity, Austrian identity.

There is something of a tendency to melodramatize Loos's admittedly struggling days in New York, during an economic depression; but this was no untrodden path. A generation earlier, on his own *Wanderjahr* in America, a young Viennese named Wittgenstein, father-to-be of the philosopher, had supported himself likewise in New York as a bartender, waiter, and saloon musician (Monk 6, 7). It is amazing to think that soon after Adolf Loos began to write for the *Neue Freie Presse*, Wittgenstein *père* was also writing for it, "articles … extolling the virtues of American free enterprise," after retiring from business in 1898 and putting his money into American investments (10): the very stuff of legend! Not that life in New York was easy even for the transplanted Czechs who were already sinking roots. It is by no means wrongheaded of Rukschcio and Schachel to appeal, for local color, to *How The Other Half Lives* (1890), by the instantly famous Danish-born investigative photojournalist Jacob Riis in substantiating Richard Neutra's relayed sense of young Loos's life in New York. Riis, who was the New York Thomas Annan, had actually called attention to the plight of poor Czech immigrants caught up in the cottage industry of cigar-rolling (met at the dock and offered a tenement apartment in which to live and work, they found their rent could not be paid unless the children worked full time). However, by the later 1890s an urban picturesqueness comparable to that of rural poverty earlier on, was actually being discovered in the same down-at-the-heels Lower East Side, notably in the aesthetic view of the German-Japanese art critic Sadakichi Hartmann, an enthusiast of Schopenhauer who recommended that neighborhood for charming, or charmingly decrepit, photographic subjects (Hartmann).

But Loos had not come to New York just to visit the Lower East Side, even if he did stay there. While all students of Loos must be grateful for Rukschcio and Schachel's formidable synthesis of biographical information, those scholars' sense of the background of immigrant life in New York in the mid-1890s does seem limited to a dubiously Brechtian downtown where apparently Loos did manage despite tight financial straits (Rukschcio and Schachel 21–31). Even specifically Czech immigrant life was not confined to 'huddled masses' on the Lower East Side, though anything Czech, let alone Bohemian or Moravian, was generally too diminutive to bother about, vis-à-vis a dominant culture hardly pleased to acknowledge even its many more Irish. No doubt this situation conditioned the formation of Loos's notion of 'Anglo' culture as ideal assimilable norm – a sort of BBC of cultural style – as a special theme in the his dialectic of imperial culture.

As Loos would soon have learned in New York, there was already considerable petit-bourgeois Czech, German and German-Jewish, life uptown. One could easily travel in a matter of minutes by the Second Avenue elevated railway from the Lower East Side straight up to the conspicuously Czech East 70s, where there was built in 1895–97, at the end of Loos's stay, on East 73rd Street, the substantial Národní Budova (Bohemian National Hall), by William C. Frohne, ardently Renaissance-revival upstairs and more crisply – more Loosian, one could say – below. Had he done so, especially after taking up music criticism, however casually, he would have passed the house on East 17th Street where Dvořák was living and composing between autumn 1892 and summer 1895 – including the *Symphony from the New World*, first performed in New York in December of 1893. But with Czechness problematically dissolved (since 1867) into Austro-Hungarian imperiality, and that subsumed unto a generic Germanic 'other,' in late nineteenth-century New York, Loos would likely have felt some ethnic ambiguity. The more one thinks on the matter, the more his characteristic tropism toward a basically eighteenth-century imperial Britishness as cultural C-major, seems like a para-ethnic, if not para-aesthetic, 'way out.'

Further uptown

Why not, then, on some pleasant afternoon in the Bohemian Upper East Side, venture a couple of miles further, through Central Park, to the site of a formidable new architectural project in a rather bulked-up, Whiggish Neopalladian, classical-revival style. Now it does seem impossible to broach the suggestion without the awkwardness of an overdue social introduction, but I have in mind what came to be called the Low Memorial Library which McKim, Mead and White designed, with Charles Follen McKim as principal, as centerpiece of their new classical Columbia University campus on Morningside Heights. For there is plausibly a more than generic similarity between the seemingly most definitive form of Loos's project for the emperor's jubilee church and this, one of the most celebrated American classical-revival buildings, which, no one would have had to explain to Loos, is bold in form while, considering its bulk, relatively reserved in ornamentation.

The visual evidence of Loos's projected Kaiser Franz Joseph church is a group of three related drawings in the Loos Archive of the Albertina, in Vienna, which show the architect experimenting with various versions of a basic, 'timeless' classical temple idea, alone and in permutations of ideas for an accompanying tower whose character fluctuates between the ancient-imperial and the modern-Eiffelesque. In this, apparently ripest, design a domed and Ionically temple-fronted central feature presides over subordinate lateral peristyles, accompanied by a non-integral tower evocative of Eiffel's modernity in form and Johann Fischer von Erlach's Habsburgian neo-Romanism of the twin monumental Roman columns in their role of accompaniment to the body of the Karlskirche, on the Karlsplatz, in Vienna. The same sheet also bears a diminutive sketch that is possibly a study for the juncture of one of the lateral elements with the body of the building, together with a more realized if seemingly irrelevant little drawing of a modern suitcase or case or box, the latter to be entertained presently.

In Loos's jubilee church, as in McKim's Low Memorial, a massive unpedimented porch projects forward from a convex quadrant (another drawing verifies the quadrant form in plan), with a blocky extension with peristyle to the left – this element longer than its equivalent in New York but interrupted in its conception by graphic interposition of the stylistically disjunct accompanying tower. The convex curve of Loos's bulging quadrant finds some equivalence in the New York building's prismatically filled-out

17. McKim, Mead and White, Low
Memorial Library, Columbia University,
New York, 1895–97. Wood engraving in
Architectural Record, May 1895.

angular corner, while a more fundamental equivalence obtains between both shallow-domed central features as presiding over their respective massings of solids, with, in each case, a grand Roman podium staircase. There is just sufficent detail in the drawing to suggest the sublimely colossal Ionic order of McKim's library porch as carrying over, complete with hefty 'rostrum' wings either side of the stairs – or even just a bit more, if one takes the seemingly casual neglect of capitals on Loos's swiftly drawn peristyle as analogous to the big volute-less pilasters which stand in for columns along the sides and rear of McKim's New York building.

Already nominated as a plausible source for Loos's Franz Joseph church design is Charles B. Atwood's Palace of Fine Arts at the Columbian Exposition, which, unlike Sullivan's Transportation Building, does uniquely survive, as the Museum of Science and Industry (Rukschcio and Schachel 24). Although he never studied at the École des Beaux-Arts (ironically, Sullivan had), this Atwood produced something quite like the academy's 1867 winning 'Palace for an Exposition of Fine Arts,' except "with most of the ornament stripped away" (Drexler 470, with illus.). Yet, while the fine arts pavilion might have

18. Loos, Competition study for the
Emperor's Jubilee Church of St Elizabeth,
Vienna, 1897.

had subsidiary pertinence, Atwood's domed central feature seems much closer
to another New York building: the Gould Memorial Library (designed 1892–
96), which McKim Mead and White, with Stanford White as principal, were
building, in 1897–99, contemporaneously with Columbia and its Low Memorial
Library but across the Harlem River in the Bronx, for the University College
campus of New York University (now occupied by the Bronx Community
College). Beneath their shallow domes both the Chicago building and the
Gould have low-slung pediments ornamenting the four sides, *versus* quasi-
Palladian thermal windows under the dome at Columbia. (The one respect
in which one can imagine the Palace of Fine Arts, which of course he knew,
having influenced Loos's design is the run-on loggia of the Chicago building in
relation to Loos's also columned side pavilion, seen to the left in the drawing,
which, however, he seems to be trimming back.) And in place of an attached
'pedimental' triangle in the other McKim, Mead and White building, almost
a mere linear molding by comparison, the cut-through thermal window is
plastically integral to the Low Memorial as a composition of cubic elements
requiring, on second thought as it were, surprisingly little classical 'ornament,'
except so far as was socially obligatory to present itself as an authoritative,
generalized-classical *gestalt*.

Even if Loos had not managed to find work as a draftsman in New York, as he did, among other odd jobs, he might well have noticed the McKim, Mead and White projected view of the Low Memorial Library as published, before construction even began, in the *Architectural Record* for May 1895. There is ideo-aesthetic significance in McKim's Low Library as a rather grandly imperial version of the Neopalladian country house, such as, of course, Lord Burlington's, the chief Neopalladian's, own Chiswick House, *c.* 1725 – a type that was the very hallmark of the eighteenth-century Whigs, with their anti-Continental (and anti-Baroque) cult of anxiously restrained good taste. Although the clientèle of the Neopalladians were effectively nouveau riches, the Anglophile Loos was not oblivious to their self-consciously simple if incorrigibly plutocratic taste. Now, here in New York, was quite a grand version of just such, quite pumped up with imperial swagger, its cornerstone laid on 7 December 1895, mere moments before Columbia assumed university status in 1896. The name 'Columbia,' granted to the former King's College by the new State of New York in 1784, had obvious nationalist overtones, as 'land of Columbus' and as an independent national, not to mention imperial, personification like Roma and Britannica, well before the chauvinistic World's Columbian Exposition.

Fortunately, a series of project photographs in the Columbia archives testifies to what Loos could actually have seen of the rising Low Library before leaving New York in the spring of 1896. Dated at intervals during the building's construction, the photos make it possible to say that between mid-January and the end of April the Low Memorial had risen from the limestone walls of its basement level, with the ground-floor (American 'first'-floor) steelwork up to most of the height of that, its principal storey (Bergdoll, illus. on 160, 161). So it was certainly possible to not only know what the library was intended to look like but also to gain some firsthand sense of its imminent grandeur. Ludwig Münz was perhaps more insightful than he knew when he wrote, apropos of Loos's church project, "It was not so much that just at the time of his stay in America ... a classical reaction had emerged ... but that the basically different American attitude to building made their structures seem so much akin to the Roman" (Münz and Künstler 175) – implying, one can infer, those Roman *engineers*.

For if Adolf Loos *had* got to see Low Library under construction, soon before sailing home to Europe, what would surely have appealed to him at just that stage of its realization would have been the active alliance between a modern, light steel framework emergent as platform upon platform at the building's core, and quasi-classical limestone facing rising independently, not in the manner of load-bearing masonry but more detachedly, more abstractly, even, as cladding. And what with the importance of forthright cladding to Loos, and Otto Wagner before him, in Vienna, it may be noted that as monumental centerpiece of McKim, Mead and White's Columbia campus, the Low Memorial Library was to be the only full-dress 'clad' building of the ensemble, that is, the only one formally dressed out in stone facing, with the other Italian Renaissance-style buildings, though punctuated with stone ornament, presenting walls so typically *Anglo*-American of bare brick. Perhaps Loos's buildings never look more 'American' than when, owing to poor maintenance, their stucco cladding falls off: even the sublime Behrensian composure of his sugar refinery at Hrušovany, near Brno, in Moravia, of 1916–19, subject in recent decades to a decrepitude more rust-belt than Communist, began to give way to the look of a disused mill floundering between reincarnations as shopping mall, condominia, or the next satellite of the multinational Guggenheim Museum (Schezen, illus. on 119–21). Not that the brick architecture of the transatlantic 'Anglo-Saxon' cultural sphere doesn't have its way of looking Roman, as with the early brick projects of Mies van der Rohe. One even recalls the unfaced brick, at least in surviving condition, of most of what those who dwell in the Roman provincial north are accustomed to see as Roman 'classical' architecture.

There is after the fact, circumstantial support for the notion of the Columbia 'American empire' project as pertinent to Loos in the magnetic field of Otto Wagner. According to the *Architectural Record* of May 1912, wherein Wagner's original 1911 *Die Grossstadt* (The Great City, or 'Metropolis') pamphlet was published in English, Professor Alfred Hamlin, of the Columbia University School of Architecture, had a part in instigating Wagner's text and its accompanying graphic projections. It seems that, well before Hamlin's invitation to address a proposed city planning congress (called "urban art") in New York in 1910, Wagner's reputation had drawn Hamlin to visit him at the Vienna Academy in 1894 (Wagner 486). Since Columbia took possession of its new site on October 1, 1894, three months earlier than originally planned (Matthews 162), and held a competition won by the plan of McKim, Mead and White, Hamlin was surely seeking out modern architecture when he visited Wagner (Columbia was also setting a course more Germanic than British in its emphasis on the doctorate); and, what is intriguing, might he, knowing the basic idea of McKim's plan, even have shown it to Wagner? In any event, within two years Wagner's *Grossstadt* idea was in formation; and then came the famous projected aerial view of his

Grossstadt layout for the XXII District of Vienna, with its central placement of a domical 'Steinhof' church as "surrounded by two lateral, U-shaped buildings," as indeed, as Sarnitz has noticed, "similar to the original campus plan for Columbia University by McKim, Mead and White" (Sarnitz 91, 101, with illus.). This Vienna district, which now contains United Nations buildings and much modern low-rise housing, lies directly across the Danube Canal from the Mexikoplatz, proposed site of the jubilee church. Although still early in its realization, the new Columbia University campus would have struck Loos all the more favorably in relation to the court of honor of the World's Columbian Exposition in Chicago – that 'White City,' as it had advertised itself, – with the Columbia plan, in its abstract-classical restraint, closer to the first-generation modernity of Wagner himself, in the Vienna to which Loos was just returning.

Something contextually pertinent can be sketched in lightly, something of which New Yorkers attuned to architecture are seldom conscious: that there are structural and ornamental 'moments' when much of the surviving urban furniture of the turn-of-the-century city of New York – which in 1898 'imperially' expanded by incorporating surrounding territory, just as Vienna had done in 1890 – takes on a curiously secessionist flavor. (The very term 'secession' circulated in New York modernism thanks to Alfred Stieglitz' foundation in 1902 of the Little Galleries of the Photo-Secession and his vital art world 'photo-secessionist' journal *Camera Work*.) This is especially true of public works that have managed to escape a latter-day 'pseudo-old' advanced by corporate real estate interests lacking all sense of historical facture or material palpability over time. Even Otto Wagner's more everyday work on the urban railways of Vienna and his grand Nussdorf Lock on the Danube Canal, 1894–98, with its duet between the old compressive architecture of stone and the new tensile architecture of steel, finds such modest counterparts as the viaduct of the Broadway subway approaching West 125th Street, near Columbia, built *c.* 1904; and many other works might be adduced.

Critical stakes

Loos left New York just as so much was happening, but it was indeed happening. He missed seeing Louis Sullivan's only building in the city (1897–99) rise on Bleecker Street; but he was definitely aware of Sullivan's critical polemics, with their radically democratic thrust. Not that he was inclined to be as political as Sullivan, especially as a visiting foreigner, as much as he would have respected his architectural thinking. Conceivably, however, he may have been struck by this major work of architectural art which was specifically despised by Sullivan.

Suppose Loos's design for the emperor's jubilee church *was* conditioned by McKim's then unfinished but already formidable New York structure. Then it should be easy enough to take the much discussed accompanying tower in the same drawing as simply an additional idea, while, more incidentally, the sketchy vignette to the upper right on the same sheet may show Loos thinking about the convex quadrant corner of the church building. What, however, can possibly be the significance of the distracting, fastidiously worked image of a simple cask or case, like a travel case with rounded corners, rotated to the right on the sheet?

A remarkable anecdote concerning Loos in New York comes down through Robert Scheu from an article in Karl Kraus's *Die Fackel* (Vienna), of 26 June 1909, which suggests a telling relation between this little image and Loos's firming up and rounding off of the already grandly coordinated blocks of his still somewhat rhetorically classical, proposed American source. It seems that, one New York day, he was quite stopped in his tracks on discovering in a shop a leather travel case of such strikingly elegant, simple design that the next day he realized, "That's the modern style!" (qu., Rukschcio and Schachel 30–31). In Scheu's account it was the radically simple travel case, seen in New York, which provided the *eureka* experience which opened to Loos how British engineering, particularly, might look virtually Hellenic, as he proceeds to maintain, conspicuously earlier than Le Corbusier on engineering as quasi-Hellenic, indeed, as early as 'Glass and China' (1898; *OC* 68–74). Fifteen years later, in the essay 'On Thrift,' the impress of that experience still registers in a remark that "in one respect the aristocrat should serve as a model to us all. I mean in his sense of material"; hence, "Not any old suitcase but one made of the very best material. A solid one, made to last for centuries ... The sole important factors for aristocrats are the materials and perfect workmanship." Explicitly, sound material, sound workmanship; implicitly, no waste, no distraction of ornamentation. The self-evidence of necessary simplicity is what accounts for the accompanying outburst: "It is Ruskin, by the way, who is to blame for all this [bad art-ware production]. I am his sworn enemy" (*OA* 183). Here Loos was being somewhat hyperbolic, for Ruskin would come to be acknowledged as one of the prophets of architectural modernity for his sense of respect for material, though in Loos's view he was mainly associated with an essentially ornamentalist cult of craft. Five years later still, in the obituary of Josef Veillich, his favorite cabinetmaker and maker of 'Chippendale' chairs, he recalls having outraged the Vienna Secession by saying he would participate in a craft exhibition there on condition that if he could include the – it is taken for granted – plain, well-made leather suitcases of a particular maker (*OA* 184).

The same essay contains a remarkable piece of evidence in the matter of ethnic definition and self-definition. Why should such a hero of Viennese modernism have embraced Czech citizenship? No doubt the American-style industrial and commercial modernity of the Czech Lands would have outweighed his constitutional distaste for the peasant culture prevalent at the easterly end of the new state. Ironically, in view of the Yankee reduction of categories to a general-purpose 'German' identity in America, the implications could be complex where Czechness and Austrianness were to be triangulated with Germanness. In an essay 'On Thrift,' more noticeable for its advocacy of using the best possible materials (and polemical rejection of Ruskin), Loos writes in 1924, "Whenever I was in Brno and saw the Deutsches Haus and the Czech Beseda Dům the character of these two buildings told me how things would eventually turn out in Brno. It's obvious!" (*OA* 181). He means that the Besdeni Dům (or Beseda House), an ethnic Czech and Moravian clubhouse built in a decent Italian Renaissance mode in 1871–73 by the Dane Theophil von Hansen right after he built the Academy of Fine Arts in Vienna, had a "dignity" lacking in the equally ethnic Deutsches Haus, of 1889–91 (destroyed 1945), as built in a picturesque German Renaissance mode still steeped in the Middle Ages. Hence, on Loosian terms this doggedly German cultural effort showed up its own provincialism, and the more cosmopolitan work, the Czech one by a Dane, won the day.

Thorsten Veblen took the sociological measure of simplified forms as 'up-scale,' compatibly with Loos's critique of ornament: according to *The Theory of the Leisure Class* (1899), with its famous chapter on 'Pecuniary Canons of Taste,' while it should be easy enough to come up with pleasing designs for serviceable objects that might be economical in the sense of "inexpensive" as well as "straightforward," with an "economic beauty of the object" predicated on "adequacy to … purpose," another social purpose is the impressing of other people, as in the quietly ostensible labor-intensiveness of the well trimmed British *lawn*. The Norwegian-American anticipates 'Ornament and Crime,' a decade later, on esteeming ingeniously devised things for "giv[ing] evidence of an expenditure of labor in excess of what would give them their fullest efficiency for their ostensible economic end" (Veblen 110), though Loos will pursue the defense that simple quality goods amortize themselves by lasting longer without going out of fashion. Interestingly, while Veblen picks up on an "endless" eclectic "variety" in façades of "the better class of tenements and apartment houses" in America, quite like Schopfer, a year later, is his proto-Loosian observation: "Considered as objects of beauty, the dead walls of the sides and back of these structures, left untouched by the hands of the artist, are commonly the best feature of the building" (111).[3]

Quite possibly, then, something of Loos's epiphany, in New York, of the finely made plain suitcase, registers in this sketch on the same sheet, in the context of thinking about rounding the central form of the church and the juncture of its masses. Just as the interest of McKim's Low Memorial would have been at least as much in its sustained formal simplicity as in its classicism, a possibility deserves to be entertained that the little sketched case not only recalls Loos's critical admiration of such unadorned Austrian leather products at the Chicago world's fair but also adumbrates a high modernist extension of formal concern to utilitarian objects, including modern objects of mechanical rather than manual craft (re)production. Thus in 1934, Clive Bell, coiner of the very term 'significant form,' in *Art* (1914), would applaud a modern case, machine-made by the Revelation Suit Case Company, plus a modern steel fitted luncheon case, in analytical comparison with a fifteenth-century German carved wooden cask and cupboard in the Victoria and Albert Museum. Bell proves a great de-mystifier of craft, in quite the spirit of Loos, before him: "Who but prefers to an arty wardrobe hand-made by a virtuous homespun craftsman somewhere in the Cotswolds and left unstained too, an elegant Rolls or a shapely, satisfying locomotive?" The problem, as Loos saw a generation earlier, is not that the craftsman should be an artist: "The fact is, the craftsman, as such, is not an artist at all." True, "the work of the craftsman, be he medieval stone-cutter or modern 'art-worker,' is important to us precisely in so far as it is aesthetically significant"; but we don't want artistic presumption any more than self-consciousness in craftsmen (Bell, *Enjoying Pictures* 102–04, with illus.).

Bell's remarks seem so utterly Loosian – even to the point of evoking Loos's amusing 1898 figure of the country-bumpkin woodcrafter Peter Pinecone (chapter 2) – as to rule out any possible connection between such cool machined appeal and the cult of crafts as associated with the name of William Morris, that one is surprised to discover, in their reflected light of 1934, points of approach between even the definitive Loos of 'Ornament and

Crime' (1909) and the definitive 'The Lesser Arts' (1877), where Morris says that craftsmen were "artists" in their own right until the division of labor set in, leaving craft work an alienated chore (Morris 37, 42). Morris hopes for "a new art of conscious intelligence" that, unlike the "unconscious intelligence" of traditional craftsmen upset by technology, might prove more responsive to it (40). He condemns contrived "fashion" (41–42) and condemns "sham work" as "hurtful" to all concerned, warning, in the spirit of Loos, that "the public in general are set on having things cheap, being so ignorant that they do not know when they get them nasty also" (50). Noticing that in the houses of the well-off, the only simple beauty is to be found in the kitchen, Morris calls for "simplicity everywhere, in the palace as well as the cottage" (52). Well, if few professed Loosians have sounded quite so like their master's voice as Bell enthusing over the suitcase with rigorously machine-rounded corners, perhaps we ought to acknowledge all over again, with good old Nikolaus Pevser, the abiding relevance of William Morris.

We ought to be careful here however, because, as Loos was aware, what we are after with the cult of craft tends to get lost in an increasingly superficial Arts-and-Crafts fair that he despised. For him, after all, even the inhibited ornamentalism of the formidable Josef Hoffmann was hopelessly arty. Closer to the mark is a thought that crossed the mind of Alban Berg, the Viennese modernist composer, while reading a passage in *Vita ipsa* (1918), by Loos's intimate, the poet Peter Altenberg: "My little inkwell is made from glass, fabulously easy to clean, costs two crowns, and moreover is called 'Bobby,' well, 'Robert' nowadays. It is thus a work of art, it fulfills its purpose, disturbs nobody and is a beautiful brown." Next to these words, Alban Berg wrote in the margin of his copy: "Loos" (Pople 32).

Clive Bell's Revelation Suitcase experience came some forty years after Loos's equivalent one in New York, though neither the Loos of the definitive 'Ornament and Crime' and 'Architecture' essays, roughly contemporary with the Looshaus, nor the Bell of *Art*, stood alone. A sense of how, at the turn of the century, American architecture looked to knowing European eyes and of basic Loosian views as less than eccentric, is conveyed in an article on New York architecture 'From a Foreign Point of View,' as of 1900, by a Jean Schopfer. One wonders if 'Schopfer' could not have been an operational pseudonym (*Schöpfer* in German meaning 'creator') because this person (1868–1931), a writer for the *Architectural Record* (New York) in the decade 1897–1907, as well as of a travel book on ancient and modern Italian art, also wrote novels (including *Mayerling*, 1930) under the pseudonym 'Claude Anet' (Anet is the name of a famous château).

Telling is Schopfer's appreciation of local craftsmanship, not only plumbing – already, it seems, a patronizing *topos* by the time Marcel Duchamp would notoriously play upon it at the New York Independents exhibition in 1917, with his *Fountain*, the notorious 'readymade' urinal – but also carpentry, many New York carpenters being, of course, European, especially vaguely 'German,' immigrants. Note, apropos of Loos: "The wood-work is nearly always in natural finish. The horror, daily to be seen with us of imitation woods, which, contracting leave white fissures at the joints of pseudo mahogany, does not exist here" (Schopfer 28).

Admired among 'semi-public monuments,' in the same article, is "the enormous arch of the new cathedral," meaning St John the Divine; while nearby it, "Columbia University possesses a library of particular refinement in the grouping of the masses ..." (29) – that is, McKim's Low Memorial Library, which the article's first illustration shows. Possibly Schopfer heard that by paying for this building and naming it after his father, who had made the family fortune as a "tea merchant" in the China trade (Passanti 77), Seth Low, the Columbia president who had already been mayor of Brooklyn before the 1898 consolidation of the city and now wanted to be mayor of New York, was using the whole project to make for himself "a civic rather than academic image" (Robson 36). This visitor does say of patronage in America: "You remember the ingenious reason Burkhardt found for the building of so many huge structures by the Italian tyrants; it appeared to him as though they desired to show by so many durable stone constructions the solidity of the tyranny they had just founded" (Schopfer 30). Shades of Sullivan.

The last illustration in Schopfer's 1900 article shows Louis Sullivan's sole New York building, the new Condict (later, Bayard) Building. Schopfer presents Sullivan's commercial loft structure under the new category of 'Steel Construction'; and indeed, it "seems ... the best yet erected," in this category of the steel-cage building which is "the newest type and the most interesting for a foreigner, because it is purely American." The one fault found is "the arcades at its summit, which are a contradiction of the logical plan of the whole." Just why, however, is Sullivan's an excellent work? Interestingly, the answer is just so slightly simplistic as to begin to obscure the Loosian sense of cladding as properly, knowingly artificial, hence non-deceitful, on which score the new Columbia building was more conservative: "Because [in it] at last architecture goes hand in hand with engineering, and instead of dissimulating the frame and cheating in the materials, or, showing us, like so many others, an imitation wall of cut stone, it draws an architectural effect from the very skeleton of the structure." Seemingly aware of Sullivan's theorizing, the writer closes with questions that would have interested Sullivan and Loos, both: "Will American architecture succeed in freeing itself and really form a new style? Will it develop in the direction of a rational treatment of construction? Will it be able to unite again the ties, broken so long ago, of architectonic decoration? These are questions of powerful interest, not only for American, but for all European architecture ..." (Schopfer 30).

But there should also be some acknowledgment of Sullivan himself on critically democratic terms. Louis Sullivan did not shrink from criticizing the threat to democracy of newly aggrandizing oligarchical forces (how familiar this seems today). He hated the imposition of plutocratic monumentality, especially, but certainly not only, when of Roman-imperial stylistic inspiration. In his *Kindergarten Chats* this shows in more than one quip about Saint John the Divine, the grand Episcopal cathedral started in 1892: "Well – St John or Mammon; it's all one in New York; and I am not sure that they are two elsewhere" (Sullivan 75). But there is also a quip in Sullivan's essay 'On Scholarship' (Sullivan, ch. xl) on the new Low Memorial Library, just a few blocks north of the cathedral at likewise establishment Columbia: "when we ask an architect to make a library building for a modern American university, and he gives us fragments of what the Greeks did, and guesses at what the Greeks might have done, he is not a scholar, he is an aimless pedant: selling his modern birthright for a pseudo-scholarly mess of classic pottage" (130). And in a little essay-chapter devoted to it (ch. xxvii), McKim's Columbia masterwork is attacked as "a show building," "precious," "modish," a product "of the wax-works of our art" (91).

An ageing Sullivan wishes the next generation could be talked out of being enchanted by such vanities. Though he seems to know he's whistling in the wind, one can imagine a young Viennese architect who would grow to feel kinship with Sullivan dandyishly toying with the older architect's very complaints and reproaches. In *Kindergarten Chats* the same essay is truncated, but the last paragraph still gives more than enough to suggest such a transvaluation in the sophisticated foreigner, including Sullivan's suspicion that in a too frigidly detached, "silent" way the building seems, if anything, unbelieving of the tradition it dares to invoke, and hence culturally deracinated:

Ah, wait until you are *blasé* of being *blasé!* ... Look at this mirage! See the Ionic columns, the entablature, the dome and so forth. Note especially the and-so-forth, for it is the untold that counts here—the

discrete silence. Some say it is eloquent; and you may say in turn
that it is indeed eloquent. So are the dumb eloquent of speech; so
is the exile eloquent of his country. As we gaze—we pass into the
land of expatriation. This, it seems, is the library building of a great
academic institution of learning how to unlearn: of learning self-
forgetfulness, self-denial. Of learning not only how to forget oneself,
to deny oneself, but to forget and to deny one's land. To learn how
to forget, to learn how to deny life cautiously, is somewhat the
fashion; and by such token this is a modish building. Men must be
scarce where such neutrality prevails. Surely we are in the land of
expatriation. Surely this is architectural nihilism. (92)

Now this is Louis Sullivan on McKim's masterpiece, not some Blue-Danube
Viennese on Loos's Museum Café or the Looshaus! Nevertheless, the building
may have fascinated the Loos who tried unsuccessfully to get Sullivan's essays
published in Europe, especially as something to *respond to*.

Although we know how it was that Loos did not consider 'fashion'
such a trivial thing, what really matters is the sense of cultural grandeur
entailed in a contemporary imperial culture – late but literal for Vienna,
newly fluorescing in New York – as expressed in clarified, elementalized
terms of Roman imperial monumentality, whether as updated by Adolf Loos
or as less subtly inflected by Charles Follen McKim. We are perhaps too
smugly satisfied by the usual self-congratulatory American reading of Sullivan
on self-making, Emersonian terms, ever proclaiming something fresh and
pure, innocent of Europe, meaning of course distastefully Continental, i.e.,
unenlightened, i.e., Catholic, Europe. After all, one can't be *too* Anglo, as
even our man Loos tended to think. But however valid the McKim, Mead
and White idea about the origins of the Franz Joseph jubilee church might
be, Loos was picking up on something new and problematic in America, a
modern American 'imperial' culture all the more curiously similar in not
being genetically akin to the imperial Viennese equivalent he might have left
behind but hardly escaped.

The grandeur of received classical or neoclassical form, as in McKim's Low
Memorial library and to a degree also Loos's emperor's memorial church,
must, on Loosian terms, be stylish, even frankly classy, not unlike the politically
democratic yet culturally elitist Loos himself. Joseph Rykwert has pointed up
the fact of Loos, a "professing democrat, even something of an egalitarian,"
being drawn to "the ceremonial display of the Viennese court" (Rykwert,
'Adolf Loos' 67). Certainly the Loosian aesthetic of radical simplification,

even of received forms, favors modern urbanity, almost regardless of 'upper' or 'lower' echelons, against any sort of petit-bourgeois charm, an urbanity that presupposes a cosmopolitanism beyond ethnicity.

Furthermore, the American-empire reading of the jubilee church offered here may find some confirmation in a later parallel, actually during the First World War, in 1917, between a patriotic Monument to Franz Joseph and a high-profile New York building, classical at that, and also by McKim, Mead and White, which by then Loos could have read about. The ziggurat capping of the square corner in one version of Loos's project happens to echo the ziggurat-capped front corners of the General Post Office (later James A. Farley Building, and now being converted into Moynahan Station), built in 1913. Loos himself had already used a ziggurat form in a 1910 project for a department store for Alexandria, in Egypt – a design otherwise, one would have thought, embarrassingly like Walter Macfarlane's then new Selfridges Department Store, 1907–09, in London, though without the ziggurat feature under discussion. One wonders how early the McKim, Mead and White post office was published, since the orthodox classicism of that great bourgeois firm with high establishment authority was so near and yet so far from what Loos, even in his Anglophilia, was really good at. If anything, the resemblances with McKim, Mead and White in America show what Loos could have done for a grand clientele here, *had he been less an artist.*

Ethnicity sublated?

One wants also to consider such other social implications of Loos's imperial jubilee project as its being a church, even a quasi-official Roman Catholic church, as well as a monument to honor his emperor, and a quite unapologetically monumental one at that – factors which have bearings on the possible influence on Loos's church project viewed here as 'American imperial.' In some measure Loos's own identity must have been at stake or in play in his personal ideological negotiations, at the turn of the century, with, apparently, American as well as Austro-Hungarian imperial culture, even in his stylistic, sometimes almost blushing, neutrality. It is ironic that such a visitor as Loos would have been all the more odd in New York because New York was newer to an imperial diversity which was already to some extent comprehended in Vienna. For instance, while the Viennese feuilletonist Ferdinand Kürnberger, whose writings interested Karl Kraus, was in general pro-German in cultural orientation, and the superiority of German culture is implied throughout his writings, even he must recognize not only that Austrian culture is not the same as German culture, for the dominant position of the German language in Vienna simply does not give a measure of the city's true character, and that the admixture of non-German elements (which he may define as 'Asiatic,' 'Slav,' 'Celtic,' or 'Jewish') "makes Austria what it is" (Bailey 66).

On the ethnic *versus* imperial side of the matter: what does it mean, even today, to be told that as much as a third of Bohemia is ethno-linguistically German, as against Czech? It sounds like a concession, but why is there not a reverse concession – that by far the large majority is Czech-identifying; and not only that, but bilingual, unlike the minority? (After all, in terms of a parallel: are not many more Québécois bilingual than other Canadians?) Within the Czech Lands of Bohemia and Moravia Loos's family would have been known as 'German,' meaning, negatively, non-Czech, but also meaning, affirmatively, German in language and Austrian in culture – not German-German, at least after 1866. In America, where many people may not be able to point to modern Austria, let alone the Czech Republic, on a map, ethnic identification was vexed well before then. In 1859, an immigrant physician in San Antonio, Texas, born in Kutná Hora, complains, in an anti-Austrian tract published in New York, that everything exceptional in Bohemia or done by Bohemians is counted as German, though there is also the usual problem of compensation for inferiority when in almost the same breath he takes Slavic culture as "higher," "advanced and superior," *vis-à-vis* German (Dignowity 9, 19). Politically, it is interesting that as a sider with the underdog the same writer has good things to say not only about Austrian common soldiers, versus officers, of course, but also about the Jesuits and even the emperor, as powers sometimes standing between tyrannical aristocrats and the oppressed, and also that he should express solidarity with another oppressed people, the blacks, notwithstanding that they are "physically less progressed" (70) – something it would be wrong to associate with Loos's remarks on stages of social development of peoples (chapter 4).

The case of Loos's option for Czech nationality with the dissolution of the empire is all the more interesting for not being at all unique. Consider Loos, in some circumstances identifying himself as 'German,' in others, 'Austrian,' and, while never 'Moravian,' electing citizenship in the republic of Czechoslovakia, though in addition to his Austrian citizenship, in 1918. How curiously similar and at the same time different from that of the poet Rilke, five years Loos's junior, who, like the still younger Kafka, is also taken without qualification as a 'German' writer, though of the two, both born in Prague, only Kafka is *also* considered Czech – and Jewish too (see Cushman). Given that Loos could not speak Czech, was this not a stubborn, 'contrary' vote for *Heimatstadt* and cosmopolitanism, both, – not so unlike Nietzsche's sometimes insisting he was Polish, considering what it often means to be German? Maybe everybody should have, such as it were, bifocal identities and know what it is not to be an insider in either; and maybe that was what a Loos, already accustomed to what Whitman called "plaudits in the capital," meant by wanting to 'be somebody' in a new little republic that was quite happy (as America had seemed to an optimistic youngster who had little or no occasion to come up against the plutocracy) about modernity.

Loos has been called a "Protestant pioneer" (Girardi), by which one understands a critically radical revisionist, if not fundamentalist; but beyond an obvious 'ascetic' aesthetic point that would better be referred to Nietzsche than to Jan Hus or Luther, the epithet is questionable because the Continental term 'pioneer' can connote, just fittingly enough to confuse the issue, the ad-hoc practicality of an army 'engineer.' In Czech circumstances, the quip has too much about it of the Woodrow Wilson-style favoring of the Hussite, *versus* Catholic, view of Czech history, including the ever applauded secularizers from Joseph II to Masaryk, in some sense belied by the fading away of the Hussite Church.

The question has substance owing to some repression of the fact, private yet obviously relevant in the imperial church project, of the apparently never-denied Catholicism of Adolf Franz Karl Viktor Maria Loos himself, who, like many a Central European Catholic man, carried the name of the Virgin in addition to his male names. That after his death the second of his three wives, Elsie Altmann Loos, seemingly less than fully invested in the question, takes signs of Adolf's religiosity trivially only underlines, now, their having been taken in stride: for, by her own testimony, he was baptized, always went to Mass at Easter, kept the Friday abstinence (even if he did love fish), and liked to "bathe his spirit" in Saint Stephen's cathedral even if one didn't see him cross himself on entering; in her own words, "Loos was not superstitious (*abergläublich*), he was believing (*gläubig*)" (E. A. Loos 130). There is also to be reckoned Loos's tombstone for his poet friend Altenberg (d. 1919), in the Zentralfriedhof, Vienna, with its plain inscribed granite stone surmounted by a large plain wooden cross. Loos was no fanatic, but an ordinary believer, by Elsie's testimony. Possibly something similar was also the case in respect to the modicum of monarchist sympathy necessary for him as a beginning architect at home in the imperial capital to be competing to memorialize His Imperial, Royal and Apostolic Majesty, in that grandly super-national title, which itself had supplanted that other, ethnically ambiguous on the highest possible level: 'Holy Roman Emperor of the German Nation.' At any rate, such identification accounts for some of Loos's abiding, if elusive, Romanism – more elusive than the imperial Romanism of Otto Wagner, yet all the more Loosian precisely in being understatedly *just enough*. Not that there would have been anything ultramontane about him; but why should there be, if Vienna *already was* his worldly Rome.

Loos's Catholic background has ethno-historical entailments because of the ecclesiastical history of the Czech Lands as being on a cusp between Western-Latin and Eastern-Slavic governances. At the time of their conversion, even the Western Slavs of Bohemia were introduced to Slavonic forms, but, some thousand years before Loos (*c.* 905–06) with the demise of Greater Moravia, Bohemia became subject to Regensberg, in what is now Germany, and Salzburg, in Austria; hence for centuries a primary cultural fact of the Czech Lands was their being general-Germanic instead of Slavic. This seeming 'prehistory' to the modern question of ethnicity and nationality would still have had meaning for the budding German-speaking cosmopolitan modernist from Brno entering a competition for a church in the capital honoring his Roman Catholic emperor: in other words, something so ecclesiastical as well as Austro-imperial also carried the deeper, older, distinction of being Western and Latinate rather than Slavic and Slavonic.

On his return home to Vienna, with the imperial capital his *Heimatstadt* of choice, Loos re-entered, perhaps more aware than ever, a complex of overlapping ethnic or national identities. He himself speaks "as a German" of "Germanness" in the foreword, itself signed as at both Vienna (August 1921) and Paris (July 1931), to *Spoken Into the Void*, where questions of Austrian nationality proliferate, mainly in regard to the German language; then too, the book was being published in France. For one born in Moravia into a German-speaking family, there was thus the contradiction of a super-national identity in which one's mother tongue coincided with one's imperial and not necessarily unfavorable 'fatherland,' in this case the polyglot but German-language-dominated Austro-Hungarian Empire.

Claire Beck Loos, the third of Adolf's wives, reports on his reaction to being told, in Prague, that Czech artists were upset by his exhibiting with Austrian artists in an international exhibition: "'The Czechoslovaks think that I am a Czechoslovak because I was born in Brno and came from there. The Austrians say I've lived in Vienna for so many years, the Germans say I am a German because I speak their language, in France they suggested that

I become a naturalized French citizen [as Le Corbusier did in 1930] because I love their country so much, my English wife always said I dressed better than an Englishman ...' and smiling: 'I am neither one nor the other. I am a cosmopolitan, and so is every true European ...'" (C. B. Loos 64).

After the demise of the empire the essentially Viennese Loos had indeed maintained a thoroughly cosmopolitan identity. Although he could not speak Czech, his 1925 lectures in Prague and Brno were advertised in Czech as well as German, billing himself as a "Czech-Anglo-French-American" cosmopolite of London, Paris, Vienna, Brno, Prague, and Zurich (illus., Šlapeta, *Adolf Loos* 16), though the German equivalent of the advertisement more suavely features no nationalities but only the roster of cities (illus., Stewart fig. 1.4 on 25). That he was unimpeachably Viennese was somehow not contradicted by his eventually proudly accepting the award of a special pension from President Masaryk of the new Czechoslovak Republic. For the most chauvinistic Moravian has the right to consider himself Czech, and especially in the imperial city every Czech had the right to be at least part-time Viennese. Architecturally speaking, even the special Slavophile modernity of the Slovene Jože Plečnik seems to arrive at Prague Castle, culturally speaking, by way of Vienna. On the other hand, Czechs must be all too accustomed to having their national identity dissolved away. The insightful postwar English art critic J. P. (Josef Paul) Hodin, himself Czech by birth as well as Jewish, points out, in discussing Oskar Kokoschka as not only Viennese and Czech, and Jewish too, but on his mother's side "Celtic" as well as Austrian, that not only Adolf Loos but also such other participants in contemporary Viennese culture as the poet Rilke, the novelists Werfel, Kafka and Musil, plus Mahler, Karl Kraus, Freud, Max Dvořák (the art historian for whom Loos designed a famous tomb) and Edmund Husserl were all born in the Czech Lands (Hodin 67), and so might on occasion, had they pleased, have also thought of themselves as attached to another smaller nation (or two, if they meant Moravia), quite distinctly from 'Austria.'

At some point, political reality must impinge. However religious or patriotic Loos may privately have been, he could not have failed to notice the increasing domination of the New World by a so-called 'Anglo-Saxon' United States, a development tinged with prejudice ever since the first generation born into its 'destiny' made it clear that, oblivious to popes, they and certainly not the empires of Spain and Portugal were ordained to oversee the American hemisphere. There followed the mid-century expansions into the territory of a weak Mexico, only recently having loosened itself from Spain, and then the great 1898 jingoistic outburst of the Spanish-American War, which Loos managed to miss.[4] Claiming hegemony over Latin America, the USA seized the Philippines as well as Cuba and Puerto Rico, all from Alfonso XIII of Spain; and though Alfonso, who was only twelve, was not a Habsburg, his mother, the regent, was. What else, after all, was the World's Columbian Exposition – during which *Harper's Weekly*, in New York, carried racist cartoons showing the fair crowded unpleasantly with foreign-looking immigrants of all types – but an exercise in national self-congratulation on assuming just such an aggressive imperial role in the world – and well beyond, considering the self-righteousness of even liberal Americans who in 1992, on the 500th anniversary of Columbus's arrival, could talk of little else than the horrors of the conquistadors, and never of Santo Domingo's having had a university a good century before Harvard.

And yet the perennial cultural idealization of antiquity sometimes underwrote a classically inspired high-mindedness even among those who knew oppression. From the turn of the century the African-American social critic W. E. B. Du Bois reports that the imperialistic aggressions of the United States "toward weaker and darker people in the West Indies, Hawaii and the Philippines" were so abhorrent as actually to discourage American blacks who had thought of moving to these territories. Nevertheless, Du Bois could write, in a manner half Whitmanesque and half classicist, "… I summon Aristotle and Aurelius and what soul I will, and they come all graciously with no scorn or condescension" (Du Bois 31, 67).

However cannily or uncannily it resembles McKim, Mead and White's Low Memorial, Loos's early project for a Franz Joseph jubilee church becomes emblematic of the promise of identifying with an imperial cultural capital – and perhaps it would be better to think that if there cannot be no empires, there should best be *more than one*. I have been told (though I have not yet found confirmation) that at some point Loos had considered changing his name because it didn't sound German enough, and might even seem too oddly Czech. I can only wonder how his Anglophilia responded to the British royal family's changing its name because it was German. But the case of Loos suggests that complex identities, provincial, national, imperial, as well as religious, might be advantageous for civilization, as against situations of one or another cultural monopoly. So let us end this speculation with a marvelously conflicted comment from that other Moravian-born Viennese Anglophile, Doctor Freud, on the approaching war: "I should be with it with all my heart if only I could think England would not be on the wrong side" (qu. Jones 2: 171).

CRITIQUE OF ORNAMENT

So much of the discourse on Adolf Loos concerns his theoretical standing as one of the founders of architectural modernism by virtue of his active opposition to ornament that for many the Loos of negative polemic is so exclusively the object of concern that they never come face to face with his work at all. Is there any modern painter or sculptor so badly off as to audience? Possibly John Cage in music; and pursuing solely his reputation, without artistic engagement with any works or performances must also lead back to the same mistaken conception – ultimately dismissive of just what we are looking for, i.e., art – of Loos as merely the Marcel Duchamp of architecture. Then again, some people listen to Cage, and many people actually look at Duchamp's readymades.

Giving Loos more of a chance as artist-architect also gives good reason for fresh reading of his two most important and problematic texts: 'Ornament and Crime' and 'Architecture,' which, ironically, require and deserve more textual attention than they usually receive – ironically because part of the problem has been a too visually oblivious, especially form-oblivious, approach to Loos, and yet his prime written texts nevertheless suffer from not being taken seriously enough as problematically textual: Loos has been approached in an overly literary way; but in respect to his actual written texts, not literarily enough. Put this way, it becomes obvious why those who only read his words, and take them as hermeneutically self-evident, are left with no solid sense of this great architect's project on any level and are as much as unqualified to vote on the question of whether or not it was or is art at all. Let us try to consider, then, more of what is at stake for modern European art in its formative phase in 'Ornament and Crime' (1909) and 'Architecture'

(1910) as differently and variously problematic as they are, in succession and as having implicit connections with other, less-known texts of the architect.[1]

The very title of the lecture and pamphlet 'Ornament and Crime' demands attention. Loos's use of the neuter Latinate '*das Ornament*,' not the masculine Germanic '*der Schmuck*,' already welcomes more general and categorical construal – even of the Romanized Greek orders as grammatical complexes passed on philologically through the Renaissance and then the classical academic system – as more than just a matter of cosmetic superfluities. Loos understood and respected the classical orders much more than the reactionaries who, still to this day, dumbly fetishize them: to him the understanding that they could no longer symbolize the essence of architecture, as no longer a matter of stone upon stone, was no reason to consider them anathema. Also, in 1909 the title 'Ornament and Crime' would have carried a touch of the edginess of Karl Kraus, who had published a critique of sexual inequality titled *Sittlichkeit und Kriminalität* (Morality and Criminality), in 1902. The note of criminality carrying over from the Kraus title would have reinforced the known historical relevance to the Loosian problem of the early criminologist Lombroso, to whom we shall return. And on the heels of Kraus had come another timely Viennese double-barreled title with an ethical ring to it: Otto Weininger's sensational *Geschlecht und Charakter* (Sex and Character), of 1903.

Young Weininger had committed suicide soon after his book appeared, as Loos's career was starting up; that might not seem pertinent, except for something Allan Janik has pointed out: that according to *Sex and Character*, criminality as such is not only anti-social but essentially *aesthetic*. In other words, though aesthetic conviction was not, for the moment, a selling point, a note of skepticism about aesthetic superficiality, specifically ornamental superfluity in architecture, quite possibly was. After all, criminality had even been toyed with in early modern aestheticism: in 1890 the dandyish American painter Whistler had promulgated in his *Gentle Art of Making Enemies* a list of revisionist aesthetic propositions, beginning with: "That in Art, it is criminal to go beyond the means used in the exercise" (Whistler 76). In Weininger's terms, criminal behavior is the result of an individual's being given monomaniacally over to pleasure as gained by any means necessary, of possessive consumption of his or her objects of desire (Janik, 'Engelmann's Role' 49). But if that meant a bad mark for aestheticism as possible motivation for a bad life, let us not miss the Loosian point of this as, if anything, a propitious occasion for the definitive pronouncement of a very rhetorically inflected anti-aestheticism. This was particularly directed against the arty sensuousness of the Secession's entire decorative arts project; and if Loos seemed like Beau Brummell arguing against the threat of fashion when he stood up to say it, that might be all the more scandalously effective.

Taking these writings simply as nihilistic or Viennese-sarcastic may be a way of dismissing them that is seriously problematic in the case of such an ironist and wit as Loos. With 'Ornament and Crime' – when virtually all literate adults still assumed that ornament was precisely what set architecture as a fine art above mere building – Loos takes the lust for ornament as symptomatic of a lack of sublimatory cultivation. Chronic complaints about the presumed unfairness of imagery which entails that tribal peoples are not as advanced as Westerners, too often miss or radically mistake the thrust and aim of Loos's literary figure, which, by means of analogy, exclusively concerns *modern city-dwellers*, however crude, merely unsophisticated, or positively decadent.

'Ornament and Crime' has become notorious for purported racism in taking a tribal people given to tattoo as an extreme of cultural inferiority, a problem which requires more literally critical attention than the dismissive moralism for which it has tended to be taken as an easy target. It is, however, not simply that the prevailing view distorts Loos's exposition by taking it out of context in a multi-imperial moment when such offenses were regrettably commonplace in European and American establishment culture, though that is true enough: no, we are not looking for a loophole by which to save Loos's reputation by, as it were, 'innocence by association,' not when the whole logical thrust of Loos's argument concerns *knowing better now*. Unfortunately, latter-day objection to the terms of the statements at issue, most often from a literary viewpoint, is so concerned with Loos's figures as not to be concerned to ascertain what Loos was actually saying on behalf of architecture by employing them, as if only literary folk are allowed to put figures to work. So it may not necessarily be reactionary for one who cares about art and architecture to want to get past a problematic imagery, after a hundred years, in order to come to terms with this 'world-historic,' if also notorious, text, the only work by our polemically inclined architect, with a high sense of irony, of which most people who have heard of him even know.

The essay stands in a certain German tradition of acerbic critique that includes Nietzsche as well as Loos's friend Karl Kraus. In 'The Use and Abuse of History for Life' (1873), for example, in the second volume of *Untimely Meditations* (or, *Thoughts Out of Season*), Nietzsche sounds quite Loosian in condemning the phoniness of culture as a mere cover, supposedly a "decoration" of life but really a "disfiguring" of it: "for all adornment hides what is adorned" (Nietzsche, *Thoughts* 99). Then in 'Schopenhauer as Educator' (1874) he speaks with Loosian sarcasm of how German culture can be expected to be Frenchified after overrunning France in the Franco-Prussian War: "[W]e have no reason to mind the French despising us for our want of interest, elegance and politeness, and being reminded of the Indian who longs for a ring through his nose, and then proceeds to tattoo himself" (loc. cit. 162).

It is bad enough when readers of Loos fail to follow through with the sense of his references to cultural backwardness and atavism (neutral conditions in pre-industrial cultures, European and otherwise) as figures critically directed at the 'barbarisms' (metaphoric but fully culpable) all too rampant in modern, supposedly refined, societies. But it is either naïve or unfair to criticize Loos's evolutionary presuppositions in the matter – which owe nothing to the horrors of 'social Darwinism,' and it is scandal-mongering to make it seem they do – without acknowledging the only available theoretical alternatives. The progressivist sense of cultural evolution appealed to by Loos, whereby differentials in cultural development are differences, parallel in the prevailing historical time, in the playing out of the same cultural scenario, rests on 'uniformitarianism' in the geology of Darwin's friend Charles Lyell, by which the forces shaping the earth today are presumed to be the same as those which shaped it in the distant past. I like to think that, given his penchant for mirror-play in interiors, Loos would have been interested in a younger Hungarian anthropologist turned Freudian analyst, Géza Róheim, a defender of cultural evolutionism who also studied folkloric 'mirror magic' (*Spiegelzauber*, 1919; Robinson 84–89). However, the only alternatives to such 'cultural evolution' or 'parallel development' were (a) diffusionism, whereby every advance in culture must be a hand-me-down from another culture, or (b) functionalism, in which the historical dimension is ignored and each culture's hardware and myths belong to a game so closed unto itself as not even to be comparable to another. So unless one would have preferred either (a) or (b) instead, one should by rights make some peace with Loos's *highly figured* appeal to some sense of cultural evolution.

Thus when Loos's German predecessor in modern social criticism of architecture, Muthesius, had written only a few years before 'Ornament and Crime,' in his *Style-Architecture* (2nd edn, 1903), as noted, of "a barbarism, such as our culture had not seen before, penetrate[ing] the substratum of the trades with little notice" (Muthesius 59), without even incidentally offending contemporary tribal peoples he was deliberately offending his own, once tribal German people. Loos even seems insistent and repetitious on this theme, which does not entail less developed peoples' being less human but does insist that some people *among us* ought to know better than to do the sorts of things that people less constrained by civilization do, and hence are distinctly *culpable* where tribal peoples are definitely not.

But the matter of tattooing in particular, especially the tattoo art of the Maori people of New Zealand, coded in a way by Loos as 'Papuans,' has special significance, though for present purposes there is no need to observe ethnological distinctions between references to Maori (Polynesians of New Zealand) and Papuan (Melanesians of New Guinea) tattoo or other ornamentation. It is enough to note that the serious ethnographic reports and collected artworks of the Maori proved to have serious artistic interest, to the great Viennese critical art historian Aloïs Riegl (Masheck, 'Vital Skin'); thus it seems likely that Loos's talk of Papuans was laterally caricatural, to some extent sending up the Western infatuation in the one case with the name of another comparable group, though Maori ornament is as a rule more curvilinear. Also, as may become evident, the Maori people were better known to Western culture, so that if anything, Loos may have turned to the less theoretically rehearsed category. Otherwise, the still looser, and more regrettable, usage 'Red Indian,' now found in some translations of Loos – most conspicuously in a quotation at the beginning of E. H. Gombrich's *The Sense of Order: A Study in the Psychology of Decorative Art* (1979) – cannot be blamed on him. However objectionable, it is a standard Britishism for distinguishing Native Americans or American Indians from what the British would more usually mean by unqualified 'Indians,' i.e., the people of India. Wherever it occurs, Loos himself used *der indianer*, the special German word for American Indians, as against *der indier* for Indian Indians (the lower case 'I' is no insult because Loos preferred to drop the usual German capitalization of nouns).

There is some consensus that Loos's attenuated tattooing trope owes something to the positivist and determinist criminology of Cesare Lombroso, which was widely read by the turn of the century: in America, an article by Lombroso titled 'Savage Origin of Tattoos' appeared in *Popular Science Monthly* for April 1896. Lombroso's classic *Criminal Man* (1876), expanded four times (5th edn, 1896–97), already contained a long chapter on that most remarkable of "criminal stigmata" (meaning marks deviating from a standard ideal of beauty), tattooing, which Lombroso finds confined to the lower classes and, especially, criminals. He thought that the word for tattooing comes from "an Oceanic language" (one doubts that this can mean the Maori *ta moko* as resembling the Italian *tatuaggio*), and observes that the only men who had tattoos on their backs or pubic areas had either been in prison or "to Oceania" (Lombroso 58). Tellingly, with a view to Loos's text: "Among Europeans, the most important reason" for being tattooed is "atavism and that other form of atavism called traditionalism, both of which characterize primitive men and men living in a state of nature." Such atavism is not simply primitivism by another name, even if primitivism appeals to it. "It is only natural that a custom widespread among savages and prehistoric peoples would reappear among certain lower-class groups," including sailors and prostitutes, the former "display[ing] the same temperament as savages with their violent passions, blunted sensitivity, puerile vanity, and extreme laziness. Sailors even adopt the habits, superstitions, and songs of primitive peoples" (61–62). Lombroso saw tattooing as closely tied to criminality even in contradistinction with insanity; and Allan Janik believes that 'Ornament and Crime' "depends entirely upon Lombroso's premises" (Janik, 'Weininger' 29). That can be factually true as a point of departure without denying that Loos's shamelessly independent wit would have found scope for play with a Lombroso phrase like "that … form of atavism called traditionalism."[2]

A case from the second edition (1878) is telling for what it says about Lombroso's sense of art. A murderer named Cavaglià decorated his prison water jug by scratching into the glaze simple drawings of his acts of murder and planned suicide; these are deemed sufficiently self-evidently inept to justify the judgment that "he told the story in a mixture of words and pictures in a way that evoked the customs of savage peoples, whose language is too poor to clearly express complicated ideas" (151). In the fourth edition (1889) Lombroso has, at his fingertips for just such situations, a new technique, 'pictography,' based on the notion that "[c]riminals tend to express their thoughts through drawings, even when they could express them in words." But this is because of something presumably atavistic as such about "a picture" versus "writing," so that, again, "[a]part from atavism, it is impossible to find another explanation for the custom of tattooing" (239).

At the same moment the Norwegian writer Knut Hamsun (later a fascist), reporting in a now sometimes disturbingly racist way on his rather negative first-hand experiences of *The Cultural Life of Modern America* (1889) – an account that would have piqued Loos's curiosity if only for its criticism of American affectations of petit-bourgeois British ways – mentions New Guinea natives in connection with cultural atavism. Human breeding, in the sense of cultivation, is likened to animal evolutionary stages: "When the fish became a bird, it learned better manners." After an observation on the curious ways New Guinea and Malay tribesmen greet one another, Americans' adoption of a suburban English 'How do you do?' is attacked as belonging to the "dog stage" of culture: this "is *their* greeting – an expression of their temperament and level of development" (Hamsun 136–37). Whether or not Loos read Hamsun, the provocative report on America by this eventually famous novelist had a place in the career of the literary topos of the backward New Guinean or Maori.

In the interest of overcoming the persistent nineteenth-century naturalist notion that 'merely' ornamental forms do not qualify as art, let us note that by 1870, in his *The Origin of Civilisation and the Primitive Condition of Man*, the tattoos of the "Polynesians" favorably reminded Sir John Lubbock, the very framer of the Paleolithic/Neolithic distinction, of Bronze Age Greek spirals (Lubbock 26). In 1885, well before Riegl's discussion of the Maori's spiral ornament as an all the more decisively formal matter in the absence of the metal tools which would have made it more readily determined, the anthropologist Otto Finsch, commenting on Papuan tattooing as *clothing* the body ('*Bekleidung*' finds an English cognate in 'cladding'), called attention to a particular kind of tattooed men's belt. Because such work was so difficult to execute without iron tools, "it must be unconditionally characterized as artwork" (Finsch 14). On the hurried, 'downtown' terms of 'Ornament and Crime' it might seem absurd to think that ornament's being extra-difficult to execute should make it more art-worthy; but in fact, this is exactly how Maori ornament would serve the more 'idealist' argument of Riegl, in *Stilfragen* (Problems of Style; 1893), against the 'materialist' view of Gottfried Semper, that this shows the Maori carvers' spirals as something they *really wanted to make*, not something that more or less *had to come out that way*, given the materials, tools, "techniques."

Problems of Style, subtitled *Foundations for a History of Ornament,* has a diffusionist theoretical thrust – diffusionism, again, being the theory that similar art forms do not arise independently but through lines of transmission. Yet Riegl's speculations on Maori ornament were ultimately in the interest of modern artists and modern art. The same cannot be said of a once classic diffusionist attempt, published shortly after Loos's death, to situate Maori ornament globally by locating its source in sophisticated Zhou dynasty Chinese ornament, calling it "a barbarized (*barbarisé*) art … that could only have been born in a high civilization" (Heine-Geldern 202). Comparing Maori with Scandinavian interlace ornament, the same scholar, though he has to admit that thought of a connecting population is far-fetched, points to Josef Strzygowski's notion of "real ties between ancient art of Northern Europe and the art of New Zealand," while he himself suggests that autochthonous Neolithic spiral ornament of Bohemia and Moravia did reach the Far East (204). It might be entertaining to imagine what Adolf Loos could have added to 'Ornament and Crime' about Bukovina as ultimate formal source for the ornamentation of the great Shang or Zhou dynasty bronzes! Here, supposedly, was the connection between the Maori and the Scandinavians: the Zhou dynasty, before it "strongly influenced the art of New Zealand," had itself inherited "Danubian" and "ultimately Mycenaean" forms; and this may well make for an indirect connection between the Scytho-Sarmatian forms of the steppes, too, and New Zealand (205). Something of a Maori sort – Loos's 'Papuans' – was stirring.

Loos was an Anglophile and proud of it, aspiring in a way to a visual equivalent of the stiff upper lip as an epitome of developmental refinement connoting an unaffected, confident civility, social but private, with a 'noble simplicity' of public restraint. This character, which also pervades his concern with tailoring, also evokes, once again, the often impassively classico-plain façades of Neopalladian country houses. The diffusion of the British Neopalladian style had extended in the later eighteenth century into Central Europe (examples include Schloss Williamshöhe, near Kassel, and Schloss Belvedere at Warsaw), although the forced spatial symmetry of the interior layouts of Neopalladian buildings, even medium-sized private houses, is something one cannot imagine Loos bearing to impose – much worse than the rigorous surface symmetry of the Papuan or Maori's facial tattoo. What might be considered proto-Loosian in the Neopalladian mode, as in turn a root of Neoclassicism, was its essentially rationalist critique of Baroque rhetoric. Thus there is something of the spirit of Loos in the chapter 'On Building Without Any Orders' in Marc-Antoine Laugier's *Essai sur l'Architecture* (1753), where the great proto-functionalist practically preaches, telling architects how not everything has to be grandly important, and how positively interesting it can be to compose a building with no classical 'order' of columns at all.

And as I have noted before, in his *Prolegomena to Any Future Metaphysics That Will Be Able to Come Forth as Science* (1783) Immanuel Kant speaks of a possible "adornment … through heightened clarity." Indeed, Loos finds something of an ally in the Kant who produced a distinctly cleansing 'critical' philosophy. In remarks appended to his 1783 *Prolegomena*, which is something of a rehearsal for the *Critique of Pure Reason*, Kant acknowledges his qualified idealism as having been provoked by the same George Berkeley even as he critiques Berkeley's "dogmatic," and in proceeding to speak against ornamentation he employs two expressions that would surely have appealed to Loos, one as it were abstract and 'sentimental,' the other, more vernacular yet 'anti-naïve.' The first concerns effecting "adornment by greater clearness (*den Ausputz durch … vergrösserte Deutlichkeit*)," while the second recasts much the same basic conception in a homey figure worthy of the farmhouse: "though the old false feathers have been pulled out, it need by no means appear poor and reduced to an insignificant figure but may be in other respects richly and respectably adorned" (Ak. 382; *Prolegomena* 122; *Werke* 4: 138).

Some of Loos's smaller, but by no means insignificant built projects, early on, show him subsuming appropriate formal influences even where, a century ago, there would not have been enough to describe as ornament. Similarly, ignoring its more exotic-eclectic side, something like a default of English Regency style also has Anglophile relevance to Loos's work. For instance, in two early boutique-sized Viennese shop fronts – the Sigmund Steiner Plume and Feather Shop (1907; demolished) and the Kniže haberdashery in the Graben (1909; 1913) – a quarter-rounding of the shop-windows at the doorway, or at the Kniže store, of plinth and showcases left and right, pays formal respects to the boutique shop-fronts of Samuel Ware's elegant Burlington Arcade, of 1819 – which may even have been under discussion at the time because the Piccadilly entrance was soon to be remodeled, in 1911 (by Beresford Pite).

Loos's Anglophilia was not peculiar in contemporary Germanic artistic culture. Muthesius' major, handsomely illustrated study *The English House* (1904–05), researched while its author was German cultural attaché in London, conveyed an impressive sense of the English 'free style' and newly 'open' planning. One of the more overlooked candidates for influence, or at least corroboration, of what would become Loos's way of thinking might be the Welsh-born *décadent* poet Arthur Symons, who was sufficiently popular in Loos's world for several of his fictional works to be translated into German and even Czech early in the new century. Symons addressed the eminently Loosian theme of the plain being all the harder to come by than the meretriciously ornamented. In an essay of 1903 on 'The Decay of Craftsmanship in England,' after criticizing the cult of the "detachable picture" together with stuck-on ornament, Symons says:

> [W]e have become specialists; the craftsman is no longer an artist, and the artist can no longer be a craftsman. What we see in the Arts and Crafts, in these ambitious attempts, is only another symptom of what we see in all the shops in London. The most difficult thing to get in London is a piece of plain carpet, without any pattern on it whatever, and when you have found it you will generally have to get it dyed to the colour you want. A piece of plain wall-paper to match it will be the next most difficult thing to get; and for both these things you will have to pay much more than you would pay for a carpet or a wall-paper covered with hideous patterns. Surely the mere printing, not to say inventing, of these patterns must cost money; why, then, cannot a

cheaper and a less objectionable thing be offered to you without them? For this reason, say the shopkeepers, that only one person out of a thousand will buy it. That the pattern is a bad pattern, no one seems to mind; there must be some scrawl for the money. (Symons 183–84)

I read this passage into the record because, as will become evident, it so closely resembles critical complaints lodged even in Loos's most famous text, 'Ornament and Crime.'

That text is a great reformist contribution to early modernism as worthily high art. It will be best to deal straightaway with the problem of its now problematic culture-evolutionary aspect, if, that is, we can for once, in this situation, keep our eyes on the ball of what Loos, despite any now objectionable terms, was actually trying to say. But if the view on which Loos leans for his sense of the cultural-evolutionary aspect of 'Ornament and Crime' was biological seems cause for concern now, at least it is one which has retained some cultural respect as a figure of thought: the notion, framed by Ernst Haeckel, that the embryological "ontogeny" of the single human being developmentally "recapitulates" the anatomical form of "the phylogeny," that is, the overall developmental species pattern of the animal kingdom at large. In its time, the theory countered the pessimistic press of destiny in the more Darwinian view. More importantly for the text at hand, it was the basis of a cultural analogy that in Loos's hands was not evidently any more tainted by racism than were most other liberal-minded middle-class Europeans in 1909, or anyone who went on to welcome the 1919 revolutionary spirit in Central Europe, or who gave serious attention to social housing. For the cruder early phases of human culture consisted by definition of the best there was at the time – just as Marx can speak well of feudalism over and against slavery; and indeed, Loos points up at the start of his text something of which most Americans have no inkling when he sets between the innocent (though not exactly noble-savage) Papuan (= age two) and Socrates (= age six), in his developmental scale of culture, the pre-feudal European "tribesman" (= age four; *OC* 167) so conveniently forgotten in the modern Euro-American's sanitized sense of his or her own origins. In any case, the thrust of Loos's figure was not to criticize anybody else's lack of sophistication but only the contemporary "stragglers" as he calls them more than once, of his own modern culture, who, he always insisted, really ought to know better.[3]

Given his critical outlook, a different sort of embryological speculation, anciently Indo-European, would have appealed to him in respect to architectural cladding as a building's embryologically final epidermis: the original Sanskrit conception of ornament as final, outermost layer of something properly crafted as it comes into its own. The great orientalist Coomaraswamy (1877–1947) explains that by linguistic devolution the Sanskrit word meaning "made adequate" came more simplistically to mean merely "embellished"; the debased usage "I adorn him" had once meant something more profound that would have appealed to Loos: "I fit him out" – as an outfitter (Coomaraswamy 378). Of special interest to our modernist architect who loved well-crafted saddlery would have been a discussion of words pertaining to harness, as where, in the Rig Veda, what matters is the *aptness*, not superficial "beauty," of the gear. Loos would agree with Coomaraswamy that mere aestheticism is childish, though not about how that matters: unless we get beyond it, we cannot comprehend the fundamental meaning of such bodily adornments as "tattooing" (380).

'Ornament and Crime,' however, does propose a progression – like the biologist Haeckel's formula of the ontogeny recapitulating the phylogeny, that is, that the human embryo recapitulates "all the evolutionary stages of the animal kingdom." "[W]hen a human being is born," Loos says, "his sense impressions are like a newborn dog's. In childhood he goes through all the stages in the development of humanity" (*OC* 167). Thus develops the present-day child: "At two he sees with the eyes of a Papuan, at four with those of a Germanic tribesman, at six of Socrates, at eight of Voltaire. At eight he becomes aware of violet, the color discovered by the eighteenth century; before that violets were blue and the purple snail was red. Even today physicists can point to colors in the solar spectrum which have been given a name, but which it will be left to future generations to discern" (ibid.). This last point is important because it implies that, like the Papuans, we moderns are not incompletely human today just because cultural development is likely to continue, culture being a process of refinement that is never over. Loos cannot be arguing that Voltaire was better than and/or superior to Socrates, which would follow analogically if the Teutonic tribesman were better than the Papuan. Then, too, there is the idealizing respect for the Papuan that a dandyish Voltaire must have for a Socrates.

But in the second paragraph the now century-old but notorious account of tattoo begins; and the present-day critical reader would do well to remember that the Maori, also like the Papuans, were cannibals, notwithstanding their undeniably beautiful ornament, including tattoo. Some confusion with regard to 'Ornament and Crime' derives from the fact that Loos is already more culturally relative than is expected: the Papuan's cannibalism cannot be fully culpable because he literally knows no better: "But if a modern person kills someone and devours him, he is a criminal or a degenerate" (ibid.). Similarly, then: "The Papuan covers his skin with tattoos, his boat, his oars, in short everything he can lay his hands on." But: "He is not a criminal." (One might have expected Loos to complete the parallelism with "nor a degenerate," but he may want to leave room for a touch of *décadence*.) "The modern person who tattoos himself is either a criminal or a degenerate" – a thought that unfurls into a wittily hyperbolic Loosian cadenza: "There are prisons in which eighty per cent of the inmates have tattoos. People with tattoos not in prison are either latent criminals or degenerate aristocrats" (*OC* 167). "If a tattooed person dies at liberty, it is only that he died a few years before he committed a murder" (*AAL* 100).

Loos obviously knows he is being outrageous; and in estimating what he is intellectually up to we should not overlook his Viennese high sarcasm. As Peter Vergo notes with uncommon boldness, "critics have failed to notice" that in this prime text Loos is "far from being entirely serious," and statements like the one of dying fortuitously before committing an inevitable murder, are "surely humorous" (Vergo 172). An amusing example from one of his early exhibition reviews, on 'Glass and China' (1898), has our subject talking about a popular engraver of drinking glasses at this exhibit of wares engraving people's names 'while-they-wait': "Particularly delightful is a goblet decorated with good-luck charms, which I am sure has a future ... What I have in mind is the delightful arrangement of the charms, which recalls the principle of decoration under Emperor Francis I" (*OC* 72). While the irony in 'Ornament and Crime' is subtler than that, it is strange that our literary friends, of all people, often seem to suppose that when this friend of Kraus, criticizing contemporary European culture, made such a statement as that someone tattooed dying at liberty would soon have become a murderer, he can possibly have been speaking with a straight face. Yet beyond the scandalous hyperbole there was important thinking here – a hundred years ago now, amazingly:

> The urge to ornament one's face, and everything within one's reach is the origin of fine art. It is the babble of painting. All art is erotic. The first ornament that came into being, the cross, had an erotic origin. The first work of art, the first artistic action of the first artist daubing on the wall, was in order to rid himself of his natural excesses. A horizontal line: the reclining woman. A vertical line: the man who penetrates her. The man who created it felt the same urge as Beethoven, he experienced the same joy that Beethoven felt when he created the Ninth Symphony. (*AAL* 100)[4]

Loos's concern is not with an absolute primitive state of nature but with a relative primitivism under supposedly advanced developmental conditions.

His observations, here, on the barbarous behavior of his more uncouth contemporaries stir up matters not only of anthropology but also of the historical and political philosophy, including Giambattista Vico's pre-Nietzschean sense of cultural progress as repeatedly broken by regression to a more primitive state, with recovery to a somewhat higher plane; and of how in the final "Age of Man" a barbarism comparable to the "second barbarism" of the early Middle Ages returns with social breakdown and "barbarism of the soul" (conclusion to *The New Science*, 1725). Closer to home, the Industrial Revolution had brought the social barbarism of alienation and cultural deprivation of a lumpenproletariat which Loos obviously has in mind without putting it quite so. Even a notorious comment on those who inscribe and bedeck with drawings public lavatory walls comes closer, in tenor, than we would expect to Engels in *The Condition of the Working Class in England in 1844* (1845) on the slums of Manchester as habitable only by "a physically degenerate race, robbed of all humanity, degraded, reduced morally and physically to bestiality" (Engels 63).

Loos finally makes a decisive and sweeping point when he insists "*We* have the art that has superseded ornament" (*OC* 174; emphasis in source). "The art, which has taken the place of ornament," the same notion of supersession and even sublimation will even extend (once there is such a thing) to abstract painting as in part adumbrated by ornamental stylization in the crafts; and this is also a good condensation of the whole case that 'Ornament and Crime' was never about how the tribal artisan doesn't know any better, and not even about how the lowly present-day cobbler doesn't know any better either, disappointed as he is when you offer to pay him more if he will just make your shoes without the absurd 'wing-tip' pattern of dots – a markedly sharp criticism on Loos's part, which has a fourth-century Eastern precedent: St John Chrysostom preaching in Constantinople: "Even the shoemaker's ... [art] stands in need of restraint, for they have lent their art to luxury, corrupting its necessity and artfully debasing art" (Homily 49 on Matthew, qu. Coomaraswamy 381). No; it is really about how *we* are remiss: "What is natural in the Papuan or the child is a sign of degeneracy in a modern adult. I made the following discovery, which I passed on to the world: *the evolution of culture is synonymous with the removal of ornament from objects of everyday use*" (*OC* 167; emphasis in source). However questionable "*they* don't know any better" as a set-up, the challenging punch line, as it were, of Adolf Loos's message was and undeniably remains "*we ought to* know better."

Yes, Loos has to report that his attempt to announce the good news that ornamentation as such is now over with, and the production of ornaments might finally cease, has not pleased but disheartened people: "What? We alone, the people of the nineteenth century, were not capable of doing something every … tribesman could do, something every age and nation before us had done!?" (*OC* 167). From this sentence I have dropped a casual and unnecessary mention of race, because, usage in such things now being more sensitive (which Loos would take as improvement), the word in question is by now, 100 years later, a distraction from the real object of Loos's analogical concern with the unsophisticated provincials of the contemporary Austrian empire as all the worse, for having less excuse, than surviving Non-European tribal cultures. Of the jubilee parade of Emperor Franz-Joseph in 1898, with its endless files of ethnically costumed imperial subjects from every corner of the empire, he says with typical outrageousness, "[W]e shuddered to learn that here in Austria we still have tribes from the fourth century. Happy the land that does not have many cultural stragglers and laggards. Happy America!" (170). It was with these "stragglers," here the peasants within the outer limits of the Austrian empire, that Loos was primarily concerned with all his imagery of the primitive in 'Ornament and Crime.' Otherwise, 'otherness' as such was hardly a distasteful condition for this cultural loose cannon who titled the short-lived journal for which he wrote the copy himself *Das Andere* – 'The Other.' As for the presumption of a modern European's necessarily patronizing pre-modern culture as backward vis-à-vis modern urbanity, Loos spoke at a moment of cresting conviction in Germanic Expressionism, which inherited a German Romantic appreciation of primitivity. As early as 1799, the *Heartful Outpourings of an Art-Loving Monk*, of Wilhelm Wackenroeder, had called tribal music as good in the eyes, or ears, of God as the chants of the Church (cf. Masheck, 'Raw Art'). That was more to the modern point than the Baltic German historical writer Carl Gustav Jochmann's essay 'The Regression of Poetry' (1828), taking primitives' scarification, probably more than tattoo as such, as plainly evil (no doubt in light of Leviticus), which Walter Benjamin seems to have rediscovered in awareness of Adolf Loos.[5]

Let us be clear: there was no onus whatever in sophisticated circles on being primitive as such – the condition was even romanticized – only on behaving inexcusably like a primitive in the middle of Vienna.

Moments after the turn of the century Aloïs Riegl, who had already written a short book on folk art, and then *Problems of Style*, which actually engages with Maori tattoo, produced the first volume of a momentous book aesthetically rehabilitating the barbarian metalwork of precisely that 'Migrations' period to which Loos referred, published by the imperial and royal press in 1901, as if in celebration of the dual monarchy itself, under the title *Die spätrömische Kunst-Industrie; nach den Funden in Österreich-Ungarn* (Late Roman Art Industry; Based on the Finds in Austria-Hungary). If concern with such 'industrial art' was, by and large, more akin to the Secessionist sense of 'decorative art' from which Loos distanced himself, other studies of the turn of the century were also influential. Consider an illustration of Maori tattoo from an influential German book whose enthusiasm for tribal art was nationalistically concerned with the new German overseas empire; but it also had the perhaps more interestingly nationalistic motivation, according to Goldwater, that hearty tribal peoples were to its author, Leo Frobenius, surprisingly German or at least appealingly unlike the French. The title, with all its implications, if not the actual book, would surely have been known to Loos: *The Childhood of Man* (1901; Englished in 1909), though the original title is more apologetic: *Aus den Flegeljahren der Menschenheit*: 'Out of Humanity's Awkward Age.'

A parallel can even be suggested between a certain Papuan or Maori tattoo type from timelessly 'outside' the European sphere and Riegl's tendril motif as amazingly genealogically continuous down through the ages in Western art. Thus can a type of wood-carved stamp (illustrated by Frobenius), which one might suppose was for textile printing but which is in fact a tattoo pattern from Borneo, compare with a mechanically printed wallpaper pattern, perpetuating the tendril motif in Loos's Vienna, in Freud's apartment at Berggasse 19, in the IX District of Vienna (between 1891/92 and 1938). Also, the otherwise culturally distinct Borneo Dayaks, Melanesian Papuans of New Guinea and Polynesian Maori of New Zealand had the practice of tattoo in common; and such stamps for tattooing occur in the latter cultures as well – more remotely from Southeast Asia, with which the diffusionist would associate the Borneo one in order ultimately to connect up, across Asia, with the Western lineage. Freud's wallpaper will simply stand for all the ubiquitous leafy scrollwork, based on the tendril motif whose formal genealogy Riegl had worked out in Freud's generation, a little ahead of Loos. It is also a good generic example of what Otto Wagner, a little bit older still, basically conceived as ornamentally claiming a wall, like a clinging vine, as a faced surface, as, so beautifully, on the façade of his great Viennese apartment block, the Majolikahaus, of 1898. Loos himself used wide, rich vegetal friezes, related to tendril ornament (with interjected tailor's shears), in the Ebenstein Tailoring Salon, Vienna I, of 1897.

Janet Stewart has explored Loos's 'Papuan' theme, associating it, reasonably enough, with the living exhibition, in a Viennese zoo in 1897, of an "'African village' peopled by Ashanti men and women," as instigating a spectacle of exotic tribal 'otherness' in the background of Loos's 1898 Jubilee Exhibition essays (Stewart 69–70) – after perspicaciously suggesting that the more remote 'otherness' of Oceanic tribal villagers may have symbolically mitigated Loos's personal situation: for though culturally 'German' (by language) and Catholic, he was a Moravian-born cosmopolite with many Jewish friends at a time when Czechs and Jews were the largest categories of 'others' in Vienna (67).

But attention needs to be paid to how the essentially ornamental-abstract Maori art became sufficiently familiar, particularly in turn-of-the-century Vienna, to be available for Loos to put it to analogous work in his famous or infamous text. Two factors were at work here: that serious Western artistic interest in native Maori art was already being taken for a long time; and the less happy fact that, as reduced to a preserve within a functionally 'Western' country, New Zealand, Maori culture was already quite 'on the map.' In 1907, before 'Ornament and Crime' was drafted, something of an intersection occurred between Maori and upper-class British culture that would have amused Loos: in honor of New Zealand's passing from British colony to dominion status, Royal Doulton produced a china pattern based on the highly curvilinear patterns of Maori house decorations. By 1910 the Maori were sufficiently part of the 'world' of Western imperial culture, however subordinated to be visited by John Philip Sousa's band on their world tour of that year (I have, from my grandfather, a souvenir photograph printed as a postcard to be sent home by members of the band, who appear standing with some Maori people before a new-looking but traditionally ornamented Maori dwelling-house).

Maori art-historiography is a happier subject than imperial conquest. Maori ornament tattoo and other curvilinear ornament has a long history of aesthetic citation in the West after Captain Cook's and Joseph Banks' collections and reports, including not only the former in Kant's *Critique of Judgment* (1790) but also, as I have pointed out, the latter in the British neoclassical sculptor John Flaxman's lecture on 'Style' (Masheck, 'Vital Skin,' 158–60; though in my previous treatment of this problem I was too skeptical of Loos's sweeping negativity, which was braced against prevailing excess). Possibly the earliest disseminations of visual evidence of Maori ornament in France were two articles in the then new *Magazin pittoresque* in 1833 (Donne 5–6), and prints of the great Romantic etcher Charles Meryon.

The American sculptor Horatio Greenough, aware of Flaxman, wrote in 'American Architecture' (1843):

When the savage of the South Sea islands shapes his war club, his first thought is of its use. His first efforts pare the long shaft, and mold the convenient handle; then the heavier end takes gradually the edge that cuts, while it retains the weight that stuns. His idler hour divides its surface by lines and curves, or embosses it with figures that have pleased his eye or are linked with his superstition. We admire its effective shape, its Etruscan-like quaintness, its graceful form and subtle outline, yet we ignore the lesson it might teach.

This artist shows a lively response to such 'primitive' ornamental art even before the New York novelist Herman Melville returned from the Pacific and stimulated popular interest in Oceanic culture with *Typee: A Peep at Polynesian Life* (1846) and *Omoo: A Narrative of Adventures in the South Seas* (1847). Greenough follows through with the Loosian-Corbusian proto-functional statement of that lesson:

> If we compare the form of a newly invented machine with the perfected type of the same instrument, we observe, as we trace it through the phases of improvement, how weight is shaken off where strength is less needed, how functions are made to approach without impeding each other, how straight becomes curved, and the curve is straightened, till the straggling and cumbersome machine becomes the compact, effective, and beautiful engine. (Greenough 59)

Maori tattoo and ornament were then taken up by Owen Jones, but then too by Lubbock and, notably, by Riegl in Vienna, of whom Loos was aware. However unfortunate for the modern legacy was the title of the first book to distinguish the Old and New Stone Ages – Lubbock's *Pre-Historic Times; As Illustrated by Ancient Remains and the Manners and Customs of Modern Savages* (1865)[6] – two illustrations of facial tattoo from his somewhat more equitably titled *Origin of Civilisation and the Primitive Condition of Man* were re-published by Riegl along with his own 1890 illustrations of Maori weaving and carving in his great anti-Semperian work of 1893, *Problems of Style*. There followed in the same line not only the expressionist theoretician and Riegl enthusiast Wilhelm Worringer, but also, in Vienna, Adolf Loos.[7]

Only a few years before Loos began to write criticism, a classic work on prehistoric art appeared, treating both Maori and Papuan ornament, which would have facilitated his effective substitution for a more longstanding topos of the Maori by his Papuans: *The Beginnings of Art* (1894), by Ernst Grosse. Papuan canoe-prow ornaments are mentioned along with Maori ornamental and figurative art, with Grosse suspending aesthetic judgment on Maori figurative work, interestingly enough, because he cannot tell whether obligations to convention have disadvantageously affected figures which seem to him less than adequately naturalistic. Grosse is generally concerned with tattoo, not particularly with Maori or Papuan practices. Of Loosian interest is his sense that tools very often go unornamented even among peoples who do tattoo their bodies, except that, in a sense, we may often "recognize embellishment not in ornamental decoration only, but in the smooth and even finish of an implement" (115). That is from a chapter on 'Ornamentation' in which reverberations of Riegl's contention with Semper can be discerned, and in which Loos would have noticed the sense of progressing developmentally "higher":

> Ornamentation has in [the] lowest stage of development only a secondary artistic character; pleasing forms attach themselves to the practical, significant features only as the tendrils of a young climbing plant to the branches of a tree. But later on the vine develops faster and more richly than the tree, and finally the form of the tree almost disappears under the dense green foliage and bright blossoms of the vine ... There is ... a great difference between the ornamentation of the primitive and that of the higher peoples in nature, and consequently in influence. The ... social influences of the higher forms of ornamentation ... are certainly not insignificant, whenever, at least, the shameful prostitution of ornamental art to the interests of our modern manufacturing enterprise has not destroyed its charm and force. (Grosse 162)

Grosse still assumes like a good Victorian burgher, if unlike Loos, that ornament fluoresces with cultural development, though he has room for such an insight as that we can respond aesthetically to "embellishment" not only in ornamentation but in, in a sense of the opposite: the smooth, even feel of a presumably plain tool.

Loos had introduced the theme before 'Ornament and Crime,' only four years after Grosse's *Beginnings of Art*:

> the great development of culture in this century has left ornamentation far behind. Here I must repeat myself: The lower the cultural level, the greater degree of ornamentation. Ornament is something that must be overcome. The Papuans and criminals decorate their skin. The Red Indian covers his canoe over and over with decoration. But the bicycle and the steam engine are free of decoration. As it progresses, culture frees one object after another from ornamentation. (*OC* 109)

That is from 'Ladies' Fashion,' 1898, revised in 1902. The bicycle motif occurs even more tellingly in other of Loos's 1898 reviews. In 'Glass and China,' even the rhetorical concession that the Greek vases are "as beautiful" as a machine or a bicycle, as cited in chapter 1, belongs, in context, to a praise of modern engineering that includes the salute to engineers (and the English) as "our ancient Greeks." In 'A Review of Applied Arts – I,' after noting the modern bentwood Thonet chair as "the fruit of the same spirit" as an elegant Greek chair, Loos praises the bicycle again, this time as worthy of comparison with ancient Greek bronze tripods: "I do not mean the votive offerings, but the ones that were put to practical use – are they not exactly like our own constructions of iron?" (*OC* 134–35).[8]

In 1907 and 1908, leading up to the lecture, the same parity of 1898 persists. In Loos's promotional tour brochure 'Guided Tours of Apartments' (1907): "*The inability of our culture to create new ornament is a sign of greatness.* The evolution of humanity goes hand in hand with the disappearance of ornamentation from objects of everyday use. Whatever our applied artists, prompted by the survival instinct, might say, for people of culture a face without a tattoo is more beautiful than one with a tattoo, even if designed by Kolo Moser himself. And people of culture also want not only their skin but also their bookbindings and bedside tables protected from the Indian ornamental frenzy of these self-appointed cultural barbarians" (*OA* 54). Again, in 'Surplus to Requirements (The German Werkbund)' (1908):

> It is a fact that the cultured products of our time have nothing to do with art … The Papuans cover their household goods with decoration … Albrecht Dürer was allowed to produce shoe patterns. But to modern man, glad he is living today and not in the sixteenth century, such a misuse of artistic talent is barbarism.
>
> This separation was a good thing for our intellectual and cultural life. The *Critique of Pure Reason* could not be written by a man with five ostrich feathers in his cap, the *Ninth* did not come from a man with a plate-sized wheel around his neck, and the room where Goethe died is more magnificent than Hans Sachs' cobbler's workshop, even if every object in the latter were designed by Dürer. (*OC* 155)

Obviously Loos does not mean that Dürer is even relatively inferior to any modern artist, so it cannot be entailed that a Papuan's ornamental design is inferior to Dürer's shoe design: no, even Dürer's shoes are on the wrong track for what is wanted in modern culture.

While the notoriety of 'Ornament and Crime,' along with the scandal among the burghers of the Looshaus, undoubtedly helped to certify the avant-gardist's controversial standing, already in 1911 Loos had to explain that people misunderstood his position if they thought he was categorically against any and all ornament. "Thirteen years ago," he wrote, i.e., in 1898, in an essay on 'Otto Wagner' (whose disciples he found worse ornamentalists than their master),

> I sent out a warning, expressing the opinion that we are no longer capable of inventing new ornamentation. (My enemies take this to mean that I am opposed to all ornamentation, while all I oppose is any kind of imitation in materials.) Anyone who wants to decorate something should therefore use old ornamentation. I do not consider the invention of new ornamentation as a sign of strength but – in cultivated people – a sign of degeneration. The Papuans can go on inventing new ornaments until they finally reach the stage when they are beyond ornament. (OA 90)

In the 1920s, writing on 'Ornament and Education' for a Czech review, Loos repeats himself on the same lines, in 1924 actually referring back to the original 'Ornament and Crime' lecture – and, if seemingly by a slip, advancing the age of the figurative Papuan: "Every child is a genius. Not only its parents and aunts know that, we all know it. But the genius of a Papuan, that is of a six-year-old child, is of no use to humanity" (OC 184).

> Form and ornament are products of the subconscious collaboration of all members of a particular culture. Art is the complete opposite. Art is the product of the genius going his own way. His commission comes from God.[9]
>
> To waste art on objects of practical use demonstrates a lack of culture. Ornamentation means added labor. The sadism of the eighteenth century, burdening one's fellows with superfluous work, is alien to modern man. Even more alien is the ornamentation of primitive peoples [another unlikely polemical equation, between the supposedly most civilized and the supposedly least], which is entirely religious or – symbolically – erotic in significance, and which, thanks to its primitive nature, comes close to art ... (185–86)
>
> Twenty-six years ago I maintained that the use of ornament on objects of practical use would disappear with the development of mankind ... By that I did not mean what some purists have carried ad absurdum, namely that ornament should be systematically and consistently eliminated. What I did mean was that where it had

disappeared as a necessary consequence of human development, it could not be restored, just as people will never return to tattooing their faces. (187)

At the end of the decade it recurs in Loos's obituary salute to Josef Veillich (1929), the stalwart craftsman who made most of the copies of eighteenth-century English chairs which he required for the interiors of his apartments and houses: "In Frankfurt-am-Main the chairman of the local branch of the German *Werkbund* said I wasn't nationalistic enough. True, as they understand the term. In those circles my remark 'Why do the Papuans have a culture and the Germans none?' is seen as anti-German, as a malicious wisecrack. That my remark comes from a bleeding German heart is something the Germans will never understand" (*OA* 188–89 n. 2).

When, if ever does one hear Le Corbusier accused of racism when he borrows effectively from Loos fifteen years later – time that, if anything, should mean, in Loosian terms, knowing all the better? His *Towards a New Architecture* (1923), the most influential architectural book of the twentieth century, is quite close to the spirit of Loos:

> Civilizations advance. They pass through the age of the peasant, the soldier and the priest and attain what is rightly called culture. Culture is the flowering of the effort to select. Selection means rejection, pruning, cleansing; the clear and naked emergence of the Essential. (Le Corbusier 128) ...
>
> Art, in a highly cultivated country, finds its means of expression in pure art, a concentrated thing free from all utilitarian motives – painting, literature, music. (132) ...
>
> Decoration is of a sensorial and elementary order, as is colour, and is suited to simple races, peasants and savages. Harmony and proportion incite the intellectual faculties and arrest the man of culture. The peasant loves ornament and decorates his walls. The civilized man wears a well-cut suit and is the owner of easel pictures and books. Decoration is the essential overplus, the quantum of the peasant; and proportion is the essential overplus, the quantum of the cultivated man. (133)

Now this seems rather like a hasty digest of 'Ornament and Crime,' complete with some equivalent to the Loosian 'Beethoven' motif. The appeal to "harmony and proportion," however, sounds much too French: Loos would never speak so glibly of proportion (as cultural conservatives often do). More important here, however, is something Le Corbusier actually does not press: a sense, not so Loosian, that somehow a house should be a "a machine for living in"[10] quite *instead of* a work of architectural art in the conventional sense. One hastens to add that looking like a sleekly beautiful machine is for Corbusier a new way to look like architectural art: the famous slogan is after all a figure of speech, coming from a new aesthetic place but aesthetic nevertheless. This was not exactly Loos's way of stating the specially qualified non-art case for architecture, but it is effectively something he in some sense stated first.

That 'Ornament and Crime' always turns out to be more challenging than one expects, concerns the difficulty of breaking through conventional presuppositions about ornament as necessarily a refinement, to which even the Papuan-Maori analogue for the cultural "stragglers" of modern times is subordinate. Loos finds it frustrating to deal with even certain made-to-order articles, such as gentlemen's shoes with 'wing-tips' perforated with curlicues – possibly the most classy English 'Papuan' fetish – to have them furnished plain, without ornamentation. The cobbler himself, however, proves sentimentally attached to the ornament he has, however absurdly, always been obliged to impose on the shoes he makes; and on the theoretical plane this must to some extent spoil a ready analogy with carpentry in building construction by which Loos wants to maintain that the craftsman knows better than the architect – certainly better than any architect who considers himself an artist and tries to impose his 'creativity' – how to make a plain good and almost by necessity beautiful thing.[11]

There does seem to be some confusion over the basically good idea of well made, simpler shoes which will not go quickly out of style, together with higher pay and shorter hours for shoemakers, as a good thing all round. The confusion is not so much in the economics as in regard to the gratification versus alienation of the at least temporarily disappointed craftsman who always *thought* he liked punching the holes of the regularized wing-tip pattern as much as the peasant woman whom Loos otherwise permits to go on unembarrassedly enjoying her needlework because Beethoven is out of her cultural reach. Well, Loos could still look forward to public education bringing Beethoven to the artisan class as the peasantry disappeared; and it is no fault of him or of modernism that his essay becomes all the more challenging now that almost no Europeans or Americans except for cooks and some artists actually make anything anymore, while educational 'pragmatism' (US sense) discourages many youngsters from bothering about Beethoven, let alone his Viennese modernist successors.

ARCHITECTURE AND ORNAMENT IN FACT

How much the critical problem of the notorious essay 'Ornament and Crime,' ironically enough, has been owed to overlooking or missing the point of Loos's sometimes quite wild and disorderly ironies. A friend quotes me from memory a remark of Kierkegaard: "The presence of irony does not necessarily mean that ... earnestness is excluded. Only assistant professors assume that" (*Concluding Unscientific Postscript to Philosophical Fragments*, 1846).[1] It is manifest fact that the less raucously ironic essay on 'Architecture' never stood in the way of Loos's producing architecturally full-fledged houses, despite rhetorical denials thereof in the interest of private domesticity, let alone unapologetic architectural *ornamentation* – creatively processed though scrupulously never 'original' (which would have meant gratuitous to Loos). It ought to clarify these matters to scrutinize two cases of undeniable architecture that is undeniably ornamented yet undeniably Loosian, the second of which, however ironically, is unashamedly a house.

Qualifying the denial of art

Regarding 'Architecture,' which dates to 1910, one reads in many places the face-value report that Loos disbelieved that building or even architecture as such should be accounted a fine art, as if that were so clear in meaning and implication, whereas in actual fact it almost invites confusion. Sometimes one can read, less sweepingly but somewhat more meaningfully, that only the house is disqualified from architecture, as rightly a private affair. There will be more on this; suffice it to say now that one has to wonder, then, if even Loos's own best-known building, the Looshaus – part commercial establishment but mostly a multiple dwelling – should by rights amount to architecture, or whether it too isn't out of bounds because a multiple dwelling, with or without commercial accompaniment, qualifies as a house and hence gets disqualified as architecture. That conclusion should be sufficiently absurd to oblige one to re-think what is at stake in the matter.

'Architecture' links up with 'Ornament and Crime' where it reiterates the crucial proposition "The evolution of culture is synonymous with the removal of ornamentation from objects of everyday use," this time embedded in a briefer 'Papuan' discussion which mentions tattoo as one of the ways the cultural primitive "covers everything he can lay his hands on with ornament" (OA 75). If there was at least room for racial superiority before, it is important to consider that now, while the same aesthetic point holds, 'our' progress is here more a matter of competing in our own league, even against ourselves. For 'we' are supposed to be "more advanced ... more sensitive, more refined" than the Europeans of the Gothic and Renaissance periods"; indeed – thanks to Jacques Ignace Hittorff, who discovered that the Greek temples had been painted in polychrome (at least the non-load-bearing features), to the horror of contemporary classicists, – we are in some sense above and beyond even the Greeks: "Our temples are no longer painted blue, red, green and white like the Parthenon, we have learned to appreciate the beauty of bare stone" (OA 75).[2] Even the blondest Greeks, then, in other words, had an architectural tattoo problem, which we have surmounted, or ought to have surmounted, just as we have tribal body ornament. (There is a certain touch of melancholy in 'Architecture,' a note of 'us' city folk as having lost something that it was still possible to escape to in the countryside of 1975, let alone 1910; but we need not go there because our task is to recognize Loos's project as a matter of high art – with which one has, as it were, to go further to find sophisticated aesthetic satisfaction than may have been possible with less self-conscious satisfactions before, while in any event there is no turning back.)

In 'Architecture' Loos's posture of preaching against architecture as art, especially domestic architecture, demands, at the least, the grain of salt that this means *architecture as he then dishearteningly and disapprovingly found it*, with its integrity seriously compromised: architecture in its pretentious turn-of-the-century bourgeois condition as a pursuit of pretentious forms and ornamental rhetoric, like so much trying on of theatrical costumes. The problem becomes even worse in translation. So many secondary sources now say that in 'Architecture' Loos argued that architecture is not, or ought not to be art, that we are hardly surprised to read the relevant passage:

> A building should please everyone, unlike a work of art, which does not have to please anyone. A work of art is a private matter for the artist, a building is not. A work of art is brought into the world without there being a need for it, a building meets a need. A work of art has no responsibility to anyone, a building to everyone. The aim of a work of art is to make us feel uncomfortable, a building is there for our comfort. A work of art is revolutionary, a building conservative. A work of art is concerned with the future and directs us along new paths, a building is concerned with the present. We love anything that adds to our comfort, we hate anything that tries to pester us into abandoning our secure and established position. We love buildings and hate art.
>
> *So the building has nothing to do with art and architecture is not one of the arts? That is so.*
>
> Only a tiny part of architecture (*der architektur* [*T* 101]) comes under art: monuments. Everything else, everything that serves some practical purpose, should be ejected from the realm of art. (*OA* 82–83)

But in actual fact, at every point here where this crucial text says "building," Loos, according to the standard edition of the text, actually wrote "*das haus*" (he liked to do without capitals). Not that Michael Mitchell's rendering as "building" is eccentric by any means: his version is now simply the most convenient example of a problem; and of course it is within the purview of a translator to determine word choice by what he or she takes to be a wider contextual meaning. But in a passage like this, which is almost as problematic as some biblical passage subject in the Reformation to polemically divergent readings, one can also consider Wilfried Wang's more literal version of 1985:

> The house has to please everyone, contrary to the work of art, which does not. The work of art is a private matter for the artist. The house is not. The work of art is brought into the world without there being a need for it. The house satisfies a requirement. The work of art is responsible to none; the house is responsible to everyone. The work of art wants to draw people out of their state of comfort. The house has to serve comfort. The work of art is revolutionary; the house is conservative. The work of art shows people new directions and thinks of the future. The house thinks of the present. Man loves everything that

satisfies his comfort. He hates everything that wants to draw him out of his acquired and secured position and that disturbs him. Thus he loves the house and hates art.

Does it follow that the house has nothing in common with art and is architecture not to be included amongst the arts? That is so. Only a very small part of architecture belongs to art: the tomb and the monument. Everything else that fulfills a function is to be excluded from the domain of art. (*AAL* 107–08)

Both translations keep the "architecture" of the second paragraph distinct from a house either as such or as a figure for building in general, so that an 'architecture proper' might be reserved to buildings public in function and monumental in scale, such as Loos's large unexecuted Viennese projects in a grand but plain, semi-classical mode, for a hotel in the Friedrichstrasse *c.* 1906; a War Ministry, 1907–08; and a Technical Museum, 1909. How, then, does their divergence on a literal "house" or somewhat looser "building" matter? The second version does not quite so sweepingly presume to entail architecture as such, but more its domestic sort, though it seems safe to say that Loos uses the term 'house' for any dwelling-place, including a multiple dwelling (in German, either *Wohnhaus* or *Wohngebaude*), with 'building' (words with forms of *bauen*, 'to build') on something of a neutral ground between the monument, with its symbolic/commemorative office, addressed to all, and the dwelling-place, which is private but interfaces with the real world and so should not obtrude. This is worth trying to sort out because Loos's famous paragraph is indeed drawing a distinction and not, after all, speaking of all architecture as 'art-building' (or not). At the opposite pole from 'house,' any substantial building not a dwelling might well be eligible to be a 'work of art': this is the meaning which seems compromised by calling a 'house' a 'building' in general.[3]

A sense of this 'Architecture' as still in some degree determined by the anti-aestheticism of 'Ornament and Crime' is apparent with a glimpse at the opposite extreme from what Loos is saying: the expressionist architect Bruno Taut's almost sanctimoniously aesthetic sense of the dwelling place in his remark in *Haus des Himmels* (House of Heaven, 1920): "A house is intended for nothing but to be beautiful. It is there for no other purpose ..." (qu., Quetglas 390).

Of course, the whole discussion of tattooing in the earlier essay, including such Western equivalents as the punctured curlicue patterns of wing-tip shoes, is an extended figure for aesthetically superfluous, yet culturally fetishized, architectural ornament – just what most Europeans and Americans in 1909 assumed both necessary and sufficient condition for an otherwise ordinary building's rating as a work of architecture and thereby of fine art. 'No ornament' had to mean 'no architecture,' and hence 'no art'; but the art of architecture was in such a bad way, owing to the ornamental misconception, that a strong rhetorical denial of art status, if necessary even in general, was architecture's only hope. For the grand assumption had been that it was historicizing ornament, above all, that certified a building at least a candidate work of the fine art called architecture. With that criterion abolished, the question arises of in what, if anything, architecture could now be expected to consist. An almost Schopenhauerean pessimism makes it seem as if almost nothing will pass muster; but somehow we as readers manage to infer that Loos's irony is not bottomless.

Since postmodernism a strange antimodernist alliance has formed, whether the participants admit it or not, between sophisticated 'anti-art' enthusiasts of Duchampian ilk and architectural reactionaries who had always wished modernism would go away. As a result, there is a curious interest in wanting this master of irony really to have meant that practically nothing modern will ever really deserve to count again as architectural art. The situation would be difficult enough for anyone concerned with the truth even without it being the case that Adolf Loos's essay 'Architecture' is more complex than we are usually prepared to acknowledge. Let us look at key passages in what is now the convenient English version of Mitchell, with an eye to the German original in Loos's *Trotzdem; 1900-1930* (1931); for even Mitchell's looser renderings helpfully oblige us to question what Loos is saying.

With this essay, the big question is what Loos really means, through and beyond the often ironic rhetoric of his discourse, by possibly denying that domestic architecture, at least, is even possible. At the risk of spoiling the fun, I would venture that what Loos meant above all in 1910 was that people (still) speaking all too glibly of the art of architecture could not expect to see what was at stake. But I also think, by extension, that much the same still applies, especially to those who would be perversely inclined to conclude that architecture might aspire to the condition of being non-art, and what an end of a great bother that would be! If Adolf Loos did once burst out, with the sarcasm that Vienna loves, that architecture is not an art at all, one thing he would seem to mean is that under the conditions of the surrounding culture it isn't an art, though by rights it ought to be.

In a sense 'Architecture' might actually seem to raise the bar for what can rate as architecture. Let us look back to another of Loos's early reviews of

1898, where architecture must be assumed to be an art because "it comes last among the visual arts," meaning, that they are accounted painting, sculpture, and architecture; however, it should certainly not be referred to the graphic arts, "[b]eing an art concerned with form and space" ('The Old and the New Style in Architecture: A Parallel with Special Reference to the Artistic Situation in Vienna,' 1898; *OA* 31). "What is it the architect actually does?" Loos asks here. "He uses materials to arouse feelings in us that are not inherent in those materials themselves. He builds a church. People should be put in a reverent mood. He builds a bar. People should feel at ease there. How do you do that? You see what buildings aroused those feelings in the past" (33). Hence there is something conservative about architecture, which tends to favor the perennial tradition, so that after stylistic deviations "there will always come a great mind, I like to call him the super-architect, who will free architecture of foreign elements and return us to pure, classical forms. And the public always greets this man with rejoicing, for our hearts and minds are imbued with classicism" (ibid.). Young Loos seems so rhetorically coaching himself to stand up to his self-assumed noble task that he almost doesn't want to face possible contradictions between aspiring to be "the architect ... revered by posterity ... who makes fewest concessions to his own age" and "the architect of the future," both "involved in the actual construction process and ... trained in classicism." This ideal new architect "must also be a modern man," in the "forefront" of contemporary culture, which he influences by his decisions, from "his conception of a ground plan through the design of fittings and furnishings." He "must also be a gentleman" (the word is in English in the original), which however threatens a contradiction, because the modern notion of an ethically non-deceptive use of materials is supported by the evidence that "the craftsman does not practice this deception," whereas "the draftsman-architect ... introduced it into architecture" (34).[4] Again: architecture as it is *versus* as it ought to be.

However, Loos has a way of purporting to set up distinctions that turn out to allow of considerable slippage or ambiguity. Where in the article 'Chairs' he says that London and Viennese cabinetmakers all think alike, but London cabinetmakers and Viennese architects certainly don't (*OC* 67; as cited in chapter 2), one catches his drift; but analysis meets a certain frustration in having to settle for the statement: Loos implies that while British and Austrian cabinetmakers are both good, Austrian architects are not as good at what they do as cabinetmakers of either nationality. Where, we have to wonder, will that leave British architects? Does it matter?

In a critical essay of 1898, it had seemed that *some* architects merit being considered artists: otherwise Loos could not say, "Sad times for art, sad times for the few artists among the architects who were forced to prostitute their art for the common herd" (*OA* 43). But then that should mean there are *some* who are architects, and some, at least, of their work must be art. This comes from 'The Principle of Cladding' – on a notion shortly to be considered in its own right.

Early on, Loos projects a situation where bathrooms and kitchens are designed from a technical point of view by specialists, while for social rooms the equivalent would be "the architect, the painter, the sculptor, or the interior designer" ('The Interiors in the Rotunda,' 1898): this sounds reasonable but it will not meet the exclusive standard of art to be set ten years later. And yet it already strikes Loos that the usual "contact in temperament" which client and designer find "does not go deep enough for the living areas" (*OC* 59). This is confusing unless what is meant is that the most private spaces, where we as individuals really do our personal living should not be overdetermined; for, as he puts it, even kings do their real living in a few simple rooms, not in the social rooms of their palace which are of course architect-designed. What proves elusive is already a sense of just-plain, unfinessed private space as happily beyond the pale of architectural calculation.

What is perhaps Loos's most famous early critique concerns the architectural eclecticism, or rather, the stylistic eclecticism of architectural ornamentation, of the Ringstrasse, the great mid- to late-nineteenth century boulevard built up following the line of the demolished city wall around central Vienna: 'The Potemkin City' (1898; *OA* 26–28).[5] But because his most Viennese trait was probably his self-presentation as *normally eccentric* rather than eccentrically normal, but also because cultural histories of fin-de-siècle Vienna linger on the pivotal moment of Loos, the cultural critic Karl Kraus, and young Wittgenstein, it deserves to be established that Loos's attitude toward the Ringstrasse was not at all idiosyncratic. Among Viennese writers who criticized the Ringstrasse were Ferdinand Kürnberger, author of a novel *Der Amerikamüde* (The America-Weary, 1855), whose writings interested Karl Kraus, and Friedrich Schlögl, who contributed a chapter on Viennese popular culture to the volume on Vienna (1886) of a great illustrated ethnic encyclopedia produced under the aegis of Crown Prince Rudolf, *Die österreichisch-ungarische Monarchie in Wort und Bild* (The Austro-Hungarian Monarchy in Word and Image). Both already "stress the destructive aspect of the rebuilding and see in the fabric

of the new Vienna a manifestation of the false values which they consider
to be invading its social, cultural, political and economic way of life. They
see everywhere the erosion of older genuine values and the triumph of
pretense. The new buildings represent not wealth but debts" (Bailey 64).
These are in addition to Camillo Sitte, who reacted against such urban
regularization as the Ringstrasse with the first classic of modern urbanism,
his *City Planning According to Artistic Principles* (1889), though Loos would
not have shared Sitte's favoring of a picturesque aesthetic which was in
effect just what his new Looshaus, which he thought was decently in tune
with Viennese urbanity, was accused of not obliging by those who wanted
it to look more like "Hicksburg" (!) ('My Building on the Michaelerplatz,'
1911; *OA* 100).

In 'Some Questions Regarding Viennese Architecture,' published in
1910, Loos poses the question of why the buildings on one stretch of Ring
are better than those on another. His answer is that though there are good
and bad works on both stretches, "both artists and philistines have taken the
architectural character of Vienna into account on the Kärntnerring, while
neither did on the Steubenring" (*OA* 66). The logical slipperiness here is
like that of the Viennese and London cabinetmakers versus only Viennese
architects. Also, with a court injunction temporarily forcing construction
of the Looshaus to cease, Loos wrote that when he had worked on the
Villa Karma, on Lake Geneva, between 1904 and 1906, and was denied
permission to build a porter's lodge because, lacking ornamentation, it
was too plain, he was thrilled to receive "a certificate stating that it was
forbidden to build such a house for reason of its simplicity and therefore its
ugliness" ('My First Building!,' 1910; *OA* 70). Pragmatically speaking, then,
he must have been an artist because he can only have been censured as an
architect understood to be one, in analogy with other censured artists of
other arts: "Now everyone, even I, had to believe it of me. I was banned,
banned by the authorities like Frank Wedekind or Arnold Schoenberg. Or
rather, as Schoenberg would be banned if the authorities could read the
thoughts behind his notes" (70–71).

It is important to comprehend what in Loos's writing is of the nature of
a complaint, a critical negation stemming from the realization that things are
not as they ought to be. In 'Architecture' the architect (in a bad, unreformed
sense), with his book-learning and skill at draftsmanship, has unfortunately
overtaken the master-builder, mason and other craftsmen in building, to the
point where "The Architect has reduced the noble art of building to a graphic
art" (*OA* 76). How this pertains to the superficial working out of ornamentation

on façades is clear; what is not, at least thus far into the text, is how much Loos means there is a better way that deserves to displace this mistaken academic sense of architecture, or if he at all nihilistically gives up on architecture and would almost rather abolish the term.

Consonant with his anti-graphic emphasis is his notion that his interiors could not be adequately represented by drawings or photographs; but here the true or reformed building, we assume, must count as architecture. The notion that modern culture was lacking its own ornamental style, as previous ages had them, and that in consequence architects ought to try to supply that need, is cast aside. The twentieth century has no style because it is assumed that styles are modes of ornament, and as the new century has as yet only seen spurious attempts to concoct new ornament, at least so far it seems to have no real architectural style, though that is not necessarily disadvantageous. Where the new century actually does show a style "in its pure form" is in fine wares produced by craftsmen: "tailors … shoemakers, the makers of bags and saddles, carriages and instruments and all those who avoided the fate of being uprooted from our culture because their craft seemed too ordinary to the false prophets to be worth reforming" (79–80), so that they did well all along quite without transient styles. Here in the context of craft, it appears that the dismissal of architecture as art is a critique of too freewheeling imagination. Hence, despite its grounding in an empirical 'workshop' view, Loos's harsh anti-arts-and-crafts view of decking out objects or buildings in 'art.' The rhetorical problem is that what might seem like an anti-art stance is a plea for an art that will manage to escape the gravitational field of all the bad architecture which *purports to be* 'art' architecture. This is very hard to sum up!

Harking back again to his critical reviews of 1898, Loos reiterates:

> I found modern paneling in the cladding of the old lavatory water tanks, I found a modern solution for the problem of corners in the chests for silver cutlery, I found locks and metal fittings on suitcases and pianos. And I found out the most important thing, that the style of 1900 [*and note that here there evidently is one*] only differs from the style of 1800 to the same extent as the tail coat of 1900 differs from that of 1800 … When I finally received a commission for a building, I said to myself, 'In its external appearance a building can at most have changed as much as a tail-coat. By not very much, that is.' (*OA* 80–81)

Perhaps, however, if a classic tail-coat is still a tail-coat, at least the older classic sense of architecture must still be architecture. Sometimes Loos's witty ironies blur the sense: where he caricatures the negative reception of his new 'Looshaus' on the Michaelerplatz by saying, "That kind of thing was all right in the privacy of someone's home, but not out in the street" (81–82), the satirical remark does bear non-satirically on the distinction he is about to frame that a house should rightly be too introverted and private to amount to architecture.

Just before the short paragraph consisting of the crucial question and answer "*So the building has nothing to do with art and architecture is not one of the arts? That is so*," in Mitchell's English translation, comes the paragraph with so many difficulties, just where one would like to distinguish as carefully as possible affirmations and denials of the key terms as house, architecture and art (*OA* 82–83). Once again: we understand that the house is private, and art is supposed to be public, hence houses are not to be works of art; and this is at base what Loos maintains, not so differently from Wittgenstein's shunning the notion of a private language, language being innately social. But somehow it doesn't seem so simple. Where we are given "A building should please everyone, unlike a work of art, which does not have to please anyone" (*OA* 82), in German the equivalent statement runs: "Das haus …" (allowing for Loos's renunciation of German noun capitalization), so that what is really said is that specifically *domestic* buildings should not be conceived as works of art (*T* 101). Eight times "das Haus" occurs in this key paragraph, each time rendered by Mitchell as "building," even in the already over-the-top exaggeration about loving one's house and by comparison hating art.

Lest we think we have all distinct at last, the next short paragraph, as conclusive as it is, remains problematic: "Only a tiny part of architecture (*der architektur*; *T* 101) comes under art: monuments. Everything else, everything that serves some practical purpose, should be ejected from the realm of art (*der kunst*)." (The related category of "tomb" is invoked less distinctly by the rather German Romantic description of finding a grave in the woods.) The more one tries to think along with Loos, his way, the more it seems that what people conventionally mean by architecture applies only to what they understand as monuments (unless they have in mind a vainly monumental house), and that in the interest of a reformed, modern view of domestic architecture (as real architecture) it may set the record straight to call a moratorium on the term 'architecture' in domestic circumstances.

"Since there are buildings (*gebäude*) in good and bad taste, people assume the former are designed by artists, the latter by non-artists. But building in good taste should be a matter of course as not putting your knife in your mouth or cleaning your teeth in the morning. People are here confusing art and culture." Formerly, "The buildings of the least master mason in a provincial town were in good taste" (*OA* 83–84; *T* 102). This, I submit, is a rhetorical way of saying that one could be a better artist-architect by giving up the customary vain ostentation of bourgeois architectural art. If architecture were sweepingly ruled out, as many now take to be the thrust of the essay, how could Loos proceed to say: "Architecture arouses moods in people, so the task of the architect is to give these moods concrete expression. A room must look cozy, a house (*das haus*) comfortable to live in. To secret vice the law courts must seem to make a threatening gesture. A bank must say, 'Here your money is safe in the hands of honest people'" (*OA* 84; *T* 103). Hence if the house as such were categorically disqualified from architecture and presumably from art in general, must it not stand, however para-architecturally, as a building category side by side with those of the most monumental courthouses and banks; and how should this matter, we may persist in wondering.

It may be telling that throughout the essay Loos has used the Latinate, classically evocative nouns *Architekt* and *Architektur*, and avoided the more Germaic *Baukunst*, literally, 'building-art,' and *Baukunstler* significantly enough, 'building-artist.' It seems odd that while, however rhetorically, Loos tends to squelch claims of architecture, and of the architect as an artist, he leaves beyond dispute that whatever buildings should manage to qualify as architecture – even if this meant no mere houses – are works of art. When Otto Wagner had published *Moderne Architektur* in 1896, Muthesius suggested that he change the title because 'Moderne' smacked too much of fashion (*die Mode*) and 'Architektur' had been spoiled by association with playing the game of styles in the nineteenth century; so the 1914 edition became *Die Baukunst unserer Zeit*, 'The Building-Art of Our Time.' But, at the end of 'Architecture,' Loos himself salutes the great German romantic classicist of *c.* 1800, Karl Friedrich Schinkel, by saying, "We have forgotten him. But the light of this great figure will fall upon future generations of [artist-]architects (*baukünstlergenerationen*)" (*OA* 85; *T* 103). All in all, and given the Loosian sense of irony and hyperbole, the thrust of the essay would seem to be that architecture nowadays is not an art, certainly not the art it has been in great past phases, but that it really ought to be, and that he, Loos, for one, is already working in his own modest way to realize that possibility again.

Later comments by Loos would appear to support this reading; but in view of a certain repetitiveness, I shall only give one, so that we can move on to two interesting cases of ornament and architecture in practice. In

'Art and Architecture,' a 1920 text in French, Loos approaches his closing with an interesting rapid-fire passage: "Architecture was an art, nowadays it is no more an art than tattooing or shoemaking ... Is this sad news I bring my colleagues?" he asks. "Have I caused them pain?" Finally, a cadenza of subtler ambiguities that can only add up to a critically buffered vote of 'yes,' that architecture is an art: "I am an architect myself and the struggle to reach this truth was painful. But I have finished struggling and today I am a happy man. I know I am a craftsman whose task is to serve mankind and the present. But by that very fact I know that art exists ... I can follow the flight of the artist as he disappears, like a condor, into the unknown—and I can pray" (*OA* 141). A decade later, in a text that seems somehow more social, almost productivist, in attitude – 'The Vienna City Council's Tenements Cannot Tolerate Criticism: A Conversation with Adolf Loos In Paris' (1930) – one must know its political occasion, and that the immediate audience knows Le Corbusier but not him, to understand the pressured, remedial concision; as if, a generation after the Looshaus, the reader had never heard any of this before, and this foreigner who has left Vienna in frustration has 'one shot' with which to explain himself:

> Only a tiny minority of architects have comprehended that they should be craftsmen and not 'artists.' For that reason tailors and shoemakers have a much more 'modern' approach than they. 'Modern,' you see, is anything that does not attract attention to itself, and is subject only to considerations of practicality and, I should add, decency ... Architects must finally see that it is not their place to be artists, but craftsmen, that their task is to work in the service of human needs, as does, say, a cook, while an artist has the right to speak through his 'superfluous' works. (*OA* 194)

A point of unexpected formalist corroboration

Loos's stance on the house as exempt from public art was early and strong, but neither unique nor eccentric; and what is more, it was perfectly compatible with artistic formalism. The dean of English formalist critics, Roger Fry, expounded a comparable view in an article in *Vogue* (London), titled with Loosian skepticism 'A Possible Domestic Architecture' (1918). Fry sets out from the proposition "Houses are either builders' houses or architects' houses" (Fry 272), though here 'builders' means commercial, speculative builders, whose architectural affectations, mired in stylism, issue in anything but timeless, non-stylistic vernacularism. Some recent architects, giving up on historicism, had "set to work merely to build so well and with such a fine sense of the material employed that the result should satisfy the desire for comeliness without the use of any style" (273), notably Detmar Blow (1867–1939), of Arts and Crafts ilk. But, like Loos with his discontent with Werkstätte design, Fry wants to get to the bottom of a problem of self-consciousness and sheer snobbery: "What if people were just to let their houses be the direct outcome of their actual needs, and of their actual way of life, and allow other people to think what they like. What if they behaved in the matter of houses as all people wish to behave in society without any undue or fussy self-consciousness"; such houses might gain in "character," and "instead of looking like something, they would ... be something" (274).

Fry had actually built himself a house in this spirit, 'Durbins,' 1909–19, at Guildford, in Surrey. He explains how he came up with as compact and economical a plan as possible, and observes: "So far then there has been no question of architecture," only, besides cost, of "solving the problem of personal needs and habits" – though with a qualification which Loos observed more in practice than he tended to admit in rhetorical statement: "the elevations are given in outline, and the only question is how the rectangle of each elevation is to be treated. Doors and windows are the elements of the design, and here ... something will already be determined by needs and tastes" (276–77). After all, even such practical considerations as window light leave some latitude for choice; "and it is through the [N.B.] artist's sense of proportion and his feeling for the plastic relief of the whole surface that a work of mere utility may become a work of art" (276–77). Far from denying the art of architecture, Fry took his experience on this project to exemplify how "a genuine architecture," perhaps even "an architectural style," might come about. Unlike Loos, he faces up cheerfully to an inevitable conspicuousness that was likely even worse in conservative suburban England than in modern Vienna and Prague; yet it is curious that the arch-formalist winds up sounding as Loosian as he does, even with some of the Loosian critical bite:

> My ... house is neighboured by houses of the most gentlemanly picturesqueness ... and naturally it is regarded as a monstrous eyesore

by their inhabitants. Indeed, when I first came here it was supposed that the ugliness of my house was so apparent that I myself could not be blind to it, and should not resent its being criticised in my presence. They were quite right, I did not resent it; I was only very much amused.

To arrive at such a genuine domestic architecture as I conceive, requires, then, this social indifference to surrounding snobbishness on the part of the owner, and it requires a nice sense of proportion and a feeling for values of plastic relief on the part of the [N.B.] artist who designs the house, but it does not require genius or even an extraordinary talent to make a genuine and honest piece of domestic architecture which will continue to look distinguished when the last 'style' but one having become *démodé* already stinks in the nostrils of all cultured people (278).

Essentially, here, the art-connoisseur and the supposed anti-artist of architecture agree in a sense, not merely on a 'par' condition for plain building, but on an ethico-aesthetic sub-par of works aiming at superiority by affectation, where total unconcern with art would have proved better in the end. The difference is that Fry, a knowing amateur (even as a painter, and respectably so), points up a visually prominent aspect of architecture – specifically façade composition – to which Loos knew very well that the art of architecture could never be reduced, yet at which he showed a conspicuous gift in practice.

A case of plain splendor

Fine material and simple form would not in themselves be enough, in a sliver of entrance wall on a busy street, to effect such modest splendor as Loos ornamentally accomplished in 1914 with his narrow but lofty entrance portal to the Anglo-Austrian Bank II, at Mariahilferstrasse 70, in the VII District of Vienna. Except for its beautiful stone, one might take this entrance frontispiece as simply a pair of insignificant pilasters linked by the form of a lintel – though once attended to, it may even raise the question of pilasters as such as 'abstract forms' of columns, which, after all, is the only reason why the lintel form, only negligibly thick and clearly not holding anything up, is not embarrassed, so to speak, to be nothing but a signboard for the name of the bank, itself as subject to change. No; what might have been a minor rhetorical entrance feature, more or less just copied from some Renaissance treatise, reveals itself as an unusually profound case of cladding in highly articulated form, consonant with Aloïs Riegl's turn-of-the-century insights into the aesthetics of 'East Roman' art, once it is understood how frankly the frontispiece presents itself as a composition in veneer – an almost preciously limited but very considered, case of literal *cladding*, that is, of the permissible, possibly even aesthetically advantageous, covering of structure by applied surface, something like drapery happily presenting itself as such on classical statuary.

On behalf of this marginal but far from minor work, let us consider its theoretical implications before entertaining an overlooked art-historical reason for its looking formally just as it does. In the important early essay on 'The Principle of Cladding' (1898), right from his initial mentions of textiles, Loos does not disguise the fact that the principle, which concerns 'dressing' a building with an outer layer, covering, but not necessarily misleading as to underlying structure, was first propounded by Gottfried Semper in his *Der Stil* (1860–63; 2nd edn, 1878–79), the long title of which means 'Style in the Technical and Tectonic Arts; or, Practical Aesthetics: A Handbook for Technicians, Artists, and Art-Lovers.' But also right from the start there is critical subtlety to be found if one is prepared to look: Semper had argued that architecture grew out of primeval textile manufacture when woven mats were hung up as space-dividers; Loos does start out talking about "carpets and wall hangings." However, in the view of the future inventor of the '*Raumplan*,' this way of telling the story invites a serious misconception, the "empirical route to art" by which architects project in imagination "not rooms but walls, the rooms being the space left inside the walls. Then they clad the internal walls with the material that seems most appropriate." That is going at it the wrong way round: "The true artist, the great architect [*a nice apposition for this supposed non-artist*], first gets a feeling for the effect he wants to produce, and then sets in his mind's eye the rooms he wants to create. The effect he wants to arouse in the observer … comes from the materials used and the form" (*OA* 42).

Having gratefully and politely put Semper in his place, Loos proceeds to reframe the Semperian conception of cladding, not as a fetish of truth to materials but as a semiotic of truth-telling simply by making a point of one's 'non-lying.' The fact is that what confuses people in Loos's theory of cladding is that it is a double negative, but it is very simply non-representational. To his way of thinking there is absolutely nothing wrong with painting wood (*contra* the low-IQ theory of truth to material), except that there is everything wrong with painting it wood-color or as *wood-grain*. (The cubists would carry this a step further by introducing 'authentically' hand-painted 'false' wood-graining 'on purpose' within painting.) So the clarified, effectively corrected law of cladding runs thusly: "there should be no possibility of confusing the cladding with the material it covers" (44). An additional statement omitted from the present edition of 'The Principle of Cladding,' which links it with Loos's discussion in another place of knit underwear ('Underwear,' 1898; *OC* 112–18), confirms the semiotic of non-mimetic surfacing: "It is thus easy to understand why the legs of our dancers when covered with knit stockingnets have such an unaesthetic effect. Woven underclothes may be dyed any color at all, just not skin color" (Loos, *Spoken* 68) – just as "iron can be tarred, painted or galvanized, but never bronzed, that is, covered with a metallic paint" (*OA* 46). Obviously *Bekleidung*, 'cladding,' still retains in German more of the textile sense of *that which clothes* than the English term does.

This notion of cladding is worthy of further consideration, beyond Otto Wagner's architectural aesthetics. Gottlob Frege, the early modern logician with whom young Wittgenstein had hoped to study when he first turned to philosophy, employs in his essay 'Logic,' drafted between 1879 and 1891, a figure of a "logical kernel (*Kern*)" encased in one or another linguistically contingent husk (without, however, ethical implication of the biblical symbolism of winnowing away worthless chaff, for which he does not use the Luther Bible's word). While we can return to this in considering Wittgenstein's architecture (chapter 8), in the present context Frege has possible pertinence for a special sense of the kernel's husk as like an encasing language so much like dress that translation of the thought-kernel from one language to another is like a change of clothing. The idea that if the same thought is to be expressed in two different languages, and thinking will be affected by the grammars of each (one could almost say, as 'software'), leads Frege to the rather cosmopolitan and Loosian idea that there is benefit for logical education in learning foreign languages as well as algebraic formal notation, for making one conscious of the "fitting out (*Einkleidung*)," in the sense of the clothing outfitter, of thoughts (Frege 6; also in the German, 6). In another text, 'Logical Defects in Mathematics,' drafted between 1898/99 and 1903, Frege sounds practically Loosian: "What use to us are explanations when they have no intrinsic connection with a piece of work, but are only stuck on the outside like a useless ornament" – where this last, "als unnützer Zierat," refers specifically to architectural ornament (Frege, 'Logical Defects' 165–66; 'Logische Mängel' 181).

But there also stood ready, if necessary, to justify Loos's Anglo-Austrian Bank frontispiece, should any modern suppose it nothing architecturally integral, only a veneer, the greatest of all nineteenth-century English architectural texts, *The Stones of Venice*, already cited for Loos on free fenestration (chapter 1). Loos had a distaste for Ruskin owing to his aestheticizing of craft as ultimately underpinning Secession 'decorative art,' which he despised. However, Ruskin, who has often been invoked on behalf of conceptions of truth-to-materials far more simplistic than Loos's, has much to say in *The Stones of Venice* about the wall as a "veil." He addresses Byzantine and Romanesque medieval stone cladding in a way that would have appealed to Otto Wagner (and Sullivan too), as well as to the author of the Looshaus with his sweet tooth for cipollino marble. But Wagner, the old author of the Postal Savings Bank – with its conspicuously riveted cladding – would especially have noted a detail of plating as visibly attached where Ruskin's justifies the "confessed *incrustation*" (his emphasis) of St Mark's, in Venice, as

> the purest example in Italy of the great school of architecture in which the ruling principle is the incrustation of brick with more precious materials ... [T]his incrusted school ... appears *insincere* at first to a Northern builder, because, accustomed to build with solid blocks of freestone, he is in the habit of supposing the external superficies of a piece of masonry to be some criterion of its thickness. But, as soon as he gets acquainted with the incrusted style, he will find that the Southern builders had no intention to deceive him. He will see that every slab of facial marble is fastened to the next by a confessed *rivet*, and that the joints of the armour are so visibly and openly accommodated to the contours of the substance within that he has no more right to complain of treachery than a savage would have, who, for the first time in his life seeing a man in armour, had supposed him to be made of solid steel. (II.IV.xxiv–xxv; Ruskin, *Stones* 2: 74–76)

As to Ruskin's cultural availability in Vienna and the Empire: by 1896–97 there was even a complete edition of *The Stones of Venice* in Hungarian.

The question of possible modern Byzantinism leads naturally, at the turn of the century in Vienna, to Riegl. Although Loos might have found too closely akin to Secessionist decorative art the embrace of Late Roman metalwork which now seems a hallmark of Riegl's great book on *Late Roman Art Industry* (1901) – for his own reasons Riegl opposed the "contempt for the crafts," as he called it, of art historians – he would have been more interested in the way Riegl set his course against then recent studies of Byzantine art as all too iconographic and insufficiently formal. This is a consequence, he thinks, of "the theory, usually connected with the name of Gottfried Semper, according to which a work of art is nothing else than a mechanical product based on function, raw material and technique." For Riegl these material factors are important, to be sure, but as vital challenges, not inescapable determinations.

A certain closeness between the ornamentalist Riegl and the (in a different sense) anti-ornamentalist Loos may not be obvious. On his return to Austria from America, in an important moment of self-definition, Loos seems to have shared something of the outlook of Riegl's book draft of 1897–98 and parallel 1899 lecture notes for the University of Vienna which have come down to us as the *Historical Grammar of the Visual Arts*. At several points the informal first text evokes the young architect from the same imperial province. "Decoration was no longer simply stretched across every available surface, as in tattoos or on the outer walls of Egyptian temples," Riegl writes of classical Greek art; "it began, rather, to respond to certain natural conditions of the work of art – what we now call the tectonic" (Riegl, *Historical Grammar* 111). With the question of the origin of artistic activity as fulfilling an immediately "decorative function" still "open," Riegl even speculates that tattoo might have possessed "some intrinsic – perhaps apotropaic – significance" (116). Loos very much shared Riegl's view of the "so-called reform movement of industrial arts" then under way, as a "desperate and clumsy attempt to reinvigorate the functional role of art by latching onto earlier periods that had been more attentive to art's practical objectives"; but perhaps now, "[w]ith increased intellectual and spiritual capacities, man may … be able to dismiss his need for decoration as merely an animalistic urge" (115). There is even an observation in the spirit of Loos's Peter Pinecone joke, that so far no one "in the furniture industry" had as yet "succeeded in 'making a chest of drawers from a pumpkin,' as an old practitioner of the now-obsolete reform movement once mockingly ordered" (183).

On other points as well, Riegl's 1899 lecture notes would seem to parallel the younger Loos (or at least they would have interested him), including the observation that "the straight beamed ceiling provided a more compelling aesthetic motivation … than the Pantheon" (Riegl 250), this partly as an adumbration of cheerfully dogmatic commitment to the flat roof. In the case of the notion of cladding, there is a likely common source in Semper (credited by Loos in 'The Principle of Cladding'). However, Riegl, Semper's theoretical opponent, might even seem to adumbrate the gloomy conclusive emphasis exclusively on tomb and monument in Loos's 'Architecture' text with his sense of "the oldest kind of architecture" as the "commemorative monument," specifically a tomb even whose rudimentary spaces of "grave chamber and ... corridor" were "necessary evils"; or a temple whose "interior does not reveal itself to the outside at all: it seems non-existent, with only a door breaking through as a necessary evil" (414).

Let us return to the beautiful as well as modestly small entrance frontispiece in sober dark granite of Loos's 1914 Anglo-Austrian Bank (or Anglo-Österreichische Bank II, later Zentralsparkasse und Kommerzialbank), the only one of several bank 'Loosification' projects to be put into effect, its interior now handsomely restored under the direction of Hermann Czech. But it is the nobly simple entrance portal, which is plain enough to be taken, even today, as only negatively ornamental, that shows ornamental virtue as possibly something more than merely a safe lack of anything bad. On the lintel face façade the bronze lettering which we see now, decent though it is, takes the place not simply of the bank's earlier name but also of an heraldic Habsburgian – and ultimately Byzantine – double-eagle device, for which a drawing survives. We can return to it after considering the portal as a whole, which I long took too much for granted as seeming conservatively close to general late Secessionism (even as comparable to a certain silver-gilt brooch from 1904 by Hoffman, as Loos would have hated to hear). Yet it turns out that Gravagnuolo was in some sense right to say that here even the casual pedestrian confronts

> the best proof of the validity of Loos' intuition of design: to impose an image of architecture along the great commercial arteries of the metropolis an absolute, severe classicity was necessary.
>
> In fact, the atemporal immutability of the classical is set up as a contrast to the speedy obsolescence of commercial products and the change of public taste. In this sense, in its deliberate opposition to the unending flow of perishable goods, the classical operates as a kind of clearing of the stage that translates into a progressive, modern communication technique. This idea will be developed further, and perhaps even more suggestively, in the unrealized project for a gigantic column (also of polished black granite), entered for the international competition held in 1922 for the construction of the *Chicago Tribune* skyscraper. (Gravagnuolo 154; cf. on the Tribune Tower, chapter 6, below)

As well put as this is, it can be queried on two points. First, there is a definite play with or against the limits of classical definition. Certainly the appeal to classicism depends here on the fluting, which we cannot say even entails proper pilasters, let alone columns, because the lintel-tablet above, rests content with being an architectural surface – though Loos proves to be very good in the handling of exterior surfaces. Here he effects plasticity by a kind of double-negative play with the inverted-pilaster idea; for in such a small area he is unable to indulge the bulk he likes except in negative, as a chunk of deep shadow set off by the crisply rectilinear frame on which he must concentrate all attention without, he knows, becoming 'graphic.' In this sense, the careful handling of the fluting is also likely an effort to avoid the decorative effect of run-on fluting as in Josef Hoffmann's then much, no doubt, discussed façade for the Austrian pavilion at the 1914 German Werkbund exhibition, at Cologne. By not respecting the columnar proportionality as defined by base and capital, Hoffmann's fluting on the exhibition hall façade might as well be just a blown-up version of the reeded stripping that even Loos used chastely in such early furniture design as his chest of drawers, *c.* 1900, now in the Victoria and Albert Museum. What good evidence, by the way, of the Loosian distinction between the private interior of the home and the formal artistic decorum demanded by the publicly architectural situation.

The Anglo-Austrian Bank's frontispiece is small but too telling to be reckoned minor. In his characterization of its generalized classicism even the rightly enthusiastic Gravagnuolo may miss something pertinent to the historical time between literal ancient classicism and the metaphorical classicism that informs much 'classic' architectural modernism. In Riegl's contemporary art-historical view, with which Loos must have been familiar, Byzantium very obviously *inherited* Rome, while what was only too obvious to mention in 1914 was that the Byzantine double-headed eagle had become the Austrian double-headed eagle. And just such, as it were, active flatness as this, this formal vitality in the sheer surface, had caught Riegl's attention in a Romano-British bronze plaque in the form of an altar, in the British Museum, and led him to speculate for nearly two pages, quite amazed that anybody would frame a pure pattern instead of a picture, on how the central field of heraldically symmetrical curls, not unlike either the Byzantine dolphins or Loos's tentative Habsburg double eagle, could be readily extrapolated out in all four directions in a fine case of what he called patternistic "infinite rapport." Here, conveniently for the Secession, ornamental art was being taken seriously; but here, advantageously for Loos, it was being taken critically.

19. Hagia Sophia, Istanbul, 532–37.
Southeast conch, southeast buttress,
marble paneling and intarsia, mid-VI
century.

20. Loos, Study for Anglo-Austrian Bank II
(later Zentralparkasse), Vienna. Entrance
frontispiece, 1914, pencil.

But I want to adduce at this point something rather more than
just another art-historical detail: a wall of marble paneling, or interior
cladding, with intarsia in one of the side-aisles, of the great Byzantine
church of Hagia Sophia, in Istanbul. Loos himself was proud to have done
intarsia work, as a young man in America (though I believe, with wood).
Here the lintel-like upper tablet and the handling of the fluting are the
obviously similar features. So flat a translation of columnar tectonics into a
compartmentalization of the surface seems in quite the spirit of Riegl, who
would have called the Byzantine example 'East Roman,' and who conveyed
such a modern sense of the breakdown and sublimation of bulk into surface
pattern in 'Late Roman' art. What a fine instance, too, of Loos's love of
naturally figured polished granite and marble as a mode of ornamentation,
at once materialistic and moved by innate beauty – *"Fine material is God's
own wonder,"* as he interjects with absolutely unironic passion in 1917 (in

21. Loos, Anglo-Austrian Bank II (later
Zentralparkasse), Vienna, 1914.
Entrance frontispiece.

'Hands Off!'), having first declared more school-masterishly, "One should remember that quality materials and good workmanship do not simply make up for a lack of ornamentation, they far surpass it in luxuriousness" (*OC* 182).

There is no need to track down the particular Alinari or Anderson standard photograph of this stretch of ground-floor interior cladding of the famous monumental church of which, at the time, most Westerners' conception of the interior would have concerned its mosaics as plastered and whitewashed over by the Ottomans, only to be revealed again under Ataturk at the end of Loos's life. The most vital evidence is in the carryover, in a preparatory sketch by Loos, of a loosely schematic lintel design. Though soon to be dropped, this consists of a brace of curves, in itself perhaps vaguely heraldic – and the double eagle of the Austrian emperors does after all derive from the Byzantines' – yet, on second thought, startlingly close in form to the brace of dolphins at the top (and bottom – where the bank doorway would intervene) of the beautifully marmoreal Hagia Sophia panels, which, though decorative, to be sure, consist of structures of principally architectural ornamental motifs.

Sometimes compositions like this are memorable moves in a great game, regardless of whether the players are even aware of the fact. What is here uncanny, however, is that looking back to Loos's project drawing undoubtedly showing the imperial Austrian eagle, the forms in question should so closely resemble the sportively paired dolphins of the Byzantine panel, which one all too casually assumed to be irrelevant. Yeats had yet to speak in his second 'Byzantium' poem of dolphin motifs in the court gold and marble-work, though Loos had already produced a chandelier type resembling a Byzantine 'candelion.' The point is not so much a plausible borrowing from Hagia Sophia as that the work of this artist who threatened to frighten the horses by ranting about how perhaps his art wasn't really art, or might be better off not being so, proves involved after all with the history of the architectural art.

Subordination of ornament to composition

Loos's Rufer House, of 1922, in the XIII District of Vienna ('Heitzing'), proves crucial for the Loosian problem of ornament, thanks most obviously to the 'quotation,' set into its street façade, of three actual-size slabs cast from the great classical Greek frieze of the Parthenon, which would seem to fly in the face of the architect's supposed abolition of ornament. (One may recall Le Corbusier's curious inlay of a blank classical plaque into the outside wall of his Villa Schwob, 1916–17, which has an even more prominent, simple but hefty cornice of concrete.) Then again, these Phidean plaques, differently sized but in an even row, participate in the irregular rhythms of the fenestration, like 'double-negative' windows, in a beautifully irregular fenestration that is different on all four sides of the square house. Set into the wall like gemstones locked into a common mount, the plaques would have pleased Aloïs Riegl, both for taking part in the fenestration, in what he considered a positive-and-negative reciprocality and also as a creative redeployment of a kind of ornament about which the modern Viennese art historian actually had reservations. For Riegl had written in the 1899 version of his *Historical Grammar of the Visual Arts*, long unpublished, but heard in lecture form in turn-of-the-century Vienna, that "even the Greeks were unable to master the conceptual purpose … [of] the frieze … When one examines the whole, one finds harmony only in the serial arrangement …" (Riegl, *Historical Grammar* 379).

Apart from supposedly contradicting Loos's own no-ornament principle, however, how anomalous really is such quotation of classical ornament in modernist circumstances, by Loos or otherwise? At least in more conventional cornice settings, Loos's quotations in cast form of classical ornamentation are no more anomalous than, for instance, Frank Lloyd Wright's installing as a cornice in the entrance hall of his own house in Oak Park, Illinois, of 1889 (expanded 1898), a strip of repeating replica casts after the 'Gigantomachy' frieze, representing the rather Loosian theme of the triumph of civilization (humans) over barbarism (giants), of the celebrated Hellenistic Altar of Zeus from Pergamon, in the Berlin Museum. The great source had been discovered in 1871, and domestic plaster versions were commercially available in America by the turn of the century.

Loos himself had something of a habit of interior classical friezes, not only the unusual vegetal example in the Ebenstein Tailor Shop, Vienna, of 1897 (retained in 1927 renovations). In at least one instance he even used repeating casts of a section of mounted horsemen from the Parthenon frieze to serve as a 'new' frieze of sorts for the large inglenook of the salon of the Boskovits apartment in Vienna, of 1910 (illus., Bock 153). There is no need to belabor the 'mechanically reproduced' aspect of Loos's resort to classical ornamental quotation, interior or exterior, not only because such casts were made by craftsmanly means, like the good hand-made reproduction furniture which Loos also liked to use, but also because he also made use of more literally 'mechanically multiple' prints, framed 'built-in,' as it were, as in the staircase of the Kniže haberdashery, or the office of the Manz Bookshop, as literally part of the interior woodwork.

More often he employed a figural, rather *quattrocento*, della-Robbian type of repeating, gracefully figural frieze, as in his Bellak apartment interior, Vienna, of 1907–13; both first and second Boskovits apartments, Vienna, 1910 and 1913; the Café Capua, Vienna I, 1913; his remodeling of the Duchnitz House, in Vienna, 1915–16, specifically the music room; the remodeling of the Strasser House, Vienna, 1918–19, specifically the dining room; and also his von Bauer apartment interior, at Brno, Moravia, 1925. Significantly for the problem of mere decoration, this more common Loosian frieze type resembles a culturally prominent contemporary type of ornamental glass produced by the great Moser firm, at Karlovy Vary (Carlsbad), in Bohemia, as Loos, already a Czech citizen (and eventual designer of glasses for the Lobmeyr firm), was likely aware. Under Leo Moser as artistic director of the glass works, the firm had developed, *c.* 1915–19, when it was trademarked – possibly from designs by Leo, who was interested in its historical roots, including Biedermeier, a line of hefty, large-faceted glass, bolder than Secession glass (such as Loos's bane, Hoffmann's) but at least as classical, and characteristically ornamented with a gilt band of figures in low relief. This so-called 'oroplastic' decoration, consisting of "wide friezes with figures of Amazons and scenes of battle between Amazons and Greeks," with such motifs "gradually joined by other variations with satyrs and nymphs" (Mergl and Pánková 99), came into its own in the first three years of the 1920s, when the Rufer House was built. In 'Pottery' (1904/08), Loos had declared against the likes of such ornamental battling: he was writing, he said, for moderns, not for people who "point to the renaissance, when people drank out of jugs with a whole Battle of the Amazons on them, either engraved or modeled in relief" (*OC* 151). Something such as Moser glass in its more handsomely modern forms may have influenced him nevertheless.

As far as the Parthenon frieze in particular was concerned, our architect was certainly aware that the literal center of Viennese artistic academicism, Theophil von Hansen's 1872–76 Academy of Fine Arts, presenting itself as an Italian Renaissance city palace on the exterior, stands a beautiful rose marble Doric basilican 'Aula,' or formal hall, banded all round, under a flat roof, with a strip of slabs cast from the Parthenon frieze. But for Loos, being opposed to academic stylism hardly meant being at odds with this touchstone of classicism as such. It was soon after building the Rufer House that he wrote, immediately after the famous sentence "An architect is a bricklayer who has learned Latin," in 'Ornament and Education' (1924): "The starting point for drawing instruction should be classical ornamentation" (*OC* 187). Why, one may well ask, if drawing from plaster casts, such as, preeminently, throughout nineteenth-century Europe and America, casts after the Parthenon frieze, belonged to the discredited old academic fine-arts system? Because these would still be exercises in correct and tried-and-true form and syntax.

And as with contemporary postimpressionist painting and early modernist 'design,' decorative friezes often have an aesthetic limitation, which, needless to say, the Parthenon frieze does not: a run-on quality, which reduces form to mere subordinate drum-beats, as it were, non-mimetic but interchangeably trivial. What Loos ordained on the Rufer House façade, however, was not a mere clipping from an on-rolling strip, as if a suburban garden slip from the Parthenon frieze in the manner of a common, yes, tendrilled, vine. That he uses three plaques of different size – in a sequence of narrow, wider, and widest – and not abutting, but with discernible gaps between, precludes any merely rhythmic on-rolling of the frieze and, by not disguising the splicing,

22. Loos, Rufer House, Vienna, 1922.

obviates any thought of 'unnaturalistic' discontinuity. That this 'ornament' can be said to be straining toward something more structurally complex as a play of continuity and discontinuity is confirmed and extended as the three rectangular plaques are seen, in stepping back, to participate in the more than surface-decorative, asymmetric-orthogonal fenestration across at least the two adjoining walls at that corner of the house.

Here, too, the 'public' quality of a classically exterior frieze, which Loos had earlier employed in rooms used for entertaining within urban domestic interiors, is shifted – inverted – to the outside wall of a modestly sided 'outer-borough' house. It is not simply the resort to classical frieze as ornament that matters, but its displacement from its normal grammatical position on/under/at or even *as* cornice, to a low position in the wall in active relation with the fenestration, even as sliced into window-sized strips. Indeed, the interplay of these slightly projecting relief slabs with the slightly recessed white window-frames on the street façade compares in poetic complexity with the virtually equational juxtaposition of horizontal mirror and horizontal window in the dining room of the early Steiner House as memorably elucidated by Frampton (Frampton, 'In Spite' 200–01).[6] In both cases, planar features essentially different in nature – even the windows as dark from without and recessed, versus opaque, and the projecting but light-toned slabs – purport, as it were, to share a common planarity. Such a device is very far from any recourse, even prior recourse by Loos, to friezes as so much run-on classical ornamentation.

What distinguishes this house among Loosians, however, is its importance as occasion for the fruition of Loos's sense of *Raumplan* on the interior. As Šlapeta recounts its development, while the origins of the *Raumplan* trace back to modifications of existing houses in the time of the First World War, the concept comes to fulfillment here in the Rufer House, for which Heinrich Kulka coined the term, and then fluoresced in the Tristan Tzara House in Paris, 1926, and attained its "consummate" realization in the Müller Villa of Prague, 1926–27 (Šlapeta, 'Summary' 78). Kulka actually introduced the term '*Raumplan*' in the first monograph on Loos's work, written in collaboration with Franz Glück and Ludwig Münz – the title of which, it should be noticed, does identify our notorious loose cannon securely as a member of the architectural profession: *Adolf Loos: das Werk des Architekten* (Adolf Loos: The Work of the Architect; 1931).

The very notion of shifting floor levels finds some Viennese cultural precedent in theatrical scenography, of the nineteenth-century but also the twentieth. The comic dramatist Johann Nepomuk Nestroy (1801–62; from whom Wittgenstein took an epigram), made dramaturgical use of up-and-down levels in a single stage-set for his play 'Zu ebener Erde und erster Stock' (On the Ground Floor and First Floor), of 1835. In modern scenography, soon after Loos built the Rufer House the Czech-Austro-American Friedrich (then Frederick) Kiesler designed his *Raumbuhne*, or 'spatial stage,' in 1924. Despite his identity as a Surrealist irrationalist, some of Kiesler's thinking corresponds with Loos, such as his sense that the architect cannot expect simply to extrapolate from the plan upward and expect functionality; or even particular comments such as this, in respect to 'Ornament and Crime': "[T]he needs

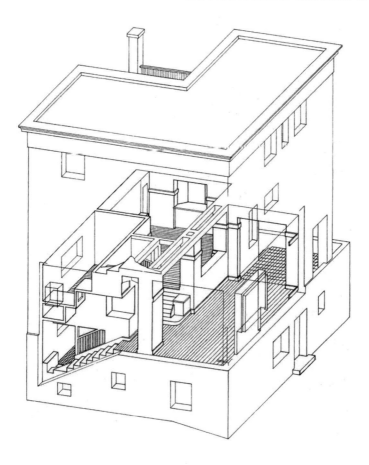

23. Loos, Rufer House. Axonometric rendering, after Heinrich Kulka, *Adolf Loos: Das Werk des Architekten* (Vienna, 1931).

of the psyche should not be repressed and projected on surface decoration" (Kiesler 735).

Commentators have often shown positive, not to say positivist, delight in saluting Loos as inventor of the *Raumplan* as a *device*, and such a clever one at that, much as Le Corbusier's 'pilotis' are often admired as the reassuringly practical product of a mysteriously incommensurable artistic talent. Every significant artistic *inventio*, however, has a prehistory. The house that in 1901 Peter Behrens built for himself and his wife, in the Mathildenhöhe artists' colony at Darmstadt, has a purpose-built music room with a floor lower than the rest of the ground floor and a ceiling raised higher than the rest of the floor upstairs. When it was new, Behrens himself wrote in a brochure for visitors to an exhibition of the artists' colony: "In order that the music room … really the principal apartment of the house – should be loftier than the rooms surrounding it, it was necessary to place the floor two steps below that of the entrance passage, and to raise the ceiling, by about as much, above the adjoining dining-room." Behrens' way of putting it, that the shift in level answered "spiritual" as well as practical need, by "lend[ing] a rhythmical movement to passage between the two rooms," was mocked in the local newspaper and satirized in the magazine *Jugend* (quotations, Windsor 20). Yet his expressed intent indicates a notable adumbration of the more radically but similarly music-adapted disposition of the music room and dining room in Loos's Rufer House. At very least Behrens' testimony disqualifies any sense that the full-fledged *Raumplan* emerged like Minerva out of the ear of Jupiter, as out of some sort of Romantic 'originality,' and (yet again) affirms this virtually trademarked Loosian device as continuous with the history of the architectural art. Beyond that, it certainly highlights Loos's bringing of the idea to decisive developmental form.

For here in the Rufer House, that categorical example of the Loosian *Raumplan,* the principal rooms spiral out, as it were, about a single square pier. Most conspicuously, what this allows is a music room, the major downstairs space, as supplemented by the dining room's opening onto it at some half a storey higher level, so that either those in the dining room might hear music performed below, or the dining room could serve as supplementary gallery for a concert in the music room proper.

Why, in this definitive case, should the musical space for music have had such a conspicuous importance? It happens that the house was built for Josef Rufer, Sr., a businessman, and his wife Maria, parents of the Josef who was a composer (Bock 218) and a pupil and amanuensis of sorts to the great modernist composer Arnold Schoenberg (see Rufer). Because the younger Rufer, who was 29 in 1922 was an intermittent pupil of Schoenberg from before to well after the house was built, between 1919 and 1929,[7] one is inclined to hypothesize a relation between this first house in which floors and ceilings were first definitively broken into independent planes in the interest of free vertical as well as horizontal disposition, and not only what Schoenberg meant by 'musical space,' but also his thinking – notably in the 1911 *Harmonielehre* (Theory of Harmony), where Schoenberg had "already pointed out that a note can be understood in both its vertical and its horizontal implications," in "musical space." In the book which he later wrote to present Schoenberg's music and theory to the world at large, *Composition with Twelve Notes Related Only to One Another* (1952), the younger Rufer stimulates us to think instead of how akin it is to Loos's new idea of the free vertical composition of room heights as well as the more commonplace composition of floor space in the single plane, inspired right here in his projection of the Rufer House, surely at least in part by the wish to make the music room higher-ceilinged and audible also from the dining room, with its higher floor as capable of serving as a balcony.

I had already entertained these ideas, and this very passage of Rufer relaying Schoenberg, in a lecture at the Edinburgh College of Art in March of 2007, when a year later an exhaustive study by the musicologist Holly Watkins showed that a Schoenberg statement in capitals, on two- and three-dimensional space in an essay drafted in 1934 and expanded in 1941, likely reflects an influence of Loos's *Raumplan* (Watkins esp. 185). A crucial shift had taken place in Schoenberg's work at about the time of the building of the Rufer House, from expressionist atonality to a very different mode of twelve-tone, complex 'spatial,' construct. Watkins points to Schoenberg's ever so Loosian figures, in *Harmonielehre*, of a carpenter needlessly "introducing flutings to enliven a smooth surface" or "certain master-mason architecture that sticks cheap stucco over every smooth, straight surface." Moreover: "Schoenberg made the source of such imagery clear at several points, mentioning his friend by name: 'This decoration with ornaments, "tattooing," as Adolf Loos says, is a childish activity'" (152).[8]

We know from his writings that when the Rufer House was built and soon after, Schoenberg was thinking about the relation of ornamentation in the musical sense – which is not so superfluous, even in his rigorous view, as it sounds, thanks largely to Adolf Loos, in respect to architecture – to structure as Schoenberg was reconceiving it. Based on texts dating from late 1922 and 1923, it is possible to say that when the Rufer House was built, as if out and about from its music room within the enclosing walls of a near-cube, Arnold Schoenberg wrote two texts dealing with ornamentation in the new music which, though not easily transposed to architecture, provoke thought on what seems like a privileged appeal to Greek architectural sculpture as potential ornament in modern circumstances.

Let us say that on the Rufer façade the row of three Greek relief tablets is a cadenza of sorts, according by size and placement with the asymmetric pattern of the fenestration. Then what Schoenberg says would apply here as just the kind of decision which would be left to the architect as supporting performer, presumably to those who build: "the continuo player" who "knows artistic ways to make the texture polyphonic without its being prescribed – a task in which "pleasure and utility combine" (Schoenberg, 'About Ornaments' 307). In other words, the Rufer façade shows Loos, otherwise refusing to rely on ornament to make for art, confident enough in the circumstances to take a performative hand and do something that uniquely complements, rather than simply obediently follows, the rules as he himself laid them down. One can even imagine Schoenberg thinking of the new house of his disciple's parents as he touches on something usually confined to the privacy of the Loosian domestic interior: "Surely people began to leave the ornaments out at a time when they still recognized them as subsidiary notes," as in polyphonic compositions with "the construction" depending on the principal notes, and "the subsidiary notes … subordinated … though in a way that is systematic, emphasizing the meaning and furthering character." An architectural figure comes to the fore, as the notion of un-scored but integral secondary material strikes Schoenberg as like "the way every house has its structural walls" (the Rufer House's exterior walls are indeed load-bearing) "and to that extent differs little from other houses of the same category. But it only becomes some particular house, belonging to some particular person with particular demands and habits, through all those thousand familiar things which are of course subsidiary from the structural point of view and yet are the only things that can in fact be of principal importance, looked at in terms which define more exactly the structure's purpose … Nobody would leave out the coat of arms, the doors, and the windows, unless he were ignorant of their purpose or had forgotten it!" (308). Amusingly apologetic for a non functional feature or two!

Watkins has noticed that eventually, in his late (1941), post-Kulka, 'Raumplan-aware' version of that essay from which, in fact, the emphatic capitalized statement, quoted first in the present discussion, derives, includes, apropos of the Parthenon frieze, "the confession that," just as much architecture is conceived merely two-dimensionally (as Loos said, merely like graphic design), except for Michelangelo "most works of sculpture strike the composer as a series of reliefs lacking integration" (Watkins 191). By then, had he forgotten, followers of Loos would have been able to remind Schoenberg of the three slices of different lengths of Parthenon frieze, like different durations in music, in the front wall of the Rufer House.

6

EVERYBODY'S DORIC

Long after his extended *Wanderjahr* in America, from 1893 to 1896, Loos, the anti-ornamentalist author of 'Ornament and Crime,' that brazen polemic against ornamental art and architecture, sent in his fairly outrageous submission to a 1922 competition for the new headquarters building for the *Chicago Tribune*. His design was rejected for reasons that used to seem more obvious when modernism was in full flower than perhaps they do today. In 'Ornament and Crime' the paradigm of superfluous ornamentation is tattooing, and while the tattoos of the cannibal Papuan and his ornamented boat and paddles are innocent, cultivated modern Europeans are supposed to be more sublimated. Even if one expected to argue that the classical orders are so integral to European architecture that they are not superadditive, or no more superadditive than other cultures' architectural ornaments, what could be more absurdly unlike any proper grammatical usage of the Greek or Roman than this proposal for a skyscraper – a distinctly modern building type – in the form of a single gigantic Doric column, on an eleven-storey cubical base. Yet while there was obviously wit in Loos's proposal, strangely enough it was not so eccentric for its time, several other entrants to the competition also having responded to the program with single monumental-column proposals. *Behold*, one might once have thought, *ornament total and absolute*, but from the man everyone thought had abolished any such thing.

A tall order

The office tower in the form of a single colossal Greek Doric column, entered in the competition for the Chicago Tribune Tower, must be Adolf Loos's at once most glaringly recognizable and yet also most enigmatic project. Maddening, no doubt, to the anthologist, is the signature piece that is anything but typical. How could it have been, if, as Loos repeats in announcing what he is presenting, the competition was for "the most beautiful and distinctive office building in the world," as distinctive, he adds, as the dome of St Peter's for Rome or the leaning tower for Pisa. In just what meaning or meanings was this response to that call grounded, one has to wonder – beyond, that is, what should be a most obvious Loosian one. For if Loos's projected monumental column for Chicago is undeniably, even exorbitantly, ironic, and amusing as such, whenever the giant column seems merely far-fetched or merely outrageous, we would do well to remember that where Loos had already speculated in 'Architecture' (1910) that nothing definitely qualifies as architecture except two categories of built work, one was the tomb, and the other, the *monument*. So, a *guaranteed* monument.

As Loos knew from personal experience, Chicago is not a subtle town; and, first thing, Loos was addressing it bluntly, very possibly in the spirit of Carl Sandburg's popular Whitmanesque poem 'Chicago' (1916): "City of the Big Shoulders …" Not that that could be the end of the matter, however, especially beyond Chicago.

This mature Loos project is in a way reminiscent, less visually than in respect to cultural history, of that other unsuccessful competition project from the very beginning of the architect's career, the church in honor of the Emperor Franz Joseph's jubilee in 1898. Loos's ideas for that work, developed on arriving home from America, include not only a massive pantheonic main building of simplified classical style – inspired, it has been suggested (chapter 3) by an important new New York building in Roman imperial style – but also, after trying out several different alternatives, an accompanying freestanding tower. The main idea is relevant to the Chicago project because it is another tower and because in its various projections Loos was obviously thinking of something monumental and monolithic in effect. In its own right, the Franz Joseph tower would have looked both vaguely ancient – as an up-dated obelisk-like shaft – and ultra-modern – Eiffel Tower-like – with its sweeping, shallow-concave (masonry) sides. One might be reminded of a certain lighthouse enlisted as proto-modern into the old 'functionalist' cause: the concrete Eddystone lighthouse, in Cornwall, by

24. Loos, Competition study for a Chicago
Tribune Building, 1922. Reconstructed
perspective.

John Smeaton, dating from 1756–59, already aesthetically admired for its unrhetorical plainness by Emerson in his 1841 'Thoughts on Art'; Siegfried Giedion mobilized it in *Architecture and the Phenomena of Transition* (1971) with the implication that it was admirable not for anything ornamental but on the contrary for its deferral to engineering. But the problem of ornament will not be dispatched so readily with Loos's Chicago proposal, which was not an engineering wonder but a sore thumb of art.

The history of art is a great 'language game' in which every significant formal move made by an artist (whether or not he or she is even aware), every engendering of a new work that takes on visual identity, at least potentially entails meaning by affiliation with similar moves already made anywhere else in the great system of works. Similarity of purpose, while unnecessary (some works take on inadvertent meanings), makes meaning likelier, especially if you are concerned with types such as the tomb and the monument. For instance, if you put a cylinder on top of a cube you are, whether you even know it or not, making a connection with the long tumbledown, so-called tomb of Cicero on the Appian Way, in Rome. But in that case you are also connecting, in more modern history, with something that would itself recall the Cicero tomb whether Robert Adam, its author, knew or remembered it or not: a rejected project for the mausoleum of David Hume (1777–78), in Edinburgh. It happens that in that case Hume was being likened to a Roman Stoic (Brown 393, with illus.); and though this might not finally connect with an early modern American office building, even there a certain no-nonsense seriousness inheres in the geometric simplicity.

In its, for him, ironically outrageous, classicism, the Chicago Tribune project combined two approaches, which as a rule Loos pursued separately: projecting a building in classical terms (not simply using columns as a formal device) and projecting a building in terms of radically de-ornamentalized volumes. Thus, in the prior year, 1921, he had designed the unexecuted Bronner Villa, with a Doric order, architraves, cornice, and double-symmetrical entrance stairs (as if deliberately re-classicizing his more 'Loosian' 1918 Director's villa built for the sugar refinery at Rohrbach, now Hrušovany, near Brno, in the Czech Republic); and also, at the other extreme, the utterly blocky and inert as well as utterly orderless, also unexecuted 1921 design for a mausoleum for the Czech-Viennese art historian Max Dvořák.

Groundings

A good century before Loos, the nineteenth-century American sculptor and architectural theoretician Horatio Greenough had insisted that the *obelisk* monument (1827–43) commemorating the Battle of Bunker Hill, early in the American Revolution, at Charlestown, now within Boston, had been his idea, specifically as against a monumental column for the same purpose and site (the obelisk form was decided upon by a "board of artists," one member of which was apparently an engineer-designer). Now one thing we do know about Loos in America was his awareness of the object of Greenough's claim, thanks to a postcard view of the Bunker Hill Monument which Loos preserved. The Loos scholar Gravagnuolo suggested that the thought of the Boston obelisk made Loos pine for the opportunity, expressed so funereally in 'Architecture' (chapter 5) to embody values transcending the mundane world of unsparing commodification, so that "Perhaps the Column designed for the 'Chicago Tribune' competition of 1922 is an even clearer testimony to the reinstatement of this idea picked up in the United States, than the picture postcard of the Obelisk at Bunker Hill so jealously guarded among his papers" (Gravagnuolo 48). While the Bunker Hill connection has also become something of a *topos* associated with the architect Aldo Rossi, as Gravagnuolo notes it was Ludwig Münz, half a century ago, who called attention to the Bunker Hill monument, publishing the postcard from Loos's papers in 1958.[1]

In the treasured image the masonry 'obelisk' stands cheek-by-jowl with a little temple-fronted orthodox neoclassical building – all the more curiously in view of Loos's early thinking about a tower to accompany the church he was designing. How "American," Münz remarked, was the abrupt disjunctness of scale and discrepancy of articulation between the two so dissimilar elements, how "*selbstheerlich* (autocratic or self-important)" in their obliviousness to one another. But this was not really so unlike the odd-couple pairing, in one drawing for the early Viennese church project, of an Eiffelesque tower with a church inspired by a contemporary 'imperial American' blow-up of a British imperial version of an imperial Roman pantheonic form on which Loos might possibly have based his church design (chapter 3).

Commonly overlooked, however, is the Bunker Hill monument's instigator, Horatio Greenough's, own homegrown American anti-ornamental theorizing in any possible relation to the sophisticated international anti-ornamentalism of Loos, with Louis Henri Sullivan maybe somewhere in between. It is not farfetched to think of Loos as having been influenced by the architectural texts of Greenough, whose own tracts against architectural ornament were to be rediscovered in the heyday of postwar 'functionalism' in American architecture and design. This was the same sculptor who had written so admiringly of the "Etruscan-like" charm of an Oceanic war-club in his *American Architecture* (1843). In an essay bearing the rather Kantian title 'Relative and Independent Beauty,' the staunchly anti-ornamental, and typically anti-Baroque, American (a type that seems to have beguiled Loos), frames, before Sullivan, a memorable statement of his principal doctrine of "Beauty as the promise of Function; Action as the presence of Function; Character as the record of Function" (Greenough 71). Advancing Greenough's general principle of beauty as happy consequence of a get-the-job-done character, such passages implicate a general pragmatic (US sense) 'all-American' aesthetic discourse of virtuously useful beauty, celebrating efficient Lamarckian adaptation to function, and ever evoking a Biedermeierish rectitude of the simple and upright.[2] Loos's buildings may look stoical, if not uprightly tasteful. No less a critic than Emerson claimed (in *English Traits*, 1856), that in what we would call his proto-functionalism Greenough anticipated the Ruskin of *Seven Lamps of Architecture* (1849); and it was alongside, in the very light as it were, of Ruskin's *Seven Lamps* that Greenough's writings were rediscovered in the mid-twentieth century heyday of functionalist theory.

Quite likely as telling, however, in the immediate wake of Greenough's 'American Architecture,' which first appeared in the *United States Magazine and Democratic Review* and was collected within a decade, is a passage in the second volume (1846) of *Modern Painters* where Ruskin says that the term beauty means two things: first, an "external quality of bodies" which typifies divine attributes, i.e., "typical beauty," "and secondarily," a "vital beauty" defined as "the *appearance of felicitous fulfilment of function* in living things, more especially of the joyful and right exertion of perfect life in man" (III.I.iii, § 17; Ruskin, *Modern Painters* 29, emphasis added). If John Ruskin himself might have read 'American Architecture,' even though it would have been an obscure source in Vienna, it could plausibly have influenced Loos at least indirectly during his American years – I have quoted Ruskin from a popular New York edition of 1885.

Sekler, mentioning the Bunker Hill obelisk as a likely stimulus to Loos, affirms the notion of Greenough's conception (Sekler 260–61), though without considering a possible implication of the fact that the admired plain prismatic obelisk was to stand specifically *instead of a column*. Greenough, however, was not the only significant nineteenth-century American architectural theorist to oppose a monumental classical column, with implications of ornamental-rhetorical vainglory. Loos may or may not have become aware of Greenough, but he has to have been aware of the more contemporaneous architectural polemics of Louis Sullivan. Not that Loos would automatically have taken to Sullivan, who might have struck him as possibly a fresh-faced new version of just what he was happy to be away from in the imperial capital, meaning, more or less, what was connoted by the Viennese situation and the whole idea of good, virtuous, artistically reformed ornament *at all*. (Escape to the other side of the world and what do you find? Another Otto Wagner.) Loos had in common with Gottfried Semper a certain respect for 'Anglo-Saxon' efficiency and businesslike rationality – a supposed virtue from a distance, but often enough patronizing when coming from old Europe.[3] Sullivan was practical too, but rather more as well! What, after all, in modernism, might be considered more like tattoo – but *good*, integral tattoo, as it were – than Sullivan's untraditional nature ornament, both crystalline and organic. There must have been on-the-spot respect for the hero of American modernism even from Loos's American years, of which he would only have been reminded when Sullivan was frustrated in his desperate effort to have his *Kindergarten Chats* published in Europe.

Especially in analogy with just what Horatio Greenough had *opposed* for the Bunker Hill Monument, i.e., a freestanding monumental column, Loos's Doric-column Chicago project may have entailed a facetious response to what *they* want – *they* being American philistines who think that architecture is the dolling up of otherwise everyday buildings with the plutocratic grandiloquence of the classical orders. It deserves reiteration that Sullivan believed the classical eclecticism of the World's Columbian Exposition of 1893, in Chicago, would set American architecture back fifty years; not until 1924, however, the year of his death, was his *Autobiography of An Idea* published, where he says so, blaming – this part of the story is not so well reported – capitalist cynicism for the world's fair's "naked exhibitionism of charlatanry in the higher feudal and domineering culture, conjoined with expert salesmanship of the materials of decay" (Sullivan, *Autobiography* 322). Now it should be recalled that one of the essays (first published in *Interstate Architect and Builder* in 1901–02) which Sullivan collected and edited (1918) as the (posthumous) *Kindergarten Chats*, a text exactly entitled 'A Doric Column' (chapter xvii) concerns a, to Sullivan, absurd proposal to memorialize the bicentennial of Detroit with the world's largest monumental Doric column. Taking the idea as fatuous, Sullivan treats it wryly enough to have delighted Loos, several times referring, in mock-deference to the diction of illiterate rubes, to the "the architek" (*sic*; Sullivan, *Kindergarten Chats* 58–60). Moreover, in the essay 'On Scholarship' (chapter xl), in the same collection, Sullivan writes: "When we ask an architect to build a memorial to the Great Lakes, the primeval forests and the hardy *voyageurs* – and he gives us a Doric Column, he is not a scholar, he is a faker! So, when we ask an architect to build a twenty-odd-story office-building, and he throws up a swaggering mass of Roman remnants, he is not a scholar but a brute" (130). So far, then, two significant American modernists of sorts, Greenough and Sullivan, have lined up *against* the idea of a freestanding monumental column, in Sullivan's case, specifically for an office building.

Given the sarcasm freely indulged in his writings on products exhibited at the World's Columbian Exposition, it is perhaps odd for it to be any less than obvious that Loos's once notorious proposal of a colossal Doric column as office tower for a major Chicago newspaper, whatever else it was, was willfully preposterous. I say once notorious because after a full architectural generation or more of postmodernism it needs to be explained all over again how this could have been pseudo-historicizing and, as such, an affront at all. And suddenly now, a modern century later, it has also become all too easy to be drawn to Adolf Loos just for being 'tough.' For his part, Sullivan, 'Mr Chicago,' who may well have influenced him in the oddball Chicago Tribune project despite his opposition to vain commemorative columns, was rather more than a sentimentally limited semi-modernist capable only of leading American modernism part way along to some sort of heartless, modernist utopia.

Both the column and its boxy base element are historically embedded. As for the great column: Loos might have appealed, for his 'inhabited column' idea, to Racine Demonville's country house built for himself in the shape of a giant fluted – though protoromantically broken – column in the garden called Le Désert, near Marly, in 1771, of which engravings had been published (in Johann Karl Krafft's *Recueil d'architecture civile*, 1812), and which indeed would eventually be included by Emil Kaufmann in his modernist classic *Von Ledoux bis Le Corbusier: Ursprung und Entwicklung der autonomen Architektur* (From Ledoux to Le Corbusier: Origin and Development of Autonomous Architecture, 1933), at the very end of Loos's life. In the text accompanying his competition submission Loos seems to have been anxious about proposing an "inhabited column," as though that were an oxymoronic idea. Part of his defense was an appeal to the precedent of Cass Gilbert's Woolworth Building, 1910–13, which he would have liked to rival in height but for a stipulated limitation in the Chicago guidelines. By 1922, however, the Woolworth Building was as much as 'taken': in 1916, Marcel Duchamp, soon after *he* arrived in New York, had the idea of claiming its rising tower, then not yet clothed in Gothic detail, as a special readymade for facilitating "fourth-dimensional" thinking by imagining the building, New York's premier skyscraper, and emblematic of

25. Sergei Chernyshev, Institute of V. I.
Lenin, Sovetskaia Square, Moscow,
1925–27.

modernity despite its Gothic ornamentation, as a giant vitrine or glass cabinet with everything visible from without presenting itself in the windows like so many three-dimensional "shadows" from the fourth-dimension (see Adcock).

To this day, the shock-value of Loos's Tribune Tower derives from the presumption that even a wildly overscaled classical column, such as it might take a Roman or a corn-fed Middle-American to conceive, is an ultimate touchstone of tradition, even of outright conservatism. While its sheer extremism, however, ought at least to qualify that presumption, Loos's conception may be, as it were, met halfway from an opposite, avant-garde extreme, if we consider a certain experimental form in which modernists were reconceiving the immemorial notion of the column, even the ideal column, such as the experiments, from about 1923, with columnar ideas, some inspired by American skyscrapers, by the 'suprematist' painter Kazimir Malevich.[4] One of the more interesting 'inhabited columns' of sorts is the Soviet avant-garde but low-tech, double-cylindrical house of stuccoed brick, which the functionalist Konstantin Mel'nikov built by himself in Moscow in 1927–29.

The plain cubical base with stepped-back uppermost stories was really, more commonsensically than one had supposed, to house the actual newspaper offices, with the 'column' element being, just as practically, a stack of small rental offices. To some extent something more than just a scale-less base for the colossal column, and more than a simple carryover from the form of Loos's 1921 project for a Max Dvořák mausoleum, this more earth-bound element finds a roster of kindred modernist buildings, from on-strike plain to class-act elegant. At the former extreme is such a stripped-down, stolidly symmetrical work as Sergei Chernyshev's plainly squared-away 'Institute of V. I. Lenin at the Central Committee of the All-Union Communist Party of Bolsheviks,' of 1925–27, as it was fully styled, in Sovetskaia Square, Moscow, exemplifying a declared 'rationalist' tendency dedicated to purifying architecture of such formal fuss as could even be found in architectural functionalism or constructivism, to which it was something of a more conservative, if not crypto-classical, counterpart. At the other are Raymond Hood's similarly blocky yet black-tie, bourgeois-luxurious British Empire Building and Maison Française, of 1933, at Rockefeller Center, in New York. Hood was in actual fact the winner of the Chicago Tribune competition – in partnership with a son of the social-realist novelist William Dean Howells (who himself was likely interested in the skyscraper, having written a play called 'The Elevator,' in 1885).

Purportedly, soon after Hood's pair of buildings any classicism in Chernyshev's work was rendered not-so-crypto by what could be considered a reactionary Soviet precocious postmodernization of 1937–44, when one Vladimir Teitel (1903–45) is said to have converted the building into a 'Young Spectators' Theatre': "The columns (sic) were given capitals, the building was crowned with a balustrade with obelisks, and relief compositions were included in the décor."[5] This account could be satirical, but it testifies to popular non-comprehension, or populistic pretense of non-comprehension, of even the dignified plainness and hypotactical yet 'open' order of the original modern work, quite apart from modernism of more demanding revolutionary ilk. In view of the later photograph, it seems that some time after its cosmetic Stalinist makeover the building (like many ex-modernist schools rendered 'yuppie-classical' in New York during the mayoralty of the philo-capitalist Michael Bloomberg) may have been fortunate to be re-simplified, perhaps as an economy.

Implications of the project

In that our Loosian theme concerns a great column of a building decidedly not built, we can begin with an idea of a negative columnar monument suggested by George Berkeley, whose eighteenth-century American house has already been considered (chapter 2). A few years before leaving for America, Berkeley had been stimulated in thinking of the London monument actually called 'The Monument' – commemorating the Great Fire of London in 1666, its authorship commonly but perhaps wrongly ascribed to Christopher Wren – that it might be good sometimes to erect *anti*-monuments, "columns of infamy" memorializing individuals whose antisocial deeds escaped less symbolic prosecution (Berkeley 79–80). And the idea of such negative monuments recurs in the fifth of the dialogues called *Alciphron; or, The Minute Philosopher*, which Berkeley largely wrote in America.

Loos would presumably have liked to win the Chicago competition, and the odd thing is that what one might have expected to be the eccentric colossal-columnar tower idea turned out to be by no means unique among the entries. Other colossal single-column towers were submitted by Matthew L. Freeman, Paul Gebhardt, and Erich J. Patelski; and Kruft has adduced some less momentous works already adumbrating the idea, including something it would have delighted Loos to 'send up': a freestanding Doric-columnar fountain by Josef Hoffmann, in the garden of the Palais Stocklet at Brussels.[6] Yet there was an edge to Loos's entry, something of a dare, with some anxiety. He closes his proposal text with a short paragraph italicized for emphasis: "*This huge Greek Doric column will be built. If not in Chicago, then in another city. If not for the Chicago Tribune, then for someone else. If not by me, then by another architect*" (*OA* 171). What, really, could be more American than this combination of idealism (it's great, so it must be done), pragmatism (if I don't do it, somebody else will), and sheer bluster. The design itself does have the busty, Chicago effrontery of a brass-band return to the America of its author's early days, where even today his renown is that of a cultural 'star.' Yes, it was 'rad,' true enough, though probably too much so for the businessmen's Chicago.

Loos's singular column-building had technical and even critical, as well as formal, precedents. It is a safe guess that before he left Vienna Loos had at least once laughed, on the Ring, at Theophil von Hansen's central-heating chimney of the Parliament building (1871), disguised as an Ionic column, which in 1902 Hermann Muthesius would mock as an unwitting "satire" on the prevailing artistic thinking of its day (Muthesius 58). Follies of Old Europe, he could have thought. Then, fascinated in New York, even before he set out for Chicago, by the new skyscraper as a type, he surely saw something more industrial than it would have been difficult in the 1890s for an architecturally curious visitor to miss, in Centre Street, near City Hall: an eight-storey shot tower rising over a conventionally rectangular factory. Built in 1855 for the McCullough Shot and Lead Company by James Bogardus, famous for his downtown cast-iron loft buildings, the tower proper was a stack of ten-sided iron frames with exposed shafts and connecting lintels and brick in-fill.[7] As for Chicago, we should not overlook, either, the opposite extreme: not the new skyscrapers but, almost on the contrary, the hyper-colossal order, or colossal stage-set of an order, in Charles B. Atwood's peristyle of the 'capitol' building at the World's Columbian Exposition, as so exemplary of the American passion for having the biggest of whatever it is as more important than authenticity.

High among possible American references should be the project of J. Graham Glover and Henry C. Carrel for another major American newspaper headquarters, the New York Herald Building, published not only in *American Architect and Building News* in 1898 but also in Germany in 1902,[8] and, for that matter, praised with a wink by Loos in his Chicago Tribune competition proposal as "true grandeur ... not characterized by petty utility" (*OA* 170). This design, however, with a fluted brick element, not really qualifying as a self-sufficient 'column,' fused to one corner of an otherwise rectangular office tower, seems not so much like the Chicago Tribune project as perhaps more loosely like cylindrical corner towers fused by Loos onto other rectangular main blocks, such as the Villa Karma, on Lake Geneva near Montreux, of 1904–06, also in a project for a House with Round Tower, *c.* 1916–17, a 1924 project for a hotel on the Champs-Elysées, and the projected house for Josephine Baker in Paris, 1927. But for the Chicago Tribune Tower, the columnar element was not to be an adjunct to the building, it was to *be* the building, for its entire upper two-thirds. Another square-towering New York office building will shortly take on greater importance under 'The Skyscraper Problem.'

We may forget that virtually all skyscrapers rising in New York and Chicago, with the most special exception of Sullivan, were expected to carry classical ornament in the mode of the École des Beaux-Arts, in Paris: that was basically what seemed to the powers that be to make architecture 'architecture': the Gothicism of the Woolworth Building was a later and exceptional metaphor for the new structural verticality. Also, a certain bourgeois anti-modernism in American architecture must have been encouraged by the two books published in 1914 already mentioned (chapter 3): Morris Hicky Morgan's translation of the *Ten Books of Architecture* of Vitruvius, and Geoffrey Scott's *The Architecture of Humanism: A Study in the History of Taste*, of which Loos at some point acquired a first edition. The latter would even more have favored a sense of high-class Rolls Royce classicism that always fascinated Loos, at the very least like a code to be cracked. Thus we cannot overlook Loos's Tribune Tower project as appealing to cultural conservatives unconcerned with subtle wit for its, to put it mildly, ostentatious classicism, despite its extremism as threatening 'good taste.'

Without getting into the Doric's old claims to a special aura: whatever terms one might prefer to account for its duality here, the column is both committed to convention and given to radical self-evidence of form. In light of Loos's critique of ornament as such, it seems that the Doric order, above all, need not stand at odds with modernity, not only in that it is the formally simplest order, innately eschewing the sort of sub-ornaments, so to speak, those ornaments *of* orders and hence ornaments of ornaments, but perhaps also insofar as it might be as unaffectedly basic, as given for the sophisticated architect as second nature for the best local practitioner (a subject Loos probably understood more profoundly than merely ultra-utilitarian Americans). Thus when the Minneapolis architect Leroy S. Buffington first conceived of the skyscraper as building type, in 1882, he imagined a hundred-storey tower like a giant Doric column, and in 1883–84, planning to patent his 'cloudscraper,' consciously presumed as a model column with vertical lines "like volutes," though this was not public knowledge.[9] In Loos's project the literal baselessness, in terms of ornamentation, of the Doric order, made the bottom element of the building significantly unadorned while respecting the protocol of the order – as plinth. (Comparably, the New York architect Richard Morris Hunt, better known as a Beaux-Arts style-monger, managed to produce something nobly massive, as if too sheerly hefty for conventional ornamentation and all the more modern for it, when faced with the task of supplying a *mere base* for the Statue of Liberty, in 1886.)

The basic form of Loos's column is so categorically Greek-classical that what also needs to be accounted for is more than its merely classic-revival formal qualities, Loos's respect for other design traditions being not overlooked but possibly underestimated. Obviously the Chicago Tribune Column would have read like a big corporate logotype from any distance; at the same time but less obviously, its single flutes would each have had Brobdingnagian fascination as great deep semicylindrical channels. There is at least one table designed by Loos which for all its elemental look of precedentless modern simplicity closely resembles 'classic' Chinese tables of late Ming to early Qing period (seventeenth century), where twin lateral 'flutes' between top and rail form a clear and typical element, plastically equivalent to the deep concave ring in the base of an Ionic column (being in proper Doric, the Chicago Tribune Column was to have no slab of a base), or indeed, columnar flutes. Joyce would have liked this, given his description, still remembered in Dublin, of Stephen Dedalus' thinking to himself of the bar in Davy Byrne's pub: "Nice piece of wood in that counter. Nicely planed. Like the way it curves there" (Joyce 173), followed by the practically purist detail, suggestive of Léger and Le Corbusier, "He drank resignedly from his tumbler, running his fingers down the flutes" (174), and then the more Loosian "His downcast eyes followed the silent veining of the oaken slab. Beauty: it curves, curves are beauty" (176). As pertinent to craft, this suggests Loos's appreciation of the already 'classic' (relative sense) modernist forms of Thonet chairs, which on at least one special occasion – for the Museum Café, in central Vienna – he was permitted sympathetically to modify, is the design, as Joyce would also have appreciated, given the amusing, mock-auctioneer's description of a Thonet chair (as seen by Stephen in juxtaposition to an overstuffed easy chair in Bloom's house) near the end of *Ulysses* (1922): "a slender splayfoot chair of glossy cane curves … its frame from top to seat and from seat to base being varnished dark brown, its seat being a bright circle of white plaited rush" (706). Otherwise apropos of non-classical tradition: the three-legged 'Egyptian' stool which is always referred to as a type indeed produced by Liberty's of London, is also a type of sub-Saharan African stool whose village production continues even today with a Loosian agelessness.

But we cannot ignore the symbolic aspect of the classical column, singular or in general, in America no more than in Europe. It is not impossible that the reason Loos chose not the obelisk idea but that of the column was that iconographically, since the old emblem books of Ripa and others, the obelisk stood, with Egyptian overtones, for princely immortality, whereas the column was, at least potentially, as decidedly democratic.

The motif of a specifically freestanding column Loos could have brought with him or found here, with a range of possible implications, including politico-cultural ones as well as individual, and modernist aesthetic autonomy. In America, there was the solitary column of Emersonian egoism: at the end of his First Series of *Essays* (1841), the celebrated 'Self-Reliance,' Emerson, recommending a self-sufficiency independent of inherited or accumulated wealth, without "foreign" or even divine assistance, and quite without political involvement, declares: "Ask nothing of men, and, in the endless mutation, thou only firm column must presently appear the upholder of all that surrounds thee" (Emerson 87). Even if he hadn't written music criticism, among other odd jobs in New York in the mid-1890s, Loos would surely have read Hanslick, the great Viennese critic of Richard Wagner, likening to "the ornamental column" (singular), in his widely read treatise *On the Musically Beautiful* (1854; 8th cdn, 1891), "[t]he beauty of a self-subsistent simple theme [that] makes itself known in aesthetical awareness with an immediacy which permits no other explanation than the inner appropriateness of the phenomenon, the harmony of its parts, without reference to any external third factor" (Hanslick 32).

On the other hand, Gottfried Kinkel, a German art historian as well as a poet who celebrated the revolutions of 1848, wrote much more socially, in an essay on the Hagia Sophia, of the column of the *schlichte* (straightforwardly plain) Greek temple as a democratic symbol: "All columns equally tall, equally strong, ornamented the same, sharing the load-bearing task, like a platoon of Spartan warriors who go decorated and festooned into battle; the absolute expression of republican equality, each part standing on its own, supporting itself, indefatigable because as simply constructed as the republican state"; even where only a couple of columns remain, they manage to retain a sense of standing stalwart (Kinkel 299). Then what are we to say, in modern times, to one huge, towering one, as singular as any Napoleonic memorializing or victory column? Especially in the context of a powerful newspaper, how can we not think, by comparison, of the plutocrat 'Citizen Kane' and his ilk. How different from the spirit of Kinkel, then, is the much more Emersonian-individualist towering individual column that Loos designed for Chicago, as if sending the natives a calculated caricature of *just what they like* – which would not have been ironic at all.

Loos's maxi-column was to be built up of blocks of black granite, highly polished on the outside. It would have cut a figure of striking elegance yet impossible to trivialize as precious because it was both ample and simple – quite in character for Loos. But this should not mean that we do not also appreciate the stroke of practically surreal genius by which he reversed the inertia of classical *cliché*, in particular the quintessentially romantic-classical *cliché* of Greek marmoreal whiteness. When Flaubert called the Parthenon "black as ebony" he was deliberately going 'over the top,' not only conveying (quite 'rationally') the sort of aftereffect of an overload of bright sunlight but connoting (quite as intuitively) an equivalent *overwhelming* (Masheck, 'Classical Sass' 173). Calling the Parthenon black was no simple negation but an overwhelming into extraordinariness: think of an immense *black pearl*, by no means defective and hardly grotesque but uniquely pure. Conceived as shiny-black, the Chicago column would have had the spiffiness of a great piece of heavy industrial equipment. Relatedly: its fluting would have pertained to the generalization of eighteenth-century rationalist forms in French purist art and design, appealing not exclusively to the political right under the French *Rappel à l'Ordre* (Call to Order) after the Great War but also to the leftist likes of Léger, such as the recapitulation of the simply faceted or fluted shapes of eighteenth-century neoclassical crystal in the 'abstract classicism' of the excellent 'Duralex' glassware, still in production – as a sort of Baccarat for everybody, like Stephen Daedalus' tumbler.

The 'skyscraper problem'

What is purportedly Loos's first sketch for the Chicago Tribune Tower (Inv. no. 0683 in the Loos Archive at the Albertina, in Vienna) shows the column idea as seeming to emerge as follow-up to a similar but less extreme idea of the tower as a fluted *square pier*, notably, raised on a high cubical base in the role of plinth. The form has a crisp *quattrocento* look to it, such as the fluted pilasters on corners, not quite free of subservience to the wall, in works of Alberti and Brunelleschi; a square pier made colossal risks losing its colossal point by simply turning into a campanile.

The part of this square-pier tower in the germination of Loos's idea is usually overlooked. Although it was left behind, it affiliated on its own with the development of the skyscraper as a type. For among the early New York skyscrapers an important one, known to Loos, was under way while he lived in the city, Bruce Prince's square-shaft-like American Surety Building (now 100 Broadway), of 1894–96, which was instant architectural news in Europe – as seen in a wood engraving published in Prague in 1895, while the building was still under construction, and eventually reprinted with obvious enthusiasm in 1922 in an anthology, *Život II*, of the important Czech functionalist journal of that name (see figure 26).

Now Loos must to some extent have been aware, even on his own, of a problem which the New York architectural critic Montgomery Schuyler had been pointing up with the skyscraper as a new and preeminently American building type. Knowing him, it has always been oddly easy to accept the peculiarity of the Chicago column proposal, and what is surprising is that other contestants, especially Americans, should also have had the idea of a single monumental column. This was possibly owing to the dissemination of the so-called skyscraper problem in Schuyler's journalistic criticism at the turn of the century, but especially after he published 'The Skyscraper Problem' in installments in the New York magazine *Scribner's*, in 1903. This was not the initial 'skyscraper problem' which Sullivan had posed and largely solved, but a secondary, critical affair of almost ancients-and-moderns implication: what was being pointed up as a new matter once the Sullivanian problem of establishing the skyscraper as a type was solved, became the new question of the skyscraper's defaulting to the look of a classical order, which, if it became unshakably representational, could hardly amount to an abstract form of classicism.

Schuyler had framed this special 'skyscraper problem' in claiming that, on one hand, much incoherence of design, especially between buildings, might have been avoided by acknowledging, with Aristotle, the necessity of a work of art's having a beginning, middle, and end, but also, on the other, that a tendency had developed to base this perhaps too literally, or, one could say, punningly, as "upon the analogy of a column, with its division into base, shaft, and capital … even conform[ing], as far as may be, to the proportions of a classic column" (Schuyler 559). Specifying the American Surety Building as a good example, Schuyler praises Sullivan's only New York building, the Bayard Building, precisely for not falling into it:

> There is nothing capricious in the general treatment of this structure.
> It is an attempt, and a very serious attempt, to found the architecture
> of a tall building upon the facts of the case. The actual structure is left,
> or rather is helped, to tell its own story. This is the thing itself. Nobody
> who sees the building can help seeing that. Neither the analogy of the
> column, nor any other tradition or convention, is allowed to interfere
> with the task of clothing the steel frame in as expressive as forms as may
> be. (572)

Schuyler recalls having tried to talk Sullivan himself, the author of 'The Tall Office Building Artistically Considered' (1895), with its advocacy of un-rhetorical functionalism, out of thinking that, because the ground floor of a skyscraper differed functionally from the floors above, there must be something equivalently special about the uppermost stories (572–73). Nevertheless, "The Bayard Building is the nearest approach yet made, in New York, at least, to solving the problem of the sky-scraper. It furnishes a most promising starting point for designers who may insist upon attacking that problem instead of

26. Bruce Price, American Surety Company
Building (100 Broadway), New York,
1894–96. Wood engraving in *Z říše vědy a
práce* (Prague), 1895.

27. Loos, Competition study for a Chicago
Tribune Building, 1922.

evading it, and resting in compromises and conventions" (574). On these terms the Tribune Tower was a bold 'evasion' indeed of the skyscraper 'problem': an extreme case of What Not to Do with an unflappable conviction of its own. Had Loos taken absurdly literally Schuyler's critical view of limitations which Sullivan himself had to transcend in practice, as just what they would like in the Chicago competition – a skyscraper as single, freestanding super-column? (Possibly the very proportional division of the building into eleven-storey cubical base surmounted by twenty-one-storey shaft reflects Schuyler's principle that what made the skyscraper possible was the elevator's doubling of the height of the commercial building, and then steel-frame construction doubling that [556, 557].)

The square American Surety tower critically exemplified what Schuyler framed as the skyscraper problem, meaning the problematic way that, once you thought about it, an office tower as a whole, with ornamented base and uppermost stories, and relatively plain through its middle extent, might inadvertently convey the sense of a single giant classical column. Loos entertained but did not, of course, decide on a square tower for his design; and this may have been why his very rejection of the possibility was significant. That his drawing shows both the square-pier and the so literally columnar final ideas suggests that one way of dealing with the problem was to literalize it before abandoning it: pushing the square tower as far as it could go, like what Schuyler tried to explain as a metaphor pushed to collapse into a mere pun.

What Montgomery Schuyler meant by the skyscraper problem was a problem because it meant that the classical paradigm from which architects like Sullivan and Loos had in their own ways boldly departed in the interest of modernist independence was back in spades. In proposing actually to build a prominent monumental building in the form of a single column Loos was, yes, being outlandish, even hilarious, as in some sense *going* impractically and outrageously *too far*, especially if by taking Schuyler's critical thinking literally – but not going in a wrong direction. There was something Nietzschean about such a whole-hog approach as an act of willful contradiction and resistance.

How ironic

Speaking of Nietzsche: in accord with a fashionable intellectual presumption, Loos's architecture is not only supposed to be nihilistic, but its nihilism is to be taken quite contradictorily as (a) a terrible thing for humanity, and (b) *so 'cool'*!

This view seems to appeal to literary people who evidently don't see much to look at in pure, non-representational art *or* non-historicizing architecture. (That seems harsh, but imagine if literary theory felt warranted to presume that all instrumental music was nihilistic compared with music with words.) Well, why should everything modern or even modernist be obliged to confess itself nihilistic or utopian anyway?

In the past twenty-five or so years there has been serious consideration of the limits of Loos's Chicago Tribune irony. Aldo Rossi thought it a European mistake to take the project as "only a game, a Viennese *divertissement*," in the face of its characteristic "application of 'style'" on a markedly American urban-monumental scale (Rossi 15).

What is rightly considered 'abstract' in Loos's approach is a drive "to represent what is essential in an architectural inheritance, to avoid idle talk"; this entails not a simplistic "omission of all historical figures" but "elimination of distracting figures," and it "works itself out through a series of filters and distillations – the flat is made flatter, the black blacker." What disallows sterile formalism is that such essentialization is historically grounded in an abiding tradition, though I would disagree with Leatherbarrow, whose terms I borrow here, in that I think that to be valid such an essentialization has somehow to be an authentic enactment or presentation, as firsthand and unironic, or not only or finally ironic, and no mere secondary "representation" (Leatherbarrow 8–9). All the more welcome, then, is Hartoonian's appreciation of the seriousness of Loos's sense of architectural tradition, which is both pervasive and perhaps double-ironically manifest in the Chicago Tribune Tower project as Gianni Vattimo-like "weak thought," not protopostmodern eclecticism (Hartoonian 54–55).

Just how serious, or alternatively, how facetious or sarcastic, was Loos's Chicago Tribune 'Column'? Frampton rightly emphasizes how a definite contrariness in Loos is manifest in this signature project: not only the confinement of the practical workings of the newspaper – presumed to be housed in the logotypic 'column' (partly a journalistic pun) – to the boxy base as updated Viennese "*Zeitungspalast*" (newspaper palace), but also the column itself as black instead of white, hollow instead of solid, and looming gigantically over the twinned three-storey 'true' columns at the entrance, already colossal by normal standards, with the whole consummating in a "transhistorical giantism of the modern American metropolis" as journalistically affiliated with the greatness of classical culture (Frampton, 'In Spite' 217). Frampton already saw the fact that the tower's "ostensibly load-bearing walls were shown as being built of coursed masonry, thereby totally denying any direct evocation of a classical order" – as "perhaps the most ironic aspect of this work, and the one that qualifies … [Loos's] bizarre but nonetheless literal application of the classical norm" (Frampton, 'Loos' 19–20).

The visible blocks of the masonry tower (the cubical 'plinth' building below was presumably to be steel-framed) need not be any more ironic, especially on such a huge scale, than the visible blocks of the would-be-monolithic nineteenth-century Bunker Hill obelisk in Boston, not to mention countless innocently homemade 'classical' columns of brick in nineteenth-century American architecture, sometimes even fluted. For the super-column to be projected in brick would not necessarily contradict the Loosian doctrine, such as it was, of truth to materials, if one is even justified in calling it that: Loos's principle was no materialistic demand for unmediated, uncompromised architectural manifestation of various materials' specific physical properties, only a non-prescriptive, rather more common-law principle by which one material was not prohibited from resembling another, only from being deceptive about it. Anyway, given that masonry is *supposed to be* load-bearing, couldn't it be a nice double-irony that the masonry 'column' actually held itself up? Also, to give credit where due: the distribution of spaces on the circular floors of the tower is hardly as crazy as it might have been: whereas one might have supposed many impractical pie-cut wedges, in floor plan only one room has no right angle.

According to Rykwert, who has expressed surprise that there weren't even more single-columnar entries than there were,[10] "Some critics have bypassed the scheme as a prank, but no one seriously interested in Loos and his work could ever maintain such a view." Rykwert refers again more categorically in a note to "the curious notion … still perpetrated … that there was something jocular about Loos' scheme." To him, Benedetto Gravagnuolo "persists in ascribing ironic intention to Loos and in considering the column a fragment torn from a context – analogous to Duchamp's celebrated urinal," whereas for Rykwert, Loos's sense that moderns, like the Romans vis-à-vis the Greeks, inherited a situation in which ornament could no longer be invented but only adapted, is "quite different from Duchamp's view of the artist's power to isolate and reveal by his or her choice" (Rykwert, *Dancing Column*, 397 n. 51). Yet perhaps it is not so different from Duchamp's attenuated fin-de-siècle sense of everything's having already been done. Earlier, Rykwert had said that the Tribune column, though "wholly serious", was "the crassest" of his resorts to classical ornament (Rykwert, 'Adolf Loos' 71). Hesitating to concede any crassness in my hero, I prefer to hold to the view that there must be some irreducible element of irony without letting irony take over, as it does with Duchamp. With Loos the 'last laugh' is not a laugh.

Rykwert is right that Loos's Doric column proposal was no *mere* joke (though again one might say that none of Loos's recorded jokes was a mere joke); but to pit Loos's design against Duchamp's readymades weakens the case rather than reinforces it because the readymades are widely understood *not only* as witticisms of a curiously concrete sort but as 'moves' in and about the game of art, which are of significance to serious aesthetics, as amusing as it admittedly is that such seemingly slight cause can produce such a formidable stir. Rykwert is certainly right that the Chicago Tribune Column is a serious work of architectural art; but we must allow that in a different, and inexhaustibly ironic yet logically respectable sense, Duchamp's readymades *only make* art-sense, if only for having nothing else to do. As for Loos, there was certainly room for spoof in view of the inevitably problematic reception he could reasonably have expected at the hands of the commercial owners of the great Chicago newspaper.

It would be impossible to maintain that the Chicago Tribune Tower was *without* irony, at least with a straight face, i.e., impossible without thereby indulging in irony oneself. Yes, one may take the Doric-columnar tower as in some sense a cultural 'return of the repressed' in relation to the basic thrust of modernism against the ornamental vocabulary of academic classicism (if not unconditionally the syntax); yet, as it should be preposterous to imagine Loos unaware of that, it should also be to think of him as unaware that there would be good reason for others to take it that way, regardless of his private intentions. But there should be no 'repressed' to speak of if only the academic legalism, but manifestly not the spirit of the law, was negated. Besides, didn't Wittgenstein say that a whole philosophy could be written in the form of a joke book?

All the irony one can detect in Loos's Chicago Tribune project only goes in the end to highlight its specialness as a building project because, however we inquire into the problem – and in light of the Schuyler theory, this work is even a problem about a problem – we see that something architecturally serious is at stake in it. As a monument *par excellence*, in one way or another to the greatest American typological contribution to architecture, the skyscraper, the Tribune Tower qualifies by the very Loosian standard which may have seemed impossibly high to demand of true architecture: that of the tomb or monument. But it qualifies by far more than a technicality by showing, exemplifying, if in an admittedly witty manner, how belonging to the art of architecture is not to be taken for granted as an ordinary, everyday, condition for a building. Dyed-in-the-wool functionalists, of whom Loos has on occasion been deemed progenitor, know something about that too, being so often in the position of denying that architecture is or should be an art, only to find themselves in the position of having to acknowledge masterpieces of their own ilk as well. So one can hardly decide if it was by a double irony or only a single one that, as soon as Loos's tower project was promulgated, it was declared by Adolf Behne, a doctrinaire German functionalist, one of the architect's "most important works" (Behne 135n).

In the wider world

What sort of *historia* is all this amounting to, anyway? I find myself arguing that Loos's giant column, which was never built in Chicago, owes something to a giant column which Sullivan did not want built in Detroit even as Sullivan, and Loos too, for that matter, were following in the line of the very Greenough who did not want a giant column built in Boston. But history is, so to speak, there already. As a modern type, the freestanding monumental column also inevitably connotes the imperial Romanism of Napoleon and as such ambivalences of him who was either the first Lenin, or else the first Hitler (and after postmodernism the difference is not even supposed to matter), that radical commoner-turned-emperor – or was it just that ultimate self-made man? There is no escaping the complexities of iconology, either: obelisks as alternatives are not simply Washingtonian and republican, antimonarchically *Europa-frei*, but also practically Hanoverian (e.g., Vanbrugh's obelisk of dynastic identification at Castle Howard) if not freemasonically Egyptoid and socially consensus-monolithic.

How all the more apt, then, in retrospect, for the first great modern instance *not* to have been Napoleon's own great column in the Place Vendôme (for whose *symbolic obliteration* during the Commune Courbet was billed) but rather that expressly anti-Napoleonic Doric 'Nelson Pillar' (1808) in the center of what is now O'Connell Street in Dublin, destroyed just a generation ago (presumably by republicans whose children may now be wizards of the merchant banks). Standing 134 feet tall until the night of 7–8 March 1966, its upper part was then eliminated, after which the rest was demolished by the army. What seems strange now are (a) that political dissociation from Britain was still so much stronger than economic re-affiliation that no one dared move to 'restore' a Nelsonian status quo (or even think of fixing the thing and putting, maybe, James Connolly on top);

and (b) that, despite the high popularity in humanist circles from the pillar's cultural moment of the romantic idea of the 'broken column,' it should not have been decided to keep it precisely as a ruin-as-such. So deep was the high-cultural *ressentiment*, however, that destructive self-deprivation somehow seemed the right thing (no doubt reinforced by the presumption that the regular army must have the last word over and against the underground army). How strange, at this distance in time, that in a country where many would have counted themselves as socialists, nobody felt that what was being effaced was theirs (had *they* not *built* it?), something they were entitled to inherit, subsume, or surmount.

Well, then, how charmingly conflicted it already was when, but one fictional century after the Nelson Pillar was erected – and only told in print in the very year of Loos's 'notion,' as the Irish say, for the Chicago Tribune offices as a gigantic newspaper 'column' – a quite counterfactual pair of spinsters in Joyce's *Ulysses* make a special day in 1904 of it, going up the Nelson Pillar so as to look down and then not wanting to look down, all in newspaper report as if at second textual hand. For Stephen Daedalus finds himself in the noisy Dublin newspaper office while stories are being composed seemingly aloud, one interrupting another, with draft headlines shouted out, one of them being 'HIS NATIVE DORIC' (Joyce 126).[11] Woven into all this is a 'human-interest' story of the two ladies' eventful day out:

> – They want to see the views of Dublin from the top of Nelson's pillar … They put on their bonnets and best clothes and take their umbrellas for fear it may come on to rain …
> – … They give two threepenny bits to the gentleman at the turnstile and begin to waddle slowly up the winding staircase, grunting, encouraging each other, afraid of the dark, panting, one asking the other have you the bawn, praising God and the Blessed Virgin, threatening to come down, peeping at the airslits. Glory be to God. They had no idea it was that high …
> – Something for you, the professor explained to Myles Crawford. Two old Dublin women on the top of Nelson's pillar.
> SOME COLUMN! – THAT'S WHAT WADDLER ONE SAID
> – That's new, Myles Crawford said. That's copy … (145, 147)

Some Doric column indeed, and some Joycean 'copy,' too (Paris to Dublin) – and as much as seconded in architecture (Vienna to Chicago) by Adolf Loos in 1922.[12]

7

ARCHITECTURELESSNESS
AND SUSTAINABLE ART

For Adolf Loos as a great modernist, the notion of a valid modern style was curiously elusive. Somehow, in his day at least, it was there for the taking all around one, in all well-handmade things whose makers' thinking never wandered into stylistics – style as such being, at least as soon as you see it as such, an affectation. Such makers only thought in a craft-based, do-the-job-right way of making things well, starting with good materials and respecting those materials in their work processes, especially by not adding ornamentation, above all not the kind of ornament supposed to be an entertaining distraction from plainness or compensation for it. On the theoretical plane, it is often said that this view derives from Gottfried Semper's materialist theory of the interplay of raw material, technique and purpose, though it might come closer to the Loosian truth to associate it, in contemporary Vienna, with Aloïs Riegl's formalist critique of Semper, in which such factors are only negative limits to art-making as something much larger and slower, with a way of its own, that is not so mechanical. Thus in *Late Roman Art Industry* (1901) the formalist Riegl sounds almost Loosian where he compares with the function or "purpose (*Zweck*)" of the ("external") iconographic content of representational art, the less meaning-beholden utilary function of craft and architectural works (Riegl, *Art Industry* 127; *Kunstindustrie* 229).

An architecturelessness beyond style?

In the face of a Loosian sense of stylelessness — a sense that if there is a valid contemporary style it is nothing novel and is somehow coming out of the woodwork, at least good woodwork, and will be seen as style only as such is put aside — one can wonder what architecturelessness might be like.[1] Like Loos going on with his work, whatever he says, we may pick up on what he means by rhetorically denying that the architect is or should be an artist, and denying that architecture should almost not have anything to do with a house. It should be all the more interesting to watch for him showing his true colors in just the sort of fix-it-up or do-the-job tasks that one might mistakenly have supposed were only quasi-architectural. In actual fact, this architect's most significant early works — the Café Museum, in Vienna, the Villa Karma, near Montreux; the Kärtner, or American Bar, in Vienna — were all remodelings. Beyond the circumstances of a career, however (including apartment interiors), the remodeling of entire houses and the design of economical social housing warrant attention in regard to extremes of artfulness and architecturelessness. Together such works begin to suggest that the citified Loos, with his rhetorical notion of almost nothing's rating as proper architecture, had a surprisingly 'green' side.

After speculating briefly on Loos's own, would-be stylelessly modern style, not as a strain of perennial classicism even though akin to the domesticated neoclassicism of the old Biedermeier, we can entertain the possibility of 'architecturelessness' as a way of coming to terms with Loos's rhetorical denial that most buildings designed by people who call themselves architects amount to architecture at all. Then we can turn, complementarily, to Loos's most practical and green works in the remodeling of existing houses in the period of the Great War — remembering that the house per se is purportedly not an occasion for architecture — and in social or 'public' housing over several postwar years. Here is a humbler Loos than we usually think about, but possibly no less an artist and certainly no less an architect.

Disassociating himself from the start from what his contemporaries considered to be architecture, above all whatever they were all too ready to consider 'modern' architecture, Loos identified with the condition of the craftsman before professed architects and 'artistic' designers went ruining the crafts by presuming to impose upon them often decadent, arbitrarily arty forms. Just what Loos meant by trying to tell himself and others that he was or was not trying to be more of a craftsman and less of an architect is problematic; but something may be gleaned of it in considering two crafted objects, both clocks, one designed by Loos himself, who probably knew that, long before the rise of engineering, clockmaking, which we think of as a mere craft, was considered by Vitruvius in *Ten Books of Architecture,* the only surviving ancient architectural treatise, along with the construction of machines and buildings, as one of only three sub-disciplines of architecture (I.iii.1). Loos's mantle clock, of brass, copper and cut glass, from *c.* 1902, exists in several examples. The other, dating from about the 1780s, is from the workshop of the great neoclassical furniture designer David Roentgen (Metropolitan Museum of Art, New York). Within the micro-architectural framing of its handsome box, the circular face of Roentgen's clock, with works hidden away behind, comes up flush with the façade, of sorts, of its boxy casing, hinting at being a thin disk resting weightlessly atop six slim brass rods which are hardly more than lines. This compares with the way Loos counterintuitively 'suspends' his cylindrical clock works, compact but weighty, by being screwed to the thick plate glass back of his canted transparent casing; and what seems truly Loosian about this is the way the technical serves a non-technical, no two ways about it, *aesthetic* effect.

In a 1929 review of a monograph on David Roentgen (and his brother) Loos has admiring words for him, and he would also have been interested in his German-speaking Moravian background, like Loos's own:

> Throughout my life David Roentgen has been one of my idols, although all I knew of him was that he lived and sold Catherine the Great a desk for 20,000 thalers, which she found so ridiculously cheap that she increased the price. Probably no one has told this story as often and as consistently as I have. I am convinced that with this kind of recognition craftwork would flourish. (*OA* 190–91)

Here he means, in line with his most famous text, 'Ornament and Crime,' patrons who would pay more for something so simply well made that it looks all the better for not harboring wasteful and distracting ornamentation. Yet he also appreciates the understated perfection of the cabinetry per se, speaking as one who enjoyed his own experience in a marquetry workshop in America, and observes in a telling passage, "in David Roentgen's time there were modern people such as only our engineers and tailors are today" (192).

Impatient non-art folk might call both works 'minimal' and be done with it; but that will not do here, neither critically nor art-historically. Historically speaking, neoclassicism allowed, in between Roentgen and Loos, for a middle-class adaptation which often proves relevant to Loos: the Biedermeier, that commonsensical, sit-up-straight, anti-French style of bourgeois rectitude, with origins in the *Empire* but eschewing Napoleonic pomposity, which thrived in Germanic Europe between the Congress of Vienna and the revolutions of 1848. Thus, for example, while neoclassicism underwrites the simple but hefty forms of Leo von Klenze's 1825 interior hall of the Bavarian Royal and National Theater in Munich (with a touch of stately sentiment that is itself Biedermeier), the public, princely grandeur of that finds a more private, chamber-music-like counterpart with much more reticent simple detail in an 1831 Biedermeier interior, painted with what is itself a limpid Biedermeier pictorial descriptiveness by one L. C. Hofmeister, of *Emperor Franz I in His Study* (Austrian Museum of Applied Arts, Vienna). Loos must have been somewhat conflicted on this subject because, while he didn't want to play the style game, Biedermeier, with the likes of Roentgen behind it, was probably something like his idea of just-plain style, the closest one could expect to come in European historical time to trans-stylistic modernity.

A good architectural example of the Germanic neoclassical on the threshold of Biedermeier has already been noted, David Gilly's Vieweg Press, at Brunswick, of 1800–07, standing as a significant precedent, at least *ex post facto*, for Loos's most famous and indeed notorious building, the Looshaus on the Michaelerplatz, in Vienna of 1909–11 (chapter 1). The lower part of the Looshaus was purpose-designed as substantial quarters for the gentlemen's tailors Goldman & Salatsch, including a tailoring school, where on the exterior one sees certain classical ornamental appointments; and then apartments above, where one sees only the plain white walls with unframed windows that everybody had such a great time pretending were hideous just because they are plain. "In what style is the building?" wrote Loos in 1911, when the building was new; "The Viennese style of 1910 … I collected features from old Viennese coffee houses and façades in order to find the modern, the truly modern style. A hundred years ago it was tailors and architects who had it. Today it is only the tailors" (*OA* 105). This last turns out to be a recurrent and important Loosian theme.

Here is where a well-known example of the conservative, anti-modern reaction to the Looshaus comes in: a contemporary Viennese journalistic cartoon satirizing Loos's masterpiece by likening its entrance façade to a pedestrian's where-have-I-seen-that-before encounter with an open sewer grating. The caption read: "The most modern of architects walked through the streets brooding about art. Suddenly he came to a stop: he had found what he had been looking for in vain for so long" (Frampton, *Modern Architecure* 8, with illus.) Obviously, this was mainly a comment on the supposedly brazenly unornamented upper stories.

The famous cartoon also peculiarly suits a critical comment of Loos himself from before he had even begun work on the building. In a 1907 promotion for a walking tour of his apartment interiors, he explains why he is inviting "joiners, decorators and interior designers" to see his work but disinviting architects. Not because he feared plagiarism: "On the contrary, I would be delighted if every architect were to work along the same lines I do. But they won't. They will only misunderstand me …" Some architects had already foolishly taken the spareness of his Café Museum as a model for domestic interiors, even though then, in 1899, there was still "something that could, if you insist, be called 'applied art.'" Next comes the uncannily prescient remark: "Since then, however, the decoration for vases and fruit bowls has been based on sewer gratings" (OA 56). Hence, before the cartoon applied the sewer-grating figure to the Looshaus, it was employed by Loos himself, possibly with special pertinence to Josef Hoffmann, whose plain, to be sure, but fussy, tabletop objects of sheet metal perforated by grids of open squares are so close in form to certain objects designed by Mackintosh, in Britain (who was admired by the Viennese decorative crowd), that at least one of the two must have learned from the other's work.

The sewer-grate cartoon may also be read in light of an ensuing critical controversy about whether Loos's splendid green cipollino marble entrance columns for the Looshaus were hypocritically deceptive for a modernist, since they really fill in ornamentally under a hidden steel beam doing the actual work of support – thanks to the engineering firm of Pittel & Brausewetter. Loos's early praise for an engineering aesthetic is sometimes taken as indicating that he thought of engineering as offering a direct route either to a finally definitively modern style or to an architectureless negation and supersession of style. But Loos never really went so far. Also, he was concerned to save a possiblity of what could be considered reformed classicism. It may substantiate this to say that in my own experience, the thing not by Loos which has struck me as most Loosian is the pair of great, heavily veined marble columns which George Gilbert Scott, Jr., erected in his late nineteenth-century extension of Wren's Pembroke College Chapel, at Cambridge, as a kind of proscenium to the apse – with Scott probably biting his Gothic Revival lip to do the thing right.

How ultimately ironic, then, that the Bauhaus functionalist Ludwig Hilberseimer's entry for the 1922 Chicago Tribune Tower competition, which he too lost, side by side with Loos, should have looked so much like Hoffmann's rather diddly little sheet-metal vases, from which it could not have been more different in every other way but formal. With his hard-nosed business tower for Chicago, gridded in three dimensions like an immense

Sol LeWitt minimal sculpture, Hilberseimer obviously didn't want to hear the word 'ornament' either; but that didn't necessarily put him on the same wavelength as Adolf Loos.

Compared with what must be Loos's second most famous and notorious building, his own unsuccessful project for the Chicago Tribune Tower (chapter 6), that skyscraper taking the form of a single colossal Doric column, the Bauhausler's tower must look less conventionally artistic but more bare bones 'functionalistic' than Loos's forever challenging entry in the same competition. After all, nobody is going to call a Doric column architectureless, though this one might be outrageously extreme *qua* architecture. Both designs posed to accommodate the headquarters of the same major American newspaper; but what is really curious is that Hilberseimer's tough-guy tower should, of all things, formally resemble, like it or not, the little Hoffmann vases and other ornamental objects of a type which it seems was already by Loos early on. The surprise is that Loos's anti-Hoffmann distaste could stretch to encompass the 'Bauhausler' Hilberseimer. Eventually he could remark that, as the "misunderstanding" of his "doctrine" got "taken over by the Weimar Bauhaus" under the rubric "New Objectivity," even Hoffmann was taking it up; and yet: "Bauhaus and constructivist romanticism is no better than the romanticism of ornament" (*OA* 197).

Possibly there is something like a state of architecturelessness, beyond. Take an often overlooked feature of Loos's Chicago Tribune design: what looks to be an eleven-storey 'base' to the shaft that we think of as the building proper. Upstaged as it is by the column, while offering the ironically correct inertness of a proper columnar base at that, maybe this will seem sufficiently inert to count as architectureless – or should it perhaps be 'zero-degree' architecture? – excusing, for the sake of argument, the more normal Doric order *in antis* at the entrance. But architecturelessness and zero-degree architecture must be different. As against something's being artlessness or architectureless in the sense of *devoid* of art or architecture, deliberately or inadvertently, and for better or worse, a degree-zero aesthetic state will somehow assert art or architecture. Unimpeded by commitments to formal articulation as well as ornament, architecture of degree-zero should thereby be all the more unquestionably *there* as architecture. Even as unbuilt, the boxy Chicago base element *isn't nothing*. It bravely squares up to any threat of architecturelessness. The pointedly stripped-down symmetrical formality of Chernyshev's elegantly solemn, and no doubt Loos-aware, Lenin Institute, for its day exemplifying a declared rationalist tendency supposed to purify architecture by favoring basic forms (degree-zero for the academy?), stands halfway between the Chicago box and the more compliantly dressed-up bourgeois elegance, in America, of Raymond Hood's twinned British Empire Building and Maison Française, in New York (chapter 6).

Perhaps no building can be considered architectureless without some reason for its exclusion. The building which in the present observer's experience most closely approximates a condition of self-evident architecturelessness is a lighthouse belonging to Hamburg, on Neuwerk Island in the mouth of the River Elbe, built as a watchtower in the fourteenth century and converted to a lighthouse in 1814. A more manageable, perhaps even definitive case, was intended from the start to stand with the most upright unpretentiousness, even, literally, to be a church without looking religious; and its initial architect, Frank Lloyd Wright, is known categorically to have abandoned and eschewed the project, taking whatever he could consider architectural, in line with his mentor Sullivan, as still too architectural for the patron. I refer to the Abraham Lincoln Center, in Chicago, which was built from 1903 to 1905 by Wright's uncle, a renegade Unitarian minister, after Wright had worked on the project for five previous years (1898–1903; see Siry). To be as clear as possible: it is not that I find *sub*-architectural this curiously beautiful building (even after alteration), thanks largely if not only, Loos would say, to the quality of the brickwork – this building, which, by Wright's walking away from it before it was executed, is by default attributed to his uncle, the patron, Jenkin Lloyd Jones. It is that it presents itself as a better candidate for possible architecturelessness of a sort pertinent to Loos than even the unassumingly boxy base of Loos's own Tribune Tower. As I understand it, *ordonnance* is a more fundamental condition than composition, and the ordonnance of Chernyshev's building would still seem fairly classical even without the string course above the ground floor as intimating pilaster capitals for the vertical strips otherwise simply articulating the rows of windows, whereas of the 'non-Frank-Lloyd-Wright' building of a generation earlier Ludwig Mies van der Rohe, who would have been familiar with it after the Second World War, might have said that it presents itself as something like one big brick, meaning that as praise.

House remodelings

I have been trying, through some examples, to think of what 'architecturelessness' would be like because in his writings Loos makes it sound simpler than it is to pretend that what you are doing is mere building and so must thereby escape being that other, artily debased thing called architecture, which pretentiously artistic people pretend uniquely to effect. One way to keep your architectural feet on the ground, however, is to busy yourself with recycling buildings which might or might not have been architectural on somebody else's good or bad terms. Given a recurrent literary theme, from Loos's early critical reviews onward, of an identification with the craft of tailors, it is more than a pun to say that his doing a number of Viennese house renovations in the 'teens suggests the role of a craftsmanly tailor making unselfconsciously and modern, meaning craftsmanly astute but stylistically unselfconscious, *alterations*. This is especially promising to consider because Loos also played down the exterior in theory, making it sound as if a house, a sub-architectural category to begin with, is so much a private interior that it would be better if it were practically unnoticeable without; and formally clever though they are, Loos's Viennese remodelings betray a certain lack of pretense in not disguising how they are make-overs. Compared with them, for example, the Bauhaus functionalist Adolf Meyer's 1925–26 remodeling of the Determann (formerly Nebe) House, at Weimar, originally built in 1899 (Jaeggi 335, with illus.), makes one wonder if the reason why the house wasn't simply torn down and replaced might only have been the cost of materials. And what Loos would likely criticize there is the way that a certain brand of modernism has been adopted wholesale as a mode in the worst sense, like buying a 'suite' of matching furniture or an outfit of clothes guaranteed to coordinate. Regardless of what the survey books say about a general negation of architecture on his part, Loos himself, all things considered (including irony and hyperbole), might well have found Meyer's remodeled Determann House architectureless in a bad sense.

Without getting into their interior specifics, I want to bring up a general problem with the house remodelings, those usually economical recyclings of preexisting buildings in that domestic category which Loos, I think rhetorically, liked to deny the standing of architectural art. Obviously there was external economic reason for house-remodeling as against house-building during the war; but on the architect's personal side, if he simply needed work he could easily have done even more apartment interiors, and all the more luxuriously too, after the scandal of Looshaus had made him a cultural 'star.' But I would like to speculate on two potentialities in the task of house remodeling which I think decidedly appealed to Loos, and which the apartment interiors did not offer: first, the opportunity to produce, against challenging but perhaps interestingly challenging limitations, a virtually new and somehow Loosian house at that, as it would present itself to the outside world; and second, the occasion to think like a craftsman, as he meant in repeatedly advocating such, ultimately, I think, on behalf of architecture.

It is sometimes said that the complications of what had to have been ordinary, continuous floor planes in these houses, into rooms with distinctly varying floor and ceiling levels, are precocious anticipations of the Loosian 'Raumplan.' Insofar as it is true this overlooks something very Loosian: the absurdly arbitrary complication and impracticality, from the constructional point of view, of building in such a way. What is more in the present context, if it is difficult enough to effect a Raumplan in building from the ground up, it must be exceedingly expensive to have room floor and ceiling heights vary, as if at whim, within somebody else's envelope. Even without getting into specifics of the interiors, which for obvious reasons are more spatially 'Loosified' than the architect's remodeled apartments, these houses can be looked at as an under-theorized but important category of Loos's production. How glaringly, once one thinks on it, they imply a limit of what might be called functionalism ad absurdum where a space is so tailored to fit its first specific purpose that its adaptability to any later modification of purpose would eventually be hampered. At least in these instances Loos got to begin with somebody else's conventional norm – not something he himself was averse to, in theory – and proceed to rework it into something special. But just imagine the task of remodeling a house that had been Raum-planned from the start.

Today, the first thing to strike us is the social benefit of recycling these family houses, dwellings as a somehow intrinsically more serious sort of enterprise than just converting the next disused industrial space into an art gallery and the next disused commercial one into a restaurant. Besides, the inventor of the Raumplan must have felt an artistic challenge in having to work with somebody else's building as architecturally, or at least structurally, given. Loos already had a few earlier Viennese house remodelings behind him when he took up these. At the Goldman House, 1909–11, and Epstein House, 1910, his interventions would seem most evidently to concern re-design of the classical entrance frontispieces and semi-helical staircases. If the outside of the gambrel-roofed Stoessl House, 1911–12, seems merely conventional, owing to post-Loosian remodeling, the unflappable Gravagnuolo manages to note one irrepressible Loosism which managed to escape effacement: a "door space hollowed out diagonally from the wall," that counts as "a genuine anticipation of the one used in 1928 for the front door of the Moller House" (Gravagnuolo 145). With a look at the latter-day front, with shutters (how can they not seem coy), and the bluntly articulated rear, it is sufficient to suppose that the guilty subsequent owner was out to normalize his or her freaky house and make it look reassuring like no real artist, fortunately, had ever touched it. That was not quite what Loos had meant by denying that the architect should consider himself an artist and that a house should be a work of art.

Other Vienna house alterations of the period of the First World War, however, show Loos rising to the occasion and designing with a creativity that must have been positively stimulated by the given limitations. In particular Loos seems to have found himself working with a villa type that marries a gabled roof with a square tower; in Victorian America this was the basic structure of many a so-called 'Italianate' villa; and though evocations of the Italian countryside in town would have struck Loos as all too 'charming,' his Duschnitz House, of 1915–16, in Vienna XIX, is saved from that. One might suppose that, during the war, the remodeling of one's old house instead of building a new one might likely have been undertaken as an austerity measure. Regrettably, in this particular case, the personal prosperity underwriting the patron's expansion of quarters, including music room with pipe organ, and study with salvaged Italian Renaissance coffered ceiling, is said to have derived from war profiteering (Sarnitz 288). Here, then, is possibly a case where Loos's aesthetic penchant for straight-faced exteriors with indulgent interiors coincided with the ethically dubious needs of the client, since even preserving the basic scale and unostentatious neighborly look of the original house had the local societal advantage of helping to keep a social boat from rocking.

From the street, the Duschnitz House looks somewhat 'vernacularly' content with its rim-of-the-city type. The square tower takes a subordinate, semi-picturesquely off-setting place in the given composition of the front. Looking up from below, this feature which Loos added in the second of two alteration stages, in 1916, and extended in height after the war, appears rather abstractly classical, something like a little domesticated part of a Greek-Revival propylaeum (e.g., von Klenze's on the Königsplatz, in Munich), with small triplet attic windows high under a wide, slim cornice like a wrap-around horizontal cap atop single large vertical windows differently subdivided from side to side. Besides more obvious fluted columns, another seemingly even more 'abstractly' classicizing feature is a radically plain but beautifully asymmetric outside entrance staircase. Inside, the very entrance hall is obviously and utterly Loosian, not only for its marble interior cladding and flooring and its handsome plain woodwork, but for its distinct vertical shift in space as movement progresses in stages, upward and forward, into the formal space of entertainment.

28. Loos (remodeled), Duschnitz House,
Vienna, 1915. Garden façade.

The rear or garden elevation, too, becomes surprisingly fullfledgedly Loosian. Here what might by itself have been merely an arbitrary, quasi-vernacular discrepancy of eave lengths on the large roof gable (as in a country house project for Prince Leo Sapieha in 1918) is justified by a horizontal 'bridge passage' connecting the 45° angle of the thus shortened roof and the perpendicular of a new attached tower. The break in roof-

29. Pavel Janák, Beneš Villa, Prague-
Střešovice, 1923–24.

line, then, formally qualifies the strength of the triangular gable as a gestalt
and so equalizes the otherwise discrepant elements, one strongly frontal,
triangular and planar, the other square in plan and cubical, as virtually to
make at least the upper part of the house seem for a moment 'half tower.'
More plastically, the protrusion of a wide music room on the ground floor
makes for a stack of three box-like forms with the smaller protruding
upstairs room and the tower. Especially with the handling of the gable and
tower – like a pair of *clichés* for the Germanic and the Italianate – Loos
here so profoundly overcomes any petit-bourgeois quasi-vernacularism of
'cottage' type that one may think forward, instead of backward, of such
a freshly modern derivation from the inherited general type as the Villa
Beneš, in Střešovice, a suburb of Prague, in 1923–24, by a then already
established Czech functionalist, Pavel Janák. If Janák's house seems better
than suburban, it is probably for its crisp rendition of the angular and the
boxy, which to a certain extent probably still entails the folkloric-local and

the constructivist-functionalist. While there is nothing to accuse of being too cottage-like in either case, the stylistic similarity would seem to concern, almost self-evidently, sophisticated handling in both works of a shared type as likely vernacular common denominator.

The Mandl House, which Loos also remodeled in 1916, was of pretty much the same suburban type, in the same (XIX) district of Vienna. Loos must have cursed its big, doltish dormer – this Loos known to have ridiculed the received wisdom of arguing for gables in Northern Europe because it is much better to shovel off a flat roof when you want to than to have a roof-full of snow fall down by chance. But what dominates towards the upper left might at least be checked by concentrated Loosian expansion at the lower right, which is also where Loos managed to get the upper hand in qualifying the fenestration – one of his favorite games, I think. The regularity of the fenestration slackens there at the entrance corner, only to resume on freer terms round the corner on the building's flank. What I take here as a fortuitous slackening may actually be thanks to at least two deviations from the street elevation as approved by the city on 16 July 1916: not only a widening of the entrance wall but also an erasure of the upper right-hand window – anticipating the similarly relaxed, and also somehow municipally approved, disappearance of an upper right-hand window of the entrance façade of the Müller House, in Prague, of 1928–30.

Beyond, at the rear corner, a square tower not as tall as the original gable helps to collect the old and new, as if to bracket '(A + B)' in suggesting the old tower type at an opposite extreme from the big old-fashioned original dormer; while on the garden side the rear of the same dormer makes friends with the new tower, accommodating its forward projection, as if pleased to enjoy the further projection of a, no doubt, new porch. There is enough of Loos in this that the rear, garden side of the Mandl can even be said to adumbrate the equivalent façade of the famous Rufer House, built, of course, from scratch, six years later in 1922. Together, the Duschnitz and Mandl exteriors suggest that something about these remodeling projects may be rather more artistically important than the re-designing of the many apartment interiors which did help Loos to establish himself professionally but already exercised a tendency to hole inhabitants up in luxuriously private interiors.

The Strasser House, of 1918–19, was and is rather different from the previous two houses. On the street front as it stands, whatever was there to begin with is subsumed into a play of forms that seems *almost* completely free: only an intimation that Loos might have preferred this or that element just a little slimmer or heftier, just a little shallower or deeper, implies a sense of some limiting condition of negative necessity. Even so, in the face of deep upper, over shallow lower, projecting bays at the left of the façade, the slim extension of the floor of the upper in the form of a shallow balcony justifies the off-centeredness of these projections by involving the large upper and lower non-projecting windows to the right. As such, Loos developed here a sense of volumetric-sculpturesque protrusion from the given plane of the wall, which stood him so well with the great right-angled, boxy bays of his later houses in Prague – the Müller, 1928–30, and Winternitz, 1931–32 – that it seems that the Strasser commission, though seemingly a mere alteration, played a constructively experimental role, whether despite or thanks to its operational limitations.

Gravagnuolo describes the complex and luxurious handling of the interior spaces, which entailed substantial reconstruction, including insertion of a whole new floor and conversion of an attic into rooms. Adumbrating the *Raumplan* as Kulka was to define it with respect to the Rufer House is a high stage of sorts, with piano, above the floor level of a music salon. Punctuating the shift of levels is a single marble column remarkable not only for its rich grain but for having entasis yet no identifying 'ornamental' features of a grammatically classical order, as if to make a point in a categorically modern way of standing 'abstractly' free of semantic commitment.

The remodeled Strasser House is extraordinary for an unexpected but major detail. Its right flank reveals a roof-line with fascinating quarter-round, eave-like ends above what might have been a big flat, doltishly unarticulated wall. Now, first of all, the eaves seem to have been a sort of counter-Mansard, suavely Loosian device to play down an extra floor, perhaps in order to conform to regulations, as with Adolf Loos's most famous private house, the Steiner, of 1910. As such it has an interesting implication of urbanity, as exact opposite, in Loos's mind, to an offensively anti-urban practice of designing legal six-storey buildings to look more cutely as if they were only five stories high, as he mentions in the 1912 essay 'Heimatkunst,' an attack on making things look too folksy. There, too, he mocks the use of artificially aged roof tiling, with a typical sarcasm daring the devotee of this mode to go further and deliberately add moss: "I can already see the time coming when our office blocks and apartment houses, our theaters and concert halls, will all be roofed with shingles and straw. *Rus in urbe* – it's a disgrace" (*OA* 115).

The crisp silhouette of this unornamented roof-line, however, crowns with reserve one of Loos's most stunningly 'hardly there' domestic façades (see chapter 9, fig. 45). At front and back the flat roof turns down in identical Loosian quarter-round swoops, with the rear eave meeting up with a similarly quarter-rounded corner on the vertical axis: doubly paired similar-but-different two- and three-dimensional forms (opposite ends the same in one plane, one end twinned as to plane and space). But this whole flank of the house offers in the plane something very different from what Loos disdained as mere 'graphic' design, namely, a pattern of fenestration both rhythmic and percussive: a straight row of windows above, framed fore and aft by a pair of smaller rectangles, in a sequence of small – double – single – double – single – double – small windows, over the most freewheeling 'notation,' as it were, syncopated by more extreme rests and fermatas in the looser fenestration of the lower floors. Loos obviously liked contrasting 'public,' formal symmetry on the front of a house, with a typically freer informality of asymmetry on the sides. Here, however, where there was limited scope for decision on the front, we see him first seeming there to suppress at least one window, slowing down the frontal fenestration, only to turn the corner and begin again with a combination of symmetry and asymmetry all his own.

In their dependence on basic, local constructional givens, these houses may have acquired something of an ironically cosmopolitan vernacular touch when Loos got his hands on them – a curious if not unexpected Anglophile aspect with its own non-local connotations of vernacularism. For especially in their most Loosian boxy overhangs, breaking out beyond lower floors on the exterior, they seem as it were abstractly reminiscent (eschewing ornamentation) of the English Queen Anne style, as in houses of Richard Norman Shaw in the late 1870s. This goes for certain forms such as square towers in respect to Shavian prismatic chimneys playing off big triangular gables. In his later houses Loos will do boxy overhangs less constrained by hand-me-down structure, as if more freely willed, though these wartime remodelings do suggest the origins. Even such overhanging features as the (supposedly semiotically 'facial') upstairs alcove protruding, front-and-center over the entrance portal of the late Moller House, in Vienna, can be considered at least quasi- or trans-vernacular. Not that we would want to imagine such an arch-Loosian form half-timbered (actually, Loos did not hesitate to introduce false 'timber' beams in interiors for vernacular effect). But William Morris's shunning of Latinate words has something contemporaneous in common with this Queen-Anne-into-'free style' which must have charmed Loos by its builderly closeness to local embodiments of traditional but not academic forms. Two architects of the mode had advocated for it, in the *Building News* for 26 February 1875, as based on seventeenth- and eighteenth-century

British brick building as a sort of domestication of the Renaissance, neither "corrupt" nor "debased," but rather "vernacular." For Basil Champneys, the very adaptation to then modern British circumstances rendered it "almost as universal and vernacular," with an interesting implication of a possible trans-vernacular, while John James Stevenson, laying down that it "should rather be homely, like colloquial talk," and "fundamentally the same as the common vernacular style, which every workman has been apprenticed to," conveys a sense of parochial dialect surmounted at least by regional dialect, if not exactly as nationalism by Loosian cosmopolitanism (qu. Girouard 61–62).

In these examples the exteriors of Loos's remodeled houses show works of remodeling as inevitably interfacing with the world beyond. Loos must indeed have gained something from the challenge of having to work with other people's givens, as if asked to take over play in a card game already under way. The situation would have encouraged him to 'lump' material conditions and get on with what only he could do. He was so much at home in the world of clothing, and especially of tailoring, in imagery as well as fact, that it is fair to say that it was likely easy for him to be constructively absorbed in something like major sartorial reconstruction, beyond mere 'alteration.' But it is also fair to say that a man of considerable ego came to learn something of the Freudian lesson that Where the Id Is, There Shall the Ego Be. Having to deal with the givens, with the way things are, the architect who had supposedly laid down the law that building a house was not properly an architectural affair seems to have managed to permit himself to be unselfconsciously architecturally engrossed in the circumscribed task of recycling a preexisting house. Two or three later remodelings in Pilsen also proved to be significant.

Remodeling was obviously a relatively humbling task for this architect whose ego-identity seems strong to this day. I sometimes think that, in view of the sartorial frame of reference in which he was so at home, it must have been all the more so for suggesting mere alteration instead of true bespoke tailoring. On the other hand, part of the dignity of this artist, which is obscured whenever we speak too loosely of 'aristocratic' taste or attitude, was in his accepting his lot (including illness and deafness) with aplomb.

This view of the remodeled houses offers an additional bonus: it helps to absolve Loos of a seeming contradiction whenever, in his writing, he denies architecture, especially modern architecture, as his contemporaries mistakenly understand it, and testifies (as, I would say, a reformed modern architect) that one's building will be better if only one whistles along and thinks like a craftsman. But despite the actual craft experience in his family background and his own practice, including his bricklaying experience in America, he is obviously not practicing any such trade, no matter how often it pleases him to talk that way. What, then, does he mean by thinking as a craftsman instead of what his contemporaries generally misunderstand as an architect? The evidence may be staring us in the face: that the mode of craft-thinking to which he felt temperamentally closest was constructive, to be sure, but that it was, in particular, tailoring: this Loos who designed more men's tailoring and haberdashery establishments, including of course Goldman & Salatsch, in the Looshaus, and a millinery shop besides, all of these except the Looshaus also being remodelings within preexisting structures – more clothing shops than any other commercial category – liked even to think of himself as thinking like a tailor. Especially as he went out of his way to manipulate his remodeled house interiors in three dimensions – an option not so available in redesigning the apartments – his house remodelings came with challenges and limited rewards, unless, that is, one can sportively take to the challenges and limitations, as Loos did: the game of doing alterations on something with materials and construction of sufficiently good quality to begin with was worth his artistic while.

I have suggested that figures of tailoring are peculiarly appropriate to Loos's work in house remodeling. Given his Anglophilia, I also suspect that Loos framed his critical 'craft' position with an awareness of Thomas Carlyle. Yes, the architectural notion of 'cladding,' even with the implication of dress, comes down from Semper and, more directly, Otto Wagner; yet doesn't Loos finally give it surprisingly little theoretical attention, beyond a basic principle of material non-deceit – of one material's not being made to look like another. Loos's Anglophile dandyism, his interest in tailoring and even in designing haberdasheries also point, I think, to a likely literary influence – that Scottish reader of German philosophy and literature, in whose *Sartor Resartus* (1833–34) an endlessly elaborated clothing imagery performs some very Loosian cultural critique. There tailoring is conceived as so architectural that one may not know at any one point which practice is metaphoric for which. For in tailoring (and even the framing of laws), man's "hand is ever guided on by mysterious operations of the mind. In all his Modes, and habilatory endeavors, an Architectural Idea will be found lurking; his Body and the Cloth are the site and materials whereon and whereby his beautified edifice, of a Person, is to be built." Continuing, with a list of historical styles, Carlyle even gets by implication, into the Loosian problem of whether there is or ought to be a specific 'modern' style: "Whether he flow gracefully out in folded mantles, based on light sandals; tower up in high headgear, from amid peaks, spangles and bell-girdles; swell out in starched ruffs, buckram stuffings, and monstrous tuberosities; or girth himself into separate sections, and front the world an Agglomeration of four limbs, – will depend on the nature of such Architectural Idea: whether Grecian, Gothic, Later Gothic, or altogether Modern, and Parisian or Anglo-Dandiacal" (I.v; Carlyle 19).

Even without tracking the complexities of internal spatial reordering, it is clear that Loos's altered houses are not architectureless by any means, what with his fitting them out with new Carlylean outfits. The more they are attended to, the more architecturally interesting they seem. Perhaps the very fact that soon before these projects he had notoriously written that houses, even when built from the ground up, aren't architecture anyway, took some of the pressure off, and allowed Loos not to feel so badly about doing such relatively modest work and even to enjoy the tailoring aspect of doing, literally, architectural alterations. In Loos's symbology the self-proclaimed modern architectural stylist stands as a glorified tattooist without the decent excuse of culture-lag: at the opposite extreme, however, the reformed architect as concerned, is like a tailor, with craft finesse in problem-solving, over and against eccentric display, honoring worthy materials, prepared to make sophisticated construction look elegantly simple, and ever avoiding style as ostentation.

Basic social housing

In the radical political fervor of 1919, Loos, with parallel contributions for other cultural fields by Karl Kraus, Arnold Schoenberg and others, composed a set of 'Guidelines' for a state arts bureau. In them he adopts an ostensibly anti-aesthetic position against planning: "Drastic changes in the character of the city should only be allowed for practical reasons, never for aesthetic reasons." He clearly favors anything built before the vain stylistic artificialities of nineteenth-century eclecticism. "Buildings done in the style of their own time are those which carry on the traditional way of building we had before the imitation of different styles came in, but with the deliberate exploitation of the latest inventions and experience." A like restraint toward inevitably misguided artistic intervention extends to the natural landscape as well, with provisions for the protection and care of monuments extending to "natural monuments," including even on occasion a single tree, as well as general preservation of the landscape by prohibition of advertising billboards in the countryside. Necessary

public works were to be built as "purely functional structures," not in any
historical style.

If anything in Loos approached the condition of architecturelessness,
while also making something of itself environmentally, it would be some of
his work in what Kenneth Frampton, notably, has long advocated for (and
even himself built) as 'low-rise, high-density' public or council housing. Loos
did not hesitate to insist, even against a rising political tide of *Gemeindebauten*,
or multiple dwellings in giant 'courts,' closer in to the center, that in this
work a prime concern was the contribution to self-sufficiency facilitated by
providing a vegetable garden for each family. So committed was he to this
principle that he justified it as a way of being liveably close to a working,
productive garden, not simply just seeing a glorified little 'allotment' garden
as an adjunct to the house.

The Loos associated with sophisticated private bourgeois domestic housing
was also strongly committed as administrator and as designer to social
housing, especially in the five years between the revolutionary moment of
1919 and his quitting the *Siedlungsamt*, or settlement (public housing) office,
of the city of Vienna in 1924. Brought into the Social-Democratic municipal
administration by Gustav Scheu – obviously pleased by the private house with
rental apartment that Loos had built for him and his wife – Loos volunteered
for the new office in 1920, and became chief architect in 1921 and head of
office as of 1923; he resigned in June of 1924 and moved to Paris. During
his tenure he took aboard a staff of architects which included Margarete
Lihotzky (later Schütte-Lihotzky), the first Austrian woman architect, who
became famous later in the 20s for designing the ultra-efficient 'Frankfurt
kitchen' and went on to work in the USSR. While in her Viennese work
Lihotzky was committed, like Loos, to developing municipal housing with
vegetable gardens, she was prepared to take over his work on the big Otto-
Haas-Hof estate when he quit (Howard 171–75).

Where Loos's otherwise favored Social Democrats clung to the vision
of grand collective dwellings around a common 'court' (*Hof*), Loos was
committed to the self-sufficiency of a workable vegetable garden for every
tenant family, as only realizable with low-rise, high-density, economical
row- or terrace-houses for single families. This view was influenced by new
British and Germanic town planning for 'new towns' or 'garden cities.' While
awareness of Ebenezer Howard's 'garden-city' movement was significant,
Loos's thinking had more to do with the primacy of the working vegetable
'allotment' garden as food source (and for bodily exercise), as developed in
Germany. Of what social housing he himself designed, beyond his supervisory

role in other projects, some was built. But between two disappointingly traditionalist interventions early on and an interesting late project, he did execute some forty row houses, all told, all intended to have integral vegetable gardens. His social housing work was predicated on a principle of economy, which entailed not only efficiently cheap construction but also some declared self-sufficiency in the individual family's being able to grow for its own use a substantial quantity of vegetables while benefitting from the rehabilitating effect, for workers used only to unvarying assembly-line and other rote work, of healthy spading and such.

Loos expounded his working-garden ideal in writing. In 'Rules for Social Housing Developments' (1920), "Every social housing development starts with the garden. The garden is the primary feature, the house secondary." The call can be quite militant: "Only people who feel the need to work in their gardens, as well as in their regular occupations, in order to produce food have a right to take up land from society for themselves … People who do not produce food belong in an apartment house." A flower garden will just not pass muster: "Personal enjoyment of a garden must consist solely of growing food. The enjoyment of a garden in the sense of aesthetic pleasure must be sought in public parks." While these guidelines are clearly social, there are important benefits for the individual: "Garden work is an antidote to the nerve-destroying division of labor which allocates the constructive and destructive processes to different people. Garden work is the essential destructive complement for every worker engaged in a constructive process. Without … [such] he will waste away, both spiritually and physically" (*OA* 142). Loos favors land ownership by a cooperative, with permission to build a house coming from outside in order to avoid favoritism; and only people who have maintained their gardens for so many years would be eligible and required to build a house – of which the state would only supply the nucleus, "which they can then transform into a complete house by buying the component parts," which are designed for simple self-assembly, one by one (143).

Another text of 1920, 'Houses for the Lainz Social Housing Development,' discusses how to economize effectively on construction costs for low-rise, high-density, publically built row housing. To save space and because the upper floor is for sleeping only, the inside stairs of row houses should be steep and narrow (the most extreme form being almost ladder-like, so called 'miller's stairs,' with alternating left-right treads), there being no reason to drag hefty armoires upstairs when built-in closets are better anyway. Ceilings can be low, with no insulational filling in the upper floor, which, as in England, also saves on heating: commercially rented tenement apartments are wastefully constructed compared with this. Practical English regulations are to be followed as to a basement "earth closet" and laundry function in the kitchen (*OA* 152). As to "site development," Loos demands "economy of layout" rather than a calculatedly "picturesque ensemble," together with "practical arrangement of the gardens for growing vegetables." His project description spills back and forth between extreme economy – such as working with an existing road in bad repair but salvageable – and confessedly "aesthetic" sensitivity to nature, such as saving "bands of trees" to either side of the road "so that the gleam of the houses will be seen through the foliage" (154). Aesthetics is even allowed to race ahead, as it were, so long as economics can catch up: excited by the prospect of "an ornamental road" from the settlement up a nearby hill, he is pleased to consider that the cost could be offset by having additional houses along it; and, then again, the new road could nicely suit the "contours of the land." In this plan long gardens are justified by economizing on water, gas, and electrical mains, which would have to be twice as long for wider houses with shorter gardens, and narrow north-south gardens prove to have gardening advantages (155–56). Finally, unlike "dreary" latter-day projects, the strings of houses were each to have their own somewhat different character.

'Social Housing Development Day,' a promotional text for a 1921 demonstration on behalf of social housing in Vienna, sees Loos elaborating on the theme of the benefits of the vegetable garden, with, again, the "destructive" manual labor involved in gardening as a refreshing psychological antidote and complement to unrelieved and alienating "constructive" tasks under the factory system (*OA* 160). Should anybody suppose that the vegetable gardens were utopian, Loos announced that 100,000,000 crowns' worth of vegetables had been produced within the city of Vienna in the previous year, 1920.

Turning to what Loos directly executed (aside from participating in city *Gemeindebauten*): at Siedlung Friedenstadt, near the Lainz zoo (XIII District), he built a few of the pleasant, if conservative, dormered row houses with continuous, laterally pitched roof, and a touch of asymmetry in the disposition of entrances and mini-dormers as well as fenestration. A founding monument and one row of houses were built by Loos in 1921; and later, between 1922 and 1924, more houses were built from his plans. He designed similarly semi-traditional hip-roofed houses for war veterans, Siedlung Hirschstetten (XXII), in 1921, but they remained projected only.

Halfway between theory and practice, as it were, in 1921 Loos patented a system of absolutely bare-bones, ultimately economical construction for attached two-storey houses: the 'House with One Wall,' following up with designs for some projected applications. Houses built on this system would be so structurally rudimentary – what with front and rear walls hanging from rafters resting on simple balloon-frame side walls resting in turn on simple footings – that if anything constructed for human habitation could be sub-architectural and hence mere building, it must be this. Still, it is one thing to posit architecturelessness in theory, and once Loos got to build one of the variations he proceeded to develop out of the basic One-Walled House conception, some 'architecturality' might have to be acknowledged. Curiously enough, while the One-Walled House shows not the slightest sign of visual art, it may be deemed entitled to inherit a high-classical literary reference: a mention in Aeschylus' tragedy *Supplices* (Suppliants) of emergency social housing for non-citizens of ancient Athens with certain rights, many of whom were moving from the country to the city (Masheck, 'One-Walled House').

As far-fetched as the One-Walled House might have seemed, it led in practice to the most actualized of Loos's garden-settlement projects, the Siedlung am Heuberg, in the XVII District of Vienna, Loos himself designed one part of the 1921 project (houses numbered 1–13 in Plachygasse are known to be by him), on which Hugo Mayer collaborated, built as far as it went between 1923 and 1924. Originally it must have looked oddly American, clad in 'clapboard' (UK, 'weatherboards'), donated, along with all other materials for this project and some for other Viennese Siedlungen, by American Quakers for postwar relief, though much of this was later replaced with asbestos. Does it follow the disposition of the original? If so, a seemingly arbitrary breaking off of the siding semiotically declares itself as such, beyond functional necessity and in conformity with Loos's theory of cladding. For in showing itself undisguisedly as a layer, by stopping so abruptly in mid-wall that it might almost be peeled off, the treatment would recall not only Professor Wagner's influential theory of cladding but also the practice of someone whose early work Loos had quickly responded to: the Czech then functionalist-to-be Jan Kotěra, who on the exterior of his Museum of Eastern Bohemia, at Hradec Krávlové, performs a willful semiotic discontinuity like that of the Heuberg houses, where one facing ends and overlaps another, highlighting, so to speak, the very nature of cladding.

The Heuberg row is interesting, but its extreme economy shows. Another project, apparently begun in 1921 but never built, avoids any hint of abjection and hints instead at a compromise with styling which may have been motivated by circumstances. This 'Project for a Settlement with Seven-Metre-Long Gardens,' as he called it, Loos had apparently designed for a congress of the International Garden Cities and Town-Planning Association, at Olympia, in London, in March 1922.[2] His design seems peculiarly attuned to the British venue: it must

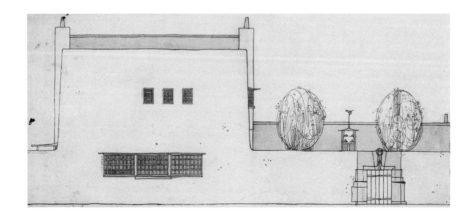

30. Charles Rennie Mackintosh, Study for a country cottage for an artist, 1901. South elevation (detail).

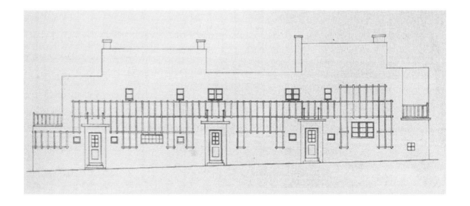

31. Loos, Study for a housing settlement with seven-metre-long gardens, *c.* 1921.

be Loos's most Mackintoshian work. Charles Rennie Mackintosh was indeed known in Vienna, where he had been invited to exhibit at the Secession, to acclaim and inevitable influence. Yet it was Mackintosh's reputation, known through photographically illustrated art magazines such as *The Studio*, which had inspired the Secessionists to invite him to Vienna in the first place. So in another form we come up again against the problem of Hoffmann – not Loos's favorite Viennese – and the Secession – not his favorite crowd in town. But in this case it seems possible that, independently of Hoffman, Loos, with a view to his reputation in Britain, was bearing in mind, to the point of *hommage*, the silhouette and elevation of Mackintosh's 1901 Country Cottage for an Artist, a project that had been published in Germany in 1902 (in particular, one of the end walls). In any case, the whole effort was yet another campaign for low-rise, high-density housing with real functioning vegetable gardens.

A most interesting compromise between that, Loos's preferred type, and the big *Gemeindebauten,* or collective dwellings whose winning of the political day indeed served to percipitate Loos's resignation from city office and his move to Paris: a 1923 'Small Dwelling-House' design for stacked-up, literally, i.e., vertically terraced, 'terrace' houses, as shown here, in two loosely parallel strips, the front one curved. Besides single studios (in the British Isles, 'bed-sitting rooms') and small flats, accommodations were to include small duplexes like the small British Victorian row or terrace houses called workmen's 'villas,' stacked up on set-back terraces as if on shelves. This salient terracing recalls the earlier stepped-back terracing, not so eccentric after all, of the upper managerial-class Scheu House, of 1912–13, built for the city lawyer who helped bring Loos into the housing administration, but also the more exotic bourgeois-luxurious set-back terracing of two unexecuted luxury projects: Twenty Villas, for the Cote d'Azur, and the Grand Hotel Babylon, at Nice. In the architect's promotion of the latter there still echoes the 'orientalizing' hostility which had greeted the Scheu House – likened above to an early modern European projection of a legendary ancient Western Asian monument (chapter 1) – which suggests possible contemporaneous induction to this project on a site for which Loos, Peter Behrens and Oskar Strnad all proposed before the Austrian Association for Housing and Small Gardens unexecuted "Terrassenwohnhäuser," at least in the basic row-house sense (Rukschcio 572). A curious contradiction in Loos's reflecting on the earlier criticism and notoriety suggests that he perhaps *liked* the exoticism, not to mention notoriety, of the 'Algerian' look, for while insisting that in designing the Scheu House he "did not have the Orient in mind at all," he wonders why a member of the city council should even try to get such stacked terraces banned; after all, "they have been usual in the Orient" (*OA* 172).

In this 1923 project the gently accelerating curve of the front block does respond in some degree to a curve in the road at the site; but it is possible that influence from a craft which meant a great deal to Adolf Loos's aesthetic sense also makes itself manifest. In itself, there was nothing eccentric about having a block of apartments curve along a curving street: Robert Kalesa's block in Margaretengürtel (District V), expanded 1922–24 by Hubert Gessner, a large and more conventional apartment complex with a façade rationalized by orderly quasi-classical compartmentalization, is an example of a municipal multiple dwelling simply following the curve of its street. But if we notice that in Loos's project the road just does not in fact bend as much as the curved building, we may be prepared to entertain a more formal source for the structure's independent and seemingly arbitrary curvature, especially in combination with a straight stretch of the same houses.

"The French curve is a worse danger than the T-square," Loos had only recently proclaimed in 1921, in connection with his low-rise row-house social housing at Lainz (in the XIII District with Heitzing; *OA* 157). He meant the French curve's facilitation of gratuitous curves, even curlicues. But by almost the same token yet also a significantly different one, another, analogous piece of craftsmanly equipment, uncommon in connection with architectural practice, would have appealed to Loos (who used shears in a tailor-shop frieze in 1897; see p. 108), one, unlike the widely available standard French curve, not sold with architect's equipment yet a tool that one can imagine as an emblem of Loos's whole outlook as an architect. I speak of the standard tailor's ruler, whose singular and slowly graduated unfurling allows accurate measurement in regular units along curved edges and seams, doing quite without, thank you, the gratuitous sinuosities of the French curve's swooning this way and that. The idea gains support from some of Loos's general remarks on tailoring and craftsmanship as model conditions for architecture, such as: "Only a tiny minority of architects have comprehended that they should be craftsmen and not 'artists.' For that reason tailors and shoemakers have a much more 'modern' approach than they" – this from a French journalistic interview of 1930: 'The Vienna City Council's Tenements Cannot Tolerate Criticism: A Conversation with Adolf Loos in Paris' (*OA* 194).

The hypothesis cannot be dismissed on grounds of simple sexist cultural stereotyping, as if the French curve were categorically feminine just in being considered French; for unlike the tailor's rule, it is a standard piece of mechanical drawing equipment, while the rule is used in ladies' as well as gentlemen's

32. Biedermeier tailor's rule, dated 1844,
hardwood, probably Austrian.

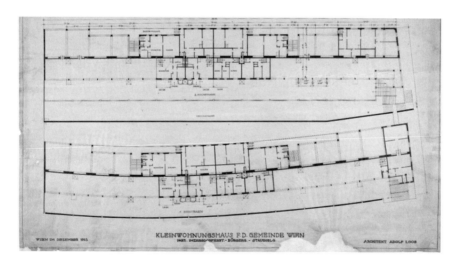

33. Loos, Study for social housing in Vienna,
1923.

tailoring. Aware of its traditionalist appeal as quasi-British as well as Austrian, I show a beautifully well-worn Biedermeier example acquired in Vienna, with recognizably the same curve as even present-day British examples. The possibility of Loos's being inspired by the steady, calmly swelling, anything but flippant asymmetric curve of the Anglo-Austrian tailor's ruler is supported by Loos's remarks on tailors as models of timeless aesthetic judgment compared with most architects.

True to style

After Loos had given up attempting to provide more mass garden housing for Vienna, and built a single terrace of fine houses (with 'miller's stairs') in 1931 at Babí, near Nachod, in the Czech Republic, which we now know were not for proletarian but for managerial workers (Tencar), and the excellent semi-detached houses-in-a-garden which he contributed in 1930–32 to the Vienna Werkbundsiedlung, he also came up with what must be his 'greenest' late project.

This was a projected luxury apartment house or hotel for Juan-les-Pins, on the Mediterranean, identified in a notice by Loos in *L'Architecture d'aujourd'hui* for October 1931 as the 'Project to Save a Pine Wood.' A stand of pine trees of some 24 x 46 meters had been sold to a developer who sought to cut down a third of it to accommodate two extended wings of a building otherwise running alongside the wood. Instead, Loos proposed (unsuccessfully) to eliminate the intruding wings and compensate for lost floor space by adding to the building's height. What is more, as the project's most conspicuous formal feature, "A large arch running a third of the length will allow the woodland to be seen" (*OA* 198). It is interesting that here he shows no compunction in mobilizing a simplified triumphal-arch form that was already not only a large-looming and repeated feature of Karl Ehn's grand Karl-Marx-Hof, a kilometer long, built in 1926 after Loos's resignation from the housing office, but also already in circulation as a stereotypic visual 'isotype' for mass housing in the 'Vienna method of image statistics,' invented by the logical positivist philosopher Otto Neurath, as in a *c.* 1928 Neurath visual graph of 'New Housing Built for the Municipality of Vienna'; yet the Loos who already felt misconstrued along lines of Bauhaus 'objectivity' could wind up misunderstood even by Adorno as a heartless functionalist, lacking awareness of form.

34. Vincenc Beer, Náměstí Republiky 22,
Pilsen, 1930–31. Loosian treatment of
staircase.

But in 1931 he produced a minor and mostly overlooked work, but one that is possibly more extensive than supposed, and remarkable. In Pilsen, where he had already remodeled and expanded the Brummel House, in 1928–29, and would project unexecuted designs for another, more extreme, the Semler House, in 1932, the latter to be entertained in respect to what would later emerge as Minimal Art (chapter 9), Loos remodeled the dental surgery office of a Dr Teichner, at Náměstí Republiky 22, with the collaboration of Kurt Unger and Norbert Krieger. An attempted visit to the apartment in the early spring of 2005, when it was said to be undergoing restoration, found it locked. But, as I reported in a talk at Cambridge University that April, and then in print (Masheck, 'Stalking Loos'), the great surprise was to realize that the staircase leading up to Dr Teichner's office in this small commercial building, with stairs winding their way up around the elevator, looked peculiarly Loosian with its wainscot of white marble framed in dark gray leading up only as far as Dr Teichner's first-floor (European-style) door. What is more, this far up the casing of the elevator is "of magnificent plate glass ... heavily beveled along the edges in the Loosian manner and framed in brass or bronze – like the elegantly sturdy clocks that Loos had produced around 1900, only on a luxuriously large scale and as 'transparently' simple and serviceable, yet also as fascinating, as if enshrining the mechanical works of the elevator like so much clockwork" (Masheck, 'Stalking Loos' 103).

Something Loosian here obtains, whoever designed this. If not only the dentist's suite but also this staircase (not impossibly, even the lobby below), this might well include a small but extraordinary staircase detail just outside Teichner's door, on the irregular quadrilateral underside of the the next landing up, is a feature which I refer to in the same article as "an amazing semantic reversal" of what on the next floor is a recession beneath the landing, but filled out "as a blocky, prismatic mass" so that a void is "invert[ed]" into "an affirmatively boxy ... device." However practically called for, this easily missed but telling detail, as I suggested, may amount to a remarkable instance of Loosian formal acuity which the Prague Linguistic Circle would have appreciated as a structural inversion: how a feature so un-'aesthetic' (if not regretted) has been "heightened or 'thickened' into artistic significance ... making something of it by poetically exploiting a lowly feature presumed to pertain to mere building as architectural 'prose'" (ibid.). So too, a device that cannot count as ornament quite deserves to count as art. Bulky as it seems, in the complete formal neutrality of its reversal from concave-negative to convex-positive, it hardly matters except as an inversion per se; and provided it proves to be by Loos when the researchers and restorers have completed

35. Beer, Náměstí Republiky 22. Loosian
treatment of staircase.

their work on Dr Teichner's office, this boxy inverted recession also points forward to the eventual problem of Loos in regard to Minimalism.

If Loos had no direct connection with this element, it must have been designed by someone with Loosian artistic sympathies. I realize that such a claim may be disputed by the new Czech antiquarians of Loos to whom we must be grateful for preservation work of extremely high material and technical standards, but it is one of the inescapably 'postmodern' ironies of East European culture since the fall of the Berlin Wall that the East still seems as constrained as during the Cold War to a positivist, one might say, *undialectical* materialist outlook that must inhibit the understanding of style, which requires some idealism for its essentialist business (see Masheck, 'Anti-Architect'). There is need, one might say, for a Vienna School revival: context, yes, but as the grounding and setting of form. I accept the possibility of some Czech student proving wrong my surmises about the Pilsen staircase by finding in an archive an invoice tendered by Vincenc Beer; I only hope he or she proves capable of engendering *better* surmises affecting artistic significance.

On a grander scale Adorno misreads Loos as a whole, taking him, of all architects, as "the sworn enemy of everything artisanal" – notwithstanding his, if anything, high idealization of the vernacular builder – and caricatures him as a technophile leading the way to a heartless and sterile detachment by "teach[ing] ... implicitly ... that real technical objects are beautiful," because he wants to say that any traditional sense of beauty "impinges on" the presumably non-aesthetic "real functionality in which functional works like bridges or industrial plants seek their law of form" (Adorno 58, 60–61; see 'Preface' to the present work). Whatever its interest for the question of later 'Minimalism' (chapter 9), such a caricature-of-a-caricature – since if anything it parodies Le Corbusier, himself never an absolute functionalist, as influenced by Loos – has little or nothing to do with the Loos who in his 'reddest' moment of 1919 (putting a formerly friendly Wittgenstein off) presciently addressed the need not only for public housing but also for the government to protect natural as well as cultural monuments. Besides billboards being forbidden in the countryside, necessary bridges and towers were forbidden to take arty forms. The point was that man is very bad at playing nature's game, and should only make respectful and never condescending interventions into the natural realm.

Yes, Loos liked what could be called blank form, simple form that, however, is hardly automatic, with materials and good workmanship altogether vital. The Juan-les-Pins project might look hasty and simplistic, like some pressured letter to the editor, which in a sense it was. I want to excuse it as a quick, admirably assured, schematic idea, just a suggestive place-holder for architecture instead of a specific architectural promise, especially in its resemblance to the isotype of Naurath, who was also sometime secretary of the Austrian Association for Housing and Small Gardens. However, something about this case seems troublesomely close to a problem of our own historical moment, namely, architectural 'solutions' being hustled along on the strength of their 'green' credentials. Already it sometimes seems as if, analogously, we were expected to favor a painting just for being painted in non-toxic and washable paint.

Unfortunately, for many people now in the early twenty-first century 'a better life' is something to look hopelessly back at. It is more than a century since Loos wrote optimistically as a young man, "The building remains, surrounded by a changing posterity" ('The Old and the New Style in Architecture,' 1898; *OA* 33). What, however, could he possibly say now, in response to the ruin of an early modernist cinema bombed out a few years ago in Kabul? Possibly that, after so much civilian suffering and death has taken place and been forgotten, those who profited in the destruction will have profited further in the rebuilding. Certainly those who destroyed the National Library of Iraq and monuments of ancient Mesopotamian architecture cannot be expected to pay any respect to *modern* architecture, being by then preoccupied making ancient works look 'better than new,' no doubt with fabulously expensive synthetic resins. Needless to say, all this will be essentially American style, though now, for the sake of heightened security as well as efficiency, lacking just that optimistic progressivism with everybody in on it for which early modern American culture was admired by the likes of young Loos and other European modernists.

Can the work of Loos somehow speak to us still in our present dilemma? Loos, dandy and beatnik; Loos the throw-back and anti-academic freak; Loos the suave anti-architect, supposedly the Marcel Duchamp of architecture: can this be one of the few who really might have understood? I do find myself unexpectedly inspired by his inventive remodelings, which even remind me that it was with a remodeling of his own modest house that Frank Gehry took off as an architect. As for his surprisingly intense commitment to the cause of social housing, taking upon himself even heavy administrative work, I have come to appreciate his frustration and his escape to Paris. Yet I have also come to see, even within the limits of his middle- and lower-class works, a sort of social sea-worthiness which, yes, entails, notwithstanding his ironies, the sustainability of the architectural art. At the very least, the limitations of

Loos's house remodelings show him not only saving existing housing stock, in the green sense, but improving the design of a house by formal attention to the rearrangement of building elements; and the projects for public housing show him working through his artful sense of possibilities for architectural art quite without anything like the superfluous rhetorical grandiloquence that many still presume transforms a mere building into a work of architecture. All with a thoroughly uneccentric sense of style.

THE WITTGENSTEIN HOUSE AS LOOSIAN

In the British colonial case of Berkeley (chapter 2), the elusive question of the authorship of a famous philosopher's house stimulated thought on Adolf Loos's own work as well as Loos's declared interest in vernacular form. The case of the house we know that Ludwig Wittgenstein in some sense built in Vienna is a different problem of overlapping sophistications. Here all concerned, including a prime Loos disciple, shared a new frame of mind in the Vienna of the acerbic cultural critic Karl Kraus, the composer Arnold Schoenberg, and other clean-slate, revisionist moderns. Loos's discontented isolation of his own architectural project from the conventional pretensions of architectural art would resemble Wittgenstein's discontented withdrawal from conventional conceptions of the philosophical task even had these two great Viennese not known and respected one another; and in the end each had modernized and in some sense reaffirmed his respective field, architecture or philosophy, though the matter is complicated by the fact of Wittgenstein's thinking of himself as adept in both fields – not to mention his conspicuously ungifted music.

Ludwig Wittgenstein, one of the preeminent philosophers of the last century, knew Loos (with Karl Kraus, one of the secret 'creative' beneficiaries of his 1914 distribution of the immense fortune of his father, who himself had patronized the Secession and Josef Hoffmann in particular). It is said that when Wittgenstein was introduced to him, in Vienna during the First World War, Loos felt sufficiently familiar with the younger man's outlook to joke, legendarily: "You are me!" During the war Wittgenstein had an army friend who was a prime pupil of Loos, Paul Engelmann, who recorded that remark, and whom it would be natural, later on, to ask to design a house for his sister Margarethe, in Vienna. Engelmann first worked, in 1917–19, on renovations of a Wittgenstein family house at Neuwaldegg, a far northwestern part of Vienna. The new house for Margarethe, or 'Gretl' (later Margaret Starnborough-Wittgenstein) was built at Kundmanngasse 19, in town, in District III, in 1926–28. Eventually, however, with the design process well under way, Engelmann was dropped from the project, and Wittgenstein took to signing the plans as "architect." Ever since, there has been ambiguity about the artistic authorship of what is known as the Wittgenstein House. While the following account diverges radically from the approach of the house's most devoted student, Bernhard Leitner, it deserves to be said that we all owe its very survival to the lifetime of scrutiny, concern and public advocacy that Leitner has devoted to this building.

It is agreed that after building the house Ludwig Wittgenstein passed from an earlier philosophical focus on logical form to a later focus on linguistic function, and that the house he in some sense built may be a fulcrum or hinge of sorts, if not a modulation, between the two projects. On his return to Cambridge in 1929, Wittgenstein did indeed pass from a consuming logical concern with forms of meaningful statement to a philosophy linguistically concerned with meaning as a function of use in discourse. Given his notion of what can be *said* as exceeded by what can only be *shown* as already operative in the *Tractatus Logico-Philosophicus*, there is a tendency to approach the house, in between, as oracular successor to that text. For a modernist building of the later 1920s, the Wittgenstein House hardly 'says' more, formally, than it 'shows' functionally; but anyone concerned with the formal aspect of Loos, the purported proto-functionalist, should find exceptionally interesting this house in which a chief Loos disciple played some elusive determining part.

Probably owing to the linguistic functionalism of Wittgenstein's later phase, the notion of this house as a harbinger of architectural functionalism has confused even Theodor Adorno. In actual fact, the Wittgenstein House proves all the more interestingly problematic if what is expected of it is a materialist functionality of blind efficiency, with or without guarantee of beauty; so that retrieving the 'true,' in some measure default-Loosian, house as a work of art becomes something like retrieving the 'true' Wittgenstein from rough cultural generalizations about logical positivism – that view in which only what is materially verifiable can stand as truth – except that Loos's denial of artistic standing to even his own houses was also the opposite of the construal or misconstrual of Wittgenstein as an artist in the history of architectural art, however open he left himself to it. Loos's self-denial was rhetorical, and ironic, but also modest.

The idea that it is not only Wittgenstein's work but of a piece with his philosophical work has led to a certain fetishization of the house, with the

36. Paul Engelmann and Ludwig
Wittgenstein, Wittgenstein House, Vienna,
1926–28.

problematic presumption that, in view of Wittgenstein's famous commitment to logical rigor, and the way he built the house to look as rigorous as possible, one might inductively access the essence of Wittgenstein simply in admiring the building's look. Such fetishization only detracts from the significant art-historical influence on the work of Adolf Loos. That influence may not be a simple matter, but (a) no work of art stands *sui generis* in art history; and (b) one looks in vain in then contemporary Vienna for houses more like this one by anybody else. At the same time, if it is easy enough for art history to say that everything takes form, and every form has antecedents, it's another matter, philosophically, for Wittgenstein to wish to produce something special (and to make something culturally visible of himself), something *unique*, yet to have to face the fact that that would not be possible if the building was to participate in the art of architecture – by much the same sense of meaning as obtains in play within a game, which he would develop in his second phase, 'post-house.'

Despite a well-established cliché of Wittgenstein's house looking 'logical,' just for looking pared-down (especially to anyone unaware that architectural modernism was already under way for a whole generation at the time), there are actually not many evident ways in which the disposition of the Wittgenstein House can be said to implicate logic. No doubt the most significant, though it is ever overlooked, concerns the multi-leaved doors, opaque, translucent, and transparent, between the great central hall and the adjacent salon or library: their various permutations, open and closed within a single doorframe, exemplify a distinctly modern logical sense of propositional quantification, distinguishing the penetration of light as 'all,' 'some' or 'none': i.e., all light, some light, no light. Ironically, perennial attempts to affiliate the house with the logical positivism of the Vienna Circle in philosophy, as supposedly a case of pure functionalism, only go to highlight a more telling parallel between Wittgenstein's withdrawal from the Vienna Circle as excessively positivist, however much he had influenced it, and Adolf Loos's standing apart from the clinically utilitarian, caricaturally 'Bauhaus' functionalism for which he, for his part, was indeed an important forerunner.

The whole problem of this famous house as a work of architecture, Loosian at that, can be approached afresh by considering certain themes: formalism and functionalism; Wittgenstein's Cambridge context; early Czech functionalism in Loos's Vienna; Engelmann's Loosian artistic identity; and proceeding to some telling fine points of the house as it stands; and, finally, by setting the project in critically longer view.

The formalist context

If form as such has no material function, function must nevertheless always assume material form. While observers often take the Wittgenstein House as standing at a 'functionalist' extreme, the present look into the formalist context has been stimulated by observing a formal similarity between an early conception of the Wittgenstein House by Paul Engelmann – a general disposition for Phase II offering a sense of volumes in mutual interrelation (illus., W 88, upper right)[1] – and a widely reproduced theoretical diagram of only a few years earlier, the Dutch abstract painter Theo van Doesburg's 1922 'Basic Elements of Architecture' – a balanced asymmetric play of boxy volumes defined by planes, which is essentially architectural on formal terms, altogether anterior to any specification of purpose or function. It is possible to say that the Engelmann composition in question is not as good as van Doesburg's, but impossible not to see the two as similar formal constructs. And in the end, Engelmann's final project (illus., W 52, right), if one only imagines it without its attic storey, still shows a resemblance to the massing of Wittgenstein's finished house.[2]

At its most general, the concept of function concerns the value of one dependent variable as pegged to another, so that when the one changes, the other changes concomitantly. A functional form is one that defers to function, purpose or utility, rather than one engendered for its own formal properties. There can indeed, however, be such a thing as a formal function, serving artistic purposes internal to a work of art, as Vasari seems to allow in remarking that in the paintings of Giotto the figures "do what they need to do (*obbedivano a quel che elle avavano a fare*)," meaning that the figures answer to artistic necessity (Vasari 2: 102). Taking architectural form and function as a polarity, we can accuse something of being formalistic – a theory as well as a building – when we consider its order affected, contrived to impress with 'produced' formal effect. Even Newtonian mathematical physics can be considered formalistic, in its anticipation of patterns of regularity; and in 1913 Lou Andreas-Salomé could applaud Max Scheler for showing up formalism in Immanuel Kant (Andreas-Salomé 177).

While the term 'function' is not problematic, according to Max Black, in the *Tractatus* Wittgenstein employs the word 'form' in no fewer than eleven different ways (Black 62–63). Now, if the house is taken as a major authorial work between Wittgenstein's earlier and later residencies in Cambridge, it is worth remarking that during Wittgenstein's five undergraduate terms there, in 1912 and 1913, Cambridge was a hotbed of new formalist aesthetics. On the functionalist side, living in G. E. Moore's old rooms in the Gothic Revival 'Whewell's Court' surely drew Wittgenstein's interest to William Whewell as a philosopher-engineer. As a youth Wittgenstein had been impressed by Heinrich Hertz's retiring of the Newtonian notion of force (in *Principles of Mechanics*, 1894), but this Whewell had written two to three generations earlier, in his *History of the Inductive Sciences from the Earliest to the Present Time* (1837), that a loss of the notion of force in Roman architecture and engineering had produced mere formalism: "destitute of mechanical truth," architecture was left with merely an "idea of … shape" (Whewell 1: 191, 247). In Whewell's Court that alone should have had Wittgenstein thinking about form and function in the modern Cambridge context.

In these early Cambridge days Wittgenstein was put off by the queer aestheticism of the proto-Bloomsbury Cambridge 'Apostles,' to which he was elected but from which he shied away. The Apostles were at the epicenter of definitive early modern formalism, with Moore its very godfather, thanks to his sense of bottom-line, unanalyzable value as advanced in *Principia Ethica* (1903). Wittgenstein cannot have moved in these circles and not known of the radically revisionist modern art exhibition organized in 1910 by the sometime Apostle Roger Fry, 'Manet and the Post-Impressionists,' patronized by Lady Ottoline Morrell, who just in 1912 began a major affair with Wittgenstein's Cambridge mentor, Bertrand Russell. Fry's formalist campaign was inescapable: he produced his 'Second Post-Impressionist Exhibition' while in residence, in 1912. Another Apostle, Clive Bell, wrote *Art* (1914), in which the ultra-formalist doctrine of 'significant form' was promulgated just after Wittgenstein left for Norway and then the war, though some of the text had already circulated privately. One might even wonder if Bell's notorious term 'significant form' influenced the terms "sinnvollen Gebrauch" (3.326) or even the crucial "sinnvolle Satz" of Prop-osition 4, in the *Tractatus*, rendered respectively as "significant use" and "significant proposition" by Ogden. Wittgenstein may have disliked the aestheticism, but his own talk in the *Tractatus* of "formal properties of objects and atomic facts … and … of formal relations and relations of structures" (4.122) is hardly at odds with the mode of thinking of these Cambridge aesthetic formalists (Wittgenstein, *Tractatus* 56 Ger./57 Eng.; 60 Ger./61 Eng.; 78 Ger./79 Eng.). Moreover, the Manchester philosopher Samuel Alexander, who had first encouraged Wittgenstein to seek out the great logician Gottlob Frege, and hence philo-sophy as such, was already interested in Bell's theory of significant form.[3]

Can one be out-of-step yet on the same wavelength? In the case of Bell, architecture, the great non-representational fine art, was important early on in the broader modernist cause. Bell challenged architects to emulate engineers, to satisfy rationalist functionalism and also, thereby, engender a beauty of rationally uncompromised form. Loos the Viennese modernist architect had already written in 1898 about engineers as the "ancient Greeks" of the modern world (*OC* 69) – a notion picked up and assimilated, as has already been noted, by Le Corbusier and disseminated in his group's journal *L'Esprit Nouveau* and his *Towards a New Architecture*, of 1923, that gospel of functionalism. But in *Art* Bell too was advancing an antiornamentalism that would have reminded any Viennese of Adolf Loos: "Only where economy has banished the architect do we see masonry of any merit. The engineers, who have at least a scientific problem to solve, create, in factories and railway-bridges, our most creditable monuments [N.B. not only the appeal to engineers but the Loosian bottom-line category of *monument*]. They at least are not ashamed of their construction, or at any rate, they are not allowed to smother it in beauty at thirty shillings a foot." Architectural thinking even spills over into the critical discourse of painting as Bell writes of modern painters' new "willingness to leave bare the construction if by doing so the spectator may be helped to the conception of the [N.B.] plan" (Bell, *Art* 148, 157).

Later on, after finishing the house, at Cambridge in 1930 and then during the same summer at a meeting of the Vienna Circle, Wittgenstein dealt with the problem of mathematical formalism as partly right and partly wrong by resolving it into a kind of functionalism, stressing the wider function of signs within some syntax or game (Waismann 102–05). After finishing the house, Wittgenstein was markedly alert to the formal aspect of architecture on his return to his old Trinity rooms. Maurice Drury reports of a visit in 1930 to Wittgenstein in Whewell's Court: "I noticed that he had altered the proportions of the windows by using strips of black paper." To his comment, Wittgenstein evidently responded, "See what a difference it makes to the appearance of the room when the windows have the right proportion. You think philosophy is difficult enough but I can tell you it is nothing to the difficulty of being a good architect" (Drury 106). This is taken as a hearty comment on the practical business of architecture; but it is also an aesthetic comment on intuiting formal value. It was even more Loosian of him in 1936 to deploy a sartorial metaphor in saying that though they were lucky to be "still living in times where a good tailor knows within a fraction of an inch how to cut his cloth," that may well become a lost art, "[j]ust as in modern architecture they don't know in what style to design a building" (130).

Architecture figures in Wittgenstein's summer 1938 aesthetics lectures, as showing up how at times the changing pragmatic of style is commonly apparent. That autumn, a review by Clive Bell in the *New Statesman* on a recent exhibition of architectural functionalism would have reminded Wittgenstein of his own work on his sister's house, what with Bell considering the role of art in the "furnishing and plenishing – for I must not say decoration – of the new functionalist buildings," with some ethico-aesthetic critique of the popularization of functionalism as abetting a "smell of conscious virtue" (Bell, 'Cubism' 767–68). By then, too, Wittgenstein may have been all the better acquainted with the modern formalist view as promulgated by Fry, who had delivered his Slade Lectures at Cambridge in 1933–34 (published as *Last Lectures*, 1939). What grounds are there for supposing that? At some point between 1937 and 1944, while working on the foundations of mathematics, Wittgenstein, speaking of depiction and symbolic representation, recorded this thought: "A theory of the placing of figures in a picture (a painting) – say on general aesthetic grounds – apart from whether these figures are engaged in fighting, love-making etc." (Wittgenstein, *Zettel* 122e). Otherwise, modernists of Loosian ilk would particularly like to know what he meant in thinking it formalism, though possibly formalism of "a good sort … [t]o regard calculation as an ornament (*Ornament*)" (Wittgenstein, *Remarks* 294).

Against the background of fluorescing formalism it is all the more telling to consider the brilliant analytical comparison by Jan Turnovský of a detail of the Wittgenstein House, namely, the handling of the front window of the little breakfast room which is reached, up a few steps from the main hall, by its own stairs. The problem is that in the circumstances the window could be centered either with respect to the exterior, with an asymmetry left and right within, which would be the solution typical of Johann Fischer von Erlach in eighteenth-century Vienna; or instead centered with respect to the interior wall, with no anxiety over the resultant left-right asymmetry without, which would be a solution typical of Loos. The material thickness of the walls necessitates a choice: you can have your window exactly centered outside, but not as seen from within, or you can have it centered on the inside wall, in the manner of Loos with his favoring of domestic interiority, ignoring the resultant asymmetry outside. Then, presumably, Wittgenstein figures out a clever way to have it both ways, but formalistically: in order to maintain symmetry on both the inside and the outside of the wall, introducing an unnecessary protrusion, like a blank pilaster in one corner, so as to equalize the interior appearance. Although as things developed this was not done, the related digging out of a niche on the wall adjacent was done (W 107). Turnovský considers the Loosian solution "in a sense more natural, more tectonically organic and less formalistic, since it reflects the actual syntactic circumstances," than Wittgenstein's (Turnovský 76).

Without actually calling the Wittgenstein idea formalistic, Turnovský says that he tried to sustain on the façade a compositional "rigour" akin to

Fischer von Erlach, the author of the eighteenth-century Karlskirsche and other major Viennese monuments and much admired of Loos, and, "want[ing] to have it both ways, to enjoy the advantages of both solutions: exterior and interior symmetry in an asymmetrical situation"; hence his device of the wall projection – which as structurally superfluous has only formal justification – "is intended to achieve the impossible. It is a curiosity, the desperate act of an amateur, timeless" (ibid. 79). No two ways about it, in architecture having something any one way means not having not only *it* some other way but also all concomitant things as well. But as Wittgenstein's very approach entails one or another manipulation of material effect – wall thickness – that is really, likewise no two ways about it, a vote for formalism as against functionalism. Insofar as this was an attempt to outdo the Loosian solution it goes without saying that it was a Loosian affair.

Wittgenstein's sense of architectural form

Of two later remarks on architecture by Wittgenstein, one reads: "In a bad period the task facing a great architect (Van der Nüll) is completely different from what it is in a good period. You must not let yourself be seduced by the terminology in common currency" (Wittgenstein, *Culture* 74e). In defending the one who stands out from fashion against the current of stylistic conventionalism, Wittgenstein refers in his aesthetics lectures to the architect Eduard van der Nüll, who with the engineer August Sicard von Sicardsburg, designed the Imperial, now State, Opera House, of 1861–68, in Vienna. When noticed at all, this remark tends to be taken as ironic or sarcastic. But both men were teachers of Otto Wagner, the grandfather of Viennese modernism and a figure much respected by Loos. In actual fact, in the opera house it is interesting how the folding in, in alternative abutments – of high, set-back attic, intermediate orthogonal wing, and low main flank – resembles an equivalent sequence of roof planes at the left side of the Wittgenstein House. This tends to confirm a point of Wittgensteinian determination, though it should have been less likely without Paul Engelmann, whose final-phase drawing looks to have set up the formal possibility of a 'van der Nüll' roof alternation if one only thinks away its attic storey.

Wittgenstein's salute to the Vienna opera house of Sicardsburg and van der Nüll at first sounds peculiarly arch, like Nietzsche citing Bizet as his favorite opera composer. Yet it entails the very shift from early nineteenth-century stylistic eclecticism to Otto Wagner's definitively modern tectonic sense; for Sicardsburg and van der Nüll were not only both Wagner's teachers but both were themselves influenced by Gottfried Semper. Within the development from Semper to Sicardsburg and van der Nüll, to Wagner, and on to Loos, van der Nüll in particular was transitional (Oechslin 84); though transitional also in a conservative way: for though he himself "had railed against thoughtless eclecticism in the 1840s, the next generation found exactly this quality in his own work" (Whyte, 'Dioscuri' 159–60, quoting Renate Wagner-Rieger), notably here in his and Sicardsburg's State Opera.

We know that Semper's vital sense of the 'cladding' of buildings derives from the imagery of a 'kernel form' hidden under the superficial 'husk' of a stylistic 'artform,' framed by the architectural historian Karl Bötticher (*Die Tektonik der Hellenen*, 1844); Frampton tracks this view back further to Goethe and the figure of the *Kern* or 'seed' in his *Naturphilosophie* (Frampton, 'Rise'). In view of the Wittgenstein House project, it is also worth highlighting a certain parallel between philosophy and architecture which concerns Frege's logical imagery of kernel and husk already familiar in the architectural realm from Gottfried Semper (chapter 5), through the progressive academician Otto Wagner, as making Adolf Loos possible, in parallel with Frege's in some sense making Wittgenstein possible. Werner Oechslin has pointed to the hope, expressed in Wagner's *Moderne Architektur* (1896; 1914), that engineer and artist-architect might share in "logical thought" (Oechslin 379).

Since on Samuel Alexander's prompting it was specifically by Frege that young Wittgenstein had first hoped to be guided on the path to the philosophical future, it is worth recalling (from chapter 5) Frege's text on 'Logic' drafted between 1879 and 1891, as tackling that eminent early Wittgensteinian subject, the confusion caused by the way grammar allows language to range beyond what logic can warrant. Gottlob Frege himself employs the Otto Wagnerian imagery of cladding. Speaking of language, he says that exact translation will be impossible if one means to carry over the "psychological shell" of what is said, for it is doubtful that the *Umhüllung*, or 'en-hulling,' of any two individuals speaking the same language, let alone two different languages, could be identical. This is why the study of foreign languages brings out both differences in the "clothing (*Einkleidung*)" of thought *versus* the common "kernel (*Kern*)" of meaning beneath discrepant claddings (Frege, 'Logic' 6; 'Logik' 1: 6). Here, in the new modern logic which inspired the young Wittgenstein, was something distictly comparable with the sense of cladding that Wagner developed out of, yet beyond, Semper in early modern architecture.

Wittgenstein's other, better known remark is on modern architecture, an expression of admiration for Alexei Shchusev's Lenin Mausoleum, in Moscow, of 1930: "You know I don't think much of modern architecture," he told Drury; "but that tomb in the Kremlin is well designed" (Drury 126). Suffice it to say, without entertaining the shift into an extreme materialist constructivism in art as paralleling the logical positivism of the Vienna Circle *versus* Wittgenstein as representing 'pure' abstraction: Shchusev's crisply massive mausoleum can be considered Loos-compatible on two counts. Not only does it virtually embody Loos's strong literary figure of tomb and monument as peculiarly definitive of the essence of architecture, in the essay 'Architecture,' but stylistically it even resembles the blocky, hefty little tomb that Loos had designed in 1921 for the art historian Max Dvořák. But the comment on Shchusev's mausoleum points up, too, a problematic boxy, crypto-classical symmetry in more doltish forms of functionalist practice, Czech or otherwise, which must be at odds with deferring freely to purpose over and against form.[4] Le Corbusier, aware of Adolf Loos, contributed a *cultus* of quasi-ethical functionalist truth-to-purpose more lyrically formal than the orthodox functionalist mode.

Early Czech functionalism in Vienna

It may clarify the matter to look to Czech functionalism, which never lost its Loosian underpinnings, even at its constructivist-materialist extreme. It was Loos who, so purgatively in 'Architecture,' had done something Wittgensteinian that is usually overlooked: to *point up more than bespeak* the metaphysical aspect of art, with tomb and monument as rock-bottom limiting cases of the *all but spiritually useless*. Somehow the question of formal composition seems moot when in head-on view the principal façade of the Wittgenstein House settles into a clean-swept blankness, with its forward projection shifted tidily into one corner. The poker-faced façade with its shy little portal lacks any pressing sense of answering 'functionally' to practical distinctions of use within. Certainly the withdrawn, sidestepping entrance 'says' nothing about a grand main floor as centered on the symmetrical central hall behind. However, in its three-by-three-unit disposition the façade compares with an earlier, four-by-four-window façade study, from 1914, by Josef Chochol, who has a place in a development from Czech 'cubism' into functionalism. His design submits a similar fenestration to articulation in obvious increments from 1 to 2 x 2 to 3 x 3 to (3 + 1), in a build-up of projecting layers, undercutting formalism, or rendering it elementary, by following a self-evident incremental compounding (illus., Krajči and Švácha 119).

A principal progenitor of Czech functionalism was a Czech student of Otto Wagner, Jan Kotěra, who, too, was born in Brno, in 1871, a year after Loos. Kotěra died young in 1923, having already taught several major Czech functionalists of the 1920s and 1930s, that, or how, "[a]rchitectural design" is not about "form and decoration" but rather about "space and construction," as "the truth of architecture," of which form is "at best" an "expression" ('On New Art,' 1900; qu. Teige 97). Ironically, Loos, like Wittgenstein, went to a German engineering school, but he earned a niche in fine-art architecture, whereas Kotěra went to Vienna and studied under Wagner, only to return to the Czech Lands to found the 'anti-aesthetic' functionalist tradition. The villa that Kotěra built for himself in Prague, in 1907–09, with soaring stair tower and integrally trimmed but unadorned brickwork (illus., Teige 101, top), makes the famous Palais Stoclet, in Brussels, of 1910, look overwrought in just the way that Loos always thought of its Vienna secessionist designer, Josef Hoffmann, as incorrigibly decorative – including, no doubt, a rather odd entrance by Hoffmann for the Wittgensteins' country place at Hohenberg in 1906–07. While Kotěra's tower is more emphatic, for the Wittgenstein House Engelmann held on, through several reconceptions, to an idea of the three-bayed main block as tower-like.

More relevantly still, between 1913 and 1916 Kotěra had built on the Hohe Warte, a great hill in the XIX District of Vienna, a large modernist urban villa in a garden, the Lemberger (or Lemberger-Gombrich) House, in which Ernst Gombrich lived as a boy. A decade earlier, in 1904, shortly before Sir Ernst was born, Loos had designed the Vienna apartment of his father-to-be. Like the Wittgenstein house, this villa too sits on the edge of a garden, but to one side of a traditionally axial *cour d'honneur*. Although one might be inclined to see the Wittgenstein House as more radically modern for lack of ornament, the Lemberger already made manifest its interior disposition on the exterior, which is not only a mark of functionalism but one respect in which the Wittgenstein House is not a functionalist building. On the courtyard flank of Kotěra's large squarish block at the left, a triplet of windows of different heights, all equally high but shorter and shorter to the right, 'expresses,' as modernists like to say, the upward rise of a flight of stairs behind, with this complemented on the adjacent wall by a row of also equally high windows

37. Jan Kotĕra, Lemberger-Gombrich Villa,
Vienna, 1913–16.

extending further and further downward as another flight of stairs descends within. Although freer of ornamentation, the Wittgenstein House is tightly trussed up, compared with the rhythmic fenestrational play of pairs and triplets, plus a pairing of pairs on the open rooftop, in a façade by that other Loosian disciple who also had a hand, simultaneously, in the Wittgenstein House, Jacques Groag: the garden façade of Loos's Moller House, in Vienna, of 1927–28, which has been called "a perfect modern counterpart" to the Wittgenstein House (W 140).

From main-line Czech functionalism, witness a fine smaller, middle-class house built in Prague-Strašnice in 1926 by Jaromír Krejcar, a student in turn of Kotěra (illus., Teige 170). Notwithstanding its straightforwardness, Krejcar's house accomplishes something formal that the Wittgenstein House, whoever's fault it may be, fails to do: it turns the corner smartly, with one tall casement of Engelmannian-Wittgensteinian type on the side initiating a triplet completed by the pair on the face, where the latter joins with other pairs of smaller windows. Despite the Sicardian, Vienna-Opera roof sequence at left, the walls of the left flank of the Wittgenstein House look conceived so independently of one another that one can image them as adjusted to fit from lengths of run-on patterns, like a garment altered rather than tailored from scratch; whereas Krejcar's work, modest as it is, puts what one might have thought coldly 'industrial' elements together to good aesthetic result.

While Loos held the notorious and rhetorically problematic view that the private house ought not even to be considered a matter of architecture, there was in actual fact almost no recent modern Viennese domestic architecture besides his that the Wittgenstein House could have resembled. Even a decade earlier, when Kotěra built the Lemberger-Gombrich House, Loos's more conspicuously spare Steiner, Stoessl, Horner and Scheu Houses were already standing as the most modern houses theretofore in Vienna.

Engelmann as Loosian

As for Loos's prime disciple, like himself Moravian-born: where was the Paul Engelmann who answered the call to help out his old army pal's sister with the Vienna house? Knowing Loos must have been a great opener for the army comradeship that began on duty in Olomouc, Moravia, in 1916; with Engelmann Wittgenstein discussed his philosophy and, surely, the work of Loos. After the war, Engelmann worked for Loos in the same town on a substantial but unexecuted project of 1919, the classically influenced Konstandt Villa. But in 1926–29, contemporaneously with the Wittgenstein House in Vienna, he also built in Olomouc a modest house for Vladimír Müller, two features of which resemble the Vienna project, adding to the latter's Engelmannian aspect, one being a type of tall, unframed 'French' window like those of the Wittgenstein House.

Twenty-five years ago the relation of the Olomouc Müller House to the Wittgenstein House was demonstrated by Vladimír Šlapeta with his publication of the right flank of the house, convincingly substantiating by virtue of this façade (not the street one) his claim that Engelmann's house "can be assumed" to have "influenced the composition (*kompozice*) of the Wittgenstein house in Vienna" (Šlapeta, *Adolf Loos* unpag.). For the device of setting a pair of shorter, squarer windows directly above a pair of taller 'French' ones, with wide margins of uninflected wall between and around, is simply a smaller, humbler, two-by-two setup that became a three-by-three composition on the front of the Wittgenstein House. This was the valid basis of Šlapeta's claim, after he had already characterized the latter as a "collaborative (*gemeinsames*) work of both friends," meaning Engelmann and Wittgenstein, with Groag giving technical advice (Šlapeta, 'Paul Engelmann' 1495), with Wittgenstein's role at first limited to minor matters, including window detailing, though later more serious "interventions" as well (ibid., 1496). Beyond Engelmann himself, the Loosian grounding of the Olomouc Müller side façade is apparent in at least one project of Loos that predates both houses: Loos's 1925 project for an exhibition hall at Tianjin (formerly Englished as Tientsin), in China, where the fenestration of the large block at the corner of the complex is basically 3 x 3 though with no windows elongated enough to look of 'French' type (and hints of three smaller attic windows above) (illus., Rukschcio figs. 123, 124 on 389).

A supporting detail for connecting Engelmann with the Wittgenstein House: Leitner offers a photographic reconstruction of a since destroyed fireplace with plain, shelf-less mantel projecting a few inches in front of the wall in Gretl's sitting room/ bedroom, its sides and top formed a continuous surface equal in width at top and sides (illus., Leitner 95) – like the more or less equal swaths of wall between and around the windows in Olomouc and Vienna. This feature was hardly unlike a smaller but similarly framed heating unit that survives in the Olomouc house: it has a slightly projecting mantel shelf; but with its tile 'surround' slightly wider than its sides, it is, if anything, more like the entrance frontispiece of the Wittgenstein House than was the lost Wittgenstein fireplace. If the latter was more elegant, as "cast out of the same dark gray, almost black artificial stone as the floor slabs – a jointless, monolithic piece" (ibid. 94), Engelmann's little heater frame looks quite as monolothic, at least after a number of humbler coats of paint. The interior staircase of the Olomouc house will be considered in respect to the Vienna house shortly. In itself, as a totality, Engelmann's small house, contemporaneous with the grand 'Kundmanngasse,' remarkably sustains the spirit of Loos on a much smaller scale than the Viennese *Stadtpalais* to which it is also, however, related.

Thanks to Wijdeveld's study, an even more structural feature of the Olomouc Müller House interior which disappeared from earlier plans in the final embodiment of the Wittgenstein House can be considered not only Engelmannian but Loosian: a characteristic cutting off of a corner, as on a landing or between two spaces at right angles, resulting in a prominent 45-degree angle, as in Engelmann's main floor plan in Phase IV of the Vienna project. Just such a device finds a counterpart in a similar 'chamfer' between two spaces at right angles on the ground floor of Engelmann's Vladimír Müller House. But it is also adumbrated in the oeuvre of Loos, including an even smaller row-house design of 1921 for social housing in Vienna (also a first-floor corner children's playroom in a 1922 design for a Vienna *palais*).

While we want to be careful not to root for Engelmann simply as underdog (a condition unknown to his old army friend), Wijdeveld's publication of the project drawings allows us to appreciate something about Engelmann's practice: the sheer pile-up of various alternative sketches, even if Engelmann's plethora of alternative drawings was instigated by successive criticisms on Wittgenstein's part, and in that sense involved the patron. How else could Engelmann keep coming up with every odd new idea until things started to crystallize? Without knowing anywhere near as much about the circumstances as such scholars of the house as Leitner and Wijdeveld, I suspect that Wittgenstein's egotism undermined a collaboration in which he might have enjoyed the complementarity of talking (and learning about) architecture with his old chum with whom he had earlier on much enjoyed talking philosophy.

Then, too, there is Loos 'in' Engelmann (just as there could also 'be' Kotěra), so that the question of the Loosian in respect to the Wittgenstein House is not as simple as they suppose who consider everything plain to be 'minimalist.' Nor is it as blindly irrelevant as Bernhard Leitner understandably supposes it to be after devoting much of his life to a building he wants to see as *sui generis*. The trouble is, the extreme nominalist view must negate architecture as art more categorically than Loos ever did, because works of art can be *sui generis* no more than there can be a 'private language,' in Wittgenstein's sense.

38. Engelmann, Vladimir Müller House, Olomouc, Czech Republic, 1926–29. Garden façade.

39. Engelmann, Müller House, Olomouc. Fireplace.

There is a possible larger point for the Engelmannian-Loosian in the house: one wonders why it was not built of steel. Karl Wittgenstein, the patriarch of the family, gained a fortune from the Bohemian steel industry. He too had run away as a youth on an extended *Wanderjahr* in Washington and New York (1865–67); on his return he studied engineering and went into the steel industry, becoming manager of the Prague Iron Works, where by 1897 – soon after young Loos's return from America – he was in control of a huge consolidated operation (Jeniček and Kruliš 27–29). A small part of his fortune went to Loos after Karl's death in 1913, when his son saw to the apportionment of his legacies to artists and writers. Presumably the family wealth still entailed the Prague Iron Works, a cartel so exclusively 'German' in its workforce as to alienate the City of Prague as a customer, yet which supplied much steel to a great building boom in the new Czech Republic (45–46, 61); so it should surely have been possible to obtain steel for Karl's daughter's house. That it was built instead of load-bearing brick and concrete, including some reinforced concrete, may lend support to the Loosian view: of Loos's own houses, all twenty tallied by Bock were built with load-bearing brick walls, with only two exceptions: the very large Looshaus, of reinforced concrete (with steel over the entrance) and the reinforced-concrete central core of the Müller Villa in Prague (see Bock). Hence, without using any steel, the Wittgenstein House was executed rather in the more Loosian manner with which Engelmann and Groag were familiar.

Fine points

Agreeing with the consensus that the philosopher took over the building of his sister's house, altered Engelmann's Loosian plans and finished the job himself encourages putting concern with formalism to rest and must tend conversely to foreground functionalism. But then, certain features prove too irrational to be functionally determined: for example, the compromise of constructional integrity where what look like identical interior piers are differently constructed in various ways difficult to tell. And what of the impractical 'distribution,' with the main floor (the whole upstairs, altered or not, being undistinguished and artistically irrelevant) consisting of, in effect, three living rooms (one sometimes called the library), a dining room but no kitchen, one little toilet at the back of a cloakroom, and a private en-suite bathroom off Margarethe's bedroom. The latter, by the way, was connected yet also blocked by Gretl's madcap bed

40. Peter Downsbrough, *Untitled Boston 02.2004*, 2004.

as installed *within* a doorway whose side walls were dummied out to fit its width, with the lady coming and going through a closet (shades of Nabokov?). Actually, the bed between rooms was an idea which, as idiosyncratic as it might seem, Thomas Jefferson had already put into effect in remodeling his house Monticello, in Virginia, *c.* 1800.

Most problematic, no doubt, is Wittgenstein's major addition at the rear of the house, to give Margarethe her self-contained *appartement* down on the otherwise stiff-necked main floor. While Wittgenstein may have put his best formal foot forward with the fine-tuning of Engelmann's roof-lines on the left side, the rear is the knottiest part of the building, excepting the exterior fenestration of the rear wall, which has something of a Czech functionalist air. (I think again of the fenestration of Krejcar's 1926 house in Prague, above.) Hermine Wittgenstein, effectively her brother's press agent, once told about how, after sparing nary a schilling, Ludwig confessed that if he ever won the lottery the one little dissatisfaction he would fix was a single window at the rear. Just one window? The whole back staircase of the rear addition is awkward even apart from an absurd subsidiary, low glass-roofed 'sewing room,' which, considering the heat of the sun, chill of winter, noise of rain, and insufficiency of headroom, does better now as a nook for house plants.

More seriously, in that it entails obliviousness to a widespread vernacular convention on the Loosian level of craftsmanly pragmatic convention: the negotiation of the diagonal treads in the corners of the stairway is inept in stubbornly forcing a riser instead of a flat tread into the corner. Loos might have said that it would take a city slicker to override a carpenter's silent avoidance of the consequent diagonal exaggeration; for even if one could have made the diagonal fall more precisely in the corner than our famously fastidious perfectionist did, that step would likely look too much wider than its mates. (Engelmann had treads run diagonally into the corners of the turns in the staircase of his Müller House in Olomouc, though a very small space and without Wittgenstein's abutting protrusions in the corners to confuse the issue.) The beautiful staircase in the Mandl House, in Vienna, which Loos remodeled in 1916, is a perfect example of the conventionally correct way to turn the corner, of which confirming evidence is found in a present-day photo-conceptual work by Peter Downsbrough, whose project is concerned with what might be called workaday architectural formalism. Furthermore, the curved ceiling above the same stairs meets adjacent angled wall planes with an awkward spatial warpage (illus., W 126, with views of the offending joins, 130 of the warped ceiling). Then too, unpleasant optical kinks occur as the handrails negotiate inside and outside corners (illus., Leitner 165, 166).

Otherwise, the privileged social space of the ground floor embraces, besides the formally fascinating 'negative capitals' of the hall (which not so negatively recall 'impost blocks' in the Renaissance classical ornamental syntax of Alberti), significant equipmental features, including severely plain lighting fixtures, doors, some with hidden metal night shutters, and door latches – ignoring for once the overworked topos of Wittgenstein's fussing over the radiators for a year, rejecting countless custom-cast fittings, the journalistic appeal of which can be easily dispelled by referencing Immanuel Kant on mere perfectionism.[5] First, there is the 'precritical' comment in the *Observations on the Feeling of the Beautiful and the Sublime* (1764) on that "spirit of minutiae (*esprit des bagatelles*) which exhibits a kind of fine feeling but aims at quite the opposite of the sublime," including a "taste for everything that is overparticular and in painful fashion orderly, although without use – for example, books that stand neatly arrayed in long rows in bookcases, and an empty head that looks at them and takes delight, rooms that like optical cabinets are prim and washed extremely clean, together with an inhospitable and morose host who inhabits them" (Kant, *Observations* 71); then, more analytically, the section of the *Critique of Judgment* (1790; 1793) propositionally titled 'A Judgment of Taste Is Wholly Independent of the Concept of Perfection' (Kant, *Critique of Judgment* 73–75).

As for the even more journalistic appeal of Wittgenstein having the salon ceiling ripped out and done over because it was a couple of centimeters too low or high, that is something of a *sensitivo* artist topos in architectural history. While building the Müller House in Prague, in 1928–30, Adolf Loos too is reported by his last wife to have had just such a fit over the overhang, presumably of mouldings on the roof parapets: after ordering half a centimetre, "He drives away. When he returns the overhang measures an entire centimeter instead of only a half. Loos is beside himself and has the extra half a centimeter taken off all the way around the house" (C. B. Loos 36). But this sort of thing is simply all that some people can manage to say in praise of architects or architecture.

Quite a few features of the house which are presumed novel or unique were things already done earlier or better by professional modernist architects. It was after first trying conical silk shades that Wittgenstein suspended from the centers of the ceilings on the main floor the single naked lightbulbs now celebrated as ever so marvelously 'tautological,' meaning simply that for once they are all a lamp is and nothing more or else – just what they need be and are. It should not, however, be overlooked that Wittgenstein's locating of his fixture in the center of a ceiling, as 'tautologically' obvious as it might be, is also a default positioning held over from the placement of the bourgeois chandelier.

If there is an implication that other lamps are by comparison compromised, needlessly complicated or obscure as to their workings, that might be true as far as it goes; but any implication that here Wittgenstein was the first to dare to use naked lightbulbs is incorrect even within Vienna, where for a generation everybody knew Papa Wagner's exposed bulbs in plain sockets in the great hall of the Postal Savings Bank, and Loos had used dangling bare bulbs in the Museum Café even before that (in about 1912–13, he produced a remarkable ceiling fixture that was a sort of electrical version of a Byzantine *polycandelon* with a ring of dangling bare bulbs). Le Corbusier's Maison Cook, outside Paris, built quite quickly in 1926, already had a bare bulb in the center of the living room ceiling before Wittgenstein's; also, Corbusier proved himself quite as fastidious as anybody by obliging his contractor to remove all the windows and replace them with plate glass when ordinary glass proved too imperfect. Frampton writes that in the Maison Cook "the world of industry was made manifest through the exposed radiators and naked light bulbs, and above all through the smooth sliding action of the metal-framed horizontal windows ..." (Frampton, *Le Corbusier* 75).

If anything, Wittgenstein's bare bulbs in their austere fixtures, with their harsh light, especially at the high wattages used, share in a certain frigid rigor that extends to the sleek, steely, virtually penal, security shutters closing off the main floor portals at night – an excess, 'simple' as it may be in form, hardly to be rationalized on grounds of domestic practicality. Unhappily, just such frigidity has become caricaturally associated with architectural modernism in general as dehumanizingly 'functionalist.' With the large iron-framed glass doors, exterior and interior, anyone could have foreseen a major problem in expecting them to stay plumb – not to mention their 'conspicuous consumption' of wasteful expense. There was no law against Wittgenstein's being as stubborn as he wanted to be in ignoring the physical properties of his material in order to make what must by default be a formalistic statement, however 'blank'; and it makes a good story that firm after firm backed down from attempting to fabricate the doors, with the last engineer succeeding after bursting into tears. But there is no functionalism in a brute insistence, especially by one who had studied engineering, on forcing something that 'doesn't want to work that way.'

Whatever may be technically impressive in the big, ever so scrupulously balanced, heavy doors with their impossibly flush fits, they are not innocent of a sublimity of sheer force, of the switched-off and inhumane, that would have been distasteful to Loos and Engelmann. One wonders if the Viennese novelist Robert Musil might have seen Wittgenstein's 'logical,' multi-leaved

41. Walter Gropius (with Adolf Meyer?),
door latch and handle, bronze: designed
1922; produced, 1923.

interior doors before writing 'Doors and Portals,' an essay begun in the 1920s, which takes a Loosian, sartorial tack in mocking the conventional sense of a door in proper door-frame as like the old detachable but obligatory shirt cuff, once ruffled but now plain and hidden by the sleeve: "This discovery must be credited to the famous architect who realized that since man is born in a clinic and dies in a hospital, he likewise requires aseptic restraint in the design of his living space" (Musil 58). This could well apply to Wittgenstein's house much more aptly than to the houses of Loos, so devoted to interior comfort, which however in other formal ways it resembles.

The question of functionalism *versus* formalism can be sharpened by comparison of Wittgenstein's admittedly elegant door latches, which are constant in circular section while bending, in one plane, in very regular curves, with a so-called 'Gropius latch' designed in 1922 by the Bauhaus director and another Bauhauser, Adolf Meyer, and excellently produced by the S. A. Loevy foundry, in Berlin.[6] Both use a shaft square in section to act as a wrench in turning the mechanism of the lock. But while both proffer themselves to the grasping hand with round handles, the Gropius latch distinguishes visibly between its grasping and wrenching functions, while the Wittgenstein latch hides its mechanical function within the door, as prestidigitationally as the hyper-sophisticated hidden mechanics of Wittgenstein's *tour-de-force*, slim but weighty doors. (Come to think of it, Would one ever have thought hidden mechanics an even *compatibly* Wittgensteinian idea?) As tersely lyrical as the curves are, their presenting a play of complementary curves on either side of a door belies the fact that Wittgenstein's latch could not work unless the hidden stretch between the handles were not *surreptitiously* square. This is worth spelling out because its sheer elegance is no tautological marvel but a matter of styling that definitely concerned form over, if not altogether against, function.

Bernhard Leitner takes the steel shutters summoned up so effortlessly from the basement at night, instead of the curtains "which Wittgenstein had 'forbidden' his sister so as not to distract from the clarity of his architectural language," as "technically succinct and convincing architectural form," and endlessly "sensually stirring." Even the great Mies was supposedly satisfied on a more prosaic level than this: "Mies van der Rohe, in contrast, did not hesitate to close up his Tugendhat House in the evening with lengths of curtain" (Leitner 121–22). Well, the Ludwig Mies van der Rohe who built the Tugendhat Villa at Brno, in the Czech Republic, soon after the Wittgenstein House, was possibly the greatest sublimator of engineering into architectural art. Now that he has been cited in the case of the polymath genius's house as wonderfully unique, he must also be allowed to testify for the other side, where the Wittgenstein House owes its style, such as it is, though not any celebrated but indiscriminate, misguided perfectionism, to Adolf Loos.

The work in longer view

But we can no more rightly override art history in order to accommodate an amateur cultural 'star' who wished to consider his artwork unique than we can suspend musicology for the sake of the boring default-romantic piano music composed by Wittgenstein. No; if Wittgenstein builds a house in Central Europe contemporaneously with Central European houses by Loos and Mies, it must stand up to theirs regardless of the wishes of its author – all the more if the same author and his fans are also in the position of suing history to have him considered the 'author sole' of a work that developed collaboratively.

Let us turn, then, for a comparative point or two, to Mies's great Tugendhat House, designed in 1928 and constructed in 1929–30, soon after the Wittgenstein House. A much more expansive feature of that building than the windows, however cleverly shuttered, of the Wittgenstein ground floor, is the entire sweeping length of the Tugendhat's living and dining areas as one wide stretch of immense plate-glass window, looking down a hillside and out to the city. This can be opened, from one end to the other, by lowering the large, heavy glass panels at the push of a button, into the above-ground basement on the downhill side of the house. In view of the mock-profundity that has long attended discussion of Wittgenstein's fussing to get his conventional radiators just perfectly so, it is worthy of note that, behind the glass, Mies has two beautiful brass railings, one at foot height and one higher, functioning as a parapet when the wall is open to the air but also, in cold weather, cleverly enough, as a radiator system.

Concern with Wittgenstein's mechanism for raising and lowering the steel shutters, versus Mies's for raising and lowering his whole enormous plate-glass wall, is a preoccupation that Leitner seems to have developed since his earlier book, *The Architecture of Ludwig Wittgenstein: A Documentation / Die Architektur von Ludwig Wittgenstein: eine Dokumentation* (1976), which still carries the excitement of discovery that many of my generation felt as it first engaged us with the house, even those of us who already knew it from the outside. Now, in *The Wittgenstein House* (2000), Leitner lingers in the basement over the doltish bulk of the massive counterweights which allow the dubiously necessary heavy steel shutters upstairs to glide up and down so illusionistically (124–25). However, a drawing in the Mies archive of the Museum of Modern Art (Mies, illus. 2.263) shows Mies's, if anything, more graceful solution to the equivalent technical problem: Mies simply hoists his enormously heavy glass plates with a device as simple as an upside-down rolling window-shade, with each panel lifted by cables winding onto an axle turned in chain-drive fashion by a motor. Although a Wittgenstein passage written in 1929–30 has been associated with just such devices as the counter-weighted shutters, for discussing how several handles in a control room, identical as handles, can activate radically different operations, such as being "always either on or off" or "a switch which permits three or more positions" (Wittgenstein, *Philosophical Remarks* § 13; 58–59), the same passage less mysteriously and quite as rationally suits a Mies drawing for the electrical control panel of his window mechanism (illus. 2.296).[7] This latter shows six simple inset buttons, also identical despite their different operational functions, in a neat vertical stack of three pairs, marked, top to bottom, "AUF" (up) / "HALT" (stop) / "AB" (down). Wittgenstein's more mechanical solution is also more like stagecraft advancing an illusion; Mies's more electrical solution effects a subtler shift from sheer transparency to literal openness, as well as being, arguably, more technically sophisticated.

Of several Wittgenstein comments on architecture collected in *Culture and Value,* one, apparently from the late 1940s, is much in the spirit of Loos's 1910 'Architecture' essay, with its rhetorical denial of architectural honor not only to the house but to everything but tomb and the monument. Wittgenstein writes, "Architecture immortalizes and glorifies something. Hence there can be no architecture where there is nothing to glorify" (Wittgenstein, *Culture* 69e, with n. 1: "Several variations in the manuscript."). The others, both concerning the notion of 'gesture,' come from a few years earlier: "Remember the impression one gets from good architecture, that it expresses a thought. It makes one want to respond with a gesture (*einer Geste*)" (*c.* 1932–43; 22e, with 22); and "Architecture is a *gesture* (*eine Geste*). Not every purposive movement of the human body is a gesture. And no more is every building designed for a purpose architecture" (1942; 42e, with 42). While it would require more philological investigation to establish this, Wittgenstein's contrast between an ordinary purposive movement and a somehow more fully-fledged *Geste,* as a significant movement, willfully made, an act, a *deed,* may illuminate Wittgenstein's remark about almost nothing being worthy of the status of architecture: then the point would be, only structures erected as worthy deeds in their own right – something like that.

More readily grasped is an opposition between gesture and gesticulation. Had Wittgenstein read the Vienna *Neue Freie Presse* as a boy (home-schooled, at ten he built a working wooden model of a sewing machine), on July 31, 1898 he could actually have read the remark of young Loos, praising a drawing for a projected classical temple by the young Czech Jan Kotěra, founder-to-be of Czech functionalism: "one architect, with a grand, simple, classical gesture, has silenced the whole army of ornamentalists with all their violent [N.B.] gesticulation (*heftig gestikulirenden ornamentisten*) ..." (*OA* 22). Wittgenstein would certainly know Loos's 'Architecture' essay early on; but Loos's early and Wittgenstein's mature distinction between the good gesture and the threat of bad gesticulation both find an antecedent in Kant. Apropos of a theme of obvious pertinence to architectural functionalism, 'The Wise Adaptation of Man's Cognitive Faculties to His Practical Destination,' Kant speaks in the *Critique of Practical Reason* (1788) of how fear of retribution might so force one not to do wrong that he or she would lose the "moral worth" that comes from doing right freely: "As long as the nature of man remains what it is, his conduct would thus be changed into mere mechanism, in which, as in a puppet-show, everything would gesticulate well (*gestikulieren*), but there would be no life in the figures" (I.II.ii.ix; Kant, *Critique of Practical Reason*, online).

Ironically, in calling upon Jacques Groag after displacing Engelmann as architect of his sister's house, Wittgenstein paralleled the Loos who in his own late houses worked not only with Groag but also with the engineering professor Karel Lhota. Likewise had the architect who coined the very phrase "Form follows function," Louis Henri Sullivan, with the engineer Dankmar Adler. Shortly before the Wittgenstein House was begun Sullivan, soon to die in obscurity, published in his *Autobiography of an Idea* (1924) a statement purportedly against logic, on behalf of art: "In his secret heart he did not believe that anything could be *proved*, but believed as firmly that many things might be *shown*" (Sullivan, *Autobiography* 224). It was with respect to showing forth of logic as such that Wittgenstein had moved, in the *Tractatus*, from saying that showing somehow *precludes* saying ("What *can* be shown *cannot* be said," 4.1212), to the singular closing proposition on remaining silent about that "[w]hereof one cannot speak" (Wittgenstein, *Tractatus* 79, 189). Soon before taking on a demanding architectural project, followed up by his later, more 'functionally' linguistic, philosophy, what he might have appreciated in Sullivan's confessional statement was its managing to affirm how the truth of the new architecture was no more an automatic (or tautological) meeting of specific needs than it had been formal indulgence, but instead might accomplish a showing forth of architecture as such.

All told, there still is some Engelmann in this house in the end legally ascribed to Wittgenstein; and in the Engelmann, at least, some Adolf Loos. Insofar as the history of art entails style, it cannot accommodate any work as altogether *sui generis*. More than that, however: this major but problematic house, however Loosian, is not as 'functionalist,' for better or worse, as is often assumed (and neither is Loos), while it is possible to maintain that if it were formally more Loosian than it is, it would be a better work. Most un-Loosian is its morbid frigidity; and in the end what is most Loosian is possibly the way it so literally bears out Loos's, one had thought, essentially rhetorical, principle that the private house ought not to aspire to be art at all. Wittgenstein himself is known to have expressed disappointment with what struck even him as a lack of vitality in the house whose design he had taken out of the hands of his old friend Engelmann, who emigrated to Israel and remained a faithful, indeed, ardent, disciple of Loos. A possible echo of the project, never discussed, also disappointed Wittgenstein: on returning to Cambridge he wrote a paper on 'Logical Form' (in the *Aristotelian Society Papers* for 1929), which he soon disavowed, but which contains a graph quantifying values wherein it may not be too far-fetched to recall the plan of the central stair hall of the Wittgenstein House – not to mention the three-bay-by-three-bay, nine-square main ground-floor space of the Looshaus.[8]

Coda

In 1994 the house proved remarkably hospitable to an exhibition of abstract art quite remote from any possible functional justification except insofar as man does not live by bread alone: the work of the Scottish painter Alan Johnston. Here structurally rigorous yet intuited non-objective images responded humanely to the spare forms and rigorous character, but perhaps also, to the aesthetic need or want of the house itself (illus., Macdonald, fig. 170; Masheck, 'Alan Johnson' 1999). The installation performed a beautiful accompaniment, allowing the architecture, to whatever extent it is finally owed to Engelmann and Groag, Wittgenstein and his sister, Margarethe, to make a more poetic point of itself, in a gesture of affirmation that was anything but superadded artistic gesticulation.

9

LOOS AND MINIMALISM

The sort of bare box which might be thought to anticipate late modern Minimalism in Adolf Loos's architecture may be illustrated by just what somebody tried to mitigate by covering up with a deftly placed philodendron plant in an old photograph of his most reproduced detail: the corner of the salon of the great Müller House, in Prague. Without the plant, however: what a strong, peculiarly Loosian sense of rectangular-prismatic forms plainly and boldly clustered, 'boxy' only in being so forthrightly volumetric. The conjunction's formal character was not and is not an appeal to tasteful beauty. Its sheer volumetric components would have seemed too doltish for that, say, to the deft placer of the plant. The question of Minimalism arises because later twentieth-century Minimal Art didn't mind looking thusly doltish to make an anti-formalist point, while for his part Loos hadn't minded being admired by anti-aesthetic functionalists. Avoiding standardly beautiful forms and compositions of form was not necessarily doing anti-art: as Loos might have said, it was art quite *trotzdem* – 'despite' – what passed as artistic. At present the predicate 'minimal' is so promiscuously applied to so many things that for the sake of Loos it might seem better to avoid it; yet reconsidering what is at stake in definitive Minimalism may bring about a clearer sense of how his work does after all belong to the prehistory of the major latter-day art movement. If so, that is another point for Loos as architectural artist; for as Minimalism was never 'non-art,' however aesthetically void it looked to start, something of the same problem may be similarly resolved in Loos's case.

42. Loos with Karel Lhota, Müller Villa, Prague, 1928–30. Salon.

43. Loos with Lhota, Müller Villa. Salon.

Prevalent misunderstanding

The latter-day art movement termed Minimalism never went after beautiful form, not even beautifully simple form. It was against all that, including the essentially spiritual notion of the architect Ludwig Mies van der Rohe, 'Less is More.' This Minimalism 'proper' was deliberately so inert that the only 'pure' thing about it was its strain to stand against anything formalistic even though self-evident basic form was the only suit it had to play. I make no claim for an objective historical connection between the architecture of Loos and the sculpture of Minimalism. But in my experience there was probably an induction, in the 1970s, from my awakening from original misconstrual in respect to Minimalism, to a gradual appreciation of Loos's work as somehow something more materially affirmative of building as such, and not just the architecture which first managed to dispose of ornament if not necessarily delight. I had learned from Minimalism something which helped me see Loos.

Minimalism or Minimal Art was an art movement committed as far as possible to mere 'object'-making, offered as sculpture, though alternative, non-formal sculpture, or even as non-sculpture, mainly in the USA, in the 1960s and 1970s. Owing to its anti-expressive, mutely uninflected elemental forms, self-evidently or 'tautologically' basic, it is sometimes extrapolated to other modes of artwork. Most such extrapolations are unwarranted, however. Certainly anything elegantly simple must be ruled out because definitive Minimalism is too pointedly an-aesthetic to be elegant. It has nothing to do with 'Less is more' because it has nothing to do with intensification, let alone spiritualization, by simplification; only with de-aestheticizing neutral, inert simplification.

Also, despite what one hears in non-art discourse, Minimalism also has nothing directly to do with the Bauhaus – though Adolf Loos had helped to open the way, and the Bauhaus propounded a constructivism which eventually had corroborating relevance to Minimalism. Even to entertain possibilities of Minimalism in architecture, however, by rights involves a figure or metaphor: an analogizing of the architecture in question to the very special, one could say, uniquely neutral and decidedly an-aesthetic forms of 1960s-to-'70s Minimal sculpture (or 'Minimal Art').

In the catalogue of an exhibition of Minimalism and its legacy, at the Solomon R. Guggenheim Museum in 2004, an essay by a British architectural critic claimed that "Minimal, or perhaps Minimalist, architecture – if there is such a thing ... is the most recent manifestation of the continual search to find ways in which to use our ability to manipulate space and structure in order to bring some sense of meaning to the chaotic shapelessness of everyday life." Such architecture was said to "demonstrate that logic and reason allow for," or even encourage, a "contemplation of space," which, "if sufficiently intense, can reveal levels of meaning about the nature of existence," and with – perish the thought – no "need to involve the semimystical poetics of Louis Kahn" (Sudjic 36). Don't worry, then, no need to take seriously any houses of worship, with their excessive social demands; nor to engage with the architects now credited with bringing this forth, since their works simply do now what the pyramids and skyscrapers did in their days, as so much "functionalism," with Ludwig Mies van der Rohe "embodying these fundamental ideas," so that "what is now described as Minimalist architecture is simply a restatement of a recurring architectural theme" (37). Skipping over the somehow kindred relevance of Zen, the Shakers, and Calvin Klein's work for John Pawson's Nový Dvůr monastery in the Czech Republic, one comes to the historical claim: "In the twentieth century, architectural minimalism is an idea that can be seen to link [Adolf] Loos – certainly a Minimalist, both in his writings and, equally, in his sensuous but restrained use of luxury materials – with Ludwig Wittgenstein, whose house designed for his sister in Vienna certainly fully lived up to [Donald] Judd's idea about 'proportion being reason made visible'" (38; on the house, chapter 8, above). In the view of the present writer practically all of this is wrong.

Suffice it to say that nothing Minimalist was sensuous, and vice versa; and that Loos's use of luxury materials was not really "restrained" (while the extremely restrained Wittgenstein House employs no known luxury materials). "[I]t is remarkable how often Judd's name comes up in architectural conversations today," we hear, though one wonders what that should mean to someone who has yet to hear of the artist; and after blurring in the names of three incompatibly different sculptors, all presumed to be aesthetically his kin, we are told that "Judd's own architectural work was a powerful example" (40), whereas all of Donald Judd's architecture was doltishly plain-Jane, and proud of it.

To begin with: in art, not all cubes are the same – that is, not all presentations or representations of a cube. What is no doubt the most famous work of Minimal Art, Tony Smith's *Die*, of 1962 (remade in 1968), a six-by-six-foot cube of sheet steel, though like many of this artist's works it was first exhibited in plywood, can be categorically distinguished from a cube as sketched by Albrecht Dürer in the 1520s (Masheck, 'Abstraction' 44–47). Dürer's drawing shows a cube like a box with its top lifted off, the 'box' being a conceptual projection and, as such, looking transparent enough to reveal two intersecting inner diagonals yet opaque enough, owing to horizontal hatching on the front and diagonal on the side, to cast a shadow. By way of comparison, as transparently crystalline as it presents itself, Dürer's drawing of a cube is also rigid and earthbound, and if crystalline, massive in the sense of quartz. No one would describe as 'light and airy' Smith's *Die*, whose title puns on the verb *to die* and the singular substantive of *dice*; but, almost hovering as it does, slightly propped on two slats, it exemplifies the modern sculptural distinction, analogous to modernist architecture's shift to tectonic structure, between mass and volume. In this connection I like to quote a passage from Smith's beloved *Ulysses* about a blind man, which itself shifts from a presumption of a block to the volume the block could occupy: "How on earth did he know that van was there? Must have felt it. See things in their foreheads perhaps. Kind of a sense of volume. Weight. Would he feel it if something was removed? Feel a gap" (Joyce 181). Tony Smith's *Die* is one of the most canonical Minimalist works: even some who would like to consider it precocious because other chief players weren't quite as ready, do not consider it a false start.

Not unlike the way we can look at and understand Smith's cube as hollow, i.e., as containing a volume, is the upshot of a famous pair of tabletop cubic models, purpose-built for their photographic illustration, as presented by the emigré Russian constructivist Naum Gabo. A good working sense of the legacy of constructivism to Minimalism may be gained by considering Gabo's pair of cubes together: at first, we might say, one unquestionable cube and one open structure of the same dimensions but consisting of top and bottom braced apart by an 'X' of two intersecting internal planes. In architectural terms that would constitute an opposition between the older extreme of stereotomy (building as a matter of mass, especially from stone-cutting) and the definitively modern extreme of open, 'tectonic' construction.

Gabo's illustration accompanied his article 'Sculpture: Carving and Construction in Space,' in the only issue of what was intended to be a British constructivist periodical, *Circle: International Survey of Constructive Art* (1937). There the two models together exemplify "the 'space problem in sculpture,'" from the point of view of that then "new Absolute or Constructive sculpture," which is to say, from that mode of geometric abstraction between the wars which often seems evoked, if not invoked, by the Minimal Art of Judd and others, two generations later. Gabo's explanation begins with a fib, the statement that the "two cubes … illustrate the main distinction between the kinds of representation of the same object, one corresponding to carving and the other to construction" (Gabo 106). The fact is that both objects were constructed to be photographed as models, the closed cube as model for a *solid*, even though we know by looking at it that it is not really solid like a gaming-piece 'die' but instead hollow like a box, though meant to stand in for a solid cube, in juxtaposition with the more forthrightly constructed and constructivist, open, "stereometrical" (107), would-be cube held together and defined by its slim interior diagonal vanes. Nevertheless, the basic point does come across, of mass on the side of the traditional sculpture and sheer volume or, as Gabo calls it, "space," on the modern side.

Of course, for Gabo's purpose in advancing the cause of a sense of spatiality that could be considered constructivist (supposedly too materialist to be metaphoric), admiration is go to the right-hand model. But one can't play dumb: what both Loos and the later Minimalists would notice here is more dialectical: how, having understood, on the right side, such things as modern construction can effect structurally, they are more than prepared to understand the left-hand cube model as itself constructed, i.e., not actually massive at all but volumetric at heart! Surely Loos's boxy small houses with their load-bearing walls are quite like the prismatic volumes of Minimalist sculptures, and even the compound boxiness of larger houses is akin to Minimalism by virtue of their elements being recognizably hollow – like Gabo's heuristic, 'metaphorically solid,' for demonstration purposes, left-hand cube – with stucco rendering on the exterior and, often enough, thin, semantically distinct stone veneer, as well as wood paneling for the 'cladding' of interior surfaces.

Adolf Loos was already known to Le Corbusier and a hero of the basically constructivist Czech Functionalists when he wrote in 1929: "Before Immanuel Kant, mankind could not think spatially ..." (*OA* 189), meaning that Kant made us conscious, at last, of space as a form of intuition allowing us to infer the disposition and relations of objects. In the second edition (1787) of the *Critique of Pure Reason* – a work that Loos appreciated even for its style in his effort to distinguish art from arty craft (it "could not be written by a man with five ostrich feathers in his cap," as he wrote in 1909 (*OC* 155)[1] – Kant's addition of the term "alongside (*neben*)" made all the more appropriate Donald Judd's stacks and rows of interchangeable unit forms and Kant's understanding of space as "presupposed" if one is to comprehend objects outside oneself as "outside and alongside one another" (A23/B38; Kant, *Critique of Pure Reason* 68); again, viewing them as "objects of our sensible intuition," we can say "that all things are side by side in space" (A27/B43; 72). Such side-by-sidedness is especially pointed in the work of both Carl Andre and Judd, among the Mimimalists, wherever Andre stacks or arranges material units in rows, and wherever Judd sets units apart by the same width as the units themselves, producing an essentially sculptural interplay of volumes and voids in which even the negatives capture, as it were, the same volume of unadulterated space that their neighbors thinly enclose.

Adolf Loos himself wanted to teach his architectural students "to think three-dimensionally, in the cube," not "in surfaces" ('My School of Building,' *OA* 121). A significant project with potential 'Minimalist' relevance looks, shall we say, deliberately boxy, but making a point of its volumetric, rather than blocky, massive, character: a two-storey villa projected for the Albanian actor Aleksander Moisi (Aleksandër Moisiu) on the Lido of Venice. Even in photographs the model, exhibited, needless to say as a work of art, at the 1923 Salon d'Automne, fascinates by the prospect of a cube as cut cubically *into* in one corner of its upper storey. Frampton, calling the design a Loosian "stripped domestic prism" ('In Spite,' 212), takes its "abstract mass" as a case of "stereotomy" (214), meaning, block-like solidity. I understand the claim, but in light of Minimalism I am led to qualify this as a Gaboesque figure allowing of an all the more metaphorical *abstraction* of mass, a boxiness that can be said to look unitary yet suggestively hollow.

If anything, the Villa Moisi model offers a provocative case of commonality between Loos's architecture and Minimal Art. By the established definition there might be a problem with saying that such closed cubical forms as the white-rendered villa or a sheet-metal or wooden 'box' sculpture by Judd is or ought to be stereotomic (as an Andre timber piece would literally be), since if it may look hollow rather than massively solid, that is not something to take lightly in respect to art-historical antecedents of Minimalism. Consider a type both formally similar and culturally remote: one of the little ancient Chinese clay house models, having a quarter-floor similarly cut out like a negative cube from one corner to the center of the upper storey. I am thinking of an example which gave me this idea, in the Asian Art Museum, of San Francisco, from the Eastern Han dynasty, AD 25–220, the outside walls of which are scored seemingly to indicate the hidden ('tectonic'?) structure within, so that one is encouraged to look at something built of slabs of clay and think about its open volumetric interior. At the time of this Lido project Loos had actually just built a fairly cubical house with upstairs cut-out quarter corner: the 1922 Rufer House, in Vienna. Together both models – the Villa Moisi and its ancient Chinese antecedent[2] – can 'second' the similarity of the Loos project to later Minimal Art in that, what might have seemed like an earthen brick itself manages to look boxlike and hollow instead: as even the negative cubic volume in either case shows itself as figuratively 'carved out' of a cubic 'mass' that we know is not really a mass at all.

What Minimalism was up to

Aesthetically speaking, the most obvious thing about Minimal Art was its obdurate objectivity. Pop Art, with its iconoclastically 'lite' attitude toward culture, was only just attaining acceptance, in the mid- to later-1960s, in reaction against the metaphysical melodrama of Abstract Expressionist high subjectivity. Suddenly this new deadpan but dead-serious, impassive, influential but understandably never popular, form of object-making came to the fore. Both were denials of the previously dominant Abstract Expressionism, but where Pop never minded being oil on canvas and having a good time with the status quo, Minimalism was the first serious threat to painting as 'top' art, in consisting of unrepentantly inert, numb, inexpressively constructed objects that seemed to regret even having to park, as it were, on the turf of sculpture.

One can compare, for instance, two such structurally similar respective works as David Smith's *Five Units Equal*, 1956 (Storm King Art Center, Mountainville, New York), made of steel, and, ten or so years later, an *Untitled Judd* relief of 1966 (as re-fabricated in 1968), consisting of wide nine-inch-high boxes of galvanized iron, set nine inches apart in a vertical stack on the wall. Admittedly, anyone unfamiliar with postwar art might even think that all abstract art was 'minimal,' much too loosely speaking; but it is easy, here, to see the differences between even first-rate pre-Minimalist modernist or abstract sculpture and Minimal Art as such. The David Smith stands with a bodily verticality, even the sense of an organic spine becoming successively slimmer as it passes, with less and less to support, to the next higher element, with the lowest, actually unequal in having half the height or thickness of the others and acting as a foot-like base. The interstices seem mutually and identically defined along with the boxes, as complementary volumes of space, so that there is structural integration without the 'relationality' whose bottom line is always intuition; instead there is pronounced mechanical repetition.[3] By comparison with Judd's plain-speak, the David Smith must look vital but temperamental, where the Judd is space-displacing but light on its feet, at once intelligent and uningratiatingly cool. Another sort of Judd relief consists of a horizontal row of small metal box-like forms hanging down from a square rod (with sizes of boxes and their interstices reciprocally decreasing in one left-right direction and increasing in the other), and obviously altogether hollow.

While this given artistic situation is not unfamiliar to some of us of a certain age, young people now doubtless need to have driven home how, in its very muteness and inertness, Minimalism both assumed a political stance and developed an articulate new and alternative aesthetic position. In my own recollection, it had a pervasive political aspect insofar as it made such a point of non-participation, in the period of the Vietnam War and its accompanying domestic repressions of dissent. In fact, complementary to the stasis of the art, as put down in surrounding, less than utopic social reality, was the typically activist political stance of the Minimal Artist. For his part, Loos seems to have been a fairly inactive Social Democrat, except in the revolutionary moment of 1919, which was in a sense Europe's first 1968.

As I recall firsthand, Minimalism did not look, so to speak, neutrally neutral; it seemed to be making a point of standing conspicuously 'switched-off,' quite *an*-aesthetically at odds with the surrounding culture, which in America was steaming along under just that 'military-industrial complex' that retiring President and former General Eisenhower had warned against. Minimalism seemed to be actively on strike, above all against the war in Vietnam. In contrast, Pop Art (which in its own way has always been *aesthetically* underestimated) was passively complicit with the status quo. Although Minimalism's oppositional integrity actually escaped me at the time, at this writing it would be laughable to look for anything oppositional in what passes popularly, for the moment, for a stylish so-called 'minimalism' in all areas of design: a blatant commodity festishism of corsetted 'taste,' all, as far as possible, in conventionally tasteful black.

Minimalist artists were markedly political: Carl Andre was a founder of the Art Workers Coalition, which began by challenging New York museums' lack of concern with contemporary art and developed an institutional critique confronting museums as establishment institutions complicit with the imperialist war effort; Dan Flavin projected pieces saluting early leftist cultural heroes and then responding to massacres of unarmed students protesting the war; and Don Judd produced an unlimited edition print of historical anti-war quotations as a benefit for the War Resisters' League. In actual fact, Judd's ideological outlook was probably more conflicted. I always thought that, as excellent an artist as he remains, he might be said to represent all those anti-metaphysical Americans who have liked to think that William Carlos Williams' "No ideas but in things," in 'Paterson' (1927), might rightly mean *No ideas, only things.* But he did stand for peace, and made a great and honest art; and in his fashion he was sustainedly critical of the status quo in America. In a text of 1991 he writes, "Know-nothingness is this time's prime feature," and of the people as "an immovable mass dominated by consumerist concerns," a condition ready for fascism as an "imposition of a middle-class idea of order," to the disadvantage of "art, architecture, music, or science" (qu., Raskin 701).

On the aesthetic front, however, let us turn to statements by two of definitive Minimalism's principal protagonists, Judd and Robert Morris. Donald Judd told Bruce Glaser in 1964 that by saying he wanted to break free of the European art tradition he meant in part breaking free of Cartesian rationalism: asked what that meant in his own antirationalist artistic practice, he answered, "The parts are unrelational." To the further question "If there's nothing to relate, then you can't be relational about it because it's just there?" he responded simply, "Yes" (Glaser and Lippard 151). Composition struck Judd as newly disposable in art, as if in emulation of Constructivism. "You keep talking about spareness and austerity," challenged Glaser; "Is that only in relation to the idea that you want your work 'whole,' or do you think there was something in Mies's Bauhaus dictum that 'less is more'?"; and by the way, "if you have space in between each one [of your elements], then it makes them parts," Glaser challenges. "Yes, it does, somewhat," is the reply; "You see, the big problem is that anything that is not absolutely plain begins to have parts in some way" (155). Judd: "You use a simple form that doesn't look like either order or disorder ... Take a simple form – say a box – and it does have an order, but it's not so ordered that that is the dominant quality. The more parts a thing has, the more important order becomes, and finally order becomes more important than anything else" (156).

A year later, in 1965, in his major text 'Specific Objects,' Judd cites the empiricist Locke's *Essay Concerning Human Understanding* (1690): "The motive to change is always some uneasiness: nothing setting us upon the change of state, or upon any new action, but some uneasiness" (II.xxi.29; Judd 181). Presumably this applies to the repeated units comprising many a Judd sculpture. What, however, can it mean for Minimal Art to pit two works of Italian Renaissance architecture against one another, a minor project by Filippo Brunelleschi and a major work of Leon Battista Alberti? "The difference between the new work [i.e., Minimalism] and earlier painting and sculpture," Judd says, "is like that between one of Brunelleschi's windows in the Badia di Fiesole and the façade of the Palazzo Rucellai [in Florence], which is only an undeveloped rectangle as a whole and is mainly a collection of highly ordered parts" (184). Two old-school authorities who would deny Brunelleschi's authorship in this matter point up more apposite reasons for Judd to admire this mid-fifteenth-century church on which several anonymous designers collaborated compatibly: ornament "stress[ing] the austere dignity of the space," as well as the fact, potentially interesting to a Minimalist sculptor, of the window frames as "hewn direct from single blocks" (Heydenreich and Lotz 40, 42). More pertinently for Loos, Judd's comparison in effect criticizes the famous façade of the Palazzo Ruccelai for what Loos accused a great deal of the architecture of his own time of being: too graphic (one can imagine what he would say of so much architecture today which looks compromisingly computer-graphic).

The passage of Locke which Judd cited carries a footnote which he ignored, to the effect that we are not really agents but are subject to the necessities of nature at large. Hence Judd's appeal to Locke leaves a certain philosophical debt, in accord with which, whatever Judd was moved to accomplish by discontent with established conceptions of art would in the end be thanks, not to him but to what Aloïs Riegl called the *Kunstwollen*, which is to say, to what art itself sort of had to do at the time, given its history and the circumstances then confronting it. There could be a movement such as Minimalism; but the most one philosophically invested could hope for in the realm of art should then be authorial neutrality, if not anonymity; and from that Judd, holding to the position of artist in the standard sense, drew back. But doesn't this suggest an analogy with the architect so often promoted as the builder of non-architecture, or supposedly the great anti-architect, the Duchamp of architecture? Doesn't it suggest a way in which Loos was hardly ironic when he made his seemingly quirky 'solutions' out to be so commonsensical – definitely not a fin-de-siècle matter of putting on a smock and having some new trademarkable oddball idea.

Robert Morris's 'Notes on Sculpture,' which began to appear in 1966, constitutes the other major theoretical contribution to the Minimalist movement. With it Morris establishes a clear sense that Minimal Art, inheriting the literalism and anti-pictorialism, as well as the geometric formal self-evidence, of the constructivist mode of sculpture, is in his view independent of architecture as well as of the figure. One would never know as Morris sets out, that, not only conservative art-lovers but, for different reasons, some Minimalists, did not want to acknowledge Minimalism as a category of 'sculpture': but Morris effectively turns the tables by announcing, as a member of the problematic new movement (whatever exactly it would finally be called), that he will speak of sculpture as such. Morris builds up a sense of the limits of Minimalism as bounded by various negations, large and small. First, whatever we call Minimal Art is definitely not non-sculpture (R. Morris 222). A sense of the affirmative virtues of this new form of art emerges with the indication that, like John Cage in music as well as Barnett Newman in painting – but also, we might interpolate, like Loos in architecture – it does without "climactic incident." Also, it is also decidedly at odds with painting's opticality, even painting of modern "structural" rather than pictorial sort, and much more akin to the tangibility of sculpture as occupying non-illusionistic space – volumetrically, one can add. With the new type of object a certain virtue of being non-rhetorical seems asserted, beyond simple intractable inertness – the visible inertness of the autonomy and literalness sought (223–24).

One thing which Minimalism proper famously entailed was 'literalism,' in opposition to all residual symbolist poeticism and expressionist angst. Hence, too, a more generalized opposition not only to painting but also to 'art,' compatibly with Loos's more rhetorical denials of his own buildings as architecture. 'Notes on Sculpture' appeared in installments over a three-year stretch in 1966–69. In the first, saluting Tatlin, Rodchenko, and the constructivists, Morris writes, "The autonomous and literal nature of sculpture demands that it have its own, equally literal space …" (R. Morris 194). At least as important is a favoring of "forms … which … do not present clearly separated parts for … relations to be established in terms of shapes" (196). "*Simple* irregular polyhedrons, such as beams, inclined planes, truncated pyramids, are relatively more easy to visualize and sense as wholes" (197). A certain inert, dare one say, Loosian unity is sought.

Morris reports with collegial approval a now well known exchange in which Tony Smith speaks of the scale of his six-by-six-by-six-foot black-painted steel cube, which first stood as a full-scale model in 1962: "Q. Why didn't you make it larger so that it would loom over the observer? A. I was not making a monument. Q. Then why didn't you make it smaller so that the observer could see over the top? A. I was not making an object" (202). Following immediately is his own surprisingly Loosian opening statement: "size range of useless three-dimensional things is a continuum between the monument and the ornament" (202). Insofar as Loos had rhetorically limited architecture proper to tomb and monument, the eschewal of monumentality left a qualification of funereal seriousness open to a six-foot cube, not only in terms of a man's height but of 'six feet under' and of bearing the ambiguously formal and emotional title *Die*. Like Loos, Morris is concerned to distinguish the private and the social: "Every internal relationship … reduces the public, external quality of the object …" (206). He also finds a way of saying that with Minimalism one does infer the hollow rather than monolithic character of the standardly boxy forms, in a way that can apply to Loos as well as Judd: "The objection to current work of large volume as monolith is a false issue. It is false not because identifiable hollow material is used" (an ambiguous phrase which is glossed over by concern with that as possibly distracting), "but because no one is dealing with obdurate solid masses and everyone knows this" (ibid.).

Minimalism may sometimes have eschewed the status of sculpture or art, but it is not 'outsider' art and inherits a share in the 'normal' history of art. Consider one of the Minimalist sculptures of Carl Andre consisting only of firebricks stacked low in neat rectangular arrays, as if by a supplier who, however, (aesthetically) liked keeping all his building materials tidily squared away. Just such a brick piece by Andre, *Equivalent VIII*, 1966, caused a famous ritual ruckus when it was bought by the British nation for the Tate Gallery in 1972. But one might have expected somebody to notice an architecturally significant way in which that work belonged formally to even specifically British art history as supposedly a special concern of the then still united Tate, encompassing both British and modern art. For the arch-Minimalist Morris had an important namesake in a British Neopalladian architect. In his *Lectures on Architecture* (1734–36) the eighteenth-century Robert Morris gives an image that has fascinated me since the early days of Minimalism. It was designed – projected, drawn, and engraved – to illustrate how variously proportioned architectural volumes could be built up from stacked brick-like unit blocks.

This plate was widely disseminated by Emil Kaufmann, along with the also Minimalistically interesting, though more sublimely simple architectural, geometries of Étienne-Louis Boullée and Claude-Nicolas Ledoux, in his posthumous *Architecture in the Age of Reason* (1955), all the more when a New York paperback reprint of 1968, still in print, interjected itself into the Minimalist situation. Suddenly all this was part of poker-faced Minimalism's *mise-en-scène* (cf. Kaufmann 22–28). So, the refugee Viennese-to-American art historian Kaufmann had already connected eighteenth-century French architectural rationalism and the high 'functionalism' notably strong in Central Europe *c.* 1930, when his later work likely contributed to the fluorescence of Minimalism in New York. He had been known to specialists as author of a strong visual case for the stripped-bare form of *c.* 1800 as pointing, in the title of his 1933 book *Von Ledoux bis Le Corbusier: Ursprung und Entwicklung der autonomen Architektur* (From Ledoux to Le Corbusier: Origin and Development of Autonomous Architecture), which makes passing reference to Loos.

Although Carl Andre's notorious 1966 brick piece is obviously too stereotomic to look volumetric, it also refuses to pose as a monolith. Even Andre's laying of flat metal plates on the floor respects and addresses the real given space – indoors, at least, as a given volume, as with Morris's claim, in Part II of 'Notes on Sculpture': "For the space of the room itself is a structuring factor both in its cubic shape and in terms of the kinds of compression different sized and proportioned rooms can effect upon the object-subject terms"

(Morris 206). Like the other Minimalists', Andre's work is decidedly non-relational and 'constructively' anti-compositional. Some may doubt this today when they see what has become the standard illustration of Andre's *Equivalents I-VIII* as installed in the Tibor de Nagy Gallery, in New York, in 1966, of which the Tate piece was one element. The standardly reproduced photograph of the installation looks so suggestively relational that it has been mistakenly compared with Mr Less is More, Mies van der Rohe's, splendid layout of the Illinois Institute of Technology campus in Chicago, as projected in a well known photo-collage of 1947.[4] So it is all the more informative to discover that other photographs of the same installation, of which at least two have been published (e.g., de Vries, pl. 2), taken from other corners of the room, show up the installation as non-relational.

Kaufmann's *Architecture in the Age of Reason* also had theoretical interest for the Minimalist cause. Its eighteenth-century Robert Morris might easily be counted proto-Loosian for several reasons, including an "experimental" (if mainly symmetrical) approach to the plan and, in his *Lectures*, an opposition to "Ornament or Dress" in favor of "Undecorated Plainness," with a sense, not only that "Structure must answer the End for which it was erected," but that any "Embellishments" should be internal rather than external (23). Where Kaufmann infers that Morris's emphasis on "*mind*" in his writings was a defense against his simple-looking work's "offending" as so much "Puritan crudeness" (26), one can think of Loos's dealings with the conservative Viennese early on in the time of the scandalous Looshaus; and Kaufmann also approaches an orthodox 1960s Minimalist sense of non-compositional assembly where he identifies a mode of "composition *ad infinitum*" (24, 71), by sheer accumulation of units (his little blocks). This principle of the first Morris's *Lectures* suits any number of pieces composed of repetitive units by Andre, Judd, or the now contemporary Morris.

One more point concerning Judd's 'Specific Objects' essay. By 'specific' in this text Judd means something as nominalistic as what Bishop Butler meant in the eighteenth century by saying that everything is itself and not another thing: no one thing is truly identical with any other – a challenging notion in connection with an art making extensive use of ostensibly interchangeable unit elements. Then too, the "new three-dimensional work" was to be taken as a between-stools kind of art object, "neither painting nor sculpture" and "not as near being simply a container" as painting as well as sculpture "have seemed to be" (in the past), though even they are "less neutral, less containers" than they once were (Judd 181). One understands a concern for reform in sculpture, with Minimalism rising to the occasion; but maybe Judd's Emersonian self-invention obscures something that would have interested Loos, something suggested by an odd awkwardness in the statements about containers – curious term for a modernist supposedly beyond an unreformed sense of *content*, i.e., that which is contained.

Given Judd's turn to art from philosophy in the early 1950s, I do find myself wondering whether, when he sat down to theorize a new mode of object that as art was in a way only sculpture by default, he didn't turn for stimulation to the early Wittgenstein, for at points in 'Specific Objects' the *Tractatus* seems to echo. Twice in the second paragraph alone Judd refers to painting and sculpture, both – not just his hollow Minimal boxes – as "containers," meaning, curiously enough for artworks, receptacles, holders – when put that way, of presumably inert content. Until recent times, it seems, simple containers were more neutral as such, whereas now they seem more "particular" as forms (181), which is something Judd would like to overcome in the new modality he was helping to open up. Now in the *Tractatus* Wittgenstein often falls back on forms of the verb *enthalten*, 'to contain,' in reference to anything logically implicit, as in saying "The truth-grounds of q are contained in those of p ..." (5.121), or "If p follows from q, the sense of 'p' is contained in that of 'q'" (5.122; Wittgenstein *Tractatus* 107). Since 'composition' was not a bad word for Wittgenstein in 1922, Judd's remark on new painting as "nearly an entity, one thing, and not the indefinable sum of a group of entities and references" (182) compares with Wittgenstein's sense of "general" propositional form: "Where there is composition (*Zusammengesetztheit*; 126), there is argument and function, and where these are, all logical constants already are" (5.47; 127). Compare Donald Judd: "Most sculpture is made part by part, by addition, composed" (183), with "hierarchies of clarity and strength and of proximity to one or two main ideas" (ibid.). Over all, the earlier Wittgenstein's strong sense of tautology is more important to Minimalism, but textual parallels may also seem to suit Loos's conglomerative compositions of volumetric 'containers.'

Before considering some actual works of definitive Minimal Art I will only add that, interestingly enough, the possibility of a Wittgenstein influence on Judd's classic essay finds some indirect encouragement from one of the philosopher's chief commentators on the *Tractatus Logico-Philosophicus*, Max Black. In 1964, the year before 'Specific Objects' appeared, an irritated Black had called attention, in *A Companion to Wittgenstein's Tractatus*, to Wittgenstein's visual imagery, notably "his picturesque imagery of propositions delimiting regions of logical space" and "of one proposition 'containing' another" (Black 17). At least all concerned would have agreed that containment implies volume rather than mass.

44. Loos, Moller House, Vienna, 1927–28.
Detail of staircase.

Minimal Art in light of Loos

There is general interest for the case of Adolf Loos in the problem of Minimalism, in that the more Loos's work is seen as part and parcel with modern art in general – with Minimalism especially important as the last significant modernist movement uncompromised by postmodernism – the more it is apparent that Loos was not just an anti-artist or anti-architect after all, even if it is meaningful to say that he was an anti-'artist'-architect. We can consider some examples of Minimal Art in relation to Loos, concentrating on works by definitive

45. Tony Smith, *Free Ride*, 1962, painted steel.

practitioners of Minimalism, and then acknowledge Judd as also having written on architecture.

Robert Morris – the present-day American one – often seems Loosian in his classic Minimal work, which has been likened to Wittgenstein for its elemental aspect, like the calling for a basic "slab" or "pillar," on behalf of language in play, in the *Philosophical Investigations* (1953). In 1961 Morris produced some simple *Untitled* prismatic boxes, subtitled or nicknamed 'Columns' despite their not being round, which find ample precedent in square piers by Loos, conspicuously clad in thin marble like his and the other Minimalists' plywood-box forms, all the more where Loos's piers proliferate, doubled, in mirror reflection, as in the marble-veneered hall at the end of the dining room of the 1928–29 Brummel House, in Pilsen. A wood-encased radiator in the adjacent salon, to be considered shortly, strikes me, with its unapologetic boxiness, notwithstanding fine material and workmanship, as one of the more proto-Minimal, 'non-formally formal,' features in later Loos. Again, Minimalism was no simple, direct descendent of either Loos or constructivism, though Loos inspired at least that notable equivalent to constructivism in architecture, the functionalism, especially Czech, which arose in the 1920s as architectural counterpart to sculptural constructivism. Later, historical constructivism-functionalism, indebted to Loos, stood prepared to corroborate Minimalism.

Carl Andre, with his unadulterated grassroots way of simply placing material units together – as with the firebricks of his *Equivalent VIII* – has pursued as radically democratic, free of European finesse, a deliberately non-dissembling, even if uningratiating, way of simply placing in rows or tiers standard, uninflected elements of straightforward, undisguised *matériel*, mainly wood or metal. Andre's posture of Emersonian self-invention has not ruled out fraternal salutes to early Russian constructivism, notably Rodchenko's undisguisedly put-together build-ups of unadulterated material. If Adolf Loos is not an artist who would generally come to mind before Andre's work, a similarity obtains between the stacked tiers in his important early *Cedar Piece*, 1959, destroyed and then re-made in 1964, and the City Hall which Loos projected for Mexico City in 1923, with a similar crisscross stepping, as a smaller pyramid impinges on the corner of a larger one, to somewhat Aztec effect. But while Andre's works do not as a rule look like Loos's, he comes close in spirit to Loos the ex-bricklayer who in 1919 proposed officially to oblige architectural students to have first had bricklaying or other construction experience.

What must be one of the best known Loosian details has long held Minimalist appeal, thanks to a photograph by Roberto Schezen of the staircase in Loos's Moller House, in Vienna, of 1927–28. When I published an essay on Tony Smith and Minimalism in *Building-Art: Modern Architecture Under Cultural Construction* (1993) the image had already been reproduced so freely that Schezen was pleased that someone should even ask permission. For those aware of Minimalism, its form as a twice-right-angled square shaft has suggested Tony Smith's *Free Ride*, of 1962; but then also later, Sol LeWitt's series 'Incomplete Open Cubes,' from 1974 onwards. Tony Smith had studied architecture with Frank Lloyd Wright. His 1950–51 project for a Catholic church on Long Island, Wrightean and non-Minimal in aspect, looks to have been stimulated by the kind of organically

46. Loos, Strasser House (alteration), Vienna, 1919.

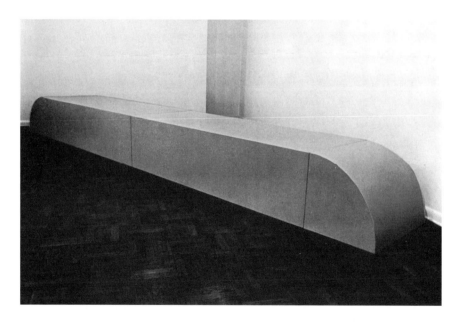

47. Robert Morris, *Untitled*, 1967.

'humane' regularity widely influenced by D'Arcy Thompson's *On Growth and Form* (1917; 2nd edn, 1942). During the sixties his sculpture, more than any other Minimalist's, played parasitic host to other architects. It always seems ironic to see his excellent 1967 work *Wandering Rocks* (named after the episode in Joyce's *Ulysses*) outside I. M. Pei's 1978 East Building of the National Gallery in Washington, with that building standing in obvious debt to such Smiths from ten years earlier as *Equinox*, 1968 – which is to say, only six years after *Free Ride*, the piece that looks so Loosian.

A peculiarly fine Minimalist work is Morris's *Untitled (Quarter-Round Mesh)*, 1966, in the Solomon R. Guggenheim Museum. The scale of the 31-inch high piece, made of by-the-yard steel mesh and taking up just over nine feet by nine feet on the floor, seems on the threshold of the architectural. Its large curved quarter-rounds about a cubical open centre look so light as only to be lending shape to the penetrating air; formally, however, the piece offers much the same swelling, simple but curvaceous profile as the large broad, inward-curving marble upstairs window-frame of Loos's 1907 Sigmund Steiner Plume and Feather Shop, in central Vienna (destroyed). Both works offered the same form in inversion, as curving inward in the one case and outward in the other, quite without formal fuss (an aspect of Loos's architecture with which Donald Judd tacitly agreed in his writings). Another Morris work, *Untitled*, 1967, which one might have thought to be as oddly unique as it is bluntly unrhetorical, perhaps settling for almost inadvertent shape in ideal form, nevertheless manages, uncannily enough, to parallel a Loosian form which in its own right must always have seemed as oddly unique as it is bluntly unrhetorical: the roof line of Loos's remodeled Strasser House, in Vienna, of 1919 – not to mention quarter-rounded stonework on other Loos shop-fronts.

Don Judd is in some ways the most irreplaceable Minimalist for purposes of generalization, even if not the only definitive one. If I say that a Loos project from 1904, well before the Looshaus, for the renovation of a Viennese bank, strikes me today as Minimalist, I will have Judd as my standard in mind. Judd also designed furniture, which he sought to keep apart from his 'art' works, though he was at pains to explain why or how, evidently not wanting to fall back on the obvious idealist explanation. In consequence, it is all the more interesting that a chaise-like late 'Wintergarden Bench,' 1980, of wood, by him (also a related design executed in sheet metal), should closely compare with the travertine bench which Loos set outside the door of his Müller House, in Prague, half a century earlier, in 1928–30. Some will say that designs so basic are nobody's 'style'; but even Judd's ostensibly styleless, homegrown American *Popular Mechanics* look winds up sophisticatedly recalling the way

LOOS AND MINIMALISM   253

Loos's houses once must have seemed almost rudely commonsensical, and the benches in question have specifically parallel non-tautological features at that.

In 1964, during the blooming of original Minimalism, Judd had written that in most contemporary architecture "[t]he only art that is involved is an idea of elegance, which is thoroughly puerile ... Architects are prone to elegance and are not especially imaginative. Much ... engineering is better than most architecture" (Judd 138). Twenty to twenty-five years later he became more involved with architecture, owing in some measure to his ongoing work on the compound he set up on a former army base; though in my view his own architecture is still less important than his furniture.

In a lecture at Yale in 1983, however, Judd sounds quite Loosian in saying, "art has been declining for fifteen years, following architecture which has already sunk into musical comedy. Many artists and a majority of architects and their clients are our internal barbarians, using Toynbee's term. A good building, such as the Kimbell Museum [by Louis I. Kahn], looks the way a Greek temple in a new colony must have looked among the huts ... The temple looks like civilization. The Kimbell is civilization in the wasteland of Fort Worth and Dallas. The Seagram Building is that in New York" (177–78). A year later in *Art in America*, he could still say, "Art has not yet been converted into commerce but architecture has, perhaps at a specific date, with the death of Louis Kahn [in 1974] ... Architecture was already a very small portion of all building [and note the rhetoric of the tomb and monument as "only a very small part of architecture" from Loos's 'Architecture' text as echoing in that phrase], even less if all of the new skyscrapers are considered merely vernacular" (178–79).

Kahn died in 1978, and if the index to Judd's *Complete Writings 1959–1975* (1975) is to be trusted, Judd, a prolific critic, had up almost to then never mentioned him in print. From Judd's viewpoint, the bad influence of postmodernism concerned the substitution of superficial (basically literary) semiotics for (crucially visual) aesthetics: "Everything is to be read; nothing is to be appreciated," he also wrote in 1984. He certainly had a point for latter-day art history. Judd could already see how the consequent ignorance of history was already blurring major critical distinctions and engendering what since have become widespread and deepset misconstruals of modernism:

> The term ... post-modernism ... is cant since the rather small influence of the 'modern' architects is held responsible for the banality of all architecture and since then this supposedly dire influence is attacked by those who claim to want something more, often some of the same authorities who debased the style of Mies van der Rohe to the

'International Style.' This is two straw men wrestling … Did the Bauhaus make A to Z look distressingly alike? Was it banal? [*Minimalism, of course, was banal on purpose and not inadvertently.*] A prominent aspect of the present is the distortion of the past … [I]t's important … that the old events look big in the history books so that it seems like a large public was excited by them. (Judd, *Complete Writings* 188)

Late Loos

Two years before designing the Moisi Villa for Venice, Loos had designed another unbuilt work, quite small, but which he could in theory have guaranteed was architecture even if none of his houses should count as such: a projected 1921 mausoleum for the Czech-Viennese art historian Max Dvořák, who died early that year. The Loos who polemically reserved, if not disqualified, the house from the category of architecture (not to mention art), had, once again, said in one of his best known flushes of extremism, in the 1910 'Architecture' essay, that only a very small part of architecture belongs to art: the tomb and the monument (chapter 5). Here then, for once, in a radically plain *mausoleum* to consist of a single square chamber of large stone blocks, with stone-block ziggurat roof: visibly just a box, with a sepulchral categorical supremacy no other building could top as unassailable architecture in the most dogmatically Loosian sense. (Loos also designed plain stone 'block' gravestones, one for the poet Peter Altenberg, 1919, surmounted by a tall plain wood cross, and at least one of two for himself [1931, *c.* 1931].) No one could possibly look at the dark funereal sublimity of the projected Dvořák mausoleum, his only actual tomb-cum-monument, and suppose that what makes it count absolutely as architecture is anything like ornamentation, however correct. Dvořák himself had written of Imperial Roman architecture, quite apart from Greek tectonics, as based on "a new awareness of both the physical effect and the weight of cubic structures … on spatial beauty, conceived in physical terms and on compact masses with natural limits" (Dvořák 7).

For a generation now it has been quite possible to look at this certified work of architectural art and to think of Carl Andre's simple layings out and stackings of bricks and other construction materials, and of Robert Morris's gray prisms, and of those black-boxy sculptures of Tony Smith which I. M. Pei, for one, obviously looked at architecturally. As heftily cubical as it is, Loos's Dvořák mausoleum looks like it definitely holds an

48. Loos, Brummel House, in Pilsen,
1928–29. Upstairs salon, radiator cover.

interior cavity. While in themselves Andre's material units never look any more hollow than the mausoleum's massive blocks, more importantly, in their (significantly unattached) assembly into works, they never look monolithic, but instead, as it were, as collectively occupying space.

As for Loos, in 1928–29 he had expanded an existing town house in Pilsen – laterally – with the collaboration of the engineer Karel Lhota. This was the Brummel House, which has certain notably proto-Minimal features, especially, upstairs, on the sort of *piano nobile*, a set of equidistant square piers, constituting a veritable modernist mini-hypostyle hall as doubled by a mirrored wall at the dining room entrance. In an adjacent salon, however, that in true Loosian form manages to accommodate a hefty 'English baronial' fireplace, one finds the more typical boxy woodwork of the large radiator cover, already noted, which can only seem more pointedly volumetric than ever after our experience of the later twentieth-century mode of 'inert' sculpture: Loos, one might say, in light of Minimalism.

In the Royal Institute of British Architects' drawings collection are 'diazotype' prints (like blueprints but positive instead of negative) from Loos's office for a town house project from nearly the end of his life; in fact, in the catalogue raisonné this is the penultimate listing. Apparently it was not necessarily the architect's declining health which halted the 1932 project so much as expensive construction complications in what had started out to be an expansion of an existing house, on a prominent street in Pilsen (Ulice Legionarska; now Klatovska), in Czechoslovakia, with assistance from Norbert Krieger and Ulrich Straub (Rukschcio and Schachel 646). The drawings, which date from late May to early June 1932, and were probably drawn by Loos's assistant Emil Ondracek, identify the house as for "Mr Engineer Oskar Semler," who was already living with his wife Hanne in an apartment in Pilsen, the interior of which had recently been designed and executed by Loos (1931–32). They give scope for speculation and possible insight into the operational aesthetics of what might be considered late Loosian 'minimal' form.

Oskar Semler and his brother Hugo were sons of the founder of a Pilsen needle factory which had become a major manufacturer of phonograph needles, packaged in tins bearing *moderne* architectural forms – rather too *Déco*-constructive for the, dare one say, more Minimal, likes of Loos, but cheerfully affirmative of techno-modernity. From a plan clearly related to the alternative elevations it is possible to gain a sense of the disposition of the interior, whether or not that was being experimented with as much as the two façades, fore and aft. In response to the difficulty of inferring the complex spatial interplay of levels in a developed *Raumplan* it is gratifying to

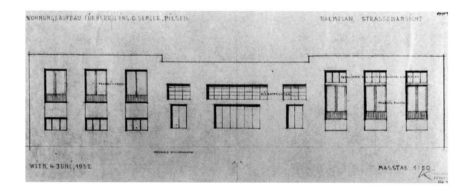

49. Loos, Print of an office drawing for projected Oskar Semler House, Legionarska, Pilsen, 1932. Street façade.

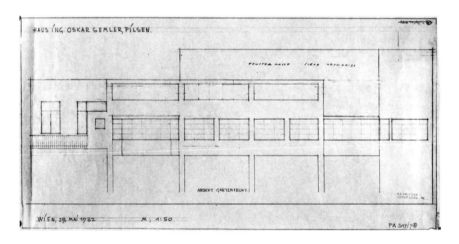

50. Loos, Print of an office drawing for projected Oskar Semler House, Legionarska, Pilsen, 1932. Garden façade.

see the clever way Loos solved the problem of indicating shifting floor levels in plan by marking them with "+" and "–" measurements from a baseline, the deviations up or down like going sharp or flat from a musical key. Reading from left to right in plan (street side up) means, more or less, on the first floor (European style) or *piano nobile*, first a partial footing or floor ("*partei Boden*," perhaps meaning broken with the rest of the floor in the interest of the *Raumplan*), then a sitting room, then a large social room or 'hall' (in the country-house sense), then a dining room, and then a pantry. In one drawing (PA397/7(2)), on what is identified as the third floor is a large lengthwise room labeled a "society room," flanked at either end by a smaller dining and sitting rooms. Obviously this was to be a substantial house, designed for major entertaining.

In designs for both street and garden façades of the Semler House there is some ambiguity beyond the basic Loosian preference for the public formality of a house as symmetrically facing onto the city street, *versus* looser fenestration elsewhere. Comparing one of each category – the categories being consistent and distinct – we might want to consider how this projected front is more Loosian and this rear, more funtionalist *instead*.

A study for the street façade of the Semler House (RIBA no. PA397/7(10)) is interesting as an example of Loosian combinational understatement under conditions of subtly modified symmetry that play down composition.[5] To begin with: it offers no doorway on what must be the house's more public face, like Loos's freestanding 1918 Director's Villa, at the Hrušovany (Rorhrbach) sugar refinery, near Brno, whose ostensibly 'outside' façade also has symmetrically disposed French windows. Here on a city street, presumably with the houses standing shoulder to shoulder, a principal side entrance seems unlikely. If it occurs on the garden side, one cannot be sure where without an associated plan because, in its shallow frontality, the drawing at hand does not bespeak wall recessions on the ground floor.

That this design is inscribed as a "*Raumplan*," referring to a freewheeling Loosian up-and-down disposition of rooms within, suggests a reason for the raised roofline, here, over the first and last triplets in what reads as a nine-unit façade: to disguise by symmetry on the front of the house what on the rear would seem to be one or another asymmetric extension upward on one side but not the other. If so, this is rationalized here on the front by having the cornice rise over the triplets of taller windows at either end, as if allotting them greater height than the lower set of mostly horizontal windows in the middle third of this façade. The tripartite division of the fenestration is symmetrical in principle but with complementary reversals of the linguistic units comprising all three clusters of three vertical pairs of windows, one above another. The upshot is so rich in permutations within the respective thirds that what purports to be as basic as A-B-A turns out to be A'-B-A", giving considerable scope to the formal interplay of signs in a qualified, in both senses, formal composition.

In the first three 'bays' (as if assuming the windows reflect structurally spacial units behind), take these elements, given as equal in width within a common frame, as: a short horizontal window of three lights, surmounted by a stretch slightly taller of blank wall, surmounted in turn by a substantially taller 'French' window; and these together as repeating a horizontal triplet of vertical triplets. By a Loosian algebra this then equates, complex for complex, with a radical redistribution of like elements in the last three bays, where each identical triplet now consists of a short stretch of blank wall, surmounted by a tall French window surmounted, like an eighteenth-century transom, a short three-light horizontal window. The reshuffling is so thorough that what had begun as a structurally nondescript basement window in the left-hand third of the façade winds up a lofty transom directly over each French window at the right. Somehow parity is maintained over all six triplets, uniform in height, notwithstanding their shifting vertical combinations.

Meanwhile, in the somewhat wider as well as shorter middle third of the façade, which looks two storeys high while both ends look to be two-and-a-half or three, a more complex but more stable arrangement of windows obtains. Below is a symmetrical triplet of vertical windows consisting of multiples of the same tall unit light: French window (two vertical lights) – wide picture window (six vertical lights) – French window (two vertical lights). Above each of these is a window shorter and wider than the windows below it, and consisting of multiple small horizontal panes, all three of these four panes high, despite the greater width of the lower central windows of the central third of the façade, so that the 2-6-2 sequence of vertical lights below, in a vertical-horizontal-vertical row of windows, is topped by a 3-wide+8-wide+3-wide sequence of horizontal lights in horizontal windows. As tedious as it seems to spell this out, it makes it possible to understand how here, on the street side of the house (and much more strongly than in a comparable a-B-a symmetry subordinated to asymmetry on the garden side) is a very characteristically Loosian fenestrational formal device: a sort of 'T-,' or *tau*-form, with upper rectangle element wider than affiliated lower rectangle – including the remarkable contradiction-in-equation of clerestory window and mirror in the dining room of the Steiner House, of 1910, and the salon windows of the Tristan Tzara House, as built in Paris in 1925, to give only two other instances.

A general difference in conception of street and garden façades in the Semler House project – more traditional on the street side and more modern in back – may be suggested by the fact that the present design for the street front specifies "normal wooden windows," except for the three upstairs horizontal windows of the central part, which resemble almost all those on the garden side and are here marked "iron windows." Alternative projects for the garden façade show Loos and his collaborators playing with alternative dispositions. Through a variety of more extreme alternatives than on the front, the rear façade remains radically asymmetric, both laterally and in its projections and recessions, with a stylistic air of functionalism that many contemporaries would have thought industrial, even as, presumably with requirements of the interior in mind, fenestrational units are tried out in a forthrightly formal manner as motifs. The larger point, in respect to both façades, is, yet again, that in actual fact the architecture of Adolf Loos is much more concerned with artistic form and with the art of architecture as such, than too many literary and cultural generalizations would have it.

The 'functionalist' look of the various versions of the garden front of the same Semler House project is a less Loosian matter of an obviously asymmetric façade as broken into recessions and projections instead of holding to a consistent plane, with unusually large areas of glass, unframed, in modified strip-window fenestration. The version shown here (PA397/7(4)) shows two parallel, almost continuous horizontal strips of window for the upper two stories, and slim piers approximating to Corbusian 'pilotis' on the ground floor. Somehow this design seems positively assertive of asymmetry. The second, third, and fourth bays project forward as a somewhat off-centered unit, with one recessed at the left and two recessed, to different depths, at right. This is not the only version with an 'L-' or *gamma*-shaped window at the far left, upstairs. Another study (PA397/7(5)) has a similar *gamma* window subsumed into an interestingly asymmetric, two-storey bay disposition, though, like a board nailed down on only one end only to pop up on the other, there the last two bays need compositional tuning up. In the present case the form is paralleled by an eighteenth-century transom-type window of the same height, with a small square window rather fussily filling out the space in the 'L.' Is this the fault of an associate being all too manneristically Loosian? Loos had just recently used his almost signature *gamma* device with more aplomb in his semi-detached houses at the Wiener Werkbundsiedlung, 1930–32, in the XIII District of Vienna, which also employs an 'L' in plan. Later, certain emphatically L-shaped or *gamma*-like sculptures by Robert Morris and others are among the major works of Minimal Art.

Such close-in formal analysis may become tedious, but here it brings us up against a certain limit, where formal richness is simply not in the end Minimalist or even proto-Minimalist, even though Loos is significant in the pre-history of Minimalism. On the other hand, such formalisms as we find here must betray what is supposed to be the worldly practicality, blissfully oblivious to art, of the constructivist-functionalist alternative. We set out with a problem of too many things seeming with deceptive simplicity to be the same: Minimal or Minimalist; but the complexity we discover threatens to disqualify the very relevance of Minimalism.

The disposition of the projected Semler street façade is fascinating as both blankly 'rationalist' and conceivably quasi-Minimal. Its symmetry is somehow too engrossing in its interplay of elements to be dismissed simply as conservatively crypto-classical. The three triplets of up-and-down paired windows offer a maximum of syntactical inflection. The central triplet of vertically paired window units recalls the Loosian *tau*-form by its shorter, wider topping of a larger but narrower window. At the same time, the taller triplets of the first and third thirds – one might not have noticed that the central third was in fact shorter, and with all short windows at that – hang together in a structural play of similarity and difference involving not only the up-and-down reversals of taller and shorter windows, all of two uniform heights, but also of blank rectangular panels, which at left might seem conventionally to fill in between the two stories but at right to count as active digital 'zeros' in the apportionment of places. At least when parsed, this seems more formally complex than eventual Minimalism will generally allow; yet perhaps it points up a crypto-formal rationalist, rather than constructivist, aspect of Loos.

Minimalism was a late-modernist art movement, specifically in sculpture; yet there are similarities between early modernist Loosian quasi-Minimalism and sculptures of Minimal, postminimal and even postmodern ilk. There is, for instance, a similarity of structural conception between certain three-dimensional grids of chamfered glass squares in such fixtures by Loos as the high cabinets for visible storage at Goldman & Salatsch, in the Looshaus, and Donald Judd's typical resort to open-ended compartmental compounding, as in a sculptural sketch of a dense honeycomb of open-ended cubic units (*No. 217*, 1969). In a way, such Loosian fittings, including even lighting fixtures, stand somewhere between the decorative extreme of Josef Hoffmann's mere patterning, in the Vienna Secession (and relatedly, Mackintosh), on one hand, and the guaranteed steeliest fenestrational grids of an arch-rationalist architect like Ludwig Hilberseimer on the other. Perhaps Judd's Minimalism stands likewise between those extremes as well.

51. Loos, Moller House, Vienna, 1927–28.

As for the postminimal: in 1968, when New York was otherwise pre-occupied, even with respect to art, the German artist Imi Knoebel, then still a student of the conceptual sculptor Joseph Beuys, produced a major sculptural installation whose very title has a Loosian ring: *Raum 19* (Raum meaning either 'space' or 'room'), reconstituted in 1986 at the Dia Art Foundation at Beacon, New York. The work consists of seventy-seven elements, all made of wood and Masonite, stacked and leaning, tidly but loosely, within some given space like a kit of prepared building elements, accouterments of life space, promising to constitute a work of architecture. Before it, anyone conversant with the works of Loos will tend to see not only panels promising to take

52. Saint Clair Cemin, *Bauhund*, 1986,
wood relief.

up their role as cladding, but prominent quarter-round volumetric forms
waiting to convey a finally admirably 'boxy' Loosian suavity. Whatever else he
accomplished alongside Kraus and Wittgenstein as major figures in Viennese
literary culture, the sheer conversancy of such an architectural sculpture as
Knoebel's with the actual architectural work, or let us say more securely now,
the architectural art of Adolf Loos, testifies to Loos's abiding accomplishment
as a fine artist within the discourse of fine art.

And for the postmodern, I present my own oblique photographic view of
the façade of the Vienna Moller House, already entertained here as happily boxy

and Minimalistic. Well before postmodernism played pseudo-semiotic games with its big, boxy, overhanging sitting nook as making for a face, it could have been pointed up as a proto-Minimal box, apparent as a hollow volume. Against this fine house I set a relief construction of wood that is neither a Rodchenko constructivist early modern piece nor a Carl Andre, orthodox Minimalist, late modern one. Instead it is a naughtily ironic, postmodern and in particular anti-Minimalist work of 1986 amusingly titled *Bauhund*, as of course a play on 'Bauhaus' (even as culture-historical cliché) by the Brazilian-American sculptor Saint Clair Cemin. At least it can be said that, by comparison with Cemin's ironic sculpture, the gap between Loos and the orthodox Minimalism of thirty years later, which some of us think of as the last unqualified modernist art movement, seems artistically narrower than we no doubt thought.

NOTES

Preface

1. Kenneth Frampton, 'Some Reflections on Postmodernism and Architecture' (1985; revised), in Lisa Appignanesi, ed., *Postmodernism: I. C. A. Documents* (London: Free Association Books, 1989), 75–87; here, 82, 86.
2. Joseph Masheck, 'A Crypto-Corbusianism in Breton's *Nadja*' (1999), in his *Texts on (Texts on) Art* (New York: The Brooklyn Rail – Black Square Editions, 2011), 36–50, here p. 45.
3. Walter Benjamin, *Selected Writings*, ed. Marcus Bullock and Michael W. Jennings, 4 vols. (Cambridge, Mass.: Harvard University Press, 1996–2003); vol. 2, *1927–1934*, trans. Rodney Livingstone et al., ed. Michael W. Jennings, Howard Eiland and Gary Smith; internal citations to this edition.
4. Benjamin, *The Correspondence of Walter Benjamin 1910–1940*, ed. Gershon Scholem and Theodor W. Adorno, trans. Manfred R. Jacobson and Evelyn M. Jacobson (Chicago: University of Chicago Press, 1994), 318.
5. This brief text is known by its first line: 'On Ships, Mine Shafts and Crucifixes in Bottles.'
6. Kent Kleinman, 'Archiving / Architecture,' in Francis X. Blouin, Jr., and William G. Rosenberg, eds., *Documentation and Institutions of Social Memory: Essays from the Sawyer Seminar* (Ann Arbor: University of Michigan Press, 2006), 54–60, esp. 58, suggests not.
7. Massimo Cacciari, 'Loos and His Angel' (1981), in his *Architecture and Nihilism: On the Philosophy of Modern Architecture*, trans. Stephen Sartarelli, Theoretical Perspectives in Architectural History and Criticism (New Haven: Yale University Press, 1993), 140–98, with notes on pp. 241–45; internal citations to this edition.
8. Theodor Adorno. *Aesthetic Theory* (1970), ed. Gretel Adorno and Rolf Teidermann, trans. and ed. Robert Hullot-Kentor (Minneapolis: University of Minnesota Press, 1997), 58–61.
9. Adorno, 'Functionalism Today' (1965), trans. Jane Newman and John Smith. Repr. from *Oppositions*, no. 17 (Summer 1979), 30–41, in Neil Leach, ed., *Rethinking Architecture: A Reader in Cultural History* (London and New York: Routledge, 1997), 5–19.
10. Adorno, *Minima Moralia: Reflections from Damaged Life* (1951), trans. E. F. N. Jephcott (London: NLB, 1978).
11. Thanks to my colleagues Charles W. Haxthausen and Pellegrino D'Acierno for stimulating advice on Benjamin and Cacciari, respectively, though neither is responsible for errors in my negotiation of the texts.
12. Allan Janik and Stephen Toulmin, *Wittgenstein's Vienna* (New York: Simon and Schuster, 1973), 93 (with citation to Karl Kraus, *Beim Wort genommen* [1955]).

Chapter 1: Loos and Fine Art

1. Furthermore: overcoming the awkwardness of a corner entrance opening into a major interior volume, the confident forward sweep of Loos's ground-floor space almost immediately within gains by taking the available diagonal in the plan as a strong straight-ahead axis for a wide and grandly rectilinear selling floor. Such an exploitation, on an irregular site, of what might have been a disadvantageous diagonal axis, by the strength of a conforming, rotating orthogonal system, has precedents in eighteenth-century tours-de-force of 'regularizing' plans on irregular sites, even for a piano nobile such as Ledoux's at the Hôtel Montmorency, Paris, of 1767–70.

2. Especially at the outset of his career, Loos obviously liked making a publicity stir. But while the public sphere became increasingly media saturated through the twentieth century, there is sometimes now a duplicitous bedazzlement with just what in this supposedly calls for critique as exploitation and manipulation. In regard to Loos, Beatriz Colomina has ably considered 'publicity' as encompassing the sense of the saturated public space of advertising and propaganda, *versus* privacy (*Privacy and Publicity: Modern Architecture as Mass Media*, 1994). However, specifically architectural distinction between publicly demonstrative exteriority and privately sacrosanct interiority also has a cultural prehistory which even includes Pietro Cataneo's Counter-Reformation call for churches to combine external simplicity with internal richness to connote, respectively, Christ's outward body *versus* inner soul (*Quattro Primi Libri di Architettura*, 1554).

3. Francis Bouvet, *Bonnard: The Complete Graphic Works*, trans. Jane Brenton (London: Thames and Hudson, 1981), cat. 72 on p. 104; William Weston, *Masterworks of Lithography: Pierre Bonnard 1867–1947: Edouard Vuillard 1868–1940* (London: Thomas Agnew and Sons, 1996), unpaginated.

Chapter 2: Loosian Vernacular

1. According to Luce's *Life* of Berkeley (q.v.), while a letter of 30 August 1729 refers to the purchase of "my land and house," another of the following March refers to "a farm-house that I have built." Berkeley could have torn down house 'A' once house 'B' was built; but because the house was at an early point added onto (long before the addition of a small kitchen under the low eave of the 'saltbox' roof), it seems likely that Berkeley's "built" simply refers to whatever building work he accomplished, even if it were all remodeling or expansion of the existing house, as '(A + B).' Of course, it would even be aesthetically significant if Berkeley had merely selected the house without modifying it.

2. It is difficult to tell if Charles-Étienne Briseux's *Architecture moderne; ou, l'art de bien bâtir pour toutes sortes de personnes, tant pour les maisons des particuliers que pour les palais* (Paris, 1728, 1729), which addresses itself to the needs of various social classes and considers the practical needs of "simple building craftsmen" (preface), is disqualified on Neopalladian grounds.

3. Apparently as early as the 1640s Rhode Island had "central-chimney, hall-and-parlor houses with rear lean-tos" like those of Connecticut and Massachusetts, and a generation later, variants in which "local builders used different English vernacular house forms to their own local ends"; and in fact, Rhode Island and neighboring Connecticut and Massachusetts were markedly "hybrid," owing to settlers from various British regional backgrounds (St George 72–74). Further: in an extensive overview of prevalent Irish building types, vernacular as well as classical, wherein the symmetrical façade fenestration with central door is commonplace, no such plan occurs: Niall McCullough and Valerie Mulvin, *A Lost Tradition: The Nature of Architecture in Ireland* (Dublin: Gandon Editions, 1987, repr. 1989); hence in this particular respect Whitehall was probably not designed by someone carrying around specifically Irish architectural presuppositions.

4. According to 'Bishop Berkeley's Gift of Books in 1733,' *Yale University Library Gazette* 8, no. 1 (July 1933), 1–41, Berkeley owned a copy of the second edition.

5. Downing and Scully, *Architectural Heritage*, pls. 29, 32, 39; the otherwise symmetrically ordered façade of the Pitt's Head Tavern, probably built by John Clarke and enlarged by Ebenezer Flagg (pl. 43), stretches so far leftward that the entire front door, frame and all, is actually right of center.

6. Cf. Eduard F. Sekler, *Josef Hoffmann: The Architectural Work: Monograph and Catalogue*, trans. Sekler and John Maas (Princeton: Princeton University Press, 1985), 174, 178, with façade illus. on p. 401.

7. According to Joseph Connors, *The Robie House of Frank Lloyd Wright* (Chicago: University of Chicago Press, 1984), 57, with figs. 44 on p. 56, 45 on p. 57, it was on the idea of another house recently built by him in Chicago, which "offered too slender a target to the perspective view," that Wright arbitrarily bulked out the Robie chimney (in part with an interior closet) "to an L-shaped design that catches the diagonal view more forcefully."

8. Thanks to Professor David Berman, of Trinity College Dublin, for pointing me to *The Querist*. The present discussion has been stimulated by Patrick Kelly, 'Ireland and the Critique of Mercantilism in Berkeley's *Querist*,' in David Berman, ed., *George Berkeley: Essays and Replies* (Blackrock and Dublin: Irish Academic Press, 1986), 101–16; also, Patrick Murray, 'Money, Wealth and Berkeley's Doctrine of Signs: A Reply to Patrick Kelly,' loc. cit., 152–56.

9. Even as Hitchcock wrote, Ludwig Mies van der Rohe was about to begin work on his campus for the Illinois Institute of Technology, Chicago, with splendidly ordered rectangular blocks in steel-framed brick and glass reminiscent of such old wooden half-timbering (in German, *Fachwerk*) as a meetinghouse in Berks County, Pennsylvania, built by a Moravian contemporary of Berkeley in the mid-1740s. And Mies himself posed the question in 1938, "Where can we find greater structural clarity than in the wooden buildings of old? Where else can we find such unity of material, construction and form?"; 'Inaugural Address as Director of Architecture at Armour Institute of Technology,' qu. in Philip C. Johnson, ed., *Mies van der Rohe* (New York: Museum of Modern Art, 1947), 192–93. In 1959, when Mies's Seagram Building was new in New York, Meyer Schapiro published his paper showing that the stone bands of Anglo-Saxon towers do after all derive from carpentry: 'A Note on the Wall Strips of Anglo-Saxon Churches,' Selected Papers, 3: *Late Antique, Early Christian, and Mediaeval Art* (New York: Braziller, 1979), 242–48. For the sentimental appeal of ersatz, non-structural half-timbering as a semiotic of idealized old-fashioned domesticity in twentieth-century British and American housing, mostly suburban, see Andrew Ballantyne and Andrew Law, *Tudoresque: In Pursuit of the Ideal Home* (London: Reaktion, 2011).

Chapter 3: Loos and Imperial New York

1. In the early Middle Ages very thinly sliced marble was sometimes used in church architecture for windows with iconographical implications of transcendent divine light, as in the eighth-century Lombard Tempietto at Friuli and the ninth-century San Zeno Chapel at Santa Prassede, Rome: Patrick Reuterswürd, 'Windows of Divine Light' (*Konsthistorisk Tidskrift*, 1982), in his *The Visible and Invisible in Art* (Vienna: IRSA, 1991), 45–56, with notes, 287–88. It might seem inappropriate to borrow such a device for such a worldly setting as a bar, and possibly all the more decadent for a bar making a Loosian point of luxurious materials. However, the preciousness of material in combination with simplicity of undecorated form in the old examples themselves relates this to a serious modernist Byzantinism (and eventually modernist admiration of Romanesque simplicity) which for Loos himself extends to a bank borrowing from the greatest Byzantine church (chapter 5).

2. Bukovina was a cultural territory politically contested between the Austrian and Russian empires. According to Russell A. Berman, *Modern Culture and Cultural Theory: Art, Politics*

and the Legacy of the Frankfurt School (Madison: University of Wisconsin Press, 1989), ch. 9, 'Imperial Encounters: The Institutionalization of Culture and Transnational Politics,' 155–74, the Austrian (Catholic) power preferred to embrace non-German Romanian culture there, and to take (Orthodox) Old Church Slavonic manuscripts as "precultural and primitive" (164), in order to counter pan-Slavism as a Russian imperial advantage.

3.   I see that I am not the first to appeal to Veblen on behalf of Loos: Eva B. Ottillinger, *Adolf Loos: Wohnkonzepte und Möbelentwürfe* (Salzburg: Residenz, 1994), mentions him and considers in particular the prestige value attaching to handwork (18, 169 n. 84). Exemplary, to Veblen, of such excess for display, is tribal ornamental woodcarving, specifically Oceanic – which was highly significant in the turn-of-the-century orbit of Loos in the investigations of the Czech-Viennese art historian Aloïs Riegl; see Joseph Masheck, 'The Vital Skin: Riegl, the Maori and Loos,' in Richard Woodfield, *Framing Formalism: Riegl's Work* (Amsterdam: G + B Arts International, 2000), 151–82, but also chapter 5, below.

4.   I have in my possession a gloating battle souvenir, a candlestick of brass inscribed: "This Metal Was Taken from Spanish Wrecked Cruiser Maria Teresa Sunk off Santiago de Cuba July 3, 1898" – relic of an imperialist campaign rationalized by the fraudulent 'Weapons of Mass Destruction' of its day.

Chapter 4: Critique of Ornament

1.   The dates conventionally given Loos's essays 'Ornament and Crime' and 'Architecture,' 1908 and 1910, respectively, prove questionable. In re-dating these key texts I follow Christopher Long in favoring 1909 for the former (as it was written out in 1909 and delivered as a lecture in the following January), while retaining the usual date for the latter as 1910, notwithstanding its expansion in 1911: 'The Origins and Context of Adolf Loos's "Ornament and Crime,"' *Journal of the Society of Architectural Historians* 68, no. 2 (June 2009), 200–23.

2.   When Loos addressed the subject the great sociologist Durkheim, aware of Lombroso, was at work on his classic study of the sociology of religion, which sees tattoo as removed from religion (even in archaic culture it is not innately totemic-religious despite sixth-century testimony of early Christians having "the name of Christ or the sign of the cross" inscribed on their skin), and clearly a matter of social position. Loos's sense of tattoo as practically identifiable with a lumpenproletarian underclass *ressentiment* is effectively seconded by Durkheim's speaking freely of tattoo as characteristic of "men of an inferior culture ... shar[ing] a common life" as "led, almost instinctively," to such practices for solidarity. Emile Durkheim, *The Elementary Forms of Religious* Life (1912), trans. Karen E. Fields (New York: Free Press, 1995), 116, 233.

3.   The problem, here, of recommending the aloof cultural non-interference of the "aristocrat," vis-à-vis his or her cultural inferiors (even allowing for the idealistic implication that anybody who cares might ascend to such taste), is similarly relative, if gentler: Loos is advocating what now seems like liberal toleration over and against any more presumptuous, pseudo-progressive cultural cleansing of the lower echelons 'for their own good.' Besides, surviving naïve folk crafts may not only be innocent of atavism but also better than the alienated industrial rubbish likely to replace them.

4.   Two of the founders of abstract painting, Wassily Kandinsky and Piet Mondrian, use the same memorable figure within a few years of 'Ornament and Crime.' After beginning *Concerning the Spiritual in Art and Painting in Particular* (1911) with the motif of art a child born into historical time, and a developmental trope of the ancient Greeks in juxtaposition with an ape pretending to read a book, Kandinsky, who had Arnold Schoenberg as a friend in common with Loos, declares that contemporary materialism "create[s] a sharp distinction between our souls and those of the 'primitives,'" and proceeds to invoke Beethoven repeatedly – as with Loos, as a great artist more advanced than the world at large. Interested from early on in folk ornament, Kandinsky writes that ornamentation "is ... either no longer comprehensible to us (ancient ornament) or else is only an illogical confusion ... a ... world in which, so to speak, grown men

and embryos are treated in the same way and play the same role in society ..."; he also mentions the sexual origins of the dance as still resonating in folk-dancing (Kandinsky 198, 197, 199). Even the Calvinist Mondrian speculates, in 'The New Plastic in Painting' (1917), that "in the duality of perpendicular opposition we see the most extreme opposites: the natural (female) element and the spiritual (male) element" (Mondrian 56). This sort of thing is often enough explained away in both artists as theosophical; but Kandinsky was living in Munich when Loos gave 'Ornament and Crime' as a lecture there (Long 213–14), and Mondrian was living in Paris in June 1913, when the first published version in any language of Loos's rather striking text appeared in *Cahiers d'aujourd'hui*, though that text shyly lacks Loos's sexual motif, as may the 1929 *Frankfürter Zeitung* version used for Mitchell's translation (*OC* 167 76).

5. Benjamin was obviously remembering 'Ornament and Crime' when, in the *Zeitschrift für Sozialforschung* for 1939–40, he published excerpts from Jochmann's 'Regression of Poetry,' e.g.: "The first care the savage takes of his body consists in its superstitious embellishment; he thinks he is adorning himself by torturing himself, beautifying himself by self-mutilation ... [He] distorts and poisons his divine spiritual image ... long before he knows how to protect and preserve that image." In Benjamin, *Selected Writings*, ed. Marcus Bullock and Michael W. Jennings, 4 vols. (Cambridge, Mass.: Harvard University Press, 1996–2003); vol. 4, *1938-1940*, trans. Edmund Jephcott et al., ed. Howard Eiland and Michael W. Jennings, 370–80, here p. 364. While one understands Benjamin's wish to find this "a new positive concept of barbarism" (p. 732) for purposes of the kind of fresh start initiated by Loos's clean sweep, there would seem to be confusion between the notion of a golden age in the past and that of a golden age to come, it being impossible to confuse Loos's conception of a high-cultural fresh start with even a metaphoric primitivism of given basics or elementals: Loosian elementals definitely had to be *worked up to*. Thanks to Charles W. Haxthausen for calling my attention to this text.

6. Cf. John Lubbock, *Pre-Historic Times; As Illustrated by Ancient Remains and the Manners and Customs of Modern Savages*. 2nd edn (London: Williams and Norgate, 1869), 3: "even the rudest savages ... are known to be very fond of personal decoration." On Lubbock's influence on Nietzsche: David S. Thatcher, 'Nietzsche's Debt to Lubbock,' *Journal of the History of Ideas* 44, no. 2 (April–June 1983), 293–309.

7. Cf. Masheck, 'Vital Skin.' In 1899 Thorsten Veblen held a less favorable view of the admittedly "well-carved handles of the ceremonial adzes of several Polynesian islands": though "undeniably beautiful" in terms of "pleasing composition of form, lines and color," and formidable as to "skill and ingenuity in design and construction," these were "manifestly ill suited to serve any other economic purpose" than social display, so much "wasted effort." But Veblen shows a Calvinist prejudice against something ceremonial as useless and wasteful, and possibly the nineteenth-century naturalistic prejudice that only representation really counts as art ("elements that would bear scrutiny as expressions of beauty"); *The Theory of the Leisure Class* (New York: New American Library, 1953), 110.

8. The bicycle and the steam-engine, and for that matter the Greek tripod which the bicycle resembles as a complex of tension and compression, leave, as it were, no room for ornament, showing their orderliness fully and self-evidently. That in their linguistic way, precisely as self-evident manifestations of order, the Greek 'orders' of columns can be said to do the same allows them, when properly deployed, not necessarily to contaminate or disqualify the blankness Loos seeks. He speaks rather indiscriminately of ornament and what could be distinguished as 'decoration'; this is a complicated subject, partly because, when such a distinction is in effect, 'decorum' may concern *ornament*. It helps to understand the importance of order to ornament, on which see Jacques Soulillou's Loos-aware 'Ornament and Order,' trans. Mark Heffernan, in Bernie Miller and Melony Ward's interesting anthology *Crime and Ornament: The Arts and Popular Culture in the Shadow of Adolf Loos* (Toronto: XYZ Books, 2002), 86–99.

9. Hence being an artist can hardly, in and of itself, be a bad thing to be.

10. On this figure, I have written 'Textual Life of the Living-Machine,' in Joseph Masheck, *Building-Art: Modern Architecture Under Cultural Construction* (Cambridge: Cambridge University Press, 1993), 77–94; with notes, 252–59.

11. Was Loos, with his modicum of Benedictine education, aware of significant late-antique Christian precedents for his imagery in this vital point of ethico-aesthetic critique? In early modern Viennese culture Augustine was of conspicuous interest to Riegl and to Wittgenstein. John Chrysostom, already briefly noted in this chapter, says that the rich man, having no worthy craft, such as metalworking, shipbuilding, weaving, or house-building, should cultivate "a better art than all those," by "learn[ing] ... to use his wealth aright, and to pity the poor," i.e., charity, which "far excels" even arts as necessary in the here and now as "house-building." Not even painting, let alone embroidery, should count as art, "for they do but throw [people] into useless expense," whereas "the arts ought to be concerned with things necessary and important to our life." Like Loos on more than men's shoes, Chrysostom observes: "the sandal-makers ... should have great retrenchments made in their art. For most things in it they have carried to vulgar ostentation, having corrupted its necessary use, and mixed with an honest art an evil craft; which has been the case with the art of building also. But even as to this, so long as it builds houses and not theatres, and labors upon things necessary, and not superfluous, I give the name of an art," whereas ornament strikes him as effeminate, and markedly exotic ornamentation stems from tribal culture. Apropos of men's shoes in particular there is found a most Loosian cadenza: "for first a ship is built, then rowers are mustered, and a man for the prow, and a helmsman, and a sail is spread, and an ocean traversed, and, leaving wife and children and country, the merchant commits his very life to the waves, and comes to the land of the barbarians, and undergoes innumerable dangers for these threads, that after it all thou mayest take them, and sew them onto thy shoes, and ornament the leather. And what can be done worse than this folly?" Making matters worse, all this amounts to so much social sin, for it is instead of helping the Christ to be found in the poor: for "how many thunderbolts must ye not deserve, overlooking Him in want of necessary food, and adorning these pieces of leather with so much diligence?" There is even a Rieglesque note where the motifs of "tendrils" (the Viennese art historian Aloïs Riegl's classic 1893 *Problems of Style: Foundations for a History of Ornament* is devoted to the evolution of tendril ornament) – as in the wing-tip shoe ornament criticized in 'Ornament and Crime' – is specifically pointed up in association with the wasteful and self-indulgent luxury of ornamenting clothing and shoes (St John Chrysostom 'Homily XLIX on Matthew,' in Early Christian Fathers: Nicene and Post-Nicene, ser. I, vol. X, sects 4-7 [http://www.ccel.org/fathers2/NPNF1-10-55.htm#P4738_1492441]).

More likely encountered would have been the *Confessions* of Augustine, Book X, which addresses more broadly the problem of the visual allure of exaggerated sensuous attractions, including superadded ornamentation. "To entrap the eyes men have made innumerable additions," as Augustine calls them, "to the various arts and crafts in clothing, shoes, vessels, and manufactures of this nature, pictures, images of various kinds, and things which go far beyond necessary and moderate requirements ..." These errors of excess are charged to some spiritual failing on the artist's part, but "higher" beauty is unscathed by private ethical disqualification; even so, when "the artists and connoisseurs of external beauty draw their criterion of judgment," they miss "a principle for the right use of beautiful things" which "is there but they do not see it, namely that they should not go to excess, but reserve their strength for holy things "and not dissipate it in delights," such as superfluous ornamentation, "that produce mental fatigue" (X.xxxiv.53; St Augustine of Hippo, *Confessions*, trans. and ed. Henry Chadwick. Oxford World Classics. Oxford: Oxford University Press, 1992, 210). These patristic sources are part of the cultural background to Loos's ethico-aesthetic critique of ornamental superfluity, with its preferential option for simplicity.

In the High Middle Ages calls to simplicity are found in thinkers as different as Peter Abelard and Bernard of Clairvaux: e.g., the former's appeal to nature against cosmetic luxury in his letters to Heloise and a famous letter of the latter against luxurious and distracting church decorations. Thomas Aquinas speaks several times against superadded ornamentation in the *Summa Theologica*.

Chapter 5: Architecture and Ornament in Fact

1. The friend is John Thornton.

2. Loos would no doubt have liked the fact that before promulgating his theory of Greek polychrome Hittorff had in 1817 designed for a British contractor named Browne a project for a classical-style theater in Vienna, consisting of a cubical stage and audience space with "forehall" having two-storey columns on its façade, and in which "[t]he architectonic formation and structure conditioned the inner disposition of space"; Kark Hammer, *Jakob Ignaz Hittorff: ein pariser Baumeister 1792–1867* (Stuttgart: Hiersemann, 1968), 91–92.

3. Where Kant distinguishes, in *The Critique of Judgment* (1790, 1793), between sculpture and architecture as plastic arts, though "dwellings" may be presumed, he specifies that what categorically "belong to architecture" are "temples, magnificent buildings for public gatherings, as well as dwellings, triumphal arches, columns, cenotaphs, and the like, [*important qualification of the preceding*] erected as memorials." Despite its seeming an opposite extreme to any such metaphysical normativity (not to mention its possibly seeming an old-fashioned holdover from the Rococo), Kant's practically delighted welcoming "domestic furnishings" under the category of architecture may also be reckoned surprisingly Loosian. For in this he salutes "the work of the carpenter and the like things for use" for the rather modernist reason that often enough – at least in his day, which was the time of Loos's admired Chippendale – they exemplify "the appropriateness of the product to a certain use [that] is essential in a work of architecture …" Immanuel Kant, *Critique of the Power of Judgment*, trans. Paul Guyer and Eric Matthews, ed. Paul Guyer, The Cambridge Edition of the Works of Immanuel Kant. Cambridge: Cambridge University Press, 2001), 200.

4. Herbert Read's essay 'Why We English Have No Taste' (1938) makes vivid in caricatural terms some of the features of Englishness that Loos admired, with such extremism that later this great advocate of modernist art, himself an English anarchist, would back down a bit, like a good sport, in a better known war-time pamphlet (*To Hell with Culture*, 1941). But it was mere moments, as it were, after the death of Loos, that Read wrote 'Why We English' in critique of just that English propriety and 'normalcy,' which compensatorily fascinated the otherwise rather wild avant-garde architect – to Read, however, as a matter of repressive and self-repressive mediocrity, especially under the sacrosanct category of the 'English gentleman.' The text still crackles critically with just what Loos, in admittedly different cultural circumstances, idealized, including the ideal of an architecturally restrained house: "The 'gentleman' is the apotheosis of the normal. Common sense is normal sense – accepted opinion, agreed conventions, perfected habits. In his house and his clothes, in his food and his women, the Englishman of the capitalist-puritan era endeavoured to attain the normal. The definition of a well-dressed gentleman is 'one whose clothes you do not remember'; a man who in every detail, from the colour of the cloth to the number of buttons on his sleeve, is so normal that he is unnoticeable, unseen. Just as a gentleman's clothes must be distinguished by their lack of distinction, so with all his possessions." Here, too, is Read in vivid reverse-caricature on the arch-Loosian theme of the understated beauty of basic English craftsmanship: "Some foreign observers puzzled by [the] complete lack of the plastic sense in the English, have attempted to find it in unexpected places. A few years ago a Danish architect made an exhibition of the real, the unrecognized, English arts. The *chef d'oeuvre* was the English football; there were English boots and English tennis-rackets, suit-cases and saddles, and probably a water-closet. In such articles, it was maintained, we showed a supreme sense of form, of abstract *form*. It was a charming idea, but the Englishman was not flattered; he laughed in his nervous manner. To him it was a *stunt*, a good joke. 'You never know,' they said to one another, 'what these foreigners will be up to next!'" (71). If Loos was such, he had, if anything, the extra-extreme enthusiasm of the convert. Herbert Read, 'Why We English Have No Taste,' in his *Anarchy and Order: Essays in Politics* (1954; Boston: Beacon, 1971), 67–73, here 70–71.

5. The Potemkin-town trope, which refers to stage-set false façades erected in Russian towns and villages to make them look nicer when Catherine the Great passed through, is one of at least two favored figures shared by the more or less social-democratic Loos and his contemporary,

the great social-democrat who turned communist in opposition to the First World War, Rosa Luxemburg, who wrote of "Potemkin villages" at least twice: in *The Accumulation of Capital: An Anti-Critique* (written 1915), and her pamphlet *The War and the Workers* (1916). Loos's choice of '*Trotzdem*' ('nevertheless') as title for his second collection of essays – *Trotzdem: Aufsätze aus dem Jahren* 1900–1930 (1931) – followed upon what many would have remembered as the last published words of Karl Liebkneckt before his and Luxemburg's dual murder in the middle of Berlin by rightist militia in 1919: "Life will be our agenda. It will reign in the world of the free. Despite everything (*Trotzalledem*)!" (Frölich 300).

6. An unforgettable Viennese instance of reflexive mirror / window conjunction in Loos's generation is found in the Freud apartment, in the IX District, where, hanging on the frame between two windows and hence breaking into the outward view, is the mirror in which Freud, stricken with jaw cancer, examined himself from day to day.

7. That is, until after a lost opera house project of Loos, discussed with Schoenberg, in Paris in late 1927 (Rukschcio and Schachel 605, cat. 190).

8. It was in seeking to account, from the musical side, for Schoenberg's passing from late-romantic expressionism to a cultivation of private emotion behind an impassive, mask-like façade, that Watkins discovered a meaningful counterpart in Loos's later houses, of the 1920s and 1930s; so that "it is to twelve-tone music and Loos's residential designs that we should look, rather than to atonality and the rejection of ornament" (Watkins 126). "Ironically, it may have been a worldly experience that gave Schoenberg the tools to formulate the spiritual ideal of musical space set forth in 'Composition with Twelve Tones'– the experience of the interiority in the houses of Adolf Loos" (179). Returning to Heinrich Kulka's very framing of the *Raumplan* concept as "free thinking in space," she notes that "Schoenberg ordered Kulka's book from the publisher in 1938, three years before settling on the multidimensional terminology of the late 'Composition with Twelve Tones' (187–88). Hence, the very words of Schoenberg, which I had quoted on Loos's behalf via Rufer's musical son, were likely already influenced by Kulka's notion of the *Raumplan*, with its definitive example of Rufer's parents' house! In pursuing her Schoenbergian course, Watkins accounts for how an ostensibly simple early eschewal of ornament – which was never, anyway, absolute, and which was expressed quite as wittily as it was earnestly in 'Ornament and Crime' – led on to the architectural complexity of Loos's mature work. She locates the pivotal theoretical shift in Schoenberg in an undated, unpublished 'Komposition mit zwöf Tönen' (Composition with Twelve Tones), said to manifest "ideas Schoenberg communicated verbally to Alban Berg (and perhaps to other students) in 1923, when he first made his new compositional approach public" (181–82) – which is to say, soon after the Rufer House was finished.

Chapter 6: Everybody's Doric

1. Benedetto Gravagnuolo, *Adolf Loos*, 48, with ref. to Ludwig Münz, "Über die Grundlagen des Baustils von Adolf Loos," *Aufbau*, no. 13 (1958), 393–95. In September 1988, the same Boston revolutionary monument was the site of a significant work of public art, *The Bunker Hill Monument Projection*, in which for three nights a video by the conceptual artist Krzysztof Wodiczko played onto the upper part of the obelisk video images of local Charlestown and South Boston residents speaking of their experiences of "life, liberty, and the pursuit of happiness"; illus., Wodiczko, 'The Bunker Hill Monument Projection,' *Assemblage: A Critical Journal of Architecture and Design Culture*, no. 37 (December 1998), 68–69, with texts on copyright page, endpapers, and covers.

2. In 'American Architecture' Greenough's praise of the functional beauty of a ship hull (Greenough 60–62) recalls Hume (e.g., *Dialogues Concerning Natural Religion*, pt. v), and not only anticipates Le Corbusier (*Vers une architecture*, 1923) but inherits Hume's utilitarian aesthetic, ever popular in Calvinist America, of the economical and the efficacious (e.g.,

'Why Utility Pleases,' in *An Enquiry Concerning the Principles of Morals*, V.i). But against Hume stand Burke and Kant. On behalf of the proposition that "Fitness Not the Cause of Beauty" (III.vi), Burke – as Greenough, who challenges "Burke on the Beautiful" (87–95), must have known – adduces a miscellany of animal features, which then should deserve to be considered beautiful: the swine's snout; the pelican's sagging bill; the hedgehog and porcupine, so well armed; the dexterous monkey's limbs; the amazingly handy elephant's trunk, etc.; also, in man and beast, "the stomach, the lungs, the liver" and "other parts ... well adapted to their purposes"; Edmund Burke, *A Philosophical Enquiry into the Origin of Our Ideas of the Sublime and Beautiful* (1756), ed. James T. Boulton (London: Routledge and Kegan Paul, 1958, repr. 1967), 105, 107. Also. "if beauty in our own species was annexed to use, men would be much more lovely than women; and strength and agility would be considered as the only beauties. But to ... have but one denomination for the qualities of a Venus and Hercules ... is surely a strange confusion of ideas, or abuse of words. The cause of this confusion, I imagine, proceeds from our frequently perceiving the parts of the human and other animal bodies to be at once very beautiful, and very well adapted to their purposes; and we are deceived by a sophism, which makes us take that for a cause which is only a concomitant ..." (106). Kant, who thinks pleasing feelings might count as useful, points out that in terms of practicality "a hen is frankly better than a parrot, a kitchen pot is more useful than a porcelain vessel, all the witty heads in the world have not the value of a peasant, and the effort to discover the distance of the fixed stars can be set aside until it has been decided how to drive the plow to best advantage"; Immanuel Kant, *Observations on the Feeling of the Beautiful and Sublime* (1764), trans. John T. Goldthwait (Berkeley: University of California Press, 1960), sect. ii, p. 73.

3. Even the *topos* of superlative American plumbing as counterpart to superlative European culture seems to belong to the larger notion that America is like unto Rome in both's imperial phases, with Europe as comparatively Greek. This includes a sense of the Roman as prosaic where the Greek is poetic, as when Hegel offers that while the Latin prose of Cicero "sounds naïve and innocent enough," even with the poetry of Virgil and Horace "we feel at once that the art is something artificial, deliberately manufactured; we are aware of a prosaic subject-matter, with external decoration added" (Hegel 2: 1010). A similar but wittier early twentieth-century assessment of Greek vis-à-vis Roman culture was drawn up by the great formalist critic Clive Bell in *Civilization: An Essay* (1928). A more modest, unexaggerated American flavor shows up where William Carlos Williams salutes the American-ordinary in the first part (1946) of the long poem *Paterson* (1948): "a basket; a column; a reply to Greek and Latin with the bare hands" (Williams 10) – a conjunction itself recalling Goethe's rather Loosian sense of a simple utilitarian Bohemian basket as practically Greek in its "synthesis of utility and beauty" (Schachel 36).

4. On experiments with columnar ideas, some inspired by American skyscrapers, *c*. 1923, by the 'suprematist' painter Kazimir Malevich, see Tatiana Mikhienko, 'The Suprematist Column: A monument to non-objective art,' in *Kazimir Malevich: Suprematism* (New York: Guggenheim Museum, 2003), 78–87, with illus. on p. 209.

5. Ivan V. Nevzgodin, '"Press: Fight for Socialist Cities!": Perception and Critique of the Architecture of Novosibirsk, 1920–1940,' in the Internet journal *Wolkenkuckucksheim / Cloud-Cuckoo-Land / Vozdushnyi zamok*, vol. 7, no. 2 (January 2003), p. 5 of 23 (16 October 2012).

6. For a remarkable range of formal precedents for Loos's Chicago Tribune design see Hanno-Walter Kruft, 'Das schönste Bürohaus der Welt: der internationale Wettbewerb für den Chicago Tribune Tower (1922),' *Pantheon* 39 (1981), 76–89.

7. Illus., James Bogardus, 'Construction of the Frame, Roof, and Floor of Iron Buildings; Specification of Letters Patent No. 7,337, Dated May 7, 1850' (United States Patent Office), in Don Gifford, ed., *The Literature of Architecture: The Evolution of Architectural Theory and Practice in Nineteenth-Century America* (New York: Dutton, 1966), 352–58, fig. 18 on p. 351.

8. Illus., Anton Schweighofer, 'Wien wäre Weltstadt, wenn ...: Zu den Arbeiten über den öffentlichen Bau von Adolf Loos,' in Burkhardt Rukschcio, ed., in *Adolf Loos* (Vienna: Grafische Sammlung Albertina, 1989), 191–215, p. 204.

9. E. M. Upjohn, 'Buffington and the Skyscraper,' *The Art Bulletin* 17 (1935), 48–70, esp. pp. 56–57.

10. This based on the wide accessibility, by then, of Sullivan's major text: 'The Tall Office Building Artistically Considered,' which had "appeared in *Lippincott's* [magazine] for March 1896, just as Loos … was leaving the United States to return to Europe," and was reprinted in May 1896, in 1905 and 1922, and included in *Kindergarten Chats*; and he relays the interesting fact, reported at first hand by Loos's student Rudolf Schindler, who emigrated to the United States, that Sullivan identified himself as "brother in the spirit" in a now lost letter to his considerably younger European colleague in about October 1920. Rykwert, 'Order,' 14–15 with 15 nn. 41, 42, depending for the account of the missing letter on Rukschcio and Schachel, *Adolf Loos*, 246–48; also Rykwert, *Dancing Column*, 19, with 397 n. 49.

11. Masheck, 'Politics of Style: Dublin Pro-Cathedral in the Greek Revival,' in his *Building-Art*, 29–46, on related matters. Tennyson, on receiving a copy of Alfred Perceval Graves' *Songs of Killarney* on its publication in 1873, was said to have characterized them to the author as "Your Irish Doric," as reported by Graves in his own *Irish Doric in Song and Story* (London: Fisher and Unwin, 1926), which is, however, to say after *Ulysses* was published.

12. Joyce is one of the cultural celebrities who supported Loos's idea of setting up an architectural school in Paris; and there is a possible allusion to him in *Finnegans Wake*: see Friedhelm Rathjen and Andreas Weigel, 'A Portrait of the Artist as an Adolf Loos Campaigner,' *James Joyce Quarterly* 42–43, nos. 1–4 (2004–06), 315–19. Thanks to Joan Ockman for directing me to this article.

Chapter 7: Architecturelessness and Sustainable Art

1. Loos himself implicitly posed the question of architecturelessness as a condition by having it seem, with typical hyperbole, in his 'Architecture' text of only a few years earlier, that practically no buildings qualify as architecture, and that that might be a good thing anyway. Certainly the question hovered over modernism. Without using the word, I have discussed various examples of the nearly-not-there state of architecturelessness posited hypothetically by Nickolaus Pevsner, where he classically opens his *Outline of European Architecture* (1942) with the pronouncement: "A bicycle shed is a building; Lincoln cathedral is a piece of architecture" (Masheck, 'Tired Tropes'). I say hypothetically because, though an architectural project need not be executed to count as architecture, it may be that no particular bicycle shed actually erected can stand outside the game of other, possibly more undeniably architectural structures to which it relates; and even that may be enough to disqualify it as architectureless. There is a possible provocation for this statement in a source with an interesting environmental aspect. In an article titled 'Art and the State,' in *The Listener* in 1937, Keynes, the great economist, arguing that it is foolishly penny-pinching of the government not to assume responsibility for preserving cultural monuments as well as to buy, outright, worthy features of the natural landscape to preserve them from destruction for short-sighted economic gain, had specifically adduced Lincoln Cathedral as quite as worthy of governmental maintenance funds as the construction, and presumably maintenance, of highways (Keynes, 'Art' 343–44).

2. It is doubtful that Loos actually presented his project at the conference, because Austria is not mentioned as represented in the accompanying exhibition; International Garden Cities and Town-Planning Association, *Report of Conference* (London, 1922), 9. Loos was also aware of the German garden-city proponent Leberecht Migge; see David Haney, *When Modern Was Green: Life and Work of Landscape Architect Leberecht Migge* (London: Routledge, 2010), to which Joan Ockman has kindly called my attention.

Chapter 8: The Wittgenstein House as Loosian

1. Paul Wijdeveld, *Ludwig Wittgenstein, Architect*, 2nd edn. Amsterdam: Pepin, 2000; abbreviated in the present chapter as 'W.'

2. In my subjective experience, at least, a domestically scaled urban building which nicely extends this Loosian-Engelmannian massing down to the present is Robert Litchfield's fine Trinity Lower East Side Lutheran Parish, of 1996, on the east side of Tompkins Square (Avenue B), in New York.

3. Further to early modern British aesthetics: Vernon Lee (pseud. of Violet Paget), in a review article 'Recent Aesthetics,' *The Quarterly Review* 199 (1904), 420–43, adumbrates Wittgenstein's idea of 'language on holiday,' commenting that non-utilitarian arts "constitute a kind of holiday in life" (423), and proves almost Loosian in calling decoration "a parasitic excrescence of play upon work" (425–26).

4. Wittgenstein would have been interested in the early modern physicist Michelson's discussion of symmetry as facilitating understanding in crystallography and as basically enforced by necessity in "the construction of buildings" (no mention of 'architecture') as well as of bridges and "engineering works in general" and machinery. While acknowledging structural symmetry and asymmetrical departure from it in art, he is excited to report, "it is a common experience that the design of a piece of machinery may be so altered as to make it symmetrical often with a surprising increase in symmetry as well as beauty"; A. A. Michelson, 'Form Analysis,' in *Proceedings of the American Philosophical Society* 45 (1906), 110–16, here p. 115.

5. Radiators deliberately left exposed were cited by Robert Scheu in 'Kennst du das Haus?' in the *Prager Tagblatt*, in about January of 1931, as "a trait of Loos which I immediately recognize"; qu. Burkhardt Rukschcio and Roland Schachel, *Adolf Loos; Leben und Werk* (Salzburg and Vienna: Residenz, 1982), 611; qu. Walter Zedniček, *Adolf Loos: Pläne und Schriften* (Vienna: the author, 2004), 179. To be sure, Loos also liked to box radiators in, even if Wittgenstein didn't.

6. The Gropius latch was made to somewhat differing designs in more than one size. In the example shown here the cylindrical handle is an extension of one leg of the right-angular bar, square in section and doubtless solid, which penetrates the door and acts as a wrench within the lock. In an example, also of 1923, in the Neue Galerie, New York, the handle meets up closer to as well as perpendicular to, the wrench-like square bar – more like an 'I' rather than the 'L' seen here – as it passes through the door.

7. I thank Barry Bergdoll for calling my attention to this fascinating drawing. Cf. Francesco Amendolagine and Massimo Cacciari, *Oikos: da Loos a Wittgenstein* (Rome: Officina, 1975), 38 n. 39.

8. One main feature of the house is akin to the most famous commercial 'public' building of Loos: the plan of the square 'hall' is related on a more modest, domestic scale, to that of the grand front sale room of the Looshaus, where four square piers divide the area into nine sub-squares, with engaged piers answering on the walls, and formal staircase rising to the mezzanine through the far center bay. Here, a grand staircase rises through the nearer of two square center bays defined by two square piers set on the central left-right axis, with half-square bays left and right, and engaged square piers also answering the supporting piers on all sides.

Chapter 9: Loos and Minimalism

1. There may be a sub-text here of Rembrandt as anti-modernist bourgeois cultural mascot; for actually imagining Immanuel Kant with ostrich feathers in his cap evokes a mental image from a century earlier, a Rembrandt self-portrait.

2. At least one piece of furniture designed by Loos, the table with rounded corners supported on round legs, with wide twin flutes running around the edge, follows a classical Chinese type (quite apart from Loos's admiration of the work of Thomas Chippendale, whose interest in China connected with Rococo *Chinoiserie*).

3. Aesthetic 'relationality' in the modernist formal sense, as akin to Bertrand Russell's '$x \, R \, y$' for the relation, as such, between x and y (chapter 1), has nothing to do with a latterday option of the term in a 'relational aesthetics' concerned with social intervention and direct interaction with otherwise would-be spectators.

    Repetition in Minimalist sculpture calls to mind Rosa Luxemburg's development, in *The Accumulation of Capital* (1913), of Marx's term "reproduction" to cover a more general and profound notion of original-repetition than even is the case with printmaking or photography, with a sense of "renewal of the process of production," as in seasonal resumptions of agricultural labor since prehistoric times; Rosa Luxemburg, *The Accumulation of Capital*, trans. Agnes Schwarzschild (London and New York: Routledge, 2003), 3. As such, reproduction is as dependent as any initial production – which is not a model but only a first instance – on prevailing social conditions. Loos himself reflects parenthetically in his obituary 'Josef Veillich' (1929): "every piece produced by a craftsman is a copy of an object from the past whether it be a month or a hundred years old" (*OA* 186). Luxemburg points up feudalism as having made possible the development of craftsmanship itself in medieval town culture (Luxemburg, op. cit. 13); afterward, capitalism introduced the profit motive; and though she does not say so, Loos for one might have been quick to point up how the realm of fine art in that respect often overly romances its conservative semblance of a pre-capitalist craft condition, with the contrived maintenance of rarity a special, inverted form of the dominant profit motive.

4. Mies's layout was (and mostly still is) superbly relational, as if the buildings were held in tense interrelation in some sort of electromagnetic field – which means, all too lively in their mutual proportionality and hence insufficiently inert, to count as Minimal. In actual fact, such relationalism within a field is tantamount to a categorical *dis*-qualification of Minimalism. Relational composition was as opposed by all orthodox Minimalists as it had been by self-identified 'constructivists' of the 1920s before them.

5. Within the broad functionalist tradition, including the Czech functionalism inspired by Loos, it is possible to distinguish a crypto-classical rationalism favoring the stability of symmetry as a neutral formalism of self-evident order (like many a Loos façade considered in detachment), from freer responses to internal anatomy, with more latitude for asymmetry and scope even for tectonic-compositional balance (like the reformed compositional formalism of Le Corbusier as itself influenced by Loos). By itself, this rationalist alternative sometimes presents itself as anti-compositional, as if that necessarily meant more constructivist; but to suppose that the perils of formal composition can be escaped by resorting to symmetry is something like thinking that the formal demands of Western musical harmony might be sidestepped by writing music only in the key of C-major. How Minimal Art has of course brought this problem to the fore is perhaps incipient in the relation of these two Loos façades.

WORKS CITED

Adcock, Craig. 'Marcel Duchamp's Approach to New York: "Find an insc for the Woolworth Building as a Ready-Made."' In Rudolf E. Kuenzli, ed., *New York Dada*. New York: Willis, Locker and Owens, 1986. Pp. 52–65.

Adorno, Theodor. *Aesthetic Theory* (1970), ed. Gretel Adorno and Rolf Teidermann, trans. and ed. Robert Hullot-Kentor. Minneapolis: University of Minnesota Press, 1997.

Andreas-Salomé, Lou. *The Freud Journal*, trans. Stanley A. Leavy. London: Quartet Books, 1987.

Bailey, L. H. 'Ferdinand Kürnberger, Friedrich Schlögl and the *Feuilleton* in Gründerzeit Vienna.' In Peter Branscombe, ed., *Austrian Life and Literature 1780–1938*. Edinburgh: Scottish Academic Press, 1978. Pp. 59–71.

Behne, Adolf. *The Modern Functional Building* (written 1923; published 1926), trans. Michael Robinson. Santa Monica, Calif.: Getty Research Institute for the History of Art and the Humanities, 1996.

Bell, Clive. *Art*. New York: Capricorn, 1958.

———. 'Cubism and Functionalism.' *The New Statesman and Nation*. 12 November 1938, pp. 767–68.

———. *Enjoying Pictures: Meditations in the National Gallery and Elsewhere*. London: Chatto and Windus, 1934.

Bergdoll, Barry. *Mastering McKim's Plan: Columbia's First Century on Morningside Heights*. New York: Miriam and Ira D. Wallach Art Gallery, Columbia University, 1997.

Berkeley, George. *Alciphron; or, The Minute Philosopher: in Focus*, ed. David Berman. Philosophers in Focus. London and New York: Routledge, 1993.

———. 'An Essay Towards Preventing the Ruin of Great Britain' (1721). In *The Works of George Berkeley, Bishop of Cloyne*, ed. A. A. Luce and T. E. Jessup, 9 vols. London and New York: Nelson, 1948–57. Vol. 6, pp. 61–85.

———. *The Querist* (1735–37). In *The Works of George Berkeley, Bishop of Cloyne*, ed. A. A. Luce and T. E. Jessop, 9 vols. London: Nelson, 1948–57. Vol. 6: 87–192.

———. *The Works of George Berkeley, Bishop of Cloyne*, ed. A. A. Luce and T. E. Jessup, 9 vols. Edinburgh: 1948–57.

Black, Max. *A Companion to Wittgenstein's 'Tractatus.'* Ithaca, New York: Cornell University Press, 1964.

Blau, Eve. *The Architecture of Red Vienna 1919–1934*. Cambridge, Mass.: MIT Press, 1999.

Blau, Eve and Monika Platzer, eds. *Shaping the Great City: Modern Architecture in Central Europe 1890–1937*. Munich: Prestel, 1999.

Bock, Ralf. *Adolf Loos: Works and Projects*, trans. Lorenzo Sanguedolce. Milan: Skira, 2007.

Bogatyrëv, Peter, and Roman Jakobson. 'Folklore as a Special Form of Creativity' (1929), trans. Manfred Jakobson. In Peter Steiner (ed.), *The Prague School: Selected Writings 1929–1946*. Austin: University of Texas Press, 1982. Pp. 32–46.

Brown, Iain Gordon. 'David Hume's Tomb: A Roman Mausoleum by Robert Adam.' *Proceedings of the Society of Antiquaries of Scotland* 121 (1991), 391–422; thanks to Graham Domke, of Inverleigh House, Royal Botanic Garden, Edinburgh, for a copy.

Carlyle, Thomas. *Sartor Resartus: The Life and Opinions of Herr Teufelsdröckh*. New York: Miller, 1866.

Chaney, Edward. *The Evolution of the Grand Tour: Anglo-Italian Cultural Relations Since the Renaissance*. London: Frank Cass, 1998.

Chroust, David. '*Bohemian Voice*: The Forgotten First Journal About the Czechs in English.' *Kosmas: Czechoslovak and Central European Journal* 14, no. 2 (Spring 2001), 1–27.

Colquhoun, Alan. 'Vernacular Classicism' (1984). In his *Modernity and the Classical Tradition: Architectural Essays 1980–1987*. Cambridge, Mass.: MIT Press. Pp. 21–31.

Coomaraswamy, Ananda K. 'Ornament.' *Art Bulletin* 21 (1939), 375–82.

Craig, Maurice. *Dublin 1660–1860*. London: Cresset, 1952.

Crane, Stephen. *Maggie: A Girl of the Streets: A Story of New York*. In *The Portable Stephen Crane*, ed. Joseph Katz. New York: Penguin, 1988.

Cushman, Jenifer. 'Rilke's Non-Nationalism: A Bohemian Model.' *Kosmas: Czechoslovak and Central European Journal* 15, no. 2 (Spring 2002), 13–26.

Czech, Hermann, and Wolfgang Mistelbauer. *Das Looshaus* (1976), 3rd edn. Vienna: Löcker, 1984.

Dal Co, Francesco. *Figures of Architecture and Thought: German Architecture Culture 1890–1920*, trans. Stephen Sartarelli. New York: Rizzoli, 1990.

Dignowity, Anthony Michael. *Bohemia Under Austrian Despotism: Being an Autobiography*. New York: the author, 1859.

Donne, J. B. 'Maori Heads and European Taste.' *RAIN* (Royal Anthropological Institute of Great Britain and Ireland), no. 11 (November–December 1975), 5–6.

Downing, Antoinette F., and Vincent J. Scully, Jr. *The Architectural Heritage of Newport, Rhode Island, 1640–1915*, 2nd edn. New York: Potter, 1967.

Drexler, Arthur, ed., *The Architecture of the Ecole des Beaux-Arts*. New York: Museum of Modern Art, 1975.

Drury, M. O'C. 'Conversations with Wittgenstein.' In Rush Rhees, ed., *Recollections of Wittgenstein*. Oxford: Oxford University Press, 1984. Pp. 97–171.

Du Bois, W. E. B. *The Souls of Black Folk* (1903). New York: Dover, 1994.

Dvořák, Max. *The History of Art as the History of Ideas* (1924), trans. John Hardy. London: Routledge and Kegan Paul, 1984.

Emerson, Ralph Waldo. 'Self-Reliance.' In his *Essays: First and Second Series*. Boston and New York: Houghton Mifflin, 1883. Pp. 45–87.

Engels, Friedrich. *The Condition of the Working-Class in England in 1844*, trans. Florence Kelly Wischnewetzky. London: Allen and Unwin, 1892.

Finsch, Otto. 'Über Bekleidung, Schmuck, und Tätowirung der Papuas der Südküste von Neu-Guinea.' *Mitteilungen der Anthropologischen Gesellschaft* in Wien 15 (1885), 12–33.

Frampton, Kenneth. 'Adolf Loos: The Architect as Master Builder.' Introd. to Roberto Schezen, *Adolf Loos: Architecture 1903–1932*. New York: Monacelli, 1966. Pp. 14–21.

———. *Le Corbusier*. New York: Thames and Hudson, 2001.

———. 'Introduction: Adolf Loos and the Crisis of Culture 1896–1931.' In Yehuda Safran and Wilfried Wang, eds., *The Architecture of Adolf Loos: An Arts Council Exhibition*. London: Arts Council of Great Britain, 1985. Pp. 8–13.

———. *Modern Architecture: A Critical History*, 4th edn. London and New York: Thames and Hudson, 2007.

———. 'In Spite of the Void: The Otherness of Adolf Loos' (written 1986). In his *Labour, Work and Architecture: Collected Essays on Architecture and Design*. London: Phaidon, 2002. Pp. 196–217.

Frege, Gottlob. 'Logic.' In his *Posthumous Writings*, ed. Hans Hermes et al., trans. Peter Long and Roger White. Chicago: University of Chicago Press, 1979. Pp. 1–8.

———. 'Logical Defects in Mathematics.' In his *Posthumous Writings*, 157–66.

———. 'Logik.' In his *Nachgelassene Schriften und Wissenschaftlicher Briefwechsel*, ed. Hans Hermes et al. 2 vols. Hamburg: Meiner, 1969–76. 1: 1–8.

———. 'Logische Mängel der Mathematik.' In his *Nachgelassene Schriften*, 1: 171–81.

Frölich, Paul. *Rosa Luxemburg: Ideas in Action*, trans. Joanna Hoomeg (1972). London: Pluto Press and Bookmarks, 1994.

Fry, Roger. 'A Possible Domestic Archtecture.' In his *Vision and Design*. New York: Meridian, 1956. Pp. 272– 78.

Gabo, Naum. 'Sculpture: Carving and Construction in Space.' In *Circle: International Survey of Constructive Art*, ed. Naum Gabo, J. L. Martin, and Ben Nicholson. London, 1937. Repr. New York and Washington: Praeger, 1971. Pp. 103–11.

Girardi, Vittoria. 'Adolf Loos: Pionere protestante (1870–1933).' Series of articles in *L'Architettura: Cronache e Storia* 9, nos. 115–22 (May–December 1965).

Girouard, Mark. *Sweetness and Light: The Queen Anne Movement 1860 1900*. New Haven. Yale University Press, 1977.

Glaser, Bruce. 'Questions to Stella and Judd' (1964), ed. Lucy Lippard (1966). In Gregory Battcock, ed., *Minimal Art: A Critical Anthology*. New York: Dutton, 1968. Pp. 148–64.

Glassie, Henry H. *Vernacular Architecture*. Philadelphia: Material Culture; Bloomington: Indiana University Press, 2000.

Gombrich, Ernst. *The Sense of Order: A Study in the Psychology of Decorative Art*. Wrightsman Lectures. Ithaca, New York: Cornell University Press, 1979.

Gravagnuolo, Benedetto. *Adolf Loos: Theory and Works*, trans. C. H. Evans. New York: Rizzoli, 1982.

Greenough, Horatio. *Form and Function: Remarks on Art*, ed. Harold A. Small. Berkeley: University of California Press, 1947.

———. 'Relative and Independent Beauty.' In his *Form and Function*. Pp. 69–86.

Grosse, Ernst. *The Beginnings of Art*. Anthropological Series. New York: Appleton, 1900.

Hamsun, Knut. *The Cultural Life of Modern America* (1889), trans. and ed. Barbara Gordon Morgridge. Cambridge, Mass.: Harvard University Press, 1969.

Hanslick, Eduard. *On the Musically Beautiful: A Contribution Towards the Revision of the Aesthetics of Music*, 8th edn (1891), trans. and ed. Geoffrey Payzant. Indianapolis: Hackett, 1986.

Harries, Karsten. *The Ethical Function of Architecture*. New Haven: Yale University Press, 1997.

Hartmann, Sadakichi. 'A Plea for the Picturesqueness of New York' (1900). In his *The Valiant Knights of Daguerre: Selected Critical Essays on Photography and Profiles of Photographic Pioneers*, ed. Harry W. Lawton and George Knox. Berkeley: University of California Press, 1978. Pp. 56–63.

Hartoonian, Gevork. *Ontology of Construction: On Nihilism in Technology in Theories of Modern Architecture*. Cambridge: Cambridge University Press, 1994.

Hegel, George Wilhelm Friedrich. *Lectures on Fine Art*, trans. T. M. Knox. 2 vols. Oxford: Clarendon Press, 1974.

Heine-Geldern, Robert. 'L'Art prébouddhique de la Chine et de l'Asie du Sud-Est et son influence en Océanie.' *Revue des Arts Asiatiques; Annales du Musée Guimet* 11 (1937), 177–206.

Heydenreich, Ludwig H., and Wolfgang Lotz. *Architecture in Italy 1400 to 1600*, trans. Mary Hottinger. Pelican History of Art. Harmondsworth: Penguin, 1974.

Hitchcock, Henry-Russell. *Rhode Island Architecture*. Providence: Rhode Island Museum Press, 1939; repr. Cambridge, Mass.: MIT Press, 1968.

Hodin, J. P. 'Oskar Kokoschka: Revolt' (1945). In his *The Dilemma of Being Modern: Essays on Art and Literature*. New York: Noonday, 1959. Pp. 67–70.

Howard, Jeremy. *East European Art 1650–1950*. Oxford History of Art. Oxford: Oxford University Press, 2006.

Ives, Colta. 'City Life.' In *Pierre Bonnard: The Graphic Art*. New York: Metropolitan Museum of Art, 1989. Pp. 93–143.

Jaeggi, Annemarie. *Adolf Meyer: der zweite Mann; ein Architekt im Schatten von Walter Gropius* (exhib. cat.). Berlin: Bauhaus-Archiv, Museum für Gestaltung, 1994.

Janik, Allan. 'Paul Engelmann's Role in Wittgenstein's Philosophical Development.' In Judith Bakacsy, Anders V. Munch, and Anne-Louise Sommer, eds., *Architecture; Language; Critique*. Studien zur Österreichischen Philosophie. Amsterdam and Atlanta: Rodopi, 2000. Pp. 40–58.

———. 'Weininger and the Science of Sex: Prolegomena to Any Future Study.' In Robert B. Pynsent, ed., *Decadence and Innovation: Austro-Hungarian Life and Art at the Turn of the Century*. London: Weidenfeld and Nicolson, 1989. Pp. 24–32.

Jeniček, Ladislav, and Ivo Kruliš. *British Inventions of the Industrial Revolution in the Iron and Steel Industry on Czechoslovak Territory*, trans. Karel Hudec. Prague: National Technical Museum, 1968.

Jones, Ernest. *The Life and Work of Sigmund Freud*, 3 vols. New York: Basic Books, 1953–57.

Joyce, James. *Ulysses*. The Modern Library. New York: Random House, 1961.

Judd, Donald. *Architektur*. Münster: Westfälischer Kunstverein, 1989.

———. *Complete Writings 1959–1975*. Halifax: Press of the Nova Scotia College of Art and Design; New York: New York University Press, 1975.

Kandinsky, Wassily. *On the Spiritual in Art and Painting in Particular*, 2nd edn, trans. Kenneth C. Lindsay and Peter Vergo. In their edn Kandinsky, *Complete Writings on Art*, 2 vols. Boston: Hall, 1982. Vol. 1 (1901–21), pp. 114–219.

Kant, Immanuel. *Critique of Judgment*, trans. Werner S. Pluhar. Indianapolis: Hackett, 1987.

———. *Critique of Practical Reason*, trans. Thomas Kingsmill. Online at http://www.gutenberg.org/cache/epub/5683/pg5683.html.

———. *Critique of Pure Reason*, trans. Norman Kemp Smith. London: Macmillan, 1956.

———. *Kritik der reinen Vernunft*, 6th edn, ed. J. H. von Kirchmann. Heidelberg: Weiss, 1884.

———. *Observations on the Feeling of the Beautiful and the Sublime*, trans. John T. Goldthwait. Berkeley: University of California Press, 1960.

———. *Prolegomena to Any Future Metaphysics That Will Be Able to Come Forward as a Science*, trans. Paul Carus, rev. James W. Ellington. Indianapolis: Hackett, 1977.

———. *Werke*, ed. Ernst Cassirer et al. 11 vols. Berlin: Cassirer, 1912–23. Vol. 4: *Schriften 1783–1788*, ed. Arthur Buchenau and Ernst Cassirer.

Kaufmann, Emil. *Architecture in the Age of Reason: Baroque and Post-Baroque in England, Italy, and France*. Cambridge, Mass.: Harvard University Press, 1955; repr. New York: Dover, 1968.

Keynes, John Maynard. 'Art and the State.' *The Listener*, 26 August 1936. In *The Collected Writings of John Maynard Keynes*, vol. 28, *Social, Political and Literary Writings*, ed. Donald Moggridge. Cambridge: Cambridge University Press for the Royal Economic Society, 1982. Pp. 341–49.

Kiesler, Frederick. 'Pseudo-Functionalism in Modern Architecture.' *Partisan Review* 16 (July 1949), 733–42.

Kinkel, Johann Gottfried. 'Die Sophienkirche von Constantinopel.' In his *Mosaik zur Kunstgeschichte*. Berlin: Oppenheim, 1876. Pp. 275–301. I owe this reference to my late teacher, Meyer Schapiro.

Knox, Ronald. 'The Contented Vagrant,' in his *An Open-Air Pulpit* (1926). Quoted in David Rooney, *The Wine of Certitude: A Literary Biography of Ronald Knox*. San Francisco: Ignatius, 2009.

Krajči, Peter, and Rostislav Švácha. 'The Architectural Avant-Garde in Prague.' In Blau and Platzer, *Shaping the Great City*. Pp. 117–24.

Král, J. J. 'Bohemia at the World's Fair.' *The Bohemian Voice* (Omaha, Neb.) 2, no. 1 (1 September 1893). Pp. 12–13. I am grateful to David Chroust for a copy.

Krell, David Farrell, and Donald L. Bates. *The Good European: Nietzsche's Work Sites in Word and Image*. Chicago: University of Chicago Press, 1997.

Kruft, Hanno-Walter. 'Das schönste Bürohaus der Welt: der internationale Wettbewerb für den Chicago Tribune Tower (1922).' *Pantheon* 39 (1981), 76–89.

Lancaster, Clay. *The Japanese Influence in America*. New York: Walton H. Rawls, 1963. Ch. 8, 'The Phoenix Villa at the World's Columbian Exposition,' 76–83, with illus.

Leatherbarrow, David. 'Interpretation and Abstraction in the Architecture of Adolf Loos.' *Journal of Architectural Education* 40, no. 4 (Summer 1987), 2–9.

Le Corbusier. *Towards a New Architecture,* trans. Frederick Etchells (1927). London: Architectural Press, 1946, repr. 1965.

Leitner, Bernhard. *The Wittgenstein House*. New York: Princeton Architectural Press, 2000.

Lombroso, Cesare. *Criminal Man*, trans. Mary Gibson and Nicole Hahn Rafter. Durham, N.C.: Duke University Press, 2006). A variorum edition.

Loos, Adolf. 'Architecture,' trans. Wilfried Wang. In *The Architecture of Adolf Loos* (exhib. cat.). London: Arts Council of Great Britain, 1985; 2nd edn, 1987. Pp. 104–09.

———. *Sämtliche Schriften*, ed. Franz Glück. Vienna: Herold, 1962.

———. *Spoken Into the Void: Collected Essays 1897–1900*, trans. Jane O. Newman and John H. Smith. Cambridge, Mass.: MIT Press, 1982.

Loos, Claire Beck. *Adolf Loos: A Private Portrait* (1935), trans. Constance C. Pontasch and Nicholas Saunders, ed. Carrie Paterson. Los Angeles: DoppelHouse Press, 2011.

Loos, Elsie Altmann. *Adolf Loos der Mensch.* Vienna: Herold, 1968.

Loran (Johnson), Erle. 'Cézanne's Country.' *The Arts* 16 (April 1930), 520–51.

Lubbock, John. *The Origin of Civilization and the Primitive Condition of Man* (1870), ed. Peter Rivière. Chicago: University of Chicago Press, 1978.

Luce, A. A. *The Life of George Berkeley, Bishop of Cloyne.* Edinburgh: Nelson, 1949.

Macdonald, Murdo. *Scottish Art.* World of Art. London: Thames and Hudson, 2000.

Masheck, Joseph. 'Abstraction and Apathy: Crystalline Form in Expressionism and in the Minimalism of Tony Smith.' In Neil H. Donahue, ed., *Invisible Cathedrals: The German Expressionist Art History of Wilhelm Worringer.* University Park: Pennsylvania State University Press, 1995. Pp. 41–68.

———. 'Alan Johnston at Haus Wittgenstein.' In *Alan Johnston: Haus Wittgenstein; Inverleith House*, ed. Paul Nesbitt. Edinburgh: Royal Botanic Garden Edinburgh, 1999. Unpaginated.

———. 'The Anti-Architect.' *Art Monthly* (London), no. 328 (July–August 2011), 11–14.

———. *Building-Art: Modern Architecture under Cultural Construction.* Cambridge: Cambridge University Press, 1993.

———. 'Classical Sass: Notes on Soft Postmodernism' (1984). In his *Building-Art*, 170–83.

———. 'A Note on Sullivan and the Rarefaction of Bodily Beauty' (1993). In his *Building-Art*, 57–68.

———. 'The "One-Walled House": A New Facet to Loos's Dodgy Classicism.' *Word & Image* 32 (2007), 270–74.

———. 'Raw Art: "Primitive" Authenticity and German Expressionism' (1982). In his *Modernities: Art-Matters in the Present.* University Park: Pennsylvania State University Press, 1993. Pp. 155–92.

———. 'Stalking Loos in Bohemia.' *Kosmas: Czechoslovak and Central European Journal* 22, no. 2 (Spring 2007), 100–06.

———. 'Steven Holl' (interview). *Bomb* (New York), no. 79 (Spring 2002), 24–29.

———. 'Tired Tropes: Cathedral versus Bicycle Shed; "Duck" versus "Decorated Shed."' In Masheck, *Building-Art*, 184–221.

———. 'The Vital Skin: Riegl, the Maori, and Loos.' In Richard Woodfield, ed., *Framing Formalism: Riegl's Work.* Critical Voices in Art, Theory and Culture. Amsterdam: G + B Arts International, 2001. Pp. 151–82.

Matthews, Brander, et al., eds. *A History of Columbia University 1754–1904.* New York: Columbia University Press, 1904.

McCoy, Esther. 'Letters from Louis H. Sullivan to R. M. Schindler.' *Journal of the Society of Architectural Historians* 20 (1961), 179–84.

Mergl, Jan, and Lenka Pánková. *Moser 1857–1997*, trans. Štěpán Suchochleb and Andreas Beckmann. Karlovy Vary: Moser, 1997.

Meyer, James. *Minimalism: Art and Polemics in the Sixties.* New Haven: Yale University Press, 2001.

Mies van der Rohe, Ludwig. *The Mies van der Rohe Archive*, ed. Arthur Drexler. Garland Architectural Archives. 20 vols. New York: Garland, 1986–92.

Moholy-Nagy, Sibyl. *Native Genius in Anonymous Architecture.* New York: Horizon, 1957.

Mondrian, Piet. 'The New Plastic in Painting.' In his *The New Art – The New Life: The Collected Writings*, trans. and ed. Harry Holtzman and Martin S. James. Boston: Hall, 1986. Pp. 27–81.

Monk, Ray. *Ludwig Wittgenstein: The Duty of Genius.* New York: Free Press, 1990.

Morris, Robert. 'Notes on Sculpture' (4 parts; 1966–69). In Gerd de Vries, ed., *Über Kunst*, 192–240 (English on even-numbered pages).

Morris, William. 'The Lesser Arts.' In *The Political Writings of William Morris*, ed. A. L. Morton. New York: International Publishers, 1973. Pp. 31–56.

Münz, Ludwig. *Der Architekt Adolf Loos.* Vienna: Schroll, 1964.

Münz, Ludwig and Gustav Künstler. *Adolf Loos: Pioneer of Modern Architecture* (1964), trans. Harold Meek. New York: Praeger; London: Thames and Hudson, 1966.

Musil, Robert. 'Doors and Portals.' In *Posthumous Papers of a Living Author* (1936), trans. Peter Wortsman. Hygiene, Colo.: Eridanos, 1987.

Muthesius, Harmann. *Style-Architecture and Building Art: Transformations of Architecture in the Nineteenth Century and Its Present Condition* (1902), trans. Stanford Anderson. Texts & Documents. Santa Monica, Calif.: Getty Center for the History of Art and the Humanities, 1994.

Nietzsche, Friedrich. *The Birth of Tragedy and The Case of Wagner*, trans. Walter Kaufmann. New York: Vintage, 1967.

————. *On the Genealogy of Morals and Ecce Homo*, trans. (with R. J. Hollingdale) and ed. Walter Kaufmann. New York: Vintage, 1969.

————. *Thoughts Out of Season*, Part II, trans. Adrian Collins (*Complete Works*, ed. Oscar Levy). Edinburgh and London: Foulis, 1909.

Oechslin, Werner. 'The Evolutionary Way to Modern Architecture: The Paradigm of Stilhülse und Kern.' In Harry Francis Mallgrave, ed., *Otto Wagner: Reflections on the Raiment of Modernity*. Santa Monica, Calif.: Getty Center for the History of Art and the Humanities, 1993. Pp. 362–410.

Passanti, Francesco. 'The Design of Columbia in the 1890s: McKim and His Client.' *Journal of the Society of Architectural Historians* 36 (1977), 69–84.

Patmore, Coventry. 'Ideal and Material Greatness in Architecture' (1886). In his *Principle in Art, etc.* (1889), new edn. London: Bell, 1898; repr. Farnborough, Hants: Gregg, 1969. Pp. 210–17.

Pople, Anthony, ed., *The Cambridge Companion to Berg*. Cambridge: Cambridge University Press, 1997.

Quetglas, Josep. *Fear of Glass: Mies van der Rohe's Pavilion in Barcelona*, trans. John Stone and Rosa Roig. Basel: Birkhäuser; Boston: Publishers for Architecture, 2001.

Raskin, David. 'Specific Opposition: Judd's Art and Politics.' *Art History* 24 (2001), 682–706.

Riegl, Aloïs. *Historical Grammar of the Visual Arts*, trans. Jacqueline E. Jung. New York: Zone, 2004.

————. *Late Roman Art Industry*, trans. and ed. Rolf Winkes. Rome: Bretschneider, 1985.

————. *Spätrömische Kunstindustrie*, 2nd edn (1927). Repr. Darmstadt: Wissenschaftliche Buchgesellschaft, 1964.

Robinson, Paul A. *The Freudian Left: Wilhelm Reich, Geza Roheim, Herbert Marcuse*. New York: Harper and Row, 1969.

Robson, John William, *A Guide to Columbia University; With Some Account of Its History and Traditions*. New York: Columbia University Press, 1937.

Rossi, Aldo. Introduction to his *The Architecture of the City*, trans. Diane Ghirardo and Joan Ockman, ed. Aldo Rossi and Peter Eisenman. Cambridge, Mass.: MIT Press, 1982.

Rudofsky, Bernard. *Architecture Without Architects*. Garden City, New York: Doubleday, 1964.

Rufer, Josef. *Composition with Twelve Notes Related Only to One Another*, trans. Humphrey Searle. London: Barrie and Rockliff, 1969.

Rukschcio, Burkhardt, ed. *Adolf Loos* (exhib. cat.). Vienna: Grafische Sammlung Albertina, 1989.

Rukschcio, Burkhardt and Roland Schachel. *Adolf Loos: Leben und Werk*, 2nd edn. Salzburg: Residenz, 1982.

Ruskin, John. 'The Influence of Imagination in Architecture' (1857). Lecture IV in his *The Two Paths; Being Lectures on Art and Its Application to Decoration and Manufactures Delivered in 1858–9*. In his *Works*, 12 vols. New York: Wiley, 1885. Vol. 8(a), 113–50, 207.

————. *Modern Painters*, 2: *Of the Imaginative and Theoretic Faculties*. New York: Wiley, 1885.

————. *The Stones of Venice*, 4th edn in 3 vols. Orpington, Kent: Allen, 1886; repr. New York: Dover, 2005.

Russell, Bertrand. *Introduction to Mathematical Philosophy* (1919). New York: Simon and Schuster, 1971.

Rykwert, Joseph. 'Adolf Loos: The New Vision' (1972; 1973). In his *The Necessity of Artifice*. Ideas in Architecture. New York: Rizzoli, 1982. Pp. 66–73.

————. *The Dancing Column; On Order in Architecture*. Cambridge, Mass.: MIT Press, 1996.

————. 'Order in Building.' *Res: Anthropology and Aesthetics*, no. 11 (Spring 1986), 5–17.

St George, Robert Blair. *Conversing by Signs: Poetics of Implication in Colonial New England Culture*. Chapel Hill: University of North Carolina Press, 1998.

Sarnitz, August, ed., *Architecture in Vienna*, trans. Ramesh Kumar Biswas et al. Vienna and New York: Springer, 1998.

————. 'Realism versus *Verniedlichung*: The Design of the Great City.' In Harry Francis Mallgrave, ed., *Otto Wagner: Reflections on the Raiment of Modernity*, Issues and Debates. Santa Monica, Calif.: Getty Center for the History of Art and the Humanities, 1993. Pp. 84–112.

Schachel, Roland. 'Adolf Loos, Amérique, et l'antiquité.' In Felice Fanuele and Patrice Verhoeven, eds., *Adolf Loos 1870–1933.* Liège and Brussels: Mardaga, 1983. Pp. 33–38.

Schezen, Roberto. *Adolf Loos: Architecture 1903–1932.* New York: Monacelli, 1996.

Schoenberg, Arnold. 'About Ornaments, Primitive Rhythms, etc., and Bird Song' (1922). In his *Style and Idea: Selected Writings*, ed. Leonard Stein, trans. Leo Black. Berkeley: University of California Press, 1975. Pp. 298–311.

Schopfer, Jean. 'American Architecture from a Foreign Point of View: New York City.' *The Architectural Review* 7 (1900), 25–30.

Schuyler, Montgomery. 'The "Sky-Scraper" Up to Date.' *Architectural Record* 8 (January–March 1899). Repr. in Don Gifford, ed., *The Literature of Architecture: The Evolution of Architectural Theory and Practice in Nineteenth-Century America*. New York: Dutton, 1966. Pp. 554–74.

Sekler, Eduard F. 'Adolf Loos, Josef Hoffmann und die Vereinigten Staaten' (1983; 1986). In *Adolf Loos* (exhib. cat.), ed. Burkhardt Rukschcio. Vienna: Grafische Sammlung Albertina, 1989. Pp. 251–67.

Siry, Joseph. 'The Abraham Lincoln Center in Chicago.' *Journal of the Society of Architectural Historians* 50 (1991), 235–65.

Šlapeta, Vladimír. *Adolf Loos a česká architektura* (exhib. cat.). Louny, Czech Republic: Galérie Benedikta Rejta, 1984 (1985). Unpaginated. I am grateful to Dr. Alica Štefančiková for a copy.

————. 'Paul Engelmann und Jacques Groag: die olmützer Schüler von Adolf Loos.' In *Bauwelt* 40 (1978), 1491–1501.

————. 'Summary,' trans. Jana Solperová. In his *Adolf Loos a česká architektura* (exhib. cat.; Louny, Pilsen, Prague, 1984). Repr. Prague: Muzeum hlavního města Praky, 2000.

Šlapeta, Vladimír, Jan Palkovský, and Dietrich Worbs. *Adolf Loos a česká architektura* (exhib. cat.; Louny, Pilsen, Prague, 1984). Repr. Prague: Muzeum hlavního města Praky, 2000.

Spechtenhauser, Klaus. 'Between Le Corbusier and Jan Kotěra, Germany, and Karel Teige: In Search of Jaromír Krejcar's Architectural Theory.' In Rostislav Švácha, ed., *Jaromír Krejcar 1895–1949*. Prague: Galerie Jaroslava Fragnera, 1995. Pp. 176–207.

Stewart, Janet. *Fashioning Vienna: Adolf Loos's Cultural Criticism*. London and New York: Routledge, 2000.

Sudjic, Deyan. 'The Pursuit of Simplicity: Recent Architectural Minimalism.' In *Singular Forms (Sometimes Repeated): Art from 1951 to the Present* (exhib. cat.). New York: Solomon R. Guggenheim Museum, 2004. Pp. 35–41.

Sullivan, Louis H. *The Autobiography of An Idea*. New York: Dover, 1956.

————. *Kindergarten Chats and Other Writings* (collected and edited 1918). New York: Wittenborn, Schultz, 1947; repr. New York: Dover, 1979.

Švácha, Rostislav. *The Architecture of New Prague 1895–1945*. Cambridge, Mass.: MIT Press, 1995.

Symons, Arthur. 'The Decay of Craftsmanship in England.' In his *Studies in Seven Arts*. London: Constable; New York: Dutton, 1906.

Teige, Karel. *Modern Architecture in Czechoslovakia* (1930). In his *Modern Architecture in Czechoslovakia and Other Writings*, trans. Irena Žantovská Murray and David Britt. Texts & Documents. Los Angeles: Getty Research Institute, 2000. Pp. 97–304.

Tencar, Jiří. 'Adolf Loos's Terrace Houses at Babí Today.' *Kosmas: Czechoslovak and Central European Journal* 20, no. 1 (2006), 81–82 with plates following.

Turnovský, Jan. *The Poetics of a Wall Projection*, trans. Kent Kleinman. Words 3. London: Architectural Association, 2009.

Vallier, Dora. *Abstract Art*, trans. Jonathan Griffin. New York: Orion, 1970.

Van Duzer, Leslie, and Kent Kleinman. *Villa Müller: A Work of Adolf Loos*. New York: Princeton Architectural Press, 1994.

Vasari, Giorgio. *Le Vite de' più eccelenti pittori, scultori ed architettori* (1550; 2nd edn, 1568), ed. Gaetano Milanese. 9 vols. Florence: Sansoni, 1878–85.

Veblen, Thorsten. *The Theory of the Leisure Class: An Economic Study of Institutions*. New York: New American Library, 1953.

Vergo, Peter. *Art in Vienna 1898–1918: Klimt, Kokoschka, Schiele and Their Contemporaries,* 3rd edn. London: Phaidon, 1993.

Vico, Giambattista. *The New Science*, 3rd edn, trans. Thomas Goddard Bergin and Max Harold Fisch. Ithaca, New York: Cornell University Press, 1984.

Vries, Gerd de, ed., *Über Kunst: Künstlertexte und veränderten Kunstverständnis nach 1965 / On Art: Artists' Writings on the Changed Notion of Art Since 1965*, trans. Wilhelm Höck and Gerd de Vries. Cologne: DuMont Schauberg, 1974.

Wagner, Otto. 'The Development of a Great City; with an Appreciation of the Author by A. D. F. Hamlin.' *The Architectural Record* 31, no. 5 (May 1912), 485–500.

Wagner-Rieger, Renate. 'Semper und die Wiener Architektur.' In Eva Börsch-Supan et al., *Gottfried Semper und die Mitte des 19. Jahrhunderts*. Basel: Birkhäuser, 1976. Pp. 275–89.

Wagstaff, Samuel. 'Talking with Tony Smith.' In Gregory Battcock, ed., *Minimal Art: A Critical Anthology*. New York: Dutton, 1968. Pp. 381–86.

Waismann, Friedrich, ed., *Wittgenstein and the Vienna Circle: Conversations*, ed. Brian McGuinness, trans. Joachim Schulte and Brian McGuinness. New York: Barnes and Noble, 1979.

Watkins, Holly. 'Schoenberg's Interior Design.' *Journal of the American Musicological Society* 61 (2008), 123–206.

Whewell, William. *History of the Inductive Sciences from the Earliest to the Present Time*, 3rd edn. 2 vols. New York: Appleton, 1859.

Whistler, James Abbot McNeill. *The Gentle Art of Making Enemies*, 2nd edn. New York: Putnam, 1982; repr. New York: Dover, 1967.

Whyte, Iain Boyd. 'Modernist Dioscuri? Otto Wagner and Hendrik Petrus Berlage.' In Harry Francis Mallgrave, ed., *Otto Wagner: Reflections on the Raiment of Modernity*. Santa Monica, Calif.: Getty Center for the History of Art and the Humanities, 1993. Pp. 156–97.

———. 'Vienna Between Memory and Modernity.' In Blau and Platzer, *Shaping the Great City*. Pp. 125–35.

Wijdeveld, Paul. *Ludwig Wittgenstein, Architect*, 2nd edn. Amsterdam: Pepin, 2000.

Williams, William Carlos. *Paterson*. New York: New Directions, 1963.

Windsor, Alan. *Peter Behrens: Architect and Designer*. London: Architectural Press; New York: Watson-Guptil, 1981.

Wittgenstein, Ludwig. *Culture and Value*, ed. G. H. von Wright and Heikki Nyman, trans. Peter Winch. Chicago: University of Chicago Press, 1984.

———. *Philosophical Remarks*, ed. Rush Rhees, trans. Raymond Hargreaves and Roger White. Chicago: University of Chicago Press, 1975.

———. *Philosophische Untersuchungen / Philosophical Investigations*, trans. G. E. M. Anscombe. New York: Macmillan, 1953.

———. *Remarks on the Foundations of Mathematics*, ed. G. H. Von Wright, R. Rhees and G. E. M. Anscombe, trans. G. E. M. Anscombe, rev. edn. Cambridge, Mass.: MIT Press, 1978.

———. *Tractatus Logicus-Philosophicus*, trans. C. K. Ogden. London: Routledge and Kegan Paul, 1922, repr. 1960.

———. *Zettel*, ed. G. E. M. Anscombe and G. H. von Wright, trans. Anscombe. Berkeley: University of California Press, 1970.

Wittkower, Rudolf. *Palladio and Palladianism*, ed. Margot Wittkower. New York: Braziller, 1974. Especially 'English Literature on Architecture' (1966), 93–112, and 'Classical Theory and Eighteenth-Century Sensibility' (1966), 191–204 .

Zetzsche, Carl. *Zopf und Empire*, 3 vols. Berlin: Kantor Mohr, 1906.

Zevi, Bruno. 'A Guide to the Anticlassical Code,' trans. Ronald Strom. In his *The Modern Language of Architecture*. Seattle: University of Washington Press, 1978. Pp. 3–85.

INDEX